CHINA, THE UNITED STATES, AND THE
FUTURE OF LATIN AMERICA

China, the United States, and the Future of Latin America

U.S.-China Relations, Volume III

Edited by

David B. H. Denoon

NEW YORK UNIVERSITY PRESS
New York

NEW YORK UNIVERSITY PRESS
New York
www.nyupress.org

References to Internet websites (URLs) were accurate at the time of writing. Neither the author nor New York University Press is responsible for URLs that may have expired or changed since the manuscript was prepared.

ISBN: 978-1-4798-9928-9 (hardback)
ISBN: 978-1-4798-2164-8 (paperback)

For Library of Congress Cataloging-in-Publication data, please contact the Library of Congress.

New York University Press books are printed on acid-free paper, and their binding materials are chosen for strength and durability. We strive to use environmentally responsible suppliers and materials to the greatest extent possible in publishing our books.

Manufactured in the United States of America

10 9 8 7 6 5 4 3 2 1

Also available as an ebook

CONTENTS

This book is the third in a series on U.S.-China relations and will explore how the U.S. and China interact in Latin America and compare those patterns to circumstances in Central Asia and Southeast Asia.

In the first volume, on *Central Asia* (NYU Press, 2015), we concluded that China and the U.S. had different goals and operating styles in the region. The U.S. has been, overwhelmingly, concerned with national security in the region, while China's focus has been resource extraction, especially oil and natural gas. Thus, there has been little direct competition between the U.S. and China in Central Asia.

In the second volume, on *Southeast Asia* (NYU Press, 2017), we noted a strikingly different type of interaction between China and the U.S. In Southeast Asia both China and the U.S. have major interests, and we found direct competition between the outside powers. We also saw a clear attempt by both Beijing and Washington to seek alignments with states in the region that would support their respective policies and goals. For example, Myanmar, Laos, Thailand, and Cambodia all tacitly support China on various regional issues; while the Philippines, Singapore, and Indonesia are all more skeptical of China and are cooperating, in various ways, with the U.S.

In this third volume, on Latin America and the Caribbean, we see an even more complex interaction between China and the U.S. Hence, what Volume III assesses is how China's rising profile is affecting both the countries of Latin America and the outside powers. China has both economic and strategic interests in Latin America. In some countries like Venezuela, Brazil, and Argentina, China's interests are directly competitive with the U.S. In other states, like Bolivia and Nicaragua, China has made major commitments, but these are not of great concern to the U.S. government.

To make the three volumes comparable and to provide a similar structure for the analysis, each book has overview chapters, discussion of interactions within the region, and discussion of the role of outside powers.

In comparing the three regions, it is clear that, over the next several decades, China will play the dominant role in Central Asia but there will be major contests for influence between the U.S. and China in Southeast Asia and Latin America. Given China's occupation of several islands/atolls in the South China Sea and its construction of airfields and military bases there, Southeast Asia is in a very precarious military situation. There is nothing that tense in Latin America yet; but, depending upon Chinese intentions, comparable circumstances might, ultimately, develop in Panama, Cuba, or Venezuela. We urge readers of this volume to peruse the other two in the series so they can make their own judgments about the three regions. In addition, at the end of the Conclusion to this volume, there is a brief comparison of U.S.-China relations in Central Asia, Southeast Asia, and Latin America.

One of the issues facing authors of policy-oriented books is how to deal with events that occur between the time the chapters are drafted and when the book is published. This is a special problem with edited volumes when chapters by authors arrive at different times.

With this particular volume, we face the further problems that a U.S. presidential election took place after the chapters were drafted and while the book was being edited. Also, for example, President Rousseff of Brazil was removed from office in that period as well. We have decided to leave the chapters mostly as they were drafted because then readers will have a consistent view of the topics—as they were seen by the authors in 2016.

Yet, we have edited some comments on one topic: the Trans Pacific Partnership (TPP). Most of the discussion on TPP has been left as the authors initially wrote it; however, some sentences that implied that TPP would be implemented shortly have been changed. The Trump administration has said it will not implement the tariff reductions and trade stimulating measures in TPP as negotiated. Nevertheless, the Trump administration has put out assorted comments on TPP, including a recent one saying that the U.S. might use the current wording of TPP as a basis for new negotiations. Since there is no way to know if TPP will ultimately proceed, we leave the authors' comments on TPP mostly as drafted so readers can judge for themselves what might have happened if TPP had proceeded as originally conceived.

* * *

Thanks go to a broad range of individuals who contributed to make this volume possible. First, I want to thank the chapter writers themselves and the other participants who made insightful comments at the June 2015 conference that launched this volume. Appreciation is also warranted for two unnamed reviewers, obtained by NYU Press, who made detailed and very helpful comments on the draft manuscript. We also received very helpful suggestions from Ilene Kalish and Caelyn Cobb of NYU Press. In addition, we got excellent copyediting arranged by Dorothea Halliday and fine indexing from Robert Swanson.

Particular thanks go to Anthony Spanakos, who helped guide me through assorted thickets in the Latin American studies literature, and to Amb. Winston Lord, who read both the Introduction and Conclusion with his eagle eye and made many suggestions for clarification and elaboration. Also, I want to thank New York University, its Center on U.S.-China Relations, and Mr. Wenliang Wang for their support as this project proceeded. Finally, deep appreciation goes to Ms. Dongbo Wang and Ms. Xing Lu, who showed great skill in helping with researching, editing, and administering aspects of this volume.

David B. H. Denoon
New York, NY
March 2017

PART I

The Context

1

China's Arrival in Latin America

DAVID B. H. DENOON

Background

In the last decade China has become the largest trading partner for more than half the countries in Latin America, and Beijing has established strategic ties, as well, with Panama, Nicaragua, Cuba, Venezuela, Bolivia, and Argentina. Some analysts see this as just normal aspects of globalization and China's need for more food and raw material imports.[1] Others, however, think China's commercial and strategic objectives are specifically designed to undercut long-standing U.S. links in Latin America.[2]

This book is the third in a series on U.S.-China relations and will explore the themes discussed below with the intent of comparing patterns in Latin America to those in Central Asia and Southeast Asia.

In the first volume on *Central Asia* (NYU Press, 2015), we concluded that China and the U.S. had different goals and operating styles in the region. The U.S. has been, overwhelmingly, concerned with national security in the region, while China's focus has been resource extraction, especially oil and natural gas. Thus, there has been little direct competition between the U.S. and China in Central Asia.

In the second volume on *Southeast Asia* (NYU Press, 2017) we noted a strikingly different type of interaction between China and the U.S. In Southeast Asia both China and the U.S. have major interests, and we found direct competition between the outside powers. We also saw a clear attempt by both Beijing and Washington to seek alignments with states in the region that would support their respective policies and goals. For example, Myanmar, Laos, Thailand, and Cambodia all tacitly support China on various regional issues; while the Philippines, Singapore, and Indonesia are all more skeptical of China and open to cooperating with the U.S.

In this third volume, on Latin America and the Caribbean, we see an even more complex interaction between China and the U.S. Hence, what Volume III assesses is how China's rising profile is affecting both the countries of Latin America and the outside powers. For the past decade, China has been a source of surging exports for Latin American states and has, increasingly, been seen as a means for anti-U.S. governments to rally toward a new outside power. Yet several developments make this scene multifaceted: (1) China's own growth rate is slowing, so exports from Latin America to China are less buoyant. (2) China's imports from Latin America are almost entirely food, raw materials, and metals and its exports to the region are predominantly manufactured goods, which compete with Latin American manufactures. So, many Latin American analysts are wondering if they are just establishing a new kind of dependency on China. (3) China was successful at initiating new strategic links with the Leftist governments in Nicaragua, Cuba, Venezuela, Bolivia, and Argentina but now the political orientation in Latin America seems to be changing. Both Venezuela and Argentina have had recent elections where conservatives have replaced Leftists; and, even in Brazil, the Left's hold on power is uncertain.

Thus, China is looking like a less attractive economic partner for Latin America than it was several years ago and the strategic ties that Beijing has established may be loosened if the current political trends continue. So, we will be exploring a scene where trends are definitely in flux.

Thus, what is the net impact of China's new profile in the Southern Hemisphere? Has China's dynamism and willingness to challenge the U.S. made it a real competitor to U.S. influence? Or is the growing Latin American resentment over trade imbalances and the recognition that the Latin American states cannot compete against Chinese manufactured goods enough to limit China's influence?

We will be exploring these issues from a number of competing perspectives. This volume is consciously designed to present authors with different ideological and empirical appraisals of these topics. The bulk of the analysis in this volume is on South America; but, of course, we have included Mexico and a chapter on Central America and the Caribbean as well.[3]

Themes of the Volume

There are five major themes that cut across the chapters in this volume:

1) In the last decade, China's reach and ambitions have become truly global. Long a major presence in Asia, China is now a key actor in the Middle East, Africa, and Latin America.
2) China's goals are to achieve prominence in a broad range of areas: economic, political, military, and technological prowess.
3) Since 1823 and the announcement of the Monroe Doctrine, the U.S. has sought to be the preeminent power in Latin America and the Caribbean. China does not currently pose a direct military threat to the U.S. or its interests in Latin America, but it does represent serious competition in the economic and diplomatic arenas. Neither the George W. Bush nor Barack Obama administrations made Latin America a top priority in their respective foreign policy agendas.
4) China's priorities in Latin America are to extract resources and sell manufactured goods, and, if it can, to advance its strategic interests at the same time.
5) In the past decade, a clear East-West split has developed among the Latin American states. Venezuela, Brazil, and Argentina became more nationalistic and anti-U.S., while Chile, Columbia, and Peru have tended to be more market-oriented and comfortable working with U.S. power.

The Economic Scene

Although China has invested a total of at least $50 billion in Latin America, its principal economic interaction with the region is through trade. In the last 15 years, Sino-Latin American trade has soared. Between 2007 and 2012 alone, combined import and export trade between China and Latin America skyrocketed from approximately $100 billion to $250 billion.[4] In that period, Latin America became the region where China's trade increased most rapidly and it even eclipsed total Chinese trade with the European Union.

As Osvaldo Rosales points out in Chapter 2 of this volume, although Sino-Latin American trade has grown rapidly since 2000, GDP growth rates in Latin America have been trending down. In the 2003 to 2011 period, Latin American GDP growth averaged 4.1% per year, between 2012 and 2014 it averaged 2.1%, and in 2015 it is expected to average about 1.5%.[5] This has created a problem which several of our authors address: Chinese exports are dominating a number of manufactured goods sectors in Latin American states and the Latin American countries are having little success at exporting manufactures to China.[6] Not only has this pattern created a serious trade imbalance, but it has also led to resentment on the part of many Latin American businessmen. The situation has further led to questions about whether Sino-Latin American trade is, essentially, a new form of dependency.[7]

It is unclear if the Latin American states will, on balance, move toward greater economic integration with China or whether they will try to slow a process where many Latin Americans feel they are losing out.[8] Many Latin Americans like China's foreign policy approach of "non-interference in the internal affairs" of the states it deals with.[9] However, there is also deep ambivalence about how to deal with the juggernaut that the Chinese state-owned enterprises and state banks represent.[10]

Because China has over $3 trillion in foreign exchange reserves and the Chinese banks can draw on that enormous reservoir of funds for an approved project, there is no way that smaller Latin American corporations and banks can compete on an equal footing. Hence, new mechanisms need to be found that can stabilize the economic imbalances at present.[11]

Diplomatic and Strategic Relations

Historians note that there was trade across the Pacific between China and Latin America during the 1600s, so some see the current revival of trade as a return to normal.[12] This view understates the context in which the current developments are occurring. China's links to Latin America are stunning because of the rapid transformation they represent—yet it is critical to place them in the global context. In the Yuan and Ming dynasties, China had modest links to Africa and the Middle East as well, but nothing on the scale of today's interactions.[13] Moreover, the historical ties were almost exclusively in trade, whereas today's links have political and strategic implications also.[14]

As Christopher Sabatini, He Li, and Haibin Niu comment in their respective chapters, China's rise today is accompanied not just with trade and investment, but with a whole host of new initiatives and institutions. The new institutions focus mostly on Asia (and warrant a separate section below), but China is proposing them at the same time that new organizations are being promoted in Latin America.

Thus, we see a whole host of new linkages that have completely outmoded the old, Latin America versus the United States approach to understanding the region. For example, Venezuela has been promoting the Bolivarian Alliance for the Peoples of Our America (ALBA) and has recruited eleven members, mostly from the Caribbean.[15] Except for Venezuela, these are mostly low-income countries so they have not been particularly influential. Yet Venezuela has close ties with Brazil and Argentina and shares their Left-wing political orientation, so this represents an important cluster of like-minded leaders and countries on the eastern half of Latin America.

Conversely, on the western side of the continent, many of the states are more conservative and market-oriented. The Andean Pact, started in 1966 as a customs union, is now the Andean Community with Colombia, Peru, Ecuador, and Bolivia as members. The Pacific Alliance was created in April 2011 (with Chile, Colombia, Mexico, and Peru as founding members) and has both an economic and political component. Economically, the group wants to encourage the free flow of goods, capital, people, and services. Politically, it requires the members to be democracies and to respect human rights.[16]

* * *

What does this mean for relations between the Latin American states, China, and the U.S.?

First, Latin America is now a complex mixture of different ideologies and approaches to foreign policy.[17]

Second, because of those differences, Latin America cannot really negotiate with either the U.S. or China as a cohesive group.

Third, as we see in Table 1.1 below, China is now one of the top two trading partners with most of the Latin American states. Since the U.S.

is the other leading trading partner, we have a clear triangular relationship where any move by a Latin American state toward either the U.S.
or China will necessarily affect the other major power.[18] That is why so
many of the chapters discuss the Latin American relationship to China
and the U.S. as a triangular interaction.

One key remaining issue is worth discussing under diplomatic and
strategic relations: the Taiwan question. Some would argue that this is
simply a relic of the Cold War and that it will, eventually, just fade away
as Taiwan and China reach some form of accommodation. That would
be satisfactory to the public in Taiwan if they were able to keep their
democratic system and autonomy, but it is not clear that China will really agree to that.[19] Also, there are now closer ties between the "Umbrella"/democracy movement in Hong Kong and comparable groups in
Taiwan, so leaders in Beijing may be concerned about making concessions to Taiwan that would be desired in Hong Kong.[20] The link to Latin
America is that 11 of the states that recognize Taiwan as the Republic of
China are in Central America and the Caribbean. The Chinese government finds this an irritant, and has alternated between offering these
governments inducements to change recognition and ignoring them.

Nevertheless, as Richard Bernal notes in his chapter, Taiwan supplies
a significant amount of aid to these Central America and Caribbean
states, so their governments are loath to give up the official recognition
of Taiwan. At present, the People's Republic of China is downplaying the
importance of this competition, but it might heat up if there were to be
some incident affecting Taiwan or the islands in the South China Sea.
Also, China may be inclined to be more forthcoming with aid to Latin
and Caribbean states while the "Taiwan recognition" issue is still extant.

New Institutions

There are three relatively new institutions that could affect Chinese and
U.S. relations in Latin America: the Union of South American States
(UNASUR); the New Development Bank, which is an outgrowth of the
BRICS (Brazil, Russia, India, China, and South Africa) agreement; and
the Trans-Pacific Partnership (TPP).

UNASUR was launched in 2005 and is an attempt to link regional
organizations from the Eastern and Western parts of South America.

It links MERCOSUR (which comprises Argentina, Brazil, Paraguay, Uruguay, and Venezuela) with the Andean Community with the goal of displacing the Organization of American States (OAS) as the principal representative of South America with the outside world.

At a time when Brazil, Venezuela, and Argentina all had Leftist and anti-U.S. leaders, it appeared that UNASUR might be a means for producing a consolidated South American set of policies. Yet, now that the Chavez supporters have lost control of the legislature in Venezuela, the Left in Brazil is in complete disarray over corruption scandals, and the Left has lost the presidency in Argentina, the original goals of UNASUR cannot be implemented.[21]

It remains to be seen if UNASUR will adapt to the new political orientation in the region or if it will fade into insignificance. If UNASUR does shift in a more conservative direction, what will its original supporters do?

In 2006, Brazil, Russia, India, and China decided to form a new organization (later adding South Africa) to represent major regional powers that were not aligned with the Western states. The organization, which eventually became the BRICS, got a great deal of press attention and held annual summit meetings. However, the basic problem with the BRICS was that the four leading states did not have strong common interests.

Although India and China have a substantial trade relationship, they are strategic competitors and neither Russia, China, nor India has particularly close relations to Brazil. Although China has pledged $100 billion as capital for the BRICS New Development Bank, Beijing has now put much more effort and political capital into its latest venture, the Asian Infrastructure Investment Bank (AIIB).[22] Also, because of declining oil and gas prices and sanctions imposed over its occupation of Crimea and Eastern Ukraine, Russia's economy has declined dramatically. Given slower economic growth rates in China, India, and Brazil, the excitement about the BRICS as a phenomenon is gone. Ironically, the investment bank that coined the term "BRICS," Goldman Sachs, has recently lost money on its BRICS mutual fund, so it closed the fund in October 2015.[23] The BRICS is likely to continue as an institution, but, until the members' economies pick up, its influence is likely to be limited.

The Trans-Pacific Partnership, started in November 2015, is too new to evaluate in depth but it could, eventually, have a significant effect on Latin America.[24] Although the TPP is essentially a free-trade pact, all but Vietnam are democracies and the intent of the members is to advocate for open economies and civil liberties. Hence, it is similar in many ways to the Latin Pacific Alliance. Moreover, in its emphasis on market-oriented economic policies, it will be a challenge to the statist policies preferred by the political Left. President Obama is presently having trouble getting Congressional approval for the TPP agreement, but it may go through at some point in the next year.[25] Then, as the TPP is being implemented, we will be able to judge its long-term impact.

Key Countries

As President-elect Macri prepared to take office in December 2015, Argentina appeared to be on the cusp of a major change in economic and foreign policy. As J. L. Machinea and L. Castro show in their chapter, Argentina has been in a downward spiral under the Kirchner, husband and wife, leadership team. When the Kirchners controlled both the executive branch and the legislature, they negotiated loans from China (to avoid meeting the terms of their creditors) and reportedly signed an agreement giving the China military the right to set up a satellite down-link station in Argentina.[26] Presumably, the terms of these arrangements will now be revealed by the incoming president, and analysts will be able to determine what exactly China received for its largesse. Therefore, we are not only likely to see major changes in Argentinian policy directions but to learn significantly more about Beijing's operating style in Latin America.

As J. A. Guilhon-Albuquerque details, Brazil is in turmoil over a massive and widespread corruption scandal involving billions of dollars in payoffs to figures in the current and prior administrations. There were frequent demonstrations calling for the resignation of President Dilma Rousseff and numerous individuals are under indictment. Rousseff has been impeached and replace by Michel Temer.

These internal troubles have already affected Brazil's aspirations to play a larger role on the global scene.[27] For example, the scandals have hurt Brazil's chances of getting a permanent set on the UN Security Council. Yet Brazil still remains the largest market in South America and thus an attractive location for Chinese economic activities. Chinese trade still vastly out shines direct investment; but, after 2009, Chinese FDI, into Brazil, has risen significantly to a rate of over $10 billion per year.[28] The Chinese government has also wanted to encourage use of its currency in international trade and thus arranged a "swap agreement" for $30 billion with Brazil, which will be using yuan instead of U.S. dollar for clearing certain of its accounts.[29] The Chinese government partially succeeded in its objective of making the yuan an international currency when the International Monetary Fund announced that the yuan would be one of the currencies included in the IMF's Special Drawing Rights (SDR). So, Brazil and China still have a close working relationship but it remains to be seen what will happen given that Temer is the president.

Mexico is the largest economy in Latin America and receives premier attention from China not only because of its size but also because Mexico provides access to the North American Free Trade Area.[30] China thus has the advantage of getting access to the U.S. and Canada by trans-shipping through Mexico and doing some assembly of products close to its final market. In addition, China is interested in Mexican oil and gas and broadening its overall access to the Mexican market.

In his chapter, E. Dussel Peters analyzes the dilemmas this poses for Mexico—as it is not in Mexico's interest to be outcompeted on manu-factured goods and both China's cost of capital and labor are less than Mexico's. Moreover, because of the scale of its economy and its special relationship to the U.S., Mexico wants to be able to keep its manufactur-ing sector viable, while enhancing its international stature through its membership in the Organisation for Economic Co-operation and De-velopment (OECD) and the Group of 20.[31] Also, because of the massive illegal immigration problem (much of it stemming from Mexico) and the passage of drugs through Mexico, relations between the U.S. and Mexican government are often strained.

It is in China's interest to keep its profile in Mexico as low as possible. Mexican workers may resent Chinese imports; and, if Chinese invest-ment is too visible, it may endanger Chinese access to the North Ameri-can Free Trade Agreement (NAFTA). Also, though Mexican economic policy is often nationalistic, Mexico does not want to be associated with the type of anti-U.S. policies that ALBA has been advocating. So, Mexico stands apart from many of its Latin neighbors and is crafting its own, unique relationship with China.

Anthony Spanakos's chapter on Venezuela evaluates a country following a very different strategy from Mexico's. Although its economy has been in deep trouble for more than five years, Venezuela has continued its ideological battles with capitalist economies and has subsidized oil prices for many of its neighbors through Petrocaribe. This has exhausted its foreign exchange reserves and produced major domestic shortages as the world's oil price turned down.

Although precise details have not been disclosed, China has loaned Venezuela over $40 billion in foreign exchange and is taking repayment in kind, through oil shipments. In addition, the China Development Bank has loaned Venezuela an additional $5 billion for infrastructure projects.[32] Thus, as Russia has cut back on its investments in and loans to Venezuela, China has increased its exposure. Presumably, leaders in Beijing have been willing to underwrite the Chavez/Maduro strategy for rallying nations to oppose the U.S.

Now, however, after the recent legislative elections, even some of the most committed Chavistas realize that the country has been on an unsustainable course. With the opposition winning handily in the legislative elections, there could well be a standoff between the legislature and the executive branch.[33] Yet, with the country's economy on the edge of collapse and fellow regimes in trouble or out in Brazil and Argentina, a grand coalition of Leftist governments in Latin America is not feasible now.[34] It is not clear how much this matters to China.

* * *

In sum, leaders in Beijing may be pleased when a U.S. sphere of influence is split between supporters and opponents of Washington's policies. Nevertheless, Latin America matters to China mostly for economic reasons, and there is little incentive for more conservative governments to turn against China. So, on balance, China is using its foreign exchange reserves skillfully to fund investments, loans, and aid, which is increasing its access and influence in Latin America. The U.S., on the other hand, has no direct military challenge from China in the Southern Hemisphere and currently benefits from disarray on the Left in Argentina, Brazil, and Venezuela.

TABLE 1.1. China's rankings with Latin America and the Caribbean as trade partner (comparing 2000 to 2012)

	Exports		Imports	
	2000	2012	2000	2012
Argentina	6	3	4	2
Bolivia	18	9	7	2
Brazil	12	1	11	1
Chile	5	1	4	2
Colombia	36	2	9	2
Costa Rica	30	8	15	2
Ecuador	18	11	10	2
Salvador	49	32	23	4
Guatemala	43	29	19	3
Honduras	54	9	21	4
Mexico	19	4	7	2
Nicaragua	35	25	20	3
Panama	31	5	25	2
Paraguay	15	25	3	1
Peru	4	1	9	2
Uruguay	4	2	7	3
Venezuela	35	2	18	2
Antigua and Barbuda	N/A	15	26	3
Bahamas	N/A	19	28	3
Barbados	42	12	9	4
Belize	N/A	11	17	2
Cuba	6	2	3	2
Dominica	N/A	25	25	4
Guyana	27	10	6	3
Jamaica	16	18	10	4
Dominican Republic	N/A	3	N/A	2

Source: Barcena, A., et.al. *Promoción del comercio y la inversión con China: Desafíos y oportunidades en la experiencia de las cámaras empresariales latinoamericanas* (Santiago, Chile: CEPAL, 2013)

NOTES

1 Devlin, R., A. Estevadeoral, and A. Rodriguez-Clare, eds., *The Emergence of China* (Cambridge, MA: Harvard University Center for Latin American Studies, 2006).

2 Fornes, G., and A. B. Philip, *The China–Latin America Nexus* (New York and London: Palgrave-Macmillan, 2012); Gallagher, K., and R. Porzecanski, *The Dragon in the Room* (Stanford, CA: Stanford University Press, 2010).

3 Central America and the Caribbean are important because so many of the states recognize Taiwan and because Cuba plays a prominent role in the region's ideological and foreign policy debates.

4 National Bureau of Statistics, *Yearbook of China's Foreign Economic Relations and Trade* (Beijing: National Bureau of Statistics, Department of Commerce and Trade, 2014).

5 ECLAC, *Economic Survey of Latin America and the Caribbean 2015* (Santiago: United Nations Economic Commission of Latin America and the Caribbean, 2015).

6 Ferchen, M., "China-Latin America Relations: Long-Term Boom or Short-term Boom?," *Chinese Journal of International Politics* 4, 2011, pp. 55–86.

7 For the classic definition of "dependency" and its effects, see A. G. Frank, "The Development of Underdevelopment," *Monthly Review* 18, 4, September 1966, pp. 17–31.

8 Inter-American Development Bank, *Shaping the Future of the Asia-Latin American and the Caribbean Relationship* (Washington, DC: IADB, 2012).

9 Jiang, S., " China's New Leadership and the New Development of China-Latin American Relations," *China Quarterly of International Strategic Studies* 1, 1, 2015, pp. 133–153.

10 Downs, E., *Inside China, Inc.: China Development Bank's Cross-Border Energy Deals*, J. L. Thornton China Center Monograph Series, No. 3 (Washington, DC: Brookings Institution, 2011).

11 Shen, S., "Online Chinese Perceptions of Latin America: How They Differ from the Official View," *China Quarterly* 209, March 2012, pp. 157–177.

12 Xiang, L., "A Geo-Political Perspective on Sino-Latin American Relations," in C. Aronson, B. Moore, and R. Roett, eds., *Enter the Dragon* (Washington, DC: Woodrow Wilson Center, 2011).

13 Ikenberry, J., "The Rise of China and the Future of the West," *Foreign Affairs* 87, 2, January–February 2008, pp. 22–37.

14 Fravel, T., et al., eds., *China's Rise and International Norms: A CJIP Reader* (Oxford and New York: Oxford University Press, 2012).

15 The members are Antigua and Barbuda, Bolivia, Cuba, Dominica, Ecuador, Grenada, Nicaragua, St. Kitts and Nevis, St. Lucia and the Grenadines, and Venezuela. Suriname is a guest country.

16 Costa Rico and Panama are now in the process of joining the Pacific Alliance as well.

17 Sullivan, M., *Latin America and the Caribbean: Key Issues for the 114th Congress* (Washington, DC: Congressional Research Service, 2015).

18 Liu, Y., "Promote China–Latin American Relations in the 21st Century," *Georgetown Journal on Globalization, Competitiveness, and Governability*, 6, 1, April 2012, pp. 107–114.

19 For a discussion of how Taiwan affects the strategic picture in Asia, see D. Denoon, "Strategic Competition among China, Japan, and Taiwan," in A. Lake and

D. Ochmanek, eds., *The Real and the Ideal* (Lanham, MD: Rowman & Littlefield, 2001), pp. 283–302.

20 Veg, S., "New Spaces, New Controls: China's Embryonic Pubic Sphere," *Current History*, 114, 773, September 2015, pp. 203–209.

21 Quintana, A., "Crisis in Venezuela: UNASUR and U.S. Foreign Policy," *Heritage Issue Brief* 4205, April 23, 2014.

22 Chin, G., "China's Bold Economic Statecraft," *Current History* 114, 773, September 2015, p. 219.

23 "BRIC Fund Ends Its Run," *New York Times*, November 24, 2015, p. H-3.

24 The members are Australia, Brunei, Canada, Chile, Japan, Malaysia, Mexico, New Zealand, Peru, Singapore, and Vietnam.

25 Editor's note: This manuscript was prepared in 2016 when TPP was considered viable. As we go to press in 2017, President Trump's opposition makes TPP less likely to proceed. However, there is some possibility that the current signatory governments of TPP would go ahead on their own (without U.S. participation).

26 The terms of the various agreements with China were not even released to members of the Kirchners' party in the legislature.

27 Trinkunas, H., "Brazil's Rise: Seeking Influence on Global Governance," *Latin American Initiative* (Washington, DC: Brookings Institution, April 2014).

28 O'Conor, T., "Chinese Investment in Brazil: An Overview of Shifting Trends," *Inter-American Dialogue*, September 2013.

29 "China and Brazil Sign $30 Billion Currency Swap Agreement," BBC News, March 26, 2013.

30 O'Neil, S., "Mexico Makes It—A Transformed Society, Economy and Government," *Foreign Affairs* 92, 2, March/April 2013.

31 For an overview of how different Latin nations see China's arrival in their arena, see R. Roett and G. Paz, *China's Expansion into the Western Hemisphere: Implications for Latin America and the United States* (Washington, DC: Brookings Institution Press, 2008).

32 "Venezuela's Maduro in China to Get a $5 Billion Loan," *Latin American Herald Tribune*, September 8, 2014.

33 Neuman, W., "Opposition in Venezuela Now Has to Fix the Ills That Led to Its Victory," *New York Times*, December 9, 2015, p. A-6.

34 Sabatini, C., "The Sad Death of the Latin American Left," *Foreign Policy*, December 10, 2015.

2

Is There a LatAm-US-China Economic Triangle?

An Economic Overview

OSVALDO ROSALES

These are bad times for emerging economies.[1] At the time of this writing, according to the International Monetary Fund (IMF), 2016 has been the sixth consecutive year of slowing expansion for emerging economies. China's slowdown, falling commodity prices, prospects of higher interest rates in the United States, and the risks of increasing dollar appreciation are dark clouds hanging over emerging economies.

Also, according to the Institute of International Finance, emerging economies faced a net capital outflow in 2015—the first time since 1988. In 2007, emerging economies attracted capital equivalent to 8% of GDP; meanwhile, in 2015 capital inflows amounted to only 2% of GDP. Thus, with capital outflows of 4% of GDP, the net impact was an outflow around 2% GDP. The Institute of International Finance estimated a net outflow for 2016, albeit in a small measure.

In April 2016, the World Trade Organization (WTO) also downgraded its forecast for global trade for the year to 2.8% and highlighted that this projection may be subject to even further downgrades; this is the fifth consecutive year where the volume of global trade grew at, or below, the rate of global GDP. This figure is noteworthy given that prior to the financial crisis trade grew at twice the rate of global GDP.

Moreover, the composition of global trade is also changing. The IMF estimated that exports from developed economies grew 2.9% during 2015; meanwhile, those of developing economies grew by only 1.5%. This is another relevant change given that, in recent years, the export growth of developing economies doubled that of developed economies.

Latin America is the developing region that is the most affected by this economic deceleration. This is due to the strong link between investment and commodity price cycles. Foreign direct investment (FDI) flows fell by 16% in 2014 and approximately 15% in 2015. Private investment, which is also linked to the commodities markets, has declined in recent years. This trend will critically affect economic growth in a region that already faces a chronic lack of investment.

In the second half of 2016, it seems clear that one development cycle in Latin America is over and another cycle is beginning. The definitive signals of the new cycle are not clear yet, but 2016 marks five consecutive years of disappointing economic growth for the region. Further, projections for the remainder of the decade present real challenges. Deceleration in China, financial volatility, a strengthening dollar, weakening commodities prices, and, lastly, devaluation and turbulence in the Chinese stock market provide some explanation for this. However, the real answer is the lack of progress made by Latin America in making structural changes that are aligned with the challenges of the global economy. In fact, after experiencing the best economic period in 40 years during the first decade of this century, Latin America is entering the second half of the second decade with the traditional constraints of regional development.

I. Near-Term Growth Prospects for Latin America

Since 2011, Latin America's deceleration has been very pronounced. It has followed the deceleration of the global economy but has surpassed it in terms of magnitude. Latin America was the developing region that grew the least during the commodities boom or "super cycle" (2003–2010) and the one that is decelerating the most in the current phase (2011–2016).

The boom phase in the region occurred between 2003 and 2008 (until September of that year, when the subprime crisis took place). The region handled the 2008–2009 crisis notably well and grew at a spectacular rate in 2010. This generated a discussion of what was called "Latin America's decade," given that, notwithstanding the worst international financial crisis since the Great Depression, the region did not face any major upheavals or, more importantly, a significant deterioration of its social indicators.

These good economic results spread throughout the region—independently of macroeconomic patterns and various modes of international insertion—which speaks of the need to ponder the relevance of the external context to explain this solid economic performance.

In effect, the Latin American boom phase coincided with high growth rates in the global economy, particularly in China and the United States. The high growth rates stimulated global trade and a solid external demand for the region's exports, high commodity prices, elevated levels of remittances, abundant international liquidity, and low interest rates. In this context, in addition to the economic dynamism in the region and a good outlook for exports of basic products, the region also experienced elevated levels of FDI flows. As such, the region's growth was stimulated by a loosening of external restrictions inasmuch as the region exhibited a surplus in the current account on the balance of payments between 2003 and 2007.

It is true that the region also had economic achievements that help explain this good performance. Among those that should be highlighted are better inflation control and public accounts, a reduction of the debt-to-product ratio, increases in tax revenue due to economic growth, tax reforms, and a greater presence of floating exchange rates that provided flexibility to the political economy in the face of external shocks. Also contributing to this solid performance was a lower degree of financial depth and complex operations relative to the industrialized world, which, together with progress in the post-crisis financial regulation of the external debt of the 1980s, prevented the financial effects of the subprime crisis from having a severe effect in the region (Machinea 2015).

A. The Economic Period between 2003 and 2011 Was the Best in the Region in 40 Years

During the period between 2003 and 2011, economic growth was 4.1% per annum and macroeconomic stability was generalized (see Table 2.1). This period was marked by low inflation, orderly fiscal and external debt balance, and a low and decreasing public debt. Export values grew

TABLE 2.1. Economic Growth in Latin America, 2003–2015 (Annual Rates of Growth, GDP)

	2003–2010	2012–2013	2014	2015	2016e
Argentina	7.4	1.1	0.5	2.0	-0.8
Brazil	4.2	0.9	0.1	-3.5	-3.5
Chile	4.1	3.8	1.9	2.0	1.6
Colombia	4.7	2.9	4.6	3.1	2.9
Mexico	2.4	1.3	2.2	2.5	2.3
Peru	6.8	4.6	2.4	2.8	3.8
Venezuela	6.6	2.0	-4.0	-7.1	-6.9
Latin America	4.2	1.7	1.2	-0.4	-0.6

e=estimate (April 2016)

Source: "Balance Preliminar de las economías de América Latina y el Caribe," Economic Commission for Latin America and the Caribbean, 2013–2016.

at double digits (16% annually between 2004 and 2008), which resulted in a significant improvement in the terms of trade for South America.

Moreover, high economic growth, low inflation, and an increase in employment and real wages resulted in a significant reduction in poverty, from 43.9% in 2002 to 28.1% in 2012. During this period, indigence—or extreme poverty—declined from 19.3% to 11.3% (ECLAC December 2014). There was an overall improvement in income distribution—a moment otherwise unseen in Latin America's modern history. Among the most noteworthy cases were Argentina, Venezuela, Ecuador, Bolivia, and Nicaragua. Similar experiences were also seen in Brazil, Mexico, Chile, Honduras, Paraguay, Panama, and El Salvador.

B. Cloudy Skies between 2012 and 2014

During the period between 2012 and 2014, Latin America faced a profound deterioration in economic growth. Growth fell to 1.5% annually and deceleration was the highest in the South American subregion. The subregion's deceleration was concentrated in the large economies, mainly Brazil, Argentina, and Venezuela. The best overall performance was seen in Central America.

During this time, export value growth stagnated. After growing 22% in 2010 and 2011 (due to the strong momentum in China's demand for raw materials), exports increased less than 1% annually between 2012 and 2014. This was due, almost entirely, to a decline in the terms of trade of mineral- and metal-exporting countries like Chile, Peru, and Brazil and, subsequently, oil- and gas-exporting countries like Bolivia, Colombia, Ecuador, Mexico, and Venezuela.

Additionally, poverty levels remained static at around 28% and indigence increased to 12%. Data from 2013 showed stalled progress in income distribution in Bolivia, Uruguay, Brazil, Argentina, Peru, El Salvador, Mexico, Chile, and Ecuador.

C. Worrying Signs for 2015 to 2020

In 2014–2015, economic growth dropped to 0.4% due to both external and internal factors. In 2015, economic growth was -0.4% for the region and -1.3% for South America. In fact, in 2015 Brazil and Venezuela were in a recession, harboring on -3.5% and -7% growth rates, respectively. Both countries remained in recession in 2016, with similar rates of decline in economic activity (ECLAC 2016). There has also been a sharp drop in the growth rate of mineral-exporting countries such as Chile and Peru; a drop in oil prices has also strongly affected Mexico, Venezuela, Ecuador, and Colombia.

Macroeconomic management is also facing several challenges. There is a resurgence in the average inflation rate (e.g., in Venezuela and Argentina), a current account deficit of approximately 3% of GDP in 2014–2015 despite a drop in imports, and a fiscal deficit of around 3% of GDP. With this deterioration in the external sector, investment rates were affected, thus increasing the volatility of economic activity.

Given that the economic slowdown in the region is explained basically by South America—and, within the region, by Brazil, Venezuela, and Argentina—the next section is dedicated to the economic performance of these countries.

D. Subregional Patterns and Noteworthy National Cases: Argentina, Brazil, and Venezuela

Estimates for 2016 show clear subregional asymmetries. While South America's GDP will fall 1.3%—due mainly to Brazil and Venezuela—Mexico will grow at a 2.3% rate and Central America at a 3.9% rate. It is worth noting that, if Brazil and Venezuela are excluded from the calculation, the rest of the region exhibits a 2.5% growth rate, that is to say, slightly lower than the global economy. Mexico is the large economy with the most growth (2.3%), while Central American countries (growing 3.9% in 2016), collectively, lead growth in the region as they benefit from lower energy prices and close ties to the United States, as is evidenced by exports, tourism, and remittances.

Mineral-exporting countries are the most affected in terms of trade but are not, however, the countries with the lowest growth. Petroleum-exporting countries are drastically affected by the decrease in commodity prices and, while Venezuela faces its fourth year of recession in 2016, Mexico will grow at 2.3%, Ecuador at 0.1%, and Colombia at 2.9%. This signifies that, together with the international context, there are domestic variables that help explain lower growth rates and understand national and subregional differences.

Trade partners also help explain some of the differences in the economic dynamism of the region's exports. On the one hand, the United States is the main export market for Mexico, the Dominican Republic, Central America (including Panama), Colombia, Ecuador, and Venezuela; on the other hand, China is the main export market for Brazil, Chile, Peru, and Uruguay.

ARGENTINA

After defaulting on its loans in the early 2000s, Argentina grew at Asian-like rates and achieved an average growth rate of 7.4% between 2003 and 2010. This was due to favorable external conditions and an expansive fiscal policy that accompanied—and surpassed—the GDP growth rate. On the external plane, the period between 2003 and 2008 constitutes one of the best periods for the global economy. The virtuous interaction between the economies of the United States and China provided an impulse to the global economy and to international trade, thus favoring elevated demand and improved terms of trade for exporters of raw materials.

A good part of the fiscal policy was focused on current expenditures with social subsidies that helped lower poverty levels. The exchange rate lag and price freeze of public utilities such as water and energy helped contain inflationary pressures that induced vigorous internal demand (basically consumption), which grew beyond a GDP that had an annual 10% growth rate.

As is evident, a fiscal policy of this nature faces limits—as did occur in 2014 and 2015. The favorable result in economic growth and poverty reduction led government authorities to risk making structural changes in the development strategy by prioritizing re-industrialization and seeking to diversify export structure. In terms of political economy, the strategy sought to take advantage of good international prices in agricultural raw materials—particularly soybeans—to subsidize the industry. Elevated retentions in agricultural and energy products were established to take advantage of high international prices and to argue that a significant portion of the gains associated with higher prices corresponded to income and not to productive or technological efforts. Beyond the fairness of this argument, what is certain is that most of these gains were oriented toward consumption and subsidies in social issues and less in infrastructure, innovation, and technological change.

The strategic thinking that dominated this industrialization effort privileged the domestic economy by closing the economy to foreign trade through the use of numerous non-tariff barriers. In this way, the valid reasons to pursue changes in the productive base resulted in turning away from the global economy. This produced a new, frustrating experience with import substitution that ignored the lessons of past periods. As such, the important issues that the government tried to pursue—such as value chains, industrial renovation, innovation, and technological change—did not manage to transcend the limits of the domestic economy. The eventual progress that could have been made was not reflected in improved rankings for Argentina in international competitiveness, innovation, and productivity.

This strategy could work while external conditions permitted it. In essence, the agricultural industry can survive inasmuch as international prices can compensate for retentions and exchange rate lag. However, when these prices weakened and the currency constraints were tightened, authorities reacted with vigorous exchange controls. On the other hand, several years of exaggerated expansion of fiscal spending and credit, as well as increases in salaries that exceeded the rate of the productivity expansion, yielded an inflation rate that neared 30% annually.[2]

In 2014, a less favorable external scenario led to the reappearance of external restrictions. Within this context, an expansive political economy has less space. The reaction of the authorities was to accentuate price and exchange controls at a time when inflation and exchange rate lags led people to take refuge in the dollar, considering, especially, that interest rates were negative.

Given Argentina's recent memory with hyperinflation as well as "corralitos"[3] and defaults in the last 20 years, it is a natural tendency for economic actors to seek refuge in the dollar in the face of economic turbulence or measures that appear as precursors to drastic actions like confiscation of private savings.

In this context, data for 2015 showed a fiscal deficit near 8% of GDP, considerable exchange rate lags, lagging rates for public utilities, and negative real interest rates. Given the expansionary fiscal policy, economic growth reached 2%. News on the international stage continues to lean toward low growth estimates for the global economy, particularly for China and Brazil—Argentina's two main trading partners. The time is approaching for the United States to normalize interest rates and, with that, reduce the volatility of currency in emerging economies given that such actions coincide with the weakening of the terms of trade for raw material–exporting countries.

As such, the economic scenario for the new government that takes power in early 2016 in Argentina is headed toward an adjustment that balances the public account, normalizes interest rates, corrects marked distortions in relative prices (exchange rates and utility rates), and reduces numerous subsidies—many of which are regressive and benefit mainly high-income and middle-income consumers of electric energy. The economic debate will be centered on a discussion regarding the gradualness of the adjustment and the policy instruments used. Both of these are fundamental issues given that there are adjustment modalities that affect investment and the potential product, thus damaging future growth perspectives and, even more so, the possibilities of transforming the productive structure.

In the second half of 2015, the government of Cristina Kirchner conducted a series of fiscal, monetary, and credit measures aimed to ensure a victory in presidential and parliamentary elections at the end of October. These measures strengthened demand, avoiding a recession that seemed inevitable. However, they also added pressures on the exchange rate and inflation. The reaction of the government was controlling the exchange rate, using the international reserves of the Central Bank and establishing strict foreign exchange controls. These measures even led to extreme limits on spending by Argentinians using their credit cards while abroad. Further, rigid price controls also supplemented foreign exchange controls.

As expected, this resulted in wide variations in the official dollar-dollar parallel—the so-called "blue dollar"—that made it virtually inaccessible. While the official dollar averaged 9 Argentine pesos, the "blue dollar" was approaching 15 pesos.

When the center-right opposition candidate Mauricio Macri won the second round, Cristina Kirchner's government carried out a series of last-minute measures to further complicate matters for the new government. It incorporated thousands of workers to the staff of various ministries and public agencies; essentially, at the last minute, the government agreed to comply with a court ruling that had previously questioned this action and which forced the central government to return a substantial amount of resources to the provinces. Lastly, the government issued a significant bonus to close the fiscal accounts of 2015—a bonus that would be withdrawn entirely in March 2016 by the new government.

Therefore, when President Macri took office in mid-December 2015, he faced a ticking time bomb that threatened the economy. This was a delicate scenario because economic challenges were compounded by significant political challenges. Indeed, the new government does not have a majority in Congress and must deal with different factions of Peronism that can create a stiff opposition to the new government and mobilize the important unions they control.

The first economic measure of the new administration was to liberalize the foreign exchange market and unify the various exchange rates that existed. This took place in parallel to eliminating retentions that had been established on agricultural exports and lowering those retentions that affected soybeans from 40% to 30%. Apparently, there were also talks with Chinese authorities to use part of the RMB credit line that Argentina holds. The market reaction was surprising because the exchange rate, while it jumped 30% with respect to the official value, came in under 15 pesos per dollar—the rate in the parallel market. In the following days, the rate stabilized around 13 to 14 pesos per dollar and, since then, has followed the trends exhibited by other Latin American economies.

The new government has just presented its goals and macroeconomic program (an advantage over the previous administration that did not do this). These goals are as follows:

TABLE 2.2. Argentina: The New Government's Macroeconomic Goals

	2015	2016	2017	2018	2019
Fiscal deficit (% of GDP)	7.1	4.8	3.3	1.8	0.3
Inflation rate	27%	20–25%	12–17%	8–12%	3.5–6.5%

The argument is that if Macri were to be elected president, he would seek to enter into an agreement with the "vulture funds," that is, accepting this macroeconomic policy applies a shock to the exchange market and opts for a gradual reduction of inflation and the fiscal deficit. To run this gradualism, it is essential to regain access to external financing to rebuild the levels of international reserves, and increase imports of capital goods in order to raise investment and productivity. This involves reaching an agreement with the so-called "vulture funds" that demanded full payment.

This agreement also required reasonableness because Kirchnerism's main supporters criticized reaching an agreement with the IMF quickly, and establishing a new "neoliberal adjustment." The current political mood is not the best for any type of agreement, though this is an urgent issue because Argentina has not been part of the international credit markets for 15 years and has not had the favorable terms of exchange in the past 6 or 7 years.

After 14 years of legal disputes, in February 2016 Argentina reached an expensive but necessary deal with the "vulture funds." Argentina will pay the creditors 75% of the principal and interest claimed as well as US$235 million to compensate debt-holders' legal fees. To pay that amount, Argentina issued bonds in the amount of US$16.5 billion, thereby permitting the return of Argentina to the international capital market.

As a result of the repressed inflation inherited by the Macri administration and price adjustments to make companies adapt to the new exchange rate, monthly inflation jumped by 3% in January 2016, making it very difficult to meet the annual goal of 20%. Moreover, the cuts to energy subsidies in the amount equivalent to 1.5 points of GDP—a subsidy that had reached an impressive level of 3% of GDP—could add about 5 more points to the annual inflation rate. With this, an initial obstacle to the new macroeconomic plan is that, as of the end of January 2016, the goal for annual inflation is no longer credible. The inflation rate in the first quarter exceeded 10% and will likely trigger pressure by unions for wage adjustments to compensate for the loss of purchasing power. Given that salaries and pensions are an important component of fiscal expenditure, these wage-pension pressures will probably raise the fiscal deficit and the need to issue bonds to finance it.

Economic goals are very exigent and the political scenario helps little. Macri's government resolved the ongoing conflict with "vulture funds" effectively and quickly; however, it may be excessively optimistic to expect fresh external financing in the short term. The IMF estimates that the Argentina economy will contract marginally in 2016, with a 0.7% drop in GDP. That decline could be higher if the crisis in Brazil, Argentina's main trade partner, deepens.

The new Argentine government expected that external resource inflows would lead to lower inflation and stimulate a recovery in economic activity. The road, however, is fraught with risks. In fact, capital inflows can lag behind the nominal exchange rate, which would help reduce inflation but would aggravate the external deficit. The temptation to rush, with greater emphasis on public investment, would encourage growth, but it would increase the fiscal deficit, thus making it more difficult to fulfill the government's goals.

The strong bet that the Argentine government has placed on economic recovery is a double-edged sword. On the one hand, it helps to contain expectations; but, on the other hand, it raises the risk of disappointing results.

The sudden rise in price levels during the first half of 2016 enabled the trade unions to exert pressure that led to collective bargaining and 30% salary increases, which, in and of itself, puts upward pressure on the year's inflation. Strong trade-union mobilization—historically led by Peronism—has forced the government to activate tax cuts to pensioners and other social measures. This will result in using up about one-third of the 3 points of GDP that the government had saved by reducing subsidies to energy, water, and transport. This fiscal decline was probably the only possible way to slow down the eventual start of new social and trade union pressures.

By the end of the first two quarters, significant sums of foreign capital income had not yet materialized and the government opted for a tax amnesty for undeclared dollars that return to the formal circuit. It is a controversial measure that has been sold as a part of increased social spending and public investment in the region—an issue that favors the relationship between Macri's government and the provinces, which adhere mostly to Peronism. In summary, the Argentine transition is highly complex and requires fine-tuning of technical measures and other political economy factors, which explains a tax gradualism due to an economy that still does not show positive growth figures, is marked by high inflation, and led by an administration that does not have a legislative majority (Fanelli 2016).

BRAZIL 2015–2016: ECONOMIC AND POLITICAL CRISIS
After growing at an average rate of 4.2% between 2003 and 2010, the Brazilian economy is slowing down drastically. Brazil either bordered on, or was in, a recession between 2012 and 2015. According to ECLAC, after an economic contraction of 3.5% in 2015, an additional contraction of similar magnitude was expected for 2016 (ECLAC 2016). That means five consecutive years (2012–2016) of economic stagnation or recession. Once interest payments are included, the total fiscal deficit for 2015 was 8 to 9% of GDP and inflation was near 10%.

For Brazil, the end of the commodity boom coincided with a large corruption scandal after years of the economy growing beyond sustainable bounds. During the commodity boom, the government increased the minimum wage well above increases in productivity and production, expanded access to credit for the poor and middle class, and expanded social components of public expenditure in a very remarkable way. Of course, the outcome was a revolution in consumption, giving millions of families access to durable goods. With rising wages, credit growth, and an expansionary fiscal policy, the obvious result in the short term is a strong aggregate demand. The impact on the GDP will depend on existing gaps in idle production capacity and the capacity to finance current account of the balance of payments. At that moment, there was excess capacity in the economy, while the growth in exports and favorable terms of trade allowed easy financing of external accounts.

Sooner rather than later, in such circumstances, supply constraints—such as, inter alia, inadequate infrastructure, logistics, and transportation, and a lack of skilled labor and critical inputs—begin to appear. This generates inflation or balance of payments pressures given the need to bridge the gap with imports. In the presence of external clearances, this process can be carried out without great difficulty. The problem arises when these external gaps disappear—the situation is even worse when those gaps become restrictions. That, in fact, is exactly what happened in 2014 and 2015: worsening terms of trade, weakening Chinese demand for commodities, and lower foreign capital inflows due to investors who turn their backs on commodities in anticipation of the effect that weakened prices will have on emerging economies during the next tightening of the United States' monetary policy.

In this context, the evolution of domestic variables has contributed to Brazil's aggravating economic scenario. The economy fell into a recession in the second quarter of 2015 when GDP contracted 1.9% from the previous quarter and 2.6% compared with the second quarter the previous year. The growth figure was the second worst since 1998—years that were marked by the Asian and Russian crises—and capped only by the immediate aftermath of the 2008 financial crisis.

Brazil is dealing with a series of interlinking problems:

i) Corruption scandals affecting Brazil's main state-owned enterprises, particularly the oil giant Petrobas, are seriously affecting the government's credibility. The Petrobas corruption scandal is also affecting investment due to the number of large private firms that are engaged in business dealings with company. Dozens of senior business executives are imprisoned and regular operations are blocked while the investigations are underway, all of this at the forefront of declining oil prices. Fixed investment fell 8.1% in the second quarter—another indication that the scandal also involved many private construction companies that are key investors (Dyer 2015).

ii) The fiscal deficit was increasing. When interest payments are excluded, Brazil faced a budget deficit of 0.3% GDP in 2015—the first time the figure has been in deficit mode since the government began publishing the statistic in 1997. The government's low popularity limited its ability to bring the budget deficit under control, which officials and the finance minister believe is necessary to begin a new cycle of growth. A proposal to cut the deficit was included during the second half of 2015 to reinstate a tax on financial transactions but the proposal met with sharp criticism from leading politicians including the Senate president.

iii) A draft budget initially sent to Congress built in a primary deficit for the first time in the hyperinflation era. The government would essentially have to borrow to cover all of its interest payments, during the recession, and with a high real interest rates and bad prospects for external financing. In September 2015, Standard & Poor's (S&P) downgraded the investment status of Brazil's debt to junk status together with dozens of big Brazilian companies, including important banks (Leahy 2015). After the S&P downgrade, the government reacted with a new draft budget that now includes a primary surplus; however, it must still be approved by Congress—a task that appears difficult.

iv) Inflation was very high. Given the historic inertial inflation in Brazil, the scenario is complex. In fact, the economy was in recession, with inflation around 10%, and the interest rate at about 14%. In other words, higher interest rates to contain inflation are less probable while fiscal adjustments also appear politically difficult. The economic and political dilemma was difficult: higher interest rates would hit investment and growth and result in aggravating the recession and fiscal gap. A harder fiscal adjustment, which is crucially necessary, will aggravate the recession in the short term, thus making it difficult to obtain the necessary political support in Congress.

v) Unemployment is also rising and reached 8.3% in the second quarter of 2015 (it was 6.8% the previous year) and 500,000 additional jobs were cut between January and September 2015. With that, household spending dropped 4.1% in the middle of 2016.

vi) Uncertainty about China's economic situation—Brazil's main trading partner—has added pessimism to the already bad economic outlook for the coming months.

Brazil was hit by a triple combination of lower commodity prices, the multibillion-dollar corruption scandal at Petrobras, and a political crisis that has made President Rousseff the most unpopular president in Brazilian history, with only 10% approval rating as of September 2015 (Lewis 2015). Hundreds of thousands of protesters took to the streets calling for her resignation, while the *real* (national currency) depreciated by 25–30%, making it one of that year's worst-performing emerging market currencies (Kynge and Wheatley 2015).

The government was also dealing with huge problems in Congress with mounting political pressure on President Rousseff and an already fragile governing coalition. The political differences within the official coalition are growing and President Rousseff's political party is divided about the necessity and features of the fiscal adjustment.

With a recession in 2015 and 2016, any economic recovery will be slow, particularly, when taking into account that growth in the past decade was aided by high commodity prices and abundant consumer credit. On the positive side, exports are slowly reacting to the devaluation and lowering the current account deficit (4.5% GDP in 2015). The external sector will lead the recovery, thus making the Brazilian economy highly dependent upon the strength of the global economy and, mainly, on China's economy.

During the first quarter of 2016, the prospects for Brazilian economy were worsening. The impact of the political events on the economy makes it difficult to recover economic certainty and complicate the adoption of the urgent fiscal adjustment measures. Fiscal indicators worsened sharply in 2015 and without a broad political pact it will be hard to avoid additional deterioration in 2016–2017 (BBVA 2016). Of course, the deterioration in fiscal indicators is having a negative impact on economic activity.

The external scenario is not helping. Slowdown in China, Brazil's main trade partner, deteriorating terms of trade, weak growth of global trade, financial volatility, and slower growth in the OECD economies is the framework of the global economy for 2016 and probably 2017.

Corruption scandals, political chaos, and the successful impeachment of President Dilma Rousseff contributed to the worst recession in 25 years in Brazil. The Petrobras scandal has hurt the economic and political domains in Brazil. Dozens of politicians, business executives of leading companies, and prominent bankers have been arrested during massive investigations that have destabilized the political system.

PMDB, the biggest political party and member of the official coalition, voted to leave the government in April 2016, which accelerated Rousseff's impeachment. Former president Lula is also being investigated for money laundering. When Rousseff invited Lula to be part of the cabinet, this appointment was broadly interpreted as a tactical move oriented to shield him from investigation, given that Brazilian law stipulates that only the Supreme Court can try high-ranking cabinet members.

The Rousseff scandal is the largest in Brazilian history, which already has imposed dozens of court sentences upon prominent politicians and businessmen. The entire political and economic system is being affected. Even worse, this scandal coincides with the worst downturn in the economic history of Brazil. The GDP for the first quarter of 2016 showed a fall of 5.4%; a 4.3% contraction of GDP was expected in 2016 overall, and a 1.7% contraction is expected in 2017 (OECD 2016). With this, Brazil could face three years of recession and experience the worst economic period in its history. At the end of 2017, the Brazil's GDP could be 8% less than GDP in 2011, making it the second lost decade in its recent history.

The Brazilian economy has worsening fiscal accounts, with a public deficit already around 10% of GDP; meanwhile, it needs a primary surplus of 2% of GDP (before interest) to gradually reduce the heavy burden of public debt. Today the primary deficit is 2% of the GDP, and although the inflation and the current account deficit are declining, this is due to the acute recession.

Brazil needs broad consensus to reduce its bulging fiscal deficit and high interest rates, and to resume growth. Reducing the deficit requires very unpopular measures like freezing or reducing public spending, including public employment, and making the costly pension system sustainable. In the present moment of tension and political confrontation, that consensus is very difficult. Without that consensus it will be difficult to improve the economic situation. For now, thanks to the devaluation of the currency, only exports are contributing to the growth. However, given the weakness of the world economy, exports alone are not enough to overcome the recessive climate.

VENEZUELA

In the first quarter of 2016, government announced a set of measures oriented to fight against "the economic war" supposedly pushed for the opposition. These measures included a new economic cabinet, a partial cut of gasoline subsidies, devaluation of the currency, and the creation of a novel two-tier exchange system to improve liquidity and fiscal accounts.

Two thousand sixteen was the third year of recession in Venezuela. Growing at a modest annual average of 1.7% in 2012 and 2013, the Venezuelan economy contracted 4% in 2014 and 7% in 2015, and was expected to contract 7% or more in 2016. The sharp drop in international oil prices has aggravated the economic and political scenario. External constraints are tightening, fostering a sharp compression on imports, exacerbating already severe shortages of basic foods and goods, raising the fiscal deficit, and plummeting international reserves. The risk of hyperinflation and debt default rose in late 2016 or early 2017.

The government seems committed to servicing its debt, but the economic scenario is worsening and the probability of a default is growing every day. Additionally, debt restructuring will be difficult without a clear shift on economic policy and signs of political détente. Both phenomena are very far from materializing today. In fact, an efficient debt restructuring requires transparency on economic data, while Venezuela is a country that has not had official data since 2014.

As of 2016, Venezuela owes over US$10 billion, nearly half of which is due in October and November. Exports in 2016 were expected to amount to US$22 billion and, with current account deficit around US$18 billion in 2015, without any external support it would appear very difficult for Venezuela to close domestic and external gaps.

Exports in 2016 show a 77% decline compared to 2012. In 2016, imports plunged by more than half of the previous year's. That, combined with price controls and multiple exchange rates, led to huge shortages and a black market for basic foods and products. In any event, any room to cut imports further without provoking social unrest is very limited.

Some analysts were expecting a contraction of 10–12% in GDP for 2016. Low oil prices, severe power shortages, an unknown but high level of inflation,[4] the black market, and severe shortages of basic foods and goods are behind these estimates.

Throughout 2016, the economic and political situation in Venezuela deteriorated in a remarkable way. There was a huge conflict among the three branches of government. During the December 2015 election, the opposition party won 112 of the 164 seats in the National Assembly (the sole legislative chamber). The seats won amount to more than the two-thirds necessary to invoke important constitutional changes, including the ability to call a plebiscite or shorten a presidential mandate. To counter this, the executive branch has relied on the Court of Justice—the top of Venezuela's judiciary branch—whose judges are comprised entirely of members of the ruling party. By way of successive court rulings, the executive has been able to continuously block the National Assembly's actions and decisions. Collectively, this is aggravating the country's institutional instability.

Faced with the possibility of an ever worsening economic situation due to shortages and the threat of hyperinflation, the government proclaimed emergency economic measures. However, these measures were rejected by the National Assembly, which led to immediate questioning by the Court of Justice of the legality of said vote and, in turn, validated President Maduro's measures. These measures were initially implemented for 60 days and were later extended for another 60 days—again, with the backing of the Court of Justice.

Venezuela's government blocked parliamentary action systematically with the goal of voiding its legislative powers. Institutional fragility and a tense political climate increased. The opposition party in the National Assembly approved the start of a recall referendum, beginning with the collection of signatures and forwarding them to the electoral tribunal for validation. After that, a date for the recall referendum will have to be determined.

The Electoral Council, ruling unanimously, excessively delayed the response. Meanwhile, President Maduro and other pro-government leaders indicated that no such referendum would take place due to allegedly fraudulent signatures. The crisis is escalated to the point that the former presidents of Spain, the Dominican Republic, and Panama arranged a meeting with representatives of the ruling party and the opposition party in Santo Domingo to bridge differences and engage in a dialogue that would prevent further escalation of the crisis.

In early June, the secretary-general of the OAS called upon ambassadors to discuss the situation in Venezuela and evaluate the application of the OAS Charter, which is activated in the event of an alteration to the constitutional order and which could result in political sanctions that would isolate Venezuela from the rest of the OAS members. Ultimately, the OAS members rejected the secretary-general's proposal and instead concluded with a mild call for dialogue, which was interpreted as a triumph by the government of Venezuela. In this context, President Maduro softened his stance against the Santo Domingo dialogue but, at the same time, announced legal action against the National Assembly for having sought support in the OAS in supposed violation of their powers. All polls indicate that if the referendum were held today, Maduro would have to leave office and there would be a call for new elections. However, if the referendum is carried out in 2017 and if the government loses the referendum, Maduro would resign the presidency and be replaced by his vice president for the remainder of the term.

The political and economic situation in Venezuela is very difficult to predict. What does seem clear, however, is that the conflict will deepen, as the executive does not show any willingness to engage in dialogue. The opposition party keeps trying institutional pathways to enact a change of government. However, the actions of the executive and the judiciary branches aim precisely to close any gaps that can lead to change. Meanwhile, the economic situation is worsening and there are no signs of improvement. On the contrary, IMF projections warn of a hyperinflationary escalation and a downturn of 7–8% in 2016.

The Santo Domingo dialogue is still underway, although its start was inauspicious. There is doubt, however, about how much the opposition party will commit to this process if it is convinced that this dialogue only appears to buy time for the government. The government succeeded in blocking the referendum in October 2016—thus taking away all the dialogue's usefulness. If so, institutional and political conflict could escalate to dangerous levels.

In 2007, Venezuela cut its linkage with the IMF, turning its financial demand to China, which has already lent it more than US$50 billion and accepts repayment in oil. Several press commentators are speculating that Venezuela is trying to seek to delay the oil payments. If China agrees, it will probably ask for access to oil and minerals on more favor-

TABLE 2.3. Chinese Loans to LAC, 2005–2015

	Number of loans	Amount (US$b.)	%
Venezuela	17	65.0	52.1
Brazil	8	21.8	17.5
Argentina	8	15.3	12.2
Ecuador	11	15.2	12.2
Other LAC	24	7.5	6.0
LAC total	68	124.8	100.0

Source: Inter-American Dialogue, 2016

able terms. With a more favorable oil market during the remainder of 2016, and with Chinese help, Venezuela could avoid defaulting on its bonds. Venezuela's current administration is betting on this.

Chinese lending activity in Latin America and the Caribbean is concentrated on energy (56.3%) and infrastructure (32.3%). The Chinese banks that committed to these loans are the China Development Bank (80% of the loans) and the Ex-Im Bank (20%).

Chinese lending to LAC was marginal until 2009, when it reached US$15.5 billion and then a yearly high of US$35.6 billion in 2010. Between 2011 and 2014 the level of lending averaged US$10 billion and jumped sharply to US$29 billion in 2015. In other words, there is a clear countercyclical trend in Chinese lending to Latin America and the Caribbean, increasing rapidly during years of bad economic performance.

The focus of Chinese lending is concentrated in Venezuela, Argentina, and Ecuador—countries that faced problems accessing global capital markets in those years—and in Brazil, a BRICS partner and the main economy in the region. But the most important partner for Chinese banks has been Venezuela, which received 17 loans between 2005 and 2015 and received 52.1% of all Chinese funds directed at Latin America and the Caribbean in a decade.

In April 2015, China provided a new loan of US$5 billion. Since 2005, China has provided around US$65 billion in loans to Venezuela in so-called oil-for-loans deals. The repayment of these loans is mostly in the form of oil and gas shipments from Venezuela to China.

China's investments and loans in Venezuela amount to more than US$70–75 billion. Perhaps the interaction over the next several years will be different. Two Chinese academics have said, "Considering the state's political and economic situation, it is inappropriate to further increase the amount of investment and loans."[5] In December 2014, the Chinese Academy of Social Sciences defined Venezuela as the second-riskiest country in a list of 36 developing countries (BBC 2016).

The most likely scenario is that China will continue supporting Venezuela because it is interested in entering the Miner Arch, an area that has gold, cotton, diamond, iron, bauxite, and other reserves. Additionally, the greater the exposure of Chinese banks in Venezuela, the harder it will be to leave its main customer in Latin America, not just for financial reasons but also for diplomatic and political reasons. In fact, a failure of Chinese loans in Venezuela would be nothing more than a political strategy failure. However, this does not mean that Chinese banks will easily give up on their returns. The Chinese are probably sympathetic to President Maduro's recent economic announcements regarding devaluation, greater exchange market unification, and a drastic reduction in fuel subsidies. In other words, China will not abandon Venezuela but will be more comfortable with changes in its economic policy so as to avoid higher financial and political costs.

E. The Return of External Constraints for Latin America's Economic Growth

Latin America grew at elevated rates between 2003 and 2008 by taking advantage of favorable external conditions and benefiting from economic reforms made in the 1990s. With a surplus in the current account and easy and cheap access to finance small imbalances, the region grew at elevated rates compared to past trends. This growth, however, was not coupled with significant improvements in classic regional bottlenecks such as savings, investment, and productivity.

When the external scenario worsens, classic external restrictions to Latin America's growth reappear. The current account deficit resurges when it is more complex to finance it and a deterioration in the prices of basic products affects private and external investment cycles. This results in a deceleration of economic growth that, in turn, narrows the space for fiscal policy inasmuch as a deterioration in the terms of trade and the valuation of the dollar weakens currency and discourages foreign investment, even inducing capital outflows. In fiscal terms, Latin America has a deficit balance that is conducive to the feared "twin deficits"—external and fiscal—which indicates that, in the current situation of external vulnerability, Latin America today has less space for countercyclical policies like those it implemented in 2009 and 2010. In the medium term, this is the result of an underdiversified export structure that is heavily reliant upon a few commodities. In the short term, this speaks of not having properly taken advantage of the "golden period" by investing in infrastructure, education, innovation, and productivity.

Latin American economies face numerous challenges in light of a global economy that will continue to lack dynamism, be highly volatile, and subject to new financial crises. Among the challenges, Latin American countries must maintain macroeconomic stability and make progress in macro-prudential measures. Additionally, countries must build a more diversified productive and export structure and make progress in distribution efforts that will broaden the internal market by taking steps to achieve productive coordination with other countries in the region to widen the space for the regional market so that it can absorb extra-regional demand shocks.

Latin America is the developing region that is expected to experience the lowest growth between 2015 and 2020. With stunted growth, the labor market will undoubtedly be affected and there will be an increase in unemployment and a drop in real wages and job creation. Lower growth will also narrow the fiscal space for more progress in social policies and public investment. Recent experiences in Latin America show that with economic growth lower than 3%, poverty and income inequality will increase. Moreover, this less favorable economic scenario between 2015 and 2020 will be met with serious challenges in political governance in several countries including corruption, drug trafficking, urban insecurity, inefficiency in public utilities, and political parties losing credibility.

The expected normalization of interest rates in the US could make external financing more costly to fund the balance of payment gap. For certain, the effect will be different depending upon the macroeconomic specificities of each country. Those countries with significant fiscal deficits in their current accounts will face more severe adjustments. Economies with a flexible exchange rate and higher levels of international reserves will be in better condition to absorb external shocks, while economies with lower inflation and more rigorous fiscal management will be able to take advantage of the devaluation of their currencies to stimulate exports. Finally, countries with significant savings abroad will have the possibility of combining financing with adjustments thus limiting the shocks. On the contrary, economies with elevated inflation and fiscal imbalance with delays in significant exchange controls, distortions in key relative prices, and less international reserves will face more severe adjustments.

In this vein, Venezuela—which has a fiscal deficit of 15% of GDP, inflation near levels of 200%, a considerable decline in its international reserves, and large gaps between the official value of the dollar and its parallel value—will likely be the most affected. With the price of petroleum falling more than 50% in 2015 and a further drop in 2016, an expected inflation rate of 700% for 2016 (IMF 2016, Table A-7), and current account deficit around 7% of GDP, the policy space is increasingly limited. After three consecutive years of a recession and a fall of GDP in 2016, the coming times will be even more complex for Venezuela. No doubt it will be the worst performing economy in the region and considering the high level of political unrest in Venezuela, this forecast could be overly optimistic.

F. Preliminary Findings

Latin America experienced its best economic period in 40 years during the first decade of this century. This was the result of both internal and external factors. Internal factors include greater macroeconomic responsibility and considerable progress in making economic reforms. Relevant external factors include robust external demand for raw materials—particularly, Chinese demand—which was highly beneficial for South America. This resulted in favorable terms of trade for several countries including Brazil (soybeans and iron), Argentina (soybeans), and Chile and Peru (copper), as well as Ecuador, Venezuela, and Colombia (oil). A significant accumulation of international reserves as well as low international interest rates and favorable access to external financing allowed for an easy funding of the external gap. Large inflows of FDI aligned with an expansive commodities cycle made financing the external gap even more accessible.

Economic growth was coupled with a reduction in poverty and inequality. However, this was attributed to external variables and not domestic factors. Although Latin America was experiencing a favorable cycle, it did not make proportional progress in infrastructure, competitiveness, innovation, and quality education. In fact, during the "golden age" of the boom, the region exhibited low performance in total factor productivity while investment and savings rates did not show significant increases.

Volatility in export values remains significant—a clear sign that the region did not make sufficient progress in addressing export diversification challenges. Latin America—albeit with the exception of Mexico and Costa Rica—shows clear indications of reprimarization of exports. The dramatic increase in exports destined for China is attributed to very few products, all of which are commodities with low technological content (except for those commodities exported by Mexico and Costa Rica).

II. Major Challenges Lie Ahead

In terms of productivity, innovation, and the quality of education, Latin America has made little progress. The region needs a modern industrial policy for an open economy that bets on innovation, a presence in regional and global value chains, and reinforces ties between natural resources, manufactures, and services. This has to be coupled with supply programs that permit qualified SMEs to incorporate into value chains through accumulation of a critical mass of qualified human resources, functional infrastructure, and new technologies like the Internet of Things (IoT), Big Data, e-cloud, and robotics in specific activities that strengthen links between natural resource activities (mining, agriculture, fishing, and forestry) with modern manufacturing and services.

The key to a new industrial policy (ECLAC May 2014) resides in its ties to regional integration with more emphasis on production coordination—e.g., business alliances, regional and subregional value chains, trade facilitation measures, plurinational convergence in certain areas such as workforce training, technical standards, and vendor programs—in specific industries.

There is extensive literature associating the swings of Latin American development—basically Mexico and South America (mainly Brazil, Argentina, Colombia, Chile, Peru, Uruguay, and Venezuela)—with the notion of the middle-income trap. This entails structural features linked to low and volatile growth, little diversification of exports, low levels of productivity and competitiveness, low-quality education, excessive inequality, a lack of social protection, and institutions that do not provide stability, transparency, or adequate state management.

Empirical features of countries that have overcome the middle-income trap exhibit 12- to 15-year-long periods wherein total factor productivity grows at 1–1.5% annually, quality education that facilitates the transmission of knowledge and spread of innovative ideas, solid physical infrastructure in both "hardware" and "software," a diversified export structure that increasingly relies on knowledge-intensive goods and services, research and development (R&D) expenditure that exceeds GDP and that double or triples the regional average and, lastly, institutions that provide stability with respect to the rules of play and generate conditions for a public-private dialogue characterized by a forward-looking and coordinated approach that can address the region's development challenges in the long term. Sadly, however, the balance shows that during the ascending phase of the supercycle of raw materials, there was little progress in these areas.

A. The Economic Relationship of Latin America with the United States

THE US ECONOMY

The United States economy appears to be the strongest in the West.[6] Growth has been steady since July 2009, unemployment has decreased, the housing market is recovering, the deficit has fallen as a percentage of the GDP, and the stock market reached historic levels. However, its growth during 2014 and 2015 was only a modest 2% and, while the recession officially ended in June 2009, many Americans still perceive the economy as being in a recession. What, then, explains this significant gap between numbers and perception?

Although the economy has grown 10.3% between June 2009 and June 2014, this is the lowest rate of recovery in the post–World War II era. During this five-year period after the end of the recession, productivity (output per hour worked) grew only 6.5% during the first 20 quarters. This compares to an average increase in productivity of 13.4% in previous recoveries, for a similar period of time.

During the recovery period—June 2009 to June 2014—the employment rate grew 6.2%, which compares poorly with a rate of 12.5% during previous recoveries. Furthermore, the quality of employment deteriorated. Workers with employer-sponsored health insurance fell from 60% in 2007 to 54% in 2013 and the percentage of private-sector workers participating in retirement plans dropped from 42% in 2007 to 39% in 2013. The low economic security afforded by the labor market requires more private savings to finance the gap, which results in a reduction of available income for consumption.

The converse of this phenomenon of social vulnerability is a major leap in income and wealth concentration. In 2013, the income of the richest 5% of families was more than nine times the income of the poorest 20%—the biggest gap since 1967, when statistics began to be recorded. In June 2014, corporate profits adjusted for inflation were 94% higher than in June 2009; meanwhile, the median household income was 8% below the pre-crisis level.

The reduction in unemployment (from 10% to 6%) has already been mentioned. However, this reduction in unemployment seems to be explained by large numbers of workers leaving the labor force. During this period, the participation rate in the labor force has fallen 4 points (from 67% to 63%). The explanation for this is that the economy is generating few jobs, thus increasing the duration of unemployment while real wages remain stagnant.

During the economic expansion of the 1990s, the economy added at least 250,000 new jobs per month more than 47 times. During the expansion—the period of 60 months between June 2009 and June 2014—creation of new jobs per month was achieved only 6 times. The figures for long-term unemployment are 50% higher than during pre-crisis levels and there are already three million unemployed workers expected for an additional year. One-third of the unemployed fall into this category.

Real wages (measured by the employment cost index, which is a more comprehensive measure than wage cost per hour) fell between 2009 and 2013 and began to rise only as recently as 2014 with small increases of only 0.15% per year.

This significant asymmetry in the distribution of the benefits associated with growth is already worrying the Federal Reserve. Indeed,

Janet Yellen, chair of the Federal Reserve, expressed concern about the growth in income inequality in the United States and described it as the most extreme since the 19th century. She referred to 2013 figures, which show that 50% of lower-income families received only 1% of the wealth (3% in 1989) while the wealthiest 5% received a 61% share (54% in 1989). The average income of the wealthiest 5% grew 38% between 1989 and 2013, while the income of the remaining 95% in those 24 years only grew slightly less than 10% (less than half a point increase per year). This undoubtedly results in substantial prosperity for a minority of the population and stagnation in living standards for the majority.

This acute process of economic concentration—also underway in the United Kingdom—is not only conducive to social and political tensions in the coming years but also becomes an obstacle to economic growth. There are real concerns regarding economies where private consumption accounts for approximately two-thirds of GDP, real wages are stagnating or declining, the labor market is characterized by low labor force participation and long-term unemployment, effective demand will remain depressed, and potential output will be lower. All of these factors will result in a continued disappointment with the dynamism of the global economy and will remain so as long as these delicate issues of political economy are not addressed.

TRADE BETWEEN THE US AND LATIN AMERICA

Latin America accounts for one-quarter of total US trade. In the past two decades, the United States' trade with Latin American countries has grown faster than the country's trade with most of its main partners, except for China. However, this trade is highly concentrated. In fact, Mexico alone accounts almost for two-thirds of total US imports from the Latin America region (see Table 2.4).

The United States is a particularly important trading partner for Mexico, Central America, and the Caribbean. Mexico's share of exports to the United States of total GDP is 27%, for the Caribbean it is 13%, and for Central America it is 9%[7] (see Table 2.5). The United States continues to be the primary destination for products originating in Mexico, Central America, Panama, Ecuador, Colombia, and Venezuela, and, conversely, the main source of imports for these same countries. The situation, however, is different for South American countries. During the first decade

TABLE 2.4. United States: Breakdown of Trade by Main Partners, 1980–2014 (*Share of total US trade and annual growth rate*)

	Region/country	Shares				Annual growth rate (2000–2014)
		1980	1990	2000	2014	
Exports	Canada	16.0	21.1	22.6	19.2	4.2
	LAC	17.1	13.3	21.6	25.8	6.7
	European Union	28.7	26.6	21.6	17.1	3.6
	Asia	19.6	24.5	21.9	21.3	5.1
	China	1.7	1.2	2.1	7.6	15.6
	Japan	9.4	12.4	8.4	4.1	0.2
	Rest of the World	18.5	14.4	12.2	16.5	7.7
Imports	Canada	16.6	18.1	18.5	14.6	3.0
	LAC	14.2	12.9	16.9	18.8	5.5
	European Union	17.2	20.2	18.7	17.7	4.4
	Asia	21.9	31.7	31.9	35.4	5.5
	China	0.5	3.1	8.6	20.2	11.4
	Japan	13.0	18.1	12.0	5.7	-0.7
	Rest of the World	30.1	17.1	14.1	13.5	4.4
Total Trade	Canada	16.3	19.6	20.6	16.5	3.5
	LAC	15.7	13.1	19.3	21.6	6.1
	European Union	22.9	23.4	20.1	17.5	4.1
	Asia	20.7	28.1	26.9	29.7	5.4
	China	1.1	2.2	5.3	15.1	12.1
	Japan	11,2	15.3	10.2	5.1	-0.4
	Rest of the World	24.3	15.8	13.2	14.7	5.7

Source: Based on the Economic Commission for Latin America and the Caribbean and COMTRADE

of the 2000s, China replaced the United States as the primary destination for exports from Brazil, Bolivia, Chile, and Peru, and a similar phenomenon occurred with respect to country of origin for imports.[8]

The United States traditionally posts a deficit in merchandise trade with Latin America. The largest deficit, of course, is with Mexico and then with Central America. The United States has a slight surplus with South America. In terms of the composition of trade, Latin America's exports to the United States present a higher share of manufactures than the region's exports to the rest of the world. Mexico has the largest share of manufactures in its exports to the US (82%); if Mexico is excluded, the

TABLE 2.5. United States' Rank as a Trading Partner for Latin American Countries

			Exports				Imports			
			1980	1990	2000	2014	1980	1990	2000	2014
South America	Mercosur	Argentina	3	1	2	3	1	1	2	3
		Brazil	1	1	1	2	1	1	1	2
		Paraguay	6	6	6	9	3	4	4	4
		Uruguay	4	2	3	6	4	3	3	4
	CAN	Bolivia	1	2	1	3	1	1	1	3
		Colombia	1	1	1	1	1	1	1	1
		Ecuador	1	1	1	1	1	1	1	1
		Peru	1	1	1	2	1	1	1	2
		Chile	3	2	1	2	1	1	1	2
		Venezuela	1	1	1	1	1	1	1	1
Mexico and Central America	CACM	Costa Rica	1	1	1	1	1	1	1	1
		El Salvador	1	2	1	1	2	1	1	1
		Guatemala	1	1	1	1	1	1	1	1
		Honduras	1	1	1	1	1	1	1	1
		Nicaragua	1	4	1	1	1	1	1	1
		Mexico	1	1	1	1	1	1	1	1
		Panama	1	1	1	1	1	1	1	1

Source: COMTRADE

share of manufactures exported by the region drops to 42%. In terms of export diversification, Latin America exports a higher number of products to the United States than to the European Union and Asia. But, except for Mexico and Brazil, the share of the top five products in total exports to the United States ranges from 40% to 97%.

KEY ELEMENTS OF THE ECONOMIC RELATIONSHIP BETWEEN THE US AND LATIN AMERICA

The United States has not had a comprehensive trade strategy toward the region since the abandonment of the Free Trade Area of the Americas (FTAA) project. It has opted instead to pursue a strategy of bilateral negotiations. However, the bilateral approach has two major problems: (i) it results in "hub and spokes," which loses the benefits of linking several free trade agreements (FTAs); and (ii) there are no clear signals to

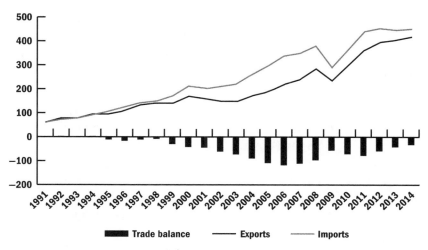

Figure 2.1. United States: Exports, Imports, and Trade Balance with LAC, 1991–2014 (Billions of dollars)
Source: Economic Commission for Latin America and the Caribbean

engage those countries in the region that are not parties to FTAs with the United States.

The most recent effort visible in the region is the Trans-Pacific Partnership (TPP), which anticipated including Mexico, Chile, and Peru. However, this is still the same strategy: a bilateral approach, albeit with an expanded focus, if the TPP proceeds. The special link that the TPP could signify for these three countries may create a clear divide with the remaining countries in the region that are not parties to the TPP. In essence, Level I countries would be those that have free trade agreements with the United States and are also signatories to the TPP (Chile, Mexico and Peru). Level II countries would be those countries that are parties to free trade agreements with the United States but are not TPP countries like, for example, Central American countries and Panama, the Dominican Republic, and Colombia. Lastly, Level III countries would be those countries that do not have free trade agreements with the United States and are not parties to the TPP (Mercosur countries, Ecuador, and Venezuela).

The overlap of trade agreements of varying scope and depth will generate transactional costs for Latin American products entering the United States. Depending on the country of origin, Latin American products will be subject to different tariffs and customs and trade facilitation treatment. Something similar will occur with trade in services and investments. If it seems that running this risk is worthwhile because the rest of the region may accede to the TPP, which is a highly improbable scenario. It is not realistic to assume that Brazil will adhere to a trade scheme in which it has not participated in the rule-creation process. Something similar can be said with respect to Argentina. As such, with the independent nature of the current governments, it is unlikely that other countries may accede to the TPP, even more so when it is evident that Brazil looks to China as a main trading partner.

The June 2015 debates surrounding renewal of trade promotion authority emphasized the importance of the TPP as a vehicle to contain China and also to improve the relative position of United States businesses in Asian value chains. This further confirms the TPP's geostrategic value. If the TPP eventually goes ahead, this may result in complications for Latin American economies that have China as their main trading partner like, for example, Chile and Peru. This is even more valid for Brazil—a BRICS member—which is China's main ally in Latin America.

The United States' economic approach to Latin America is based on various free trade agreements and does not take into account special funds for infrastructure or symbolic megaprojects such as those that appear in China's cooperation proposal with the region like, for example, an interoceanic railway that will connect Brazil and Chile (the "Twin Ocean Railroad") and a trans-Andean railroad project that will link Argentina and Chile.

Of course, the most important link that is absent in the United States' Latin America policy is Brazil—the biggest country in the region, member of the G20 and the BRICS. It seems, in fact, like an important omission, but now may be less significant because Washington is hesitant to proceed with the TPP. Given the defining role of Brazil in South America and in UNASUR—and by extension in the Community of Latin American and Caribbean States (CELAC)—a policy toward the region that does not emphasize Brazil is incomplete and ineffective.

Moreover, this strategy is to seemingly "divide and conquer" and does not incorporate the increasing need for regional integration in Latin America. In essence, it seems ever more clear that it is not a good idea to foster a division between the Atlantic (Mercosur) and the Pacific (Pacific

Alliance)—and not just for ideological reasons, but rather for strictly economic ones. Increasing intraregional investment flows associated with the expansion of Trans-Latins, a growing number of tourists and intraregional migrants, and mobility of specialized and nonspecialized labor begin to build a case for more regional integration or, at least, the need to make progress in regulatory convergence in investment and services in key sectors as well as take initiatives to participate in regional and global value chains.

Furthermore, a majority of the region's manufactures have as their primary export markets other countries in the region. Any serious industrialization efforts should prioritize the expansion of intraregional trade (Rosales 2015). This trade, however, has a low component of intraindustrial trade—pieces, parts, and components—which characterizes the type of trade that takes place within value chains. As such, if the region wants to diversify exports in order to broaden the space for manufactures and services as well as develop value chains, it must engage in more, and better, intraregional trade.

In this sense, the Pacific Alliance has taken important steps forward. Among them is the integration of Colombia's, Chile's, and Peru's stock markets—which will soon be joined by Mexico's stock market. The possibility of engaging in market transactions in each of these stock markets is a step forward in market development. This has not gone unnoticed by Brazil given that the joint capitalization of these stock markets surpasses that of São Paulo. This explains why a major bank in Brazil has purchased significant shares of stock in Santiago's Stock Exchange.

For members of the Pacific Alliance, it is abundantly clear that a friendly link must be established with both Brazil and the Atlantic rim. Each time there is dialogue between the Pacific Alliance and China, it is clear what the founding purpose of the Pacific Alliance is. Essentially, it is to coordinate and accomplish a joint insertion of Latin America into China and Asia-Pacific. To fulfill this objective, the Pacific Alliance needs a collective approach that encompasses both the Atlantic and Pacific rims. For reasons of scale and market opportunities, a collective approach to Asia-Pacific would be more beneficial if countries from both rims were engaged.

In terms of foreign direct investment, the United States remains the largest single foreign investor in the region. Latin America's share in

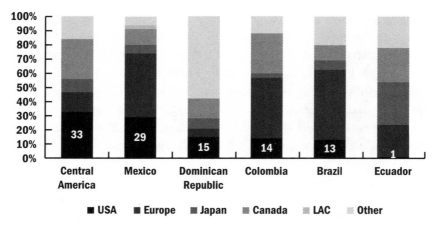

Figure 2.2. Foreign Direct Investment Flows into Latin America and the Caribbean
Source: Economic Commission for Latin America and the Caribbean, based on
official figures

total United States FDI flows is about 8%. The main recipients are Central America and Mexico (see Figure 2.2). In comparison with FDI flows originating in other regions, the United States remains the largest investor in Central America. It has, however, been displaced by the European Union in Mexico, Brazil, and Colombia.

The US investment stock in the region continues to be highly concentrated in Mexico and, to a lesser extent, in Brazil. It is worth noting that the US investment in Argentina is similar to that in Central America and only one-third of that destined for Chile. In the event the multimillion-dollar cooperation funds offered by China for infrastructure, agriculture, industry, and new technologies come through, this investment scenario will stimulate close commercial ties to China.

STRENGTHENING ECONOMIC AND TRADE COOPERATION BETWEEN THE US AND LATIN AMERICA

In the field of FTAs, the United States has the opportunity to allow accumulation of origin across all of its FTAs in force with countries in the region and thus foster productive integration and the development of regional value chains oriented toward the United States market. The United States should take the initiative because if the European Union concludes its trade agreement with Mercosur, that could lead to accumulation of origin across all European Union FTAs in the region, which are geographically broad in scope and include Mexico, Central America, the Dominican Republic, Caribbean countries, Colombia, Ecuador, Chile, Peru, and the four economies of Mercosur (Brazil, Argentina, Uruguay, and Paraguay). It is only a matter of time before it is known which actor will take the first step in this direction.

In general terms, the United States should ensure an adequate balance between outcomes on emerging issues and traditional issues. The new issues are intellectual property, investment, services, regulatory coherence, state-owned enterprises, labor, and the environment. The traditional issues that are of interest to Latin American countries include antidumping, agricultural market access, movement of natural persons, transport services, and public procurement.

There are also other strategic initiatives available to the United States in trade negotiations with Latin American countries, including: (i) incorporating Mexico in the Transatlantic Trade and Investment Partnership (TTIP) negotiations; and (ii) promoting accession to the TPP for all interested Latin American countries. In fact, given that Mexico, Central America, the Caribbean, Colombia, Ecuador, Chile, and Peru have FTAs with the European Union, future advances in the TTIP could undermine the benefits that Latin American and Caribbean countries have with the European Union and with the United States. The same is true for Central America and Colombia, which have FTAs with the United States but will see a decrease in benefits when TTIP negotiations conclude.

In the medium term, the United States should promote the convergence of all hemispheric trade agreements, mainly dominated by US and European Union templates. Taking into account the new spirit that Brazil has exhibited in pursuing an agreement with the European Union, this convergence in the next ten years looks plausible.

Moreover, the United States should consider establishing an integrated hemispheric program of economic cooperation funded by national governments as well as national and regional development banks. This program should cover areas such as: (i) transport and logistical infrastructure across the Americas (ports, airports, roads); (ii) trade facilitation, including reducing red tape in Latin American countries and assisting countries in fulfilling United States security requirements; (iii) funding to implement programs in Latin America to train and retrain workers who might have lost their jobs due to import competition similar to the Trade Adjustment Assistance program; and (iv) establishing specific programs oriented to support SMEs with export potential (Rosales 2015).

The impact of these kinds of programs would be very relevant and would likely contribute not only to improving the image of the United States in the region but also to strengthening the export-oriented nature of Latin America's economic policy. As the region is the main partner of United States in consolidated terms, these programs make sense both for the United States and for the region.

B. Latin America's Economic Relationship with China

There has been an impressive change in Latin America's trade matrix in the last ten years. China has transformed itself from a minor actor to a highly relevant trade partner. In aggregate terms, China is the region's second-largest import source (behind the United States) and the third-largest export destination (behind the United States and the European Union). In bilateral cases, China is the top trading partner for Brazil, Chile, and Peru and the second export market for Argentina, Colombia, Peru, and Venezuela. It is also the first or second import supplier for a dozen Latin American countries.

Between 2000 and 2014, trade in goods between Latin America and the Caribbean and China increased 22-fold, from just over US$12 billion to nearly US$270 billion. During the same period, China's share of the region's exports climbed from 1% to 10% and its share of imports rose from just over 2% to 16%. In 2014, merchandise trade between Latin America and China decreased by 2%—the first fall since 2009. The Chinese deceleration severely affects dynamism of trade with Latin America. Between 2000 and 2013 the value of merchandise trade grew at an average rate of 27% per year. Between 2011 and 2013, it grew at just 5% per year and, by 2014, declined by 2%. In order to reach US$500 billion around 2023–2024, bilateral trade would need to expand by 6% annually in the next years.[9]

All Latin American countries—except for Venezuela, Brazil, and Chile—have a trade deficit with China. Mexico accounts for 85% of

Latin America and the Caribbean's entire deficit with China. In 2013, Mexico's trade deficit with China was US$55 billion. Latin America as a whole maintains a growing trade surplus in commodities and natural-resource-based manufactures, especially those produced in South America. In contrast, the region as a whole, and without any country exceptions, has a growing deficit with China in other manufactures (ECLAC 2015).

The composition of trade with China remains a cause for concern in the region. In fact, Latin America's export basket to China is much less sophisticated than its exports to the rest of the world and is concentrated in a small number of products. For all countries in the region—except Mexico—the five main products accounted for 80% or more of the total value exports to China in 2013. In 2016, commodities accounted for 73% of the region's exports to China compared to 41% of its worldwide sales.

China is a key factor in the current "reprimarization" or "recommodi-fication" process of the Latin American export sector. The strong commodity bias in Latin America's exports to China may be an obstacle for the region to upgrade to a more diversified and knowledge-intensive export structure (ECLAC 2015). On the other hand, the high concentration of Latin America's exports to China in primary sectors raises social and environmental concerns because these exports support fewer jobs, generate more net greenhouse gas emissions, and use more water than other Latin American exports (Ray and Gallagher 2015).

Chinese competition in manufactures—both in domestic and third markets—is more and more relevant, as can be seen from the experiences of Mexico, Brazil, Colombia, and Argentina (Rosales 2012). The sectors that experienced the greatest impact in all four countries—all of which was negative—were industrial machinery and equipment, office machinery, electrical equipment, and metal products. The four countries have seen their market share decline in both high- and low-tech products in the United States and in Latin America. To measure the impacts of Chinese competition in domestic markets, it is also necessary to add industrial sectors like wood, pulp and paper, textiles and apparel, and footwear.

By 2010, approximately 22% of the combined industrial exports of the four selected countries to the two major regional markets (United States and Latin America) were threatened by competition from China. As for competition in the domestic market, the three countries for which it was possible to calculate the coefficient showed a rise of imports in apparent consumption from 6% to 11% in all the manufactures, with the above-mentioned sectors (office machinery, metal products, wood pulp, etc.) being the most affected ones (Rosales 2012).

There is an excess of capacity in key manufacturing sectors—i.e., steel, cement, glass, aluminum, construction equipment—which induce more Chinese exports in these sectors, thus affecting the international prices of these products and the profitability of their competitors. In light of this excess capacity—which in the case of steel surpasses all of Latin America's production—the steel sector in Latin America has been facing a significant decline in its share. This is an issue that should form part of the dialogue and cooperation agenda with China.

China's investment in Latin America remains limited in scope. Chinese foreign direct investment (FDI) in Latin America was very limited until 2010. Since then, Chinese companies have invested on average about US$10 billion per year. Of course, with this amount, China is not one of the main foreign investors in Latin America but it still has a substantial presence in natural resource related activities, particularly oil and mining.

Almost 90% of estimated Chinese investment in Latin America is concentrated in natural resources (ECLAC 2013). Chinese companies are among the most relevant foreign players in oil and gas extraction in Argentina, Brazil, Colombia, Ecuador, Venezuela, and, to a lesser extent, Peru. In mining, they have a visible presence in Peru and, to some degree, in Brazil. Manufacturing investment is concentrated in Brazil and mostly in the automotive and electronic sectors and focused on producing for domestic markets.

There are two challenges in relation to Chinese FDI in Latin America: (i) the still limited amounts involved represent a clear asymmetry with trade levels and difficult business alliances; and (ii) there is regional pressure to diversify this investment toward non-extractive industries such as manufacturing, services, and infrastructure with a view of enhancing the diversification and productivity of Latin American economies.

Latin America's main challenges with respect to the economic relationship with China may be summarized in three areas: (i) diversifying exports and the need to obtain a greater trade balance equilibrium; (ii) increasing and diversifying Chinese investments in Latin America, particularly in infrastructure, manufactures, and services; and (iii) boosting regional investment in China and Asia-Pacific.

In order to better deal with these challenges, Latin American governments urgently need to combine efforts to define and agree on regional priorities and discuss them with China. These priorities should be of a regional or subregional nature or, at the very least of a multicountry nature, with less focus on unilateral initiatives. However, the real challenge is how to link domestic agendas of innovation and competitiveness with renewed economic ties with China and, more generally, with Asia-Pacific (ECLAC 2015).

THE IMPACTS OF CHINESE ECONOMIC REFORMS IN LATIN AMERICA

The "new Chinese normal" is economic growth at 6 to 7% annually for the next five years. The impact of this growth suggests that international prices for Latin America's commodities will be similar to current levels or slightly lower for the rest of the decade. Weaker currencies may help in efforts for export diversification if efficient industrial policies are implemented.

Economic reforms in China will promote urbanization, more sophisticated industrialization, and an important expansion of the middle class. This process opens up ample space for Latin America's export diversification to China: healthy and secure foods with international certification, changes in urban diets with less consumption of grains and cereals and more meat consumption (e.g., beef, turkey, pork, and poultry), seafood, wine, and services of different kinds (ECLAC 2015).

China's "Going Global" strategy will promote more foreign direct investment into Latin America and will probably feature a higher component of private and small and medium enterprise investment. There is an opportunity to diversify Chinese investments if Latin America's governments and chambers of commerce implement activities, jointly with Chinese agencies such as the Chinese Council for the Promotion of International Trade (CCPIT), with the goal of providing information and coordinating business opportunities.

CHINA'S NEW COOPERATION PROPOSALS

The first ministerial meeting of the China-CELAC Forum was held in January 2015, an event described by President Xi Jinping as a "grand gathering in the history of China-Latin America and the Caribbean relations." The primary purpose of the meeting was to join efforts to promote a China–Latin America and Caribbean partnership of comprehensive cooperations. It was during this ministerial meeting that the Cooperation Plan 2015–2019 was approved. This plan builds upon the "1+3+6" cooperation framework proposed by China that seeks to get the three engines of trade, investment, and financial cooperation to run at full speed as well as develop cooperation projects in the six areas of energy and resources, infrastructure, agriculture, manufacturing, innovation in science and technology, and information technologies (Xi 2015). A visit by Chinese prime minister Li Keqiang in May 2015 to South America provided renewed impetus for these cooperation efforts.

These China–Latin America cooperation initiatives are creating new funds to enhance productive capacity, innovation, and technological capabilities, and to diversify exports in pursuit of a trade balance equilibrium. They are also an attempt to increase and diversify Chinese investment through infrastructure, energy, logistics, Internet and broadband, the bioceanic railway (Brazil-Peru), and the trans-Andean railroad project (Argentina-Chile).

The economic interaction with China is more and more relevant in Latin America and, particularly, in South America. China has surpassed the United States as the most important destination for South American exports. Therefore, one point of Chinese GDP is more relevant for South America's economic growth than a similar point in the United States' GDP.

Examining the evolution of the official meetings between China and Latin America, China is more proactive in presenting proposals and gives the impression that it has a clear strategy for Latin America. Latin America, on the other hand, looks more passive, discoordinated, and without any strategic guidelines. Until now, CELAC has not proved up to the challenge. The region should be more proactive.

The amounts of Chinese cooperation so far committed exceed several times the figures of the United States–led Alliance for Progress. Currently, there are symbolic initiatives in infrastructure, millions of funds for technological improvements in agriculture and manufacturing, and plans for sectoral and ministerial forums that would meet every two years (agriculture, manufacturing, science and technology, infrastructure). This cooperation, if well managed, could address the region's integration needs in infrastructure and technological upgrading, and foster intraregional trade and regional value chains.

China is beginning to occupy important areas of influence in Latin America, among them, finance in Venezuela, Ecuador, and Argentina, as well as trade in South America. Until now, the United States has done nothing comparable. While China underlines the presence of CELAC, the United States policy for the region is centered on bilateral dialogue. While China promotes a trilogy—trade, investment, and cooperation— with a marked political pragmatism, the United States prefers to focus on a few privileged partners (primarily Mexico, as Chile and Peru have been engaged mostly for purposes related to the TPP). The U.S. also demands hard commitments in delicate public policy areas. For the United States, the main topics of the Latin America agenda are drugs and immigration. While the United States needs to "de-Mexicanize" its agenda with Latin America, China needs to "de-Brazilianize" its agenda with the region.

A Final Reflection: What about Regional Integration?

The drastic change in South America's economic cycle is also reflected in significant political changes. In a scenario of strong economic slowdown, we have seen changes in Argentina's government and a temporary substitution in Brazil that, when coupled, substantially alter Mercosur's scenario. Deepened economic and political crises in Venezuela, compounded by the sharp drop in international oil prices, makes it unable to continue promoting ALBA by selling subsidized oil operations.

Political changes in Brazil and Argentina tend to reinforce the previous ABC—Argentina, Brazil, and Chile—and the link between Mercosur and the Pacific Alliance (PA). Uruguay and Chile are already negotiating a free trade agreement, surpassing the commitments contained in the Economic Complementation Agreement that currently binds them. The authorities of both countries have pointed out that the objective is to achieve a modern agreement with comprehensive coverage and depth, probably with an aim to advance Uruguay's entrance to the PA, where it is currently an observer state.

This new scenario demonstrates that Argentina and Brazil are much more willing to move forward with the Mercosur and EU negotiations, although Brazil has exhibited this proactivity since the beginning of 2015. The new Brazilian authorities have reinforced this initiative and exhibited a proclivity toward establishing more intense business and investment relationships with its main extra-regional partners. Since Paraguay and Uruguay have had this approach for several years, it is possible to predict a major renewal in Mercosur that may also be supported by strategic links with the PA.

In this sense, the successful conclusion of an EU-Mercosur agreement could play a decisive role and would be the best news for regional integration (Rosales 2016). First, the EU currently has free trade agreements in the region with many states in the region. If an agreement with Mercosur were to come to fruition, only Bolivia, Cuba, and Venezuela would be left out of this web of agreements.

If an EU-Mercosur agreement is reached, 30 countries in the region would have trade agreements with the EU that contain very similar commitments in services, investment, and public procurement, among others—topics that are not in the purview of the majority of intra-regional agreements.

Second, the next step would be to follow the patterns that we have committed to with the EU. This would be a decisive step for effective regional integration supported by a free movement of goods, services, investment, and people. This move does not have to be drastic. It can be gradual and include exceptions and specific terms for phasing out certain standards. Here tariff concessions are the least relevant, given that they are current or can be negotiated later. What is most relevant is the convergence of rules, disciplines, and a dispute settlement mechanism—these are the foundations for an expanded regional market with converging standards in trade in goods, services, and investment.

Third, an additional step would be to link the accumulation of origin contained in all of the EU agreements with the countries in the region. The EU allows this buildup of its agreements with several subregions. With such accumulation of origin, exports from any country in Latin America and the Caribbean could use inputs coming from any country in the region that has an agreement with the EU. This would create new spaces for the formation of regional value chains. The regional market is key for manufacture exports. With a unified regional market, like that which would result from the consolidation of trade agreements with the EU (including an agreement with Mercosur), intra-regional trade would benefit. As this is the most SME-friendly trade, this would not only encourage growth but also would promote equity and diversify export companies and suppliers.

In reaching an agreement with Mercosur, the EU would have forged ahead of China and the United States in concluding the first agreement with (nearly) an entire continent. This would be a success for EU international policy, ahead of the FTAA that the United States promoted and in the face of Chinese competition. Apart from short-term economic and political troubles in Argentina and Brazil, no serious investor could underestimate the market potential in goods and services in these economies, as well as the prospects for growth of their respective middle classes. In the medium term, such prospects, together with the favorable effect on regional integration, are more attractive than those of Europe.

It is true that the current situation helps little to make progress toward this agreement. Yet these decisions are not taken with a short-term lens. On the contrary, they are strategic decisions where intelligence and foresight should dominate. Once Brazil recovers, and given its new export-oriented approach, it will be even more valuable to be close to the relaunch of Brazilian trade and investment, the architects and expansionists of the multilatins.

Strategic challenges have never been easy. The new economic situation in Argentina may help to considerably improve the scenario. This agreement would also improve the economic climate in Brazil and Argentina as well as the rest of South America. It would also generate good business opportunities in goods, services, and investments for Europe, exempt from the common external tariff that would affect exports from the United States or China and with regulations that favor their investments.

Unfortunately, negotiations with Mercosur are not on the EU agenda. More regional support is required for this to occur. The task that looms is not easy. The EU has failed to curb its protectionist agricultural pressures. However, the opportunity exists and must be pressed so that the window does not close. It is not wise to bet on a last-generation agreement. The important thing is to promote a flexible agreement, although partial, to try to resize EU-Mercosur relations in a new way that is more compatible with the weight of both groups in the global economy.

In any case, it is possible to project that in the coming years a pragmatic rapprochement between Mercosur and the Pacific Alliance could occur, thus improving the chances for a major integration effort. To the extent that these efforts move forward, the region's bargaining power and attractiveness would rise. In the current international environment, the trend toward mega-blocs and inter-regional trade agreements is clear. In this way, a more integrated Latin America, along with improved development options, would improve the region's capacity for negotiations and dialogue with its main extra-regional partners, that is, with the United States, China, and the European Union.

NOTES

1 I appreciate the effective collaboration of Tania García-Millán in the preparation of this paper.

2 It is worth nothing that these are nonpublic figures given that, after the Official Statistics Institute reformulated its price indicator and lost legitimacy, the *Economist* opted not to consider this index.

3 "Corralitos" is the informal term used to refer to the economic measures taken by Argentina in early 2001 to freeze bank accounts and force dollar accounts to be converted into devalued pesos. See, for example, "Here Comes the Corralito?," *Economist*, May 17, 2012.

4 The official inflation rate for 2015 reported by the Central Bank was 161%, but the weighted sum of its sectoral components came to 249% (www.econolatin.com). Anyway, the IMF expects the 2016 inflation rate will be around 700%.

5 Xue Li and Xu Yanzhou, "Why China Shouldn't Get Too Invested in Latin America," *Diplomat*, March 31, 2015.

6 Figures are from "Economic Snapshot: September 2014" and "The State of the U.S Labor Market: Pre-October 2014 Jobs Release," both from the Center for American Progress.

7 The data for Central America is based on 2009 figures.

8 In the case of Bolivia, Brazil displaced the United States as the primary export market.

9 This is a goal included in the China–Latin America and Caribbean 2015–2019 Cooperation Plan.

BIBLIOGRAPHY
BBVA. BBVA Research: Brazil Economic Outlook, 1st Quarter 2016, Latin America Unit.
Brandimarte, Walter. "Brazil Downgraded to Junk Rating by S&P, Deepening Woes."
   Reuters, September 9, 2015. www.reuters.com.
———. "Brazil Opts Not to Support World's Worst-Performing Currency." *Reuters*,
   March 13, 2015. www.reuters.com.
Dyer, Geoff. "Brazil's Economy Slips into Recession." *Financial Times*, August 28, 2015.
ECLAC (Economic Commission for Latin America and the Caribbean). Santiago,
   April 2016. www.cepal.org.
———. *First Forum of China and the Community of Latin American and Caribbean
   States (CELAC): Exploring Opportunities for Cooperation on Trade and Investment.*
   LC/L.3941. Santiago, January 2015. www.cepal.org.
———. *Panorama Social de América Latina: 2014.* Santiago, December 2014. www.cepal
   .org.
———. *Regional Integration: Towards an Inclusive Value Chain Strategy.* LC/G2594.
   Santiago, May 2014. www.cepal.org.
———. *Chinese Foreign Direct Investment in Latin America and the Caribbean: China-
   Latin America Cross-Council Taskforce, Working Document.* Presented at the World
   Economic Forum Summit on the Global Agenda in Abu Dhabi, November 18–20,
   2013.
———. *The United States and Latin America and the Caribbean: Highlights of Economy
   and Trade.* LC/G.2489. Santiago, March 2011.
Fanelli, José María. "Argentina: esperando el segundo semestre." *Observatorio
   Económico de la Red de Mercosur,* June 2, 2016.
Gallagher, Kevin P., and Margaret Myers. "China-Latin America Finance Database,"
   2014. *Inter-American Dialogue.* www.thedialogue.org.
International Finance Institute (IFI). *Capital Flows to Emerging Markets.* Washington,
   DC, 2015.
International Monetary Fund (IMF). *World Economic Outlook: Too Slow for Too Long,.*
   Washington, DC, April 2016.
———. *World Economic Outlook: Adjusting to Lower Commodity Prices.* Washington,
   DC, October 2015.
Kynge, James, and Jonathan Wheatley. "Emerging Markets: Fixing a Broken Model."
   Financial Times, August 31, 2015.
Leahy, Joe. "S&P Cuts Brazil's Credit Rating to Junk." *Financial Times*, September 10, 2015.
Lewis, Jeffrey. "Brazilian President Dilma Rousseff's Approval Ratings Languish." *Wall
   Street Journal*, September 30, 2015. www.wsj.com.
Machinea, José Luis. "América Latina: el vaso medio lleno o medio vacío."Presented at
   Seminario de Economistas CAF-SEGIB in Segovia, Spain, July 2015.
Organization for Economic Development and Cooperation (OECD). *Sub-Par Global
   Growth and Slowdown in Emerging Economies Requires a Shift in Policy Action.*
   Paris, 2015. www.oecd.org.

————. Economic Outlook, June 2016.

Ray, Rebecca, and Kevin Gallagher, "China-Latin America Economic Bulletin." *Boston University Global Economic Governance Initiative* 9 (2015). www.bu.edu.

Rosales, Osvaldo. "El acuerdo Mercosur–Unión Europea y la integración regional," *La Nación* (Buenos Aires), February 23, 2016.

————, comp. *Globalización, integración y comercio inclusivo en América Latina, Textos Seleccionados 2010–2014* (United Nations, 2015). www.cepal.org.

————. "Trade Competition from China. The Impact of Chinese Exports on Four Countries in the Region." *Americas Quarterly*, Winter 2012. www.americasquarterly.org.

Rosales, Osvaldo, and Sebastian Herreros. "Mega-Regional Trade Negotiations: What Is at Stake for Latin America?" Presented at the Inter-American Dialogue in Washington, DC, January 14–15, 2014.

World Trade Organization (WTO). "Falling Import Demand, Lower Commodity Prices Push Down Trade Growth Prospects," September 30, 2015. www.wto.org.

Xi Jinping. "Jointly Write a New Chapter of Comprehensive Cooperation between China and Latin America and the Caribbean." Address delivered at opening ceremony of the First Ministerial Meeting of the China-CELAC Forum, Beijing, January 2015.

3

The New and Not-So-New Foreign Policies in the Americas

CHRISTOPHER SABATINI

In the past 15 years, a number of Latin American states have established more active and assertive foreign policies, seeking a broader role regionally and globally. From Brazil's efforts to establish itself as a leader of the new Global South, to Chile's efforts to link its economy in an array of extra-hemispheric free trade agreements and to Mexico's accession to the OECD, Latin American countries have, in varying ways and degrees, become global players. The diversity of goals and strategies itself reflects the space for independent action within the region, a far cry from when many countries tended to look inward or northward or court an extra-hemispheric ally to offset the predominance of the United States. And although the collapse of the global commodities prices has cooled the region's economic growth (in countries like Peru, Chile, Bolivia, Colombia, and Mexico) has brought a number of countries to economic crisis (Argentina, Brazil, Ecuador, and Venezuela), and even has contributed to political upheaval (Brazil and Venezuela), more independent and assertive foreign policies in the region will remain. The basic regional and global context have changed in ways that, irrespective of the ideological orientations of governments, states are defining their national interests more broadly than before at the same time that the scope for diplomatic initiative and economic interaction and alliances is far greater.

Four related factors have driven this growth of foreign policy initiative and change in the region. The first of these has been the economic and diplomatic emergence of the Global South, marked by China's impressive economic growth but also the growing network of south-south diplomatic initiatives and collaboration. The second, in a reflection of the proliferation south-south contacts generally, has been the emergence of regional groups in the Western Hemisphere that pointedly exclude the hemisphere's developed neighbors to the north, the United States and Canada. Groups such as the Union of South American States (UNASUR) and the Community of Latin American and Caribbean States (CELAC) have both served as points of contact to collaborate with other regional groups in the Global South and provided a forum for Latin American and Caribbean neighbors to resolve their issues without the United States. How well they've done that is a matter of dispute that I discuss below. The third has been the perceived decline of U.S. power, in the hemisphere and globally. Whether real or permanent, that perceived waning of U.S. hegemony over the region has led to governments in the region to contest U.S. policies, challenge traditional diplomatic channels and institutions, such as the Organization of American States (OAS), and economically and diplomatically court extra-regional powers. Last has been the expansion of non-state ties globally. Businesses, educational exchanges, nongovernmental organizations, and cultural relations have expanded beyond the hemisphere, piquing popular attention and connections, often outstripping the policies of hidebound diplomatic services, and shifting policy attention to new countries. Below I discuss each of these factors in more detail, but first it's worth discussing the importance and context of the U.S.'s declining unipolar role in the region.

The U.S.'s shadow has stretched over the hemisphere's southern nations since their independence. The bold assertion of U.S. predominance in the 1823 Monroe Doctrine—stating the "American continents . . . are henceforth not to be considered as subject for future colonization by any European powers"[1]—set the tone for foreign policy toward and in the region for more than 150 years. Intended as a warning to England, France, and the Holy Alliance of Austria, Prussia, and Russia and wrapped in the rhetoric of a shared democratic destiny among the former colonies in the Americas, the Monroe Doctrine defined the U.S. policy of defending its strategic interests from extra-hemispheric and—later—ideological interlopers. After 1850, the doctrine was used directly and indirectly to justify U.S. territorial claims over Mexico and the Caribbean; and from 1898 until the end of the cold war the U.S. intervened in more than 30 different instances mostly in Central America and the Caribbean, including in the Spanish American War and in Cuba, after the forced passage of the 1901 Platt Amendment in Cuba's post-independence constitution. That amendment permitted the U.S. to overturn a government not to its liking.

Later, during the cold war, the U.S. intervened directly, staged proxy interventions or backed governments and their militaries against communist-inspired insurgencies in Guatemala, Cuba, El Salvador, Honduras, Bolivia, and Colombia, to name a few. Leftist governments that courted the Soviet Union and the Eastern Bloc, soon found themselves the target of U.S. efforts—tacit or explicit—at destabilization. This included the Central Intelligence Agency's backing of a coup in Guatemala that removed President Jacobo Arbenz and led to the country's bloody civil war that by 1996 had led to the death of more than 200,000 citizens, and the disastrous, failed Bay of Pigs invasion of Cuba in 1961.

During this long history until the end of the cold war, the U.S.'s overwhelming presence and power in the hemisphere defined foreign policies for the countries to its south. Calculations of Mexican, Brazilian, Argentine, and Chilean—to name a few—foreign policies were shaped by degrees of independence from the United States. Even their decision to seek outside alliances was done with an eye to the colossus to the north. Governments built alliances with outside states to offset the power of the U.S., whether it was Brazil and Argentina's improving trade and connections with the European Union to the full-on embrace of the Soviet Union by Cuba and Nicaragua to sustain and protect their anti-U.S. revolutionary governments. (After the Bay of Pigs invasion and the U.S.'s promise not to intervene in Cuba to help to end the Cuban Missile Crisis, U.S. interference and even aggression took a more covert form, but never ended nor remained all that hidden.)

While the end of the cold war reduced the ideological dimension and the risk for governments in straying too far from the U.S.'s sphere of influence without a committed benefactor, it was several decades before states in the region really broke out of the post–cold war unipolar world. In fact, in the immediate aftermath of the cold war, the U.S.'s influence in the region became even greater. The collapse of the Soviet Union brought a brief moment, in the words of the Inter-American Dialogue, of consensus and convergence in the hemisphere around economically liberal concepts and policies of free trade and democracy. The confluence of market policies and democracy led to the 1994 Summit of the Americas in Miami that brought together all the elected heads of state in the hemisphere, which at the time included every country except Cuba, and announced a plan to create a Free Trade Area of the Americas (FTAA) by 2005. The ambitious economic initiative was to link all of the economies of the region into one market, building on the North American Free Trade Agreement (NAFTA) between Mexico, the U.S. and Canada. As unlikely as it seems 20 years later, the plan for the hemispheric trade platform was the result of lobbying by governments south of the U.S. border that wanted to anchor their economies to the U.S. market.

The same period also brought a brief consensus and series of actions and regional commitments to defend democracy. In 1991, at the OAS General Assembly meeting in Santiago, Chile, the foreign ministers from the hemisphere agreed to collectively defend democracy. The Santiago Declaration—later approved as OAS Resolution 1080—committed OAS-member states to convene when there was an unconstitutional interruption of power (read: coup d'état) and discuss whether to take actions to defend the democratic regime, including suspension from the body and voluntary, individual sanctions. Those measures were soon put in practice in Haiti (1991), Peru (1992), and Guatemala (1993), among other countries.

When Resolution 1080 wasn't sufficient to trigger collective action as former president of Peru Alberto Fujimori steamrolled the checks and balances of democratic government, hemispheric leaders re-upped with the Inter-American Democratic Charter, which more sharply defined and committed member states to protect representative democracy and minority rights. The charter was approved on September 11, 2001, in Lima, Peru. But by then the consensus that had defined the past 12 years had already started to fray, and convergence in foreign policy goals increasingly became divergent.

What Happened?

For one, the two-plus decades of democratic elections had brought to power a set of governments that saw their future less tied to the U.S. and less committed to economic orthodoxy. Part of this came about through the media's-coined term of the "pink tide" of leftist and center-left governments that were elected from 1998 (with the election of Hugo

Chávez in Venezuela) to 2006, and included Argentina (with the election of Néstor Kirchner in 2003), Brazil (with the elections of Luiz Inácio Lula da Silva in 2002 and his successor, Dilma Rousseff, in 2011), Bolivia (with the election of Evo Morales in 2005), Nicaragua (with the election of Sandinista leader Daniel Ortega in 2006), and Ecuador (with the election of Rafael Correa in 2006). Coming from the self-proclaimed left, these leaders—in varying degrees—brought a deep distrust of the United States and sought to rebalance power in the hemisphere away the colossus to the north. For some of the leaders—such as Chávez, Ortega, and Correa—part of the effort to distance their countries' foreign policies away from the United States was to avoid criticism and collective action against their efforts to consolidate personal power at the expense of democratic institutions and political and civil rights.

For Brazil and Argentina the pursuit of a foreign policy away from the U.S. represented a recalculation of these countries' national interest. At a broader conceptual level, this new crop of elected presidents were seeking to foster a broader rebalancing of the global order that would give them greater scope of action for their own independent policies, domestic and international. Embedded in this was a realization that the rise of the economies of China, India, and Russia—as well as other, smaller ones such as those of Vietnam and South Africa—represented an opportunity to both diversify their trade and investment relations away from the U.S. and also gain diplomatic leverage in various multilateral forums. The best example was in December 2003 in Miami when Brazil changed its negotiating strategy in the FTAA discussions to demand greater national control over its own development policies. Their demands to set the conditions for their entry into the proposed free trade area of the Americas and promote their own manufacturing base effectively scuttled the whole hemispheric plan. Only months earlier in the Doha Round of the World Trade Organization (WTO) talks in Cancún, Mexico, President Lula of Brazil forged a coalition of 20 developing countries that stiffened their positions on agricultural subsidies in developed countries.[2] In both cases, the Lula administration had decided that it was no longer in the country's economic interest to accede to a trade agreement dictated by the U.S. on the terms of liberal, trade-friendly NAFTA between the U.S., Canada, and Mexico or an updated world trade agreement that continued to crowd out Brazilian agricultural products because of developed-country subsidies to their farmers. The gloves were off.

For Brazil, the strategy of leading a coalition of developing countries—including its neighbors as well as countries in Africa and Asia—fits into its longstanding aspiration of becoming a global power. It is the path to do so was becoming a vehicle for the demands of the Global South. The fifth-largest country by land mass and by 2010 the seventh-largest economy in the world, Brazil had long seen itself as a future world power, and calculated that it could never do so in the shadow of the United States.

Under the direction of Foreign Minister Celso Amorim, Brazil sought actively in Lula's two terms to check U.S. power and influence in the hemisphere and in multilateral institutions. The strategy was more than just a power play. Brazil's foreign policy elite also saw themselves as the champion of the weak states in the global order, and in this role sought to strengthen international norms and institutors to protect national sovereignty.[3] (Arguably, in some cases, they have done this at the expense of respect for human rights and popular sovereignty, but that's another matter.) The idea that Brazil could serve as a moderating influence on the global tendency toward conflict and sanctions was the justification of its last-minute efforts—together with Turkey—to negotiate with Iran over its nuclear program to head off UN sanctions and its abstentions on UN Security Council votes—as a temporary member—condemning Syria for the use of chemical weapons and for the intervention to prevent Muammar Gaddafi's slaughter of Libyan citizens.

Overall, most of the countries in the region came to place a greater emphasis on regional and south-south solidarity within their calculations of national interest. Part of this stemmed from the ideological disposition of the more active governments in the region and a deep historical current in the region toward solidarity among the Latin American nations. But part of it was also that the U.S. appeared to offer less: as a market, as a source of development assistance, and as a leader on many world issues that the developing world held dear—reduction of agricultural subsidies, rebalancing multilateral institutions, improving access to medicines, and protecting national sovereignty. The one country that continued to hew to U.S. policy was Mexico, whose economy and vision has traditionally been directed northward, and Colombia under President Alvaro Uribe (2002–2010), who was locked in a partnership with the U.S. in his war on drugs and the country's two insurgent groups, the Fuerzas Armadas Revolucionarias de Colombia (FARC) and the Ejercito de Liberacion Nacional (ELN). For the others, though, regional and south-south ties and diplomatic solidarity became a higher priority in national interest calculations. Even Chile, which since the transition to democracy in 1989, has consistently placed a greater emphasis on its economic development through free trade agreements—as of 2013, totaling 27—succumbed to the call of greater regional solidarity, pledging to slow down the integration of the Pacific Alliance, which comprises the more free-trade-oriented Chile, Peru, Colombia, and Mexico—to allow the other more protectionist, inward-looking countries to catch up.

Why the Shift?

The historic post-2001 shift in foreign policy was shaped by four related factors.

The first of these, alluded to above, was the post-2000 economic and diplomatic emergence of the Global South. The most obvious of this new club of emerging economies was China. The Middle Kingdom's economic ascendency not just provided an economic updraft for the commodity-exporting countries in South America, it also offered an alternative economic model more conducive to the leftist governments that came to power after 1999 and a diplomatic ally. At the same time, the economic and diplomatic rise of India, South Africa, Turkey, and Russia provided a set of diplomatic and economic ties and benefits that created a new sense of multipolarity. It also appeared that the Global South had arrived and a long-overdue global rebalancing was occurring, both ideologically and in economic and political power.

The collapse of the Berlin Wall brought an overwhelming sense of unipolarity, of a world system dominated by the U.S. and western, post–World War II–created structures and norms. After several decades of International Monetary Fund (IMF) and World Bank–recommended and–enforced neo-liberal economic policies—the now much-maligned Washington Consensus of fiscal restraint, reducing the role of the state in the market, and throwing open the doors of the country to the global economy by reducing tariff barriers and subsidies and floating the local currency—China and India's state-centric economic model provided a welcome alternative. More than just present a promising trade and investment partner for Latin America, China also provided a new model, what at the 2001 Davos conference became known as the Beijing Consensus.[4] Countries such as Venezuela, Ecuador, Argentina, and Brazil no longer had to embrace the U.S. market and swallow the medicine of economic orthodoxy from the north; they could benefit from economic demand for their products and investment from a set of countries more aligned with their state-centric economic development focus.

There was little threat to U.S. interests from China's investment in the region and its consumption of the hemisphere's natural resources. Unlike its own region, China has no geostrategic designs on the hemisphere and has consistently made it clear that its interests in Latin America and the Caribbean are primarily economic. That became clear in May 2016, when China told one of its closest economic allies, Venezuela—in the midst of an economic meltdown and faced with the threat of defaulting on its sovereign—that Beijing saw Caracas's economic woes as a domestic issue. In other words, despite granting the Chávez and Maduro governments in Venezuela loans at concessionary rates and becoming a large export market for its petroleum, the Chinese were not about to bail out the economically and politically prostrate government, even if that government considered China an ideological comrade.

Instead, the effects of China's rise in the world and increasing economic role in the region were indirect. With the global economic and ideological diversification has come a still-nascent structural rebalancing, with the nations of the south asserting a greater presence globally, whether in multilateral institutions and politics (as in UN votes or last-ditch efforts to head off UN sanctions on Iran over its nuclear program), the growing network of south-south semi-formal alliances (such as the Brazil, Russia, India, China, and South Africa loose alliance—BRICS—or the India, Brazil, and South Africa forum—IBSA) or in planned investment and development banks and organizations (such as the proposed BRICS bank—named the New Development Bank—or the planned Asia Infrastructure Investment Bank—AIIB). These new channels have both presented alternative forums in which the states of the Global South—including Latin American governments—can air their global concerns outside the more traditional, developed-world-dominated platforms, as well as expand and deepen diplomatic and economic relationships. In particular, the new development banks, the BRICS bank and the AIIB, offer an alternative to the U.S.- and European-dominated World Bank and IMF, not just in terms of a fresh source of cash for investment and currency shortfalls, but also for Brazil to both assert its economic development view and gain more political say over multilateral development policy. In the go-go days of Brazil's economic growth and public profligacy, the Brazilian state development bank, BNDES, expanded its budget and role regionally to finance development projects. Most of those were tied to procurement from Brazil's huge infrastructure companies like Odebrecht and Andrade Gutierrez. Those companies were later discredited in massive bribery scandals with Brazil's semi-state oil company Petrobras. Later, as Brazil struggled under a declining economy and need to reduce fiscal expenditures, it cut BNDES's budget, seriously reducing its role domestically and internationally. The promised BRICS bank—which now has a basic financial commitment from members and a governing structure and headquarters in Shanghai—will permit Brazil to serve as the regional bridge to the new bank, representing and bringing in new investment, without all the strings typically attached to IMF, World Bank, or Inter-American Development Bank (IDB) loans. In April 2016 the New Development Bank issued its first loans: $300 million to Brazil, $81 million to China, $250 million to India and $180 million to South Africa, all for projects related to renewable energy. Though, given China and Brazil's economic downturn, it remains an open question whether the bank will meet the founders' original expectations of providing up to $100 billion for infrastructure and sustainable development.

The second factor that has shaped Latin American foreign policy post-2001 has been the proliferation of regional organizations and platforms. A similar phenomenon has occurred globally. Many of these new southern-generated multilateral organizations have served as platforms to forge ties with other south-oriented multilateral groupings. Within Latin America, the region has become an alphabet soup of new regional groupings or plans for new associations. While some of these platforms include the U.S., others do not, and collectively they represent a trend among countries in the region to solve local problems locally, without the influence of the U.S. or Canada. So, whether it is the Union of South American States (UNASUR), the Community of Latin America and the Caribbean (CELAC), or the pointedly (though increasingly hobbled) anti-American Bolivarian Alliance of Our Americas (ALBA) there are now more forums for discussing intraregional disputes, railing against perceived and real U.S. transgressions, and reaching out to extra-hemispheric partners beyond the traditional post–World War II institutions formed by the Rio Pact, the Organization of American States (OAS), and the 30-year-old pan-hemispheric Summit of the Americas.

Some of these are more effective than others. UNASUR has successfully ended a few regional disputes. Some of those were trumped up, such as Venezuela's charges that a plan to expand the U.S.'s right to have landing rights to more Colombian airbases was a stepping stone to a U.S. invasion of Venezuela or the series of presidential summits convened during the Edward Snowden revelations and controversies over the National Security Agency's spying activities. There have been other more substantive and serious results, however. UNASUR member states helped cool tensions between Colombia and Ecuador after Colombian planes strafed and then troops invaded a FARC camp in Ecuadorian territory, and in 2015 UNASUR helped resolve a standoff between Venezuela and Colombia provoked by the Venezuelan military sending undocumented Colombian immigrants back across the border. UNASUR has also leveraged its collective membership and market share to negotiate better rates for access to medicines, effectively circumventing the more traditional Pan-American Health Organization, the regional office of the World Health Organization in which U.S. pharmaceutical companies play a large role. In some of these cases UNASUR has provided a welcome diplomatic forum for the U.S. in which it can free ride on its efforts to resolve regional issues. In others—such as election monitoring—however, it has disappointed.

While its home office is located in Quito, Ecuador, UNASUR is largely a creature of Brazil. Originally created in 2003, the body—which joins a long list of past efforts at regional integration, including the now marginal South American parliament—was an effort by member states to create a parallel forum to the OAS. Brazil has underwritten the lion's share of the organization's budget, which is minimal since it consists only of a small office in Quito, with few regular diplomatic staff and little in the way of regional infrastructure or protocol. Nevertheless, Brazil's support for UNASUR was instrumental, first as a smaller diplomatic forum in which it could assert its regional power outside the sphere of the U.S. and, later, as a way of containing Venezuelan president Chávez and his more strident ALBA alliance—again marginalizing the U.S. and making it more of a regional issue.

ALBA, created in 2001 by Chávez, originally had a more ambitious, anti-American agenda. Underwritten almost entirely by Venezuelan petro-largesse, the eight-member ALBA[5] had great plans, including establishing a joint currency (resurrecting the defunct Ecuadoran sucre, which had been abandoned for the U.S. dollar), creating a development bank, Banco del Sur (Bank of the South), and integrating member economies. None of those ever came to fruition, and by 2014 the alliance had all but ceased to function as a coordinated diplomatic forum. While President Morales of Bolivia, Rafael Correa of Ecuador, Daniel Ortega of Nicaragua, the Castro brothers of Cuba and—for a short time, until he was removed by a coup in 2009—Manuel Zelaya of Honduras shared Chávez's general ideological orientation, they were hardly acolytes or working in lockstep with the former lieutenant colonel from Venezuela. For the other beneficiaries of Chávez's petro-diplomacy members of the alliance, particularly those in the Caribbean, it was all about oil. While not officially members of the alliance, countries such as the Dominican Republic—which received 30,000 barrels of oil per day (BPD) in 2011—Jamaica—50,000 BPD—and Haiti—14,000 BPD—their daily gifts helped buy their support for Venezuelan issues in multilateral forums, such as the UN and the OAS.

While perhaps doomed to fail, especially in the embrace of the broader and less ambitious UNASUR, ALBA in its heyday helped to fuel the momentum of a region that was breaking free of U.S. hegemony. As empty as the denunciations of supposed U.S. transgressions or intentions, the street theater protests against the FTAA at the 2005 Mar del Plata Summit of the Americas, or the offers of asylum to Snowden may have been, ALBA became a focal point for countries in the region to pursue an aggressive, in-your-face independent line vis-à-vis the United States that claimed to challenge not just its influence but its national interests. That included countries like Venezuela, Ecuador, and even Brazil receiving non-hemispheric leaders openly opposed by the United States including Iranian presidents Mohammad Khatami and Mahmoud Ahmadinejad at least three times in total, as well as Russian president Vladimir Putin.

In a similar way, the more expansive CELAC—which includes all Latin American and Caribbean countries—has also served as a forum for the region to relate to outside actors. Similar to UNASUR in serving as a series of presidential summits, CELAC unites heads of state south of the Rio Grande. In 2015 CELAC held a meeting of its ministers in Beijing, which came with a pledge by the Chinese government to financially support the forum. (How much remains a mystery.) More than just the original idea behind the idea of creating CELAC as an OAS without the U.S. and Canada, it has become a modern, trans-hemispheric, south-south multilateral institution, which rather than bridging southern countries with the powers to the north seeks to bridge them to the powers in the south. A reflection of part of this new ideological solidarity between China's diplomatic ethos and Latin American solidarity was the declaration from CELAC's 2014 summit, held pointedly in Havana, Cuba. At the time the U.S. still had not established diplomatic relations with the revolutionary state (that would occur in the summer of 2015). One of the statements coming out of the Havana CELAC summit supported member states' right to determine their own form of government without interference. The statement, though downplayed later by some participating governments, stood in sharp contrast to the OAS's and the U.S.'s commitment to human rights and to the region's collective defense of representative democracy only 13 years before.

These new diplomatic, multilateral organizations have eroded the centrality of the 70-year-old OAS. Created in 1948, the OAS was the aggregation of a number of intra-regional treaties and alliances. For most of its life the body has served as an instrument for U.S. influence in the region. This was particularly true during the cold war, when the U.S. succeeded in getting member governments to approve the 1954 intervention in Guatemala, strong-armed them into kicking the Cuban revolutionary government out of the OAS after the Castros (Fidel and Raúl) came to power, and convinced member governments to endorse the U.S. invasion Grenada in 1984. (The regional body also only expressed its "regret" over the U.S. invasion to remove General Manuel Noriega in December 1989.) Despite the U.S.'s outsized influence in the organization's more political positions, the OAS's inter-American human rights system, comprising the Inter-American Commission on Human Rights in

Washington, DC, and the Inter-American Court in San José, Costa Rica, remained independent and became a vocal, well-respected defender of human rights in the region.

The end of the global ideological battle between the U.S. and the Soviet Union injected the OAS with a new energy and purpose. But it was brief. The DC-based multilateral organization was hobbled by a number of issues. First among them was its association with the past U.S. interventions. As one former—though unnamed—president from the region declared to a friend as they got out of a limousine in front of the OAS's marble, Greek Revival building on Constitution Avenue in Washington, "Welcome to the temple to U.S. imperialism in the hemisphere." While an exaggeration, once the consensus over democracy and human rights began to fracture, governments played on that history and perception to challenge the OAS's authority, in matters of inter-state conflict and human rights and democracy. When a grouping of the ALBA countries attempted to weaken the inter-American system of human rights— triggered largely by a series of reports and recommendations citing the deterioration of human rights and freedom of expression in Ecuador and Venezuela—one of their proposals was to move the commission out of Washington, where, presumably, it was doing the bidding of the U.S.[6] The second was the leadership of the OAS during the time of the shift in hemispheric relations. The OAS secretary general from 2005 to 2015, José Miguel Insulza, had served as the chief of staff to former president of Chile Ricardo Lagos. Unlike past secretaries general, Insulza had neither the prestige of having held a national elected office or of having served as a senior diplomat. In a difficult, polarizing time in the hemisphere, Insulza was criticized by conservatives for not doing enough to counter the anti-democratic power grabs of leaders like Chávez and Correa; and when he spoke out against violations of democratic rights in Venezuela or Ecuador, the left criticized him for intervening in domestic affairs. Apart from being buffeted by member states, Insulza was also criticized internally, with OAS staff accusing the secretary general of being more preoccupied with running for the presidency of Chile than in running the OAS's massive, inefficient bureaucracy. Last was the weight of the OAS itself, which by the early 2000s had become overstaffed with politically well-connected bureaucrats and overstuffed with different mandates, each donor selecting a favorite initiative to support rather than underwrite the organization's ballooning operating expenses.

The creation of UNASUR and CELAC has allowed states in the region to "forum shop" for a multilateral organization that would more likely support their policy or preferences. For a number of countries such as Venezuela and Nicaragua, that has meant searching for a less prying human or political rights–based body. So, while the OAS's election observation efforts in the 1990s and 2000s were widely respected and studied around the world for their independence and technical sophistication, UNASUR established a competing election observation effort. But unlike the OAS's, which had to be invited and adhered to the highest standards of working electoral integrity—including working with local civil society groups—UNASUR's election observation programs were explicitly to accompany the member state's electoral commission on election day. Such a standard, if applied to elections in Nicaragua (1990), the Dominican Republic (1994), and Peru (2000), would have sanctioned infamously fraudulent electoral processes. The option of a UNASUR election observation became a welcome one for Venezuela, which invited a UNASUR accompaniment mission for its presidential election in 2013 and legislative elections in 2015. Similarly, ALBA member states also started to push for a human rights system in UNASUR that could compete with the OAS's independent, professional set of institutions. To this day, none has been created, and, in the context of UNASUR's institutional formation, it is unlikely to happen.

All of this leaves open the question of the future role of the OAS. Certainly, it has lost its central place in matters of summit platitudes, regional problem solving, and election observation, and even human rights. But the OAS has an advantage that many member states—particularly Brazil and Venezuela—have tried to use against it: the presence of the U.S. Aside from inter-state spats and the deterioration of democratic institutions, U.S. policy issues remain central across the hemisphere. On issues of immigration, narcotics, crime and insecurity, trade, and even climate change, the U.S. retains its central role in Latin American policy making. It may not be able to dictate its policy preferences as it did before—more on that later—and in many of those cases U.S. policy preferences are more a problem than the solution, but for countries in the region, addressing their most pressing issues demands that the U.S. is at the table. Similarly, creating forums that exclude the U.S. may benefit the larger, more powerful states in the region, but disadvantages the smaller states. Mexico, Colombia, Chile, Brazil, and Peru may be able to get an audience with high-level officials and even a meeting with the U.S. president for their issues. Smaller countries in Central America or the Caribbean do not have that luxury or pull. And for many of them the primary challenges do not relate to the aspiring regional powers such as Brazil or the emerging extra-hemispheric powers like China, India, or Russia. They relate directly to the United States. As a Caribbean diplomat asked me rhetorically, "In what forum other than the OAS do we get to negotiate and even extract concessions from the United States?" That power is helped in no small part by the OAS's normative quirk that requires all decisions to be made unanimously or by consensus, giving a disproportionate weight to the small Caribbean republics on matters of the election of the OAS secretary general and the OAS's budget allocation process.

In short, these other sub-regionally and extra-regionally oriented forums that exclude the U.S. may provide a platform for the resolution of issues and development of relations outside the orbit of U.S. influence and issues. But they cannot entirely replace bilateral relations with the U.S. or even multilateral relations though the OAS. As weakened as it has become by history, bureaucracy and subpar leadership, the OAS remains a forum for some regional and bilateral issues, though admittedly those are narrowing—a result of the rise of countries in the south and increasing resistance to U.S. policy.

Which raises the fourth issue that has contributed to the assertive, independent, and divergent foreign policies south of the United States: the perception of the decline of U.S. power, in the region and globally. Here, though, it is necessary to untangle the dimensions of that perceived decline and reality. It is undoubtedly true that the U.S. can no long invade a country—as it did the Dominican Republic in 1916 and 1965 and Grenada in 1984—at will, nor can it not-so-covertly support a proxy force to unseat a government as it did in 1954 in Guatemala or in 1961 in Cuba. But those past excursions have little to do with the U.S.'s absolute power; it still has the military and financial resources to do so. Rather, the tying of the U.S.'s hands over intervention has more to do with the strengthening of international norms to defend democracy and protect against intervention and the relative increase in power of other states to use multilateral organizations to denounce flagrant, unilateral transgressions of national sovereignty. And there is also the intangible, though important, shift: the U.S. simply no longer thinks in those militaristic, interventionist terms.

Where U.S. power has shifted in a more subtle and meaningful way has been in its ability to unilaterally dictate its policy preferences. In areas such as the U.S. policy in anti-narcotics or toward the Castro regime in Cuba, in the past ten years Latin American governments have pushed back and in some cases have changed U.S. policy. At the one extreme are countries like Venezuela, Bolivia, and Ecuador, which have—in different cases—kicked out the U.S. Drug Enforcement Agency (DEA) from U.S. embassies, declared the USAID persona non grata, reduced the presence of U.S. embassy officials, or even declined to accept a U.S. ambassador, and—in the case of Ecuador—refused to renew a U.S. base there to combat narcotics trafficking. On the other are stalwart allies like Colombia challenging U.S. policy toward Cuba or publicly questioning the efficacy of U.S. anti-narcotics policy and refusing to continue the U.S.-supported crop spraying program. This change was aided in part by the Obama administration's own domestic policy shift on drugs, including increasing the budget for programs to treat drug abuse as a health problem and its decisions to allow Washington, Colorado, and other states to proceed with their efforts to decriminalize marijuana. The overall effect of this is still unclear, but the pushback even from U.S. trade partners and allies on its war on narcotics—including not just Colombia but also Mexico— signals a genuinely new dynamic in inter-American relations over drug policy and the war on drugs.

In ways that go beyond the grandstanding of Bolivia, Venezuela, and Ecuador, other Latin American countries are finding their voice in trying to renegotiate a relationship with the U.S. that balances the terms of partnership to a genuine partnership in which they can express and even pursue their own policy preferences. The more extreme antics of the ALBA countries have opened up space for the more pragmatic pushback of countries like Colombia and Mexico. Their policy preferences have also been given greater weight by President Barack Obama's emphasis on partnership with countries to the south, stated in his first foreign trip as president to the 2009 Summit of the Americas meeting in Trinidad and Tobago. More striking than the willingness of governments to challenge U.S. policy preferences and tools in matters related directly to them—such as anti-narcotics or trade policy—has been their challenges to U.S. policy on topics that don't relate directly to them. At the 2011 Summit of the Americas in Cartagena, Colombia, participating governments issued a demand that Cuba be invited to the next summit in Panama City. The United States and Canada refused to sign the statement. Yet in December 2014, four months before the Panama Summit, President Obama announced a series of executive actions to loosen the U.S's 53-year-old embargo on Cuba and in doing so signaled that it would accept the presence of Cuba at the U.S.-created forum. Remarkably, the U.S. had responded to pressure from its southern neighbors—aided in part by shifts in the U.S. electorate regarding Cuba policy—for a policy change, a stark contrast to when the U.S. exerted its influence to get Latin American governments to end diplomatic relations with the Castro government (all complied except Mexico) and suspend the government from the OAS.

This is not to say that the region—despite conventional wisdom—remains solidly anti-American or that the carrots of integration and preferential access to U.S. markets and diplomatic exchanges have lost their currency. According to surveys conducted by Vanderbilt University's Latin America Public Opinion Project (LAPOP) and analyzed by Andy Baker and David Cupery,[7] in comparison to other regions in the world, the U.S. remains popular in Latin America and the Caribbean. Across the region, well over half of its citizens view the U.S. positively, including in the ALBA countries of Venezuela, Bolivia, and Ecuador. And though the appeal of the U.S. market for free trade faded after the rise of China and other fast-growing economies of the Global South, many countries—such as Peru, Panama, and Colombia—continued to pursue deeper trade relations, all three signing free trade agreements with the United States in the mid-2000s that were eventually approved by the U.S. Congress. Those countries, minus Colombia, with Mexico joined the U.S. in the negotiation of the 12-member Trans-Pacific Partnership—a demonstration of the U.S's ongoing power to link the region globally in broader pluri-lateral relations. Moreover, as China's economy cools and takes the commodity-heavy economies of Argentina, Brazil,

Ecuador, and Venezuela with it, the debate over the wisdom of pursuing such a China-focused trade relationship without broader structural reforms and trade relations has opened up. Deepening trade relations with the U.S. market, either directly or through the TPP, may reassert the U.S.'s predominant economic weight and power in the hemisphere, though it no longer carries the same weight that it did in 1994 at the announcement of the now-moribund FTAA. To achieve that leverage, the U.S.—as it has done with the TPP—needs to broaden its economic appeal.

There is a last factor, though it is admittedly smaller, that has helped shaped the region's foreign policy. Latin America and the Caribbean's economic and political actors have brought a range of informal and non-state contacts that shaped countries' foreign policies, sometimes outside the control of the official foreign policy apparatus. As scholars such as Sikkink and Keck and Sassen have demonstrated,[8] foreign relations today are driven a range of social, nongovernmental, and commercial interactions and relations. In many cases those have outstripped formal state relations, and helped to move governments in directions that state bureaucracies would not normally steer themselves: commercial connections, student exchange agreements, or adherence to human rights standards.

The best example of this is the importance of Brazil's large multinational corporations in shaping the country's foreign policies, companies such as the semi-state mining company Vale and the semi-state oil company Petrobras, as well as its powerful infrastructure companies (such as Odebrecht and Andrade Gutierrez) and its agribusinesses. Those companies have helped pull Brazil into both trade relations in Africa and the Near East, as well as push for the incorporation of Venezuela in the southern cone common market, MERCOSUR. In the latter case, Brazilian infrastructure and agribusiness companies saw a large market advantage in granting Venezuela access to the southern cone customs union for which the revolutionary, state-centric government was never prepared to enter—and remains so. But Brazil's foreign service corps (the famous Itamaraty) and establishment yielded in part to the pressure of economic groups. The contacts and economic interests of Vale, Petrobras, and others helped spawn the opening and expansion of Brazil's embassies around the world, as Brazilian diplomatic missions became important advocates for the country's economic and private sector's commercial interests. In just one example, Brazil now has more embassies in Africa than Great Britain does—a reflection not just of the country's diplomatic ambition of being a leader of the Global South but also the economic interests of its national companies. In these ways, Brazil's global private sector helped shape a new foreign policy in ways that the hidebound Brazilian professional foreign service would have been slow to do.

Cultural and academic ties between the hemisphere and the outside world also mattered. In the past decade the Chinese government has fostered a series of cultural diplomatic initiatives and exchanges, directly and indirectly through its Confucius Institutes. The institutes offer Mandarin classes and social events. The Chinese government has also actively sought out academics and civil society actors in Mexico, Brazil, Peru, and Argentina for travel to the country and for participation in academic conferences. Those contacts, part of a broader state strategy at cultural diplomacy, helped build new ties that diversified the traditional orientation of academic institutions and civil society toward the developed north. Similarly, IBSA has also engaged in academic and cultural exchanges, including one in which a delegation from India visited Brazil to study the latter's successful conditional cash transfer program, Bolsa Família, and an exchange on tax policy. All of these have helped to build the sense of connectivity between these countries of the Global South. And through multiple extra-hemispheric trade agreements, businesses in countries like Chile and Peru have built commercial and personal relations that did not exist even 20 years ago. While it is difficult to measure the import of these informal, multifaceted relations, it is clear that they have helped to create contacts and relationships outside the traditional patterns of north-south relations that have fostered a more diverse and at times independent foreign policy in Latin America.

Will It Last?

The cooling Chinese economy has triggered an economic downturn in Latin America and even recession in Argentina, Brazil, Ecuador, and Venezuela. In Brazil and Venezuela economic distress has brought political upheaval, further prolonging the economic downturn. The economic crises and political backlash raise the question of whether this new era of diplomatic muscularity will just be a passing phenomenon.

Arguably, given clear limits to the economic boom that many of these countries experienced in the 2000s—dependent as they were on the riskiness of commodities—countries such as Brazil and Argentina will need to tone down their global diplomatic profiles to concentrate on economic and social problems at home. Indeed, the most obvious and public forms of international adventurism, from Brazil's efforts to insert itself into global negotiations with Iran or Venezuela's courting of Iran to build allies in the hemisphere, have likely run their course. But the era of a new foreign policy independence in the Western Hemisphere is here to stay.

Ultimately, over the long term, the economies of the Global South will return to economic growth, even if not at the rate that they did in the 2000s and they, along with China and other developing countries, will continue to rebalance the global economy away from the developed north. That growth will sustain demands for a diplomatic and political reform in the UN and in the IMF and the World Bank, and for the creation or strengthening of new parallel institutions. Through that process of economic growth and change, Latin American governments' political and economic calculations have changed. The U.S. may remain an important market for exports to the north, but export markets, even in the decline of demand for commodities, exist in a global marketplace. As long as states calculate their national interest as economic interests, their calculations will diversify away from the U.S. Even in the case of the TPP, the U.S.'s leverage in bringing in Chile, Peru, and Mexico—and potentially Colombia and perhaps other countries—depends on the U.S.'s weight with the other countries of the potential free trade agreement, not just the allure of the U.S. market.

The past two decades in which Latin American governments have sought to diversify their foreign policies from U.S. hegemony tapped a longstanding desire in the hemisphere to achieve independence from U.S. prerogatives. That is an historic sentiment that will not be easy to put back in the bottle. Venezuela and Ecuador's aggressive anti-Americanism and courting of rogue regimes will run its course and quite possibly end. But building alliances with non-hemispheric allies will remain a powerful way of balancing U.S. influence, especially as those economies pick up steam again. The trend is not limited to avowed antagonists to U.S. power. Chile will continue to remain engaged with the European Union and economies such as Turkey's and the European Union's with whom it has free trade agreements. Mexico, Peru, and Colombia, who have a range of close economic and diplomatic relations globally, will do the same.

Last, there is the issue of policy pushback by U.S. allies. Colombia, Uruguay, and Mexico—all countries close to U.S. policies in other matters—have emerged as leaders in the challenge to U.S. drug policy. Their assertion of their domestic prerogative to set local policies on matters of legalization or decriminalization of drugs is a recognition of their own priorities and resistance to the perceived failure of U.S. drug policy. Whether on Cuba or on the U.S. war on drugs, the failures of past policies are becoming evident and at a time when the U.S. increasingly needs to shore up its friends in the region. Countries have found a voice, and have pointed out the real failings of U.S. policies. As a result, increasingly the U.S. is finding itself in a position as a partner—rather than a unilateral decision maker—on a range of hemispheric policy issues, primary among them the 30-year-old war on drugs that has cost hundreds of thousands of lives south of the border and its miserably ineffective attempt to isolate Cuba to improve human rights.

NOTES

1 Perkins, Dexter, "The Monroe Doctrine, 1823–1826," in LaRosa, Michael, and Frank O. Mora (eds.), *Neighborly Adversaries: Readings in U.S.-Latin American Relations*, Second Edition, (Oxford: Rowman & Littlefield, 2007), p. 55.

2 Amorim, Celso, "Reflections on Brazil's Global Rise," *Americas Quarterly*, Spring 2011, Volume 5, Number 2, pp. 50–55.

3 Patriota, Antonio de Aguiar, "International Cooperation or Gridlock," *Americas Quarterly*, Spring 2014, Volume 8, Number 2, pp. 40–44.

4 Bennhold, Katrin, "What Is the Beijing Consensus," *New York Times,* January 28, 2011, www.nytimes.com.

5 ALBA membership has been in flux depending on individual governments, but at its peak it included Bolivia, Cuba, Ecuador, El Salvador, Honduras, Nicaragua, and Venezuela.

6 While the U.S. unfortunately has never signed the Inter-American Convention of Human Rights, which forms the basis of the inter-American system, it participates in the system and in a majority of cases abides by its recommendations and decisions.

7 Baker, Andrew, and David Cupery, "Anti-Americanism in Latin America: Economic Exchange, Foreign Policy Legacies, and Mass Attitudes," *Latin American Research Review*, 2014, Volume 48, Number 2, pp. 106–130.

8 There is a rich and growing body of literature on this subject. For two of the seminal and best works, please see, Keck, Margaret and Kathryn Sikkink, "Activists beyond Borders: Advocacy Network and Foreign Relations," (Ithaca, NY: Cornell University Press, 1998), and Sassen, Saskia, *Losing Control? Sovereignty in an Age of Globalization* (New York: Columbia University Press, 1996).

4

Latin American Views of Chinese and U.S. Policy

BENJAMIN CREUTZFELDT

Introduction

Ever since the Spanish conquest in the sixteenth century, the peoples of Latin America have found themselves in a position of reacting to outside influence, rather than being protagonists in the global agenda affecting them. That experience, together with the heterogeneous mix of cultures accumulated over time, has led to repeating cycles of a search for identity and modernity and manifested itself in what the Mexican Nobel laureate Octavio Paz described as a deep fear of being eternally defeated or conquered.[1] While independence gave the United States a genuine sense of liberation and the power to self-govern and self-determine, and the successful struggles for decolonization in twentieth-century East and South Asia allowed those nations to reconnect to their traditions and cultural identities, the countries of Latin America have struggled to achieve a position of leadership in global affairs, let alone regional cohesion.

The present chapter picks up on these themes provided by history: the ambiguous relationship with foreign powers present in the region, and the lack of national and regional cohesion, resulting in an inadequate comprehension of, and response to, the new and growing presence of China, after a century of United States dominance. Following some brief historical background to embed these themes and draw out their relevance and possible parallels today, this chapter offers a contextualized characterization of China's foreign policy toward Latin America between 2008 and 2016, and subsequently delineates key traits of U.S. foreign policy over the same period. These two outlines provide points of departure for the ensuing segment, which focuses on Latin American views of China and the U.S. from two perspectives: a vertical panorama seeks to present the differences within the populations of Latin America, considering the divergence of economic conditions and values, and a horizontal panorama broadly presents the views across countries. The discussion is informed by a broad reading of media and current academic literature and, in the interest of achieving an overview, loosely groups the countries into some of their regional organizations: the Pacific Alliance countries of Mexico, Colombia, Peru, and Chile; the Bolivarian Alliance for the Peoples of Our America (ALBA) countries of Venezuela, Ecuador, and Bolivia; and the full members of Mercosur, including again Venezuela alongside Uruguay, Paraguay, Brazil, and Argentina.[2]

Historical Precursors

In the first half of the nineteenth century, the United States was well positioned thanks to precedent—as a pioneer in revolution—to provide orientation and protection for the newly independent nations of the South, which it expressed in the Monroe Doctrine of 1823. Conceived as an expression of solidarity with those countries, and with the endorsement of the leading naval power of the period, the United Kingdom, it had the effect of generating a sense of security and political affinity with the United States and led many of them to base their new constitutions on the North American model. But although the historian John Crow argues that it was "never intended to be a charter for concerted hemispheric action" (1992, p. 676), its shadow loomed large over the North-South relationship: it cannot be dissociated from U.S. expansionism during the nineteenth century in Mexico, Panama, and Puerto Rico, armed interventions in Nicaragua, Haiti, and Cuba, and the primacy the United States assumed in economic and critical political affairs of the hemisphere in the course of the twentieth century, often in the form of very real interventions in domestic matters. The most notorious of these left a permanent stain on many bilateral relationships, being associated frequently with the support of right-leaning regimes or movements in Cuba, Chile, Nicaragua, Panama, Colombia, and Venezuela, as well as the suppression of labor unrests and the protection of corporate interests.

More positively, however, the hemispheric cohesiveness pursued by successive U.S. governments originally materialized in the Organization of American States (OAS). The OAS is the world's oldest regional organization, with roots dating back to the First International Conference of American States, held between October 1889 and April 1890 in Washington, DC. This led to the establishment of the International Union of American Republics, setting the stage for the design and articulation of the institutions that were to govern the OAS. Nonetheless, many Latin Americans maintained an edgy wariness of U.S. presence in their region, and hostility toward the United States was evident in many countries. President Franklin Roosevelt's Good Neighbor Policy of the 1930s was an important catalyst for improved relations by expressly proclaiming a policy of mutual non-aggression and non-intervention. The OAS came into being with the signing of its charter in Bogota in 1948. These are some of the elements U.S. leaders and analysts have in mind when they describe the regional ties as conditioned by geography, economy, and family (e.g., Ellis 2015).

As for Chinese contact with Latin America, historically traceable contact began with the trade during the early Spanish colonial empire in the sixteenth century, and continued for more than three centuries by means of the Manila galleons.[3] Documented contact between China and the countries of Latin America dates to the Qing Empire in the century of its gradual decline. The nineteenth century saw a first occasion for China and a number of Latin American countries to look each other in the eye. Subsequently a confluence of trends led to the emergence of labor movement—from China to the plantations and early infrastructure projects of Latin America. The chaos and poverty in rural China and the phasing out of black slavery in the Americas led to the importation of several hundred thousand "coolies" from South China. The laborers worked in the sugarcane plantations of Cuba and Jamaica, as well as the silver mines, coastal plantations, and guano collecting industry of Peru (McKeown 2001). The miserable treatment many suffered during transport and at their destination forced a reluctant and inward-looking Qing government to expand the horizon of its Zongli Yamen, created in 1961 as a precursor to a foreign ministry, and to negotiate its first formal relations with several Latin American countries: the first of these was Peru in August 1875, followed by Brazil in 1881, and Mexico in 1899.

After the establishment of the People's Republic in 1949, the new leadership principally sought cultural, people-to-people, and limited trade relations with the countries of Latin America (Zheng, Sun, and

Yue 2012). Bill Ratliff hints at a more ambitious agenda at the heart of the approach in the 1950s and 1960s, when he argues that "a disorderly but important foundation was laid for the explosive expansion of PRC–Latin American ties" in the twenty-first century (Ratliff 2012, p. 33). Beijing's cultural diplomacy consisted of promoting cultural and political links to Latin American individuals and organizations of all political orientations, but not, generally, to governments. Building such links was inexpensive and did little to offend hostile governments, but nonetheless tended to make a deep and lasting impression on their beneficiaries. While it can be said that the policy driving this informal diplomatic exchange was largely "value free," it was of course ideologically inspired, and most visitors met with Chairman Mao, Premier Zhou, or another top leader.

There were only limited ties between China and Latin America in the 1970s and 1980s and trade was minimal, but following Deng's reform and opening-up, China soon began to nurture its relations with Latin America, and welcomed the gradual realignment of most remaining South American countries from official relations with Taipei to Beijing. Initially, this meant abandoning any political agenda or ideological preferences, even establishing relationships with several neoliberal military dictatorships. At the end of 1985, Premier Zhao Ziyang embarked on what was the first ever high-level leadership visit to Latin America. China reached out to "third world" nations of Latin America and made known its intention to become the representative of the developing world. Zhao also offered "peace and friendship, mutual support, equality and mutual benefit, and joint development" ("Zhao in L. America" 1985), thus offering at least a rhetorical path toward collaboration.

Since the turn of the twenty-first century, economic and trade relations between the People's Republic of China and Latin America have grown exponentially and, as a result, so has the influence of China in the region at the political level. While China is actively involved in multilateral organizations, and indeed promotes new institutions in the spirit of "greater democracy in international relations" ("Chinese President" 2014), Beijing also increasingly stimulates direct bilateral relationships: with Brazil as a member of the BRICS group and its position as a regional power, with Venezuela and Ecuador as major suppliers of hydrocarbons, with Chile, Peru, and Costa Rica for the multifaceted exchange of goods facilitated by their free trade agreements, with Mexico for its particular position within NAFTA, and so on. But what motivates policy and its strategists in one country does not necessarily match the goals of the opposite side; although there is considerable consistency in China's policy toward Latin America, this does not accurately reflect the disparate and conflicting identities within the region. Conversely, the importance that some countries in Latin America give their relationship with China does not always find an echo on the other side of the Pacific. What is more, behind this scenario looms the presence of the "Northern hegemon"—the United States has a long history of close involvement in the affairs of its traditional "backyard" and this shadow, whether real or imagined, influences attitudes and decision making, initiatives, and responses. More imagined, perhaps, as a 2008 report to the U.S. Congress suggests, that "for all of the attention being paid to China's rise and its attendant economic, environmental, security, and political consequences, we still have a very imperfect understanding of China's power and motivations or how the rest of the world is responding to China's integration" (Congressional Research Service 2008).

In the search for an understanding, North American analysts often succumb to the temptation of viewing China's engagement with Latin America in the light of a potential threat to U.S. interests, or as part of an "emerging division of labour [in which] the U.S. will continue to promote democracy, market reforms, and rule of law in the region, while China will do the heavy lifting with trade expansion, [and] infrastructure investment" (Wise 2012, p. 134). Evan Ellis, one of the most prolific commentators on China's relations with Latin America and a contributor to the present volume, tends to take the sentiment to a more blatantly competitive level when he states for instance that "China has recklessly provided billions of dollars in financial support" to ALBA states, and that "Chinese actions in Latin America help expand political and economic turmoil and criminality [weakening] democratic institutions [. . .] and the refugees and criminals will continue to come" to the U.S. (Ellis 2014). Even the *Economist* magazine feed rhetorically into a threatening image of China, as a linguistic or discourse analysis of recent columns suggests, though the editors redeem themselves intermittently with nuanced notes, stating for instance that it "would be wrong to blame China [alone. . . .] it is up to Latin America to become as effective as its new partner in defending its interests in the relationship ("Chinese Chequebook" 2015). The evolving story we are witnessing as the twenty-first century wears on is more complex, more multidimensional, and potentially more significant. The purpose of this chapter is to offer some insights into how governments, publics, and business communities view their countries' relationships with China and the United States, and how they are attempting to position themselves between those two powers.

Chinese Foreign Policy toward Latin America, 2008–2016

Three cornerstone documents may be identified that encapsulate China's Latin America policy in the early twenty-first century: the Chinese government's November 2008 *Policy Paper on Latin America and the Caribbean* (*China's Policy Paper* 2008); Premier Wen Jiabao's speech in Santiago de Chile in June 2012 (Wen 2012); and President Xi Jinping's address to the First Ministerial China-CELAC Summit in Beijing in January 2015 (Xi 2015). These three documents are both useful and relevant because they set out broad targets and were widely circulated within China's government and diplomatic circles, received broad coverage in the national and overseas press, and have been quoted repeatedly by representatives of the Chinese government in subsequent summits and bilateral encounters.[4]

The first two frame a period from 2008 to 2012 that witnessed a transformed China in a transformed world. Within China, the buildup to 2008 was monumental, but while the Beijing Olympics were an unmitigated success that created a new imagery for novice observers of the P.R.C., other events were unplanned and unwelcome. The first was a popular uprising by Tibetan monks and supporters of Tibetan independence, which descended into violence in mid-March and was quelled by China's armed forces. The second was the devastation caused by the Wenchuan earthquake in Sichuan Province in May, which led to the deaths of an estimated eighty thousand people, a considerable portion of which were children buried beneath collapsed school buildings. At the end of the year, a campaign by intellectuals criticizing the Chinese Communist Party rule made headlines internationally and led to reprisals by the government against some of the signatories, including most famously the professor, writer, and human rights activist Liu Xiaobo, who was later awarded the Nobel Peace Prize *in absentiam*. All these events, led by the Olympic Games, generated a significant rise in global media coverage of China, both positive and critical. The financial world and most Western economies, in the meantime, were coming to terms with the fallout of the sub-prime crisis in the United States, leading to a slow-down that affected financial markets and GDP growth figures in many parts of the world. Beijing published its *Policy Paper* on Latin America on November 5, carefully timed for the day after the election of Barack Obama as the forty-fourth president of the United States.

Around the same time, Xi Jinping was named as China's vice president, paving his path for succession to the presidency five years later. China's Going Out campaign, launched in the 1990s, was by this time in full swing, fomenting the interest of Chinese companies, both state-owned and private, to invest abroad and otherwise seek involvement in all regions of the world—some of China's largest overseas acquisitions fall into this period (Lopez and Sam 2015). Trade in commodities was similarly buoyant throughout this period, with iron, soybeans, copper, and crude oil accounting for the bulk of Latin American exports to China; when the 2008 financial crisis impacted global trade and led to recession in the U.S. and the European Union, the immediate effects on Latin America were muted, as China picked up much of the slack.

The 2008 *Policy Paper* for Latin America and the Caribbean was a canvas of intentions and set out broad terms for bilateral cooperation. The explicitly stated core objective was to "clarify the goals of China's policy in this region, outline the guiding principles for future coopera-tion . . . and sustain the sound, steady and all-around growth of China's relations with Latin America and the Caribbean." Reiterating its com-mitment to the Five Principles of Peaceful Coexistence, the paper de-scribes Latin America and the Caribbean as "an important part of the developing world and a major force in the international arena. . . . [T]he Chinese Government aims to further clarify the goals of China's policy in this region, outline the guiding principles for future cooperation be-tween the two sides in various fields and sustain the sound, steady and all-round growth of China's relations with Latin America and the Carib-bean." It states four broad goals, which are to be promoted by means of policies and ties in the following fields: political, economic, cultural-social, and what it calls "peace, security and judicial affairs." The broad goals are the promotion of mutual respect, trust, and "understanding and support on issues involving each other's core interests and major concerns"; the deepening of economic cooperation for the benefit of both sides, with China and Latin American nations each leveraging "their respective strengths"; the expansion of cultural and people-to-people links with the aim of promoting "development and progress of human civilization, and the insistence on the One-China principle as the political basis for cooperative relations."

In 2010, the Chinese People's Institute of Foreign Affairs (CPIFA) hosted the first China, Latin America, and the Caribbean Think Tank Forum in Beijing. As part of its multilateral approach to Latin America (Noesselt and Soliz-Landivar 2013), China joined the Inter-American Development Bank (IDB) in January 2009, and the increasing frequency of Chinese leadership visits to the region saw President Hu Jintao attend the APEC summit in Lima in 2008 and was crowned by Premier Wen Jiabao's address to the UN's Economic Commission for Latin American and the Caribbean (ECLAC) in June 2012. Wen's address, under the heading "Trusted Friends Forever," raised the character of the connection to something akin to poetic destiny. He highlighted the common cultural roots of the nations of Latin America, mentioning some of their most famous literary figures, and drew parallels of historical longevity between the Chinese and the Inca and Aztec cultures. He went on to outline four specific proposals for furthering cooperation, focusing on political links, economic development, food security, and human and scientific exchange, backing these up with loans, funds, and financial targets. Press coverage of these pronouncements were a far cry from the attention paid to Chinese leadership visits to the U.S., Germany, or the U.K., but they were nonetheless encouragement for Chinese companies seeking diversification and new markets.

The period from 2013 to 2016 corresponds to the initial period of the fifth generation of Chinese leadership, under President and Party Chairman Xi Jinping and Premier Li Keqiang. This was a widely expected handover and thought of both inside China and among external observers to represent a sign of stability and continuity. In many ways, this new period has been just that, and continuity has meant continued economic growth, a continued rise in overseas investment, a foreign policy often described as "assertive" since 2009, and a continued rise in military spending. On the other hand, the new leadership has been more centralized in a strong president than was previously the case, and China's (re)stating of borders in the South China Sea has caused friction with neighbouring countries as well as the United States. At a domestic level, the government has orchestrated a more thorough crackdown on corruption than previously seen, one result of which was the removal of Zhang Kunsheng, the foreign ministry official in charge of Latin American and Caribbean affairs, in early 2015 ("China despidió" 2015).

In a bold predictive study published in 2013 whose results have been largely corroborated by events since, the authors use a political psychology approach to compare and evaluate Hu Jintao's and his successor Xi's "operational code beliefs." In this way, they are "bringing leaders back in" to the analysis of national policy and foreign policy decision making and they emphasize the role of leaders' belief systems in connecting leaders' policy decisions with the external material and ideational worlds. Their results allow them to suggest "that even though Chinese leaders hold a cooperative and optimistic worldview about the political universe and intend to maintain the status quo, they will behave assertively when facing serious external challenges" (He and Feng 2013, p. 231). The doubts or tensions in the U.S.-China relationship have not had noticeable repercussions on transpacific trade issues or other vested interests that either power has in Latin America.

In the course of the year 2014, the most emblematic institution of the ever-closer relations between China and Latin America came into being, in the form of the China-CELAC Forum. This was modelled on the Forum of China-African Cooperation (FOCAC) that had been created formally in the year 2000 during a summit in Beijing. While CELAC meets independently of China and has also held talks with the EU, China's interest in and support of the China-CELAC Forum has been emphatic ever since President Xi sent a congratulatory message to the CELAC summit in Caracas in January 2014, presided over a ministerial meeting for the official inauguration of the Forum in Brazil that July, and hosted the inaugural ministerial summit in Beijing in January 2015.

President Xi Jinping's opening speech at that summit is the most recent example of China's official state rhetoric toward that region, and the "Beijing Declaration" issued at the Forum reaffirmed China's win-win and South-South strategy, which dates back to the earliest days of the

P.R.C. and echoed the earlier papers referenced. While there has been much speculation how the recent historic drop in commodity prices might affect the burgeoning relationship, such concerns have been challenged by a doubling of trade and investment pledges, with goals announced of US$500 billion and US$250 billion respectively. This emphasis on continued Chinese support serves as an ostensible road map for the rapidly growing political and economic ties between China and Latin America, and was reinforced by government representatives at the Ninth China-Latin America Business Summit in Guadalajara, Mexico, in October 2015. Slower economic growth in China will not directly impact on this pledge, in part because it is only a comparatively small sliver of China's projected global activities, and in part because China's economy—still in large part directed centrally from Beijing—seeks to transform its domestic growing pattern and shift industrial overcapacity to other parts of the world, including Latin America.

Premier Li Keqiang's May 2015 tour of the region, visiting Brazil, Colombia, Peru, and Chile, was a further iteration of this focus. The situation report prepared by ECLAC to coincide with the state visit emphasizes that "China recognises the strategic character of its relationship with Latin America and the Caribbean" (CEPAL 2015a, p. 80). This is particularly true when it comes to Beijing's energy security strategy, which is central to its domestic needs and global interests (Zhang and Zhang 2012). The ECLAC document echoes and celebrates the priorities declared by Beijing, including the growth of bilateral trade, the reduction of poverty, the building of infrastructure, and the internationalization of the emerging economies. Further goals include the "reversal of the worrying reprimarisation of exports" (CEPAL 2015a, p. 6), advances in productivity, and capacity building in terms of human resources.

The principal driving factor in China's engagement with the countries of Latin America is trade, followed by investment. The trade has been driven in the first place by China's need for primary products to feed the rapid and sustained growth of its economy and the industry-heavy character of that growth, and to feed the evolving consumer habits of its population. The impact of China's trade with the region was an early concern of the group of analysts who found in 2007 that "China's trade impact on Latin America is mostly positive, both directly, through an export boom, and indirectly, through better terms of trade." They went so far as to claim that "China looks like a 'trade angel' and a 'helping hand' as well as being an outlet for commodities from the region" (Santiso 2007). The fact that China's foreign policy is essentially guided by its domestic focus (Fenby 2012) and the domestic priorities have been rapidly adapting to the post-crisis slowdown in China's top export markets, the U.S. and the EU, means that significant changes have occurred in the trade patterns since 2008, with further modifications generated by the Twelfth Five-Year Plan (2011–2015) and the change of leadership in early 2013: the Plan "frames the social and economic challenges facing China within the context of an unstable global economic environment [and] contends that the world is now characterised by 'continuous and complex changes'" (Myers and Yang 2012).

The second driver of transpacific trade is Latin America's potential as a market for goods manufactured in China, ranging from cars and cell phones to clothes and short-lived, high-turnover consumer goods. While this is true globally, Jiang Shixue has underscored that "expanding its market share in Latin America has been part of China's objective to reduce its dependence upon the United States, Japan, and Europe" (Shixue 2007, p. 46). Chinese manufacturing is also particularly consequential for Latin America in the sense that China "is simultaneously out-competing Latin American manufacturers in world markets—so much so that it may threaten the ability of the region to generate long-term economic growth" (Gallagher 2010a).

In sum, China's foreign policy toward Latin America is driven by domestic priorities and framed outwardly by the ideas of international cooperation for mutual benefit, non-intervention in internal affairs, growth of trade exchanges, and investment that combine Chinese financial and technological capacity with the developmental needs of most Latin American countries. These expressions of goodwill are reminiscent of Washington's Good Neighbor Policy of the 1930s, but the cultural affinities are thin, and only time will tell whether China's extant and growing commitment to increasing economic involvement will be able to change this.

U.S. Foreign Policy toward Latin America, 2008–2016

During the presidency of George W. Bush, attention and resources were given primarily to the Middle East—though the so-called War on Terror concomitantly broadened the War on Drugs by pouring further funds into Plan Colombia for the eradication of drugs and enemies of the state—and observers soon decried Washington's "bad neighbor policy" (Carpenter 2003) in sarcastic reference to Roosevelt's 1930s approach. Barack Obama, however, turned a page in his April 2009 speech at the Summit of the Americas Opening Ceremony in Trinidad and Tobago (Obama 2009). In the jovial manner that is the insignia of U.S. leaders of our age, he appeared to speak among friends of an equal partnership, "common interests and shared values." He underscored the goals of reducing inequality and of sustainable economic growth, and pledged funds for emergency aid and microfinance. A key policy announcement was for the Energy and Climate Partnership of the Americas (ECPA), which indeed materialized in November of that year. Similarly, he hinted at a warming of relations toward Cuba, a policy shift that was subtly put into practice under the direction of Secretary of State John Kerry and led to the reestablishment of diplomatic relations in 2015, simultaneously weakening the influence of Venezuela in the region.

In addition to the 2009 remarks by the U.S. president, two further texts essentially parallel in time and scope to those cited for Chinese foreign policy, above, are Obama's remarks at the CEO Summit of the Americas in Cartagena, Colombia, in April 2012 (Obama 2012), and his remarks at the First Plenary Session of the Summit of the Americas in Panama City in April 2015 (Obama 2015). It is a remarkable trait that in every one of the three speeches, Obama underscores that he is younger than many other leaders and the issues that have soured hemispheric relations. He implicitly distances himself and his government from past policies, and his emphasis on change and potential contrasts with the ideas of continuity and longevity of culture that Chinese leaders like to bring to bear in their rhetoric.

In terms of the U.S. policy toward Latin America, the time between 2009 and 2015 has been aptly described by some analysts as a hiatus, despite the young president's well-worded intentions expressed in his 2009 address (Horsley 2015), a period during which Washington continued to keep Latin America on a slow burner. This is only true, however, in terms of headlines. As the Cuban diplomatic initiative, the ratification by Congress of the Colombia-U.S. FTA, and the encouragement given to the formation of the Pacific Alliance show, Obama's government was able to follow through on many of the pledges made early in his first term. Given the United States' high level of dependency for domestic oil security, with Mexico and Venezuela among the top four suppliers, energy cooperation has long been central to U.S. strategy toward Latin America. Following Venezuelan president Chávez's offer to cash-strapped Caribbean nations of preferential rates for oil purchases, Washington aimed to win over Central American and Caribbean countries through the ECPA initiative, in a bid to overcome their dependence on oil. The Caribbean Energy Security Initiative announced in late 2014 was a further move in the same direction.

Feinberg, Miller and Trinkunas describe core U.S. interests in Latin America as "(1) progressive, resilient political democracies with respect for human rights; (2) reasonably well-managed, market-oriented economies open to global trade and investment; (3) inter-state peace among nations; (4) and the absence of credible threats to the United States from international terrorism or weapons of mass destruction" (2015, pp. 1–2). These are valid priorities but insufficient to fully explain U.S. approaches to the region, which have powerful economic motives also. There is evidence that support is given to some democracies more than others: in the case of Colombia, politically motivated crimes of the state have been understood by U.S. authorities but not sanctioned (Evans 2009), while in the case of Cuba, relations have warmed despite the absence of democratic principles in that country. Another shift that does not seem to coincide with Washington's declared policy of bringing the region closer comprises the sanctions announced against Venezuela in December 2014, which were unanimously rejected by the CELAC member countries: alongside the rapprochement with Cuba, it has been described as "one step forward, one step back" (Main 2014). The likely calculation was that by isolating Venezuela on multiple fronts, and strengthening the relationships with its allies (Cuba, the Caribbean countries, and to some extent Brazil) as well as its antagonists (Colombia and other countries of the Pacific Alliance), the United States will succeed in exerting once again a significant influence in the region, while changing the global energy landscape in an important way. It became evident in the run-up to the 2015 Americas Summit, however, that this was a decision at odds with the preferences of the community of Latin American states and their leaders.

Overall, U.S. foreign policy toward Latin America is made to sound as principled as China's is benign and value-free; the public emphasis is on human and political values while China's is on development and economic prosperity. In practice, both are interested in promoting and protecting environments in which their corporations and citizens can operate freely and with adequate assurances of protection (see, for instance, Chavarro 2016). The U.S. has reduced its presence either voluntarily or under pressure in Ecuador and Venezuela, but remains among the top three trading partners and sources of FDI for almost every country in the region (cf. CEPAL 2015b). If protectionist tendencies promoted by the administration of President Donald Trump hold sway over time, the U.S. footprint in the region will likely shrink in relative terms, as will the goodwill of Latin American governments.

Latin Views: A Vertical Panorama

Most of the countries of Latin America are still defined today by substantial inequality in terms of income and opportunity, limited government control over outlying areas, and weak regional integration. These social and political tensions have been sharpened by the recent income boom from China that has benefited the extractive industry and, to some extent, agricultural sectors, reduced the attention by governments to their manufacturing industries, and further enriched national elites. Environmental challenges are increasingly acute and civil society, whose interests are underrepresented or inadequately addressed by central governments, has divergent priorities and values expressed in forms that regularly lead to conflict with authorities or outside investors, or both. Given these conditions, the countries continue to be, by and large, preoccupied with internal processes, but the shifting balance of power in the global order is enabling them to engage more broadly and in a more balanced and selective way with the rest of the world, and with each other. A vertical panorama refers to Latin American views toward U.S. and Chinese foreign policy from the political and business elite, and the broader public, respectively.

It is safe to assume that Latin American elites will continue to benefit from China's economic involvement in their countries, in the same way that they have tended to benefit in the past from trade and investments by Spain, Great Britain and the United States. The Latin American people as a whole can benefit too, but only if their own governments, pressed and supported by the people, invest heavily in physical and intellectual infrastructures for the future, as the Chinese have done at home for thirty years, and some other Asian reformers have done for fifty years, while Latin Americans generally have not. However, as a report of October 2015 by the UN Economic Commission for Latin America and the Caribbean points out, the entrenching of the region's natural resource specialization over the previous ten years, and its persistently low-tech production structure are likely to adversely affect the possibilities for development and equitable growth. The region must therefore deepen its economic integration. Policies aimed at improving regional integration by promoting common rules, creating production linkages, and implementing industrial and technology policies in order to diversify and increase productivity are "the only mechanism capable of galvanizing long-term growth, which is essential for creating jobs and reducing inequality" (CEPAL 2015b, p. 7).

As Chinese firms and their representatives are new to the region and relatively unknown, there is overall considerable reluctance on the part of the political and business elites to engage with them. The interests of political elites determine the level of bilateral dialogue, while the owners of small and medium enterprises travel in droves to the supply centers in Guangzhou, Yiwu, and elsewhere for low-priced goods with high turnover in their home countries. Whereas leaders in Peru, Brazil, Ecuador, and Venezuela have been proactive in responding to China's advances and policy offers, and have used the relationship to reduce or balance their reliance on the U.S., those in Colombia have not significantly altered their traditionally held position. The dominant responses to the new possibilities offered by China are evident in the institutions representing business interests: in Colombia, the National Industry Association (ANDI) resists close engagement with China, which is perceived as risky and threatening to corporate interests, whereas the National Commercial Federation (Fenalco) has a more delicate task of defending small manufacturing business against dumping of low-cost goods from China, and supporting traders of consumer goods who have found new opportunities in Chinese manufacturing.[5]

According to two regional opinion polls conducted in 2014, the broader public in Latin America is more consistently favorable toward the U.S., and still skeptical toward China. A Pew opinion poll showed that the U.S. remains considerably more popular among Latin Americans than does China, with favourable views of U.S. foreign policy at 64%, versus 48% for China (Pew Research Center, 2014). In another poll, the LAPOP Survey, respondents from twenty-two countries in the region were asked about China's influence in their own country; an overall average of 63% responded "very positive" or "positive," 23% were neutral, and only 12.5% considered it to be "negative" or "very negative," while a mere 1% answered there was no Chinese influence where they live (LAPOP 2014). Fluctuations in the public opinion surveys are inevitable, but clear trends are not hard to identify: comparing data from both the aforementioned surveys to their earlier editions in 2012, it can be seen that China's development model lost some of its earlier appeal, as it slipped to third place in 2014, behind the U.S. and Japan. Ambitious declarations by Beijing leaders at the China-CELAC Forum were probably designed to shore up confidence and optimism in Latin America, but the slowing Chinese economy is bound to dampen enthusiasm (Lynch 2016). Ariel Armony and Nicolas Velásquez (2015) offer further insights into public opinion toward China through their analysis of online statements in five countries across Latin America. They offer the insight that public opinion on China, rather than being a reflection of Chinese influence in the region, is instead an expression of public concern over domestic development and the inability of those countries' own governments to successfully address social and economic challenges.

Latin Views: A Horizontal Panorama

The relationship with the People's Republic of China has gained in importance for all countries in Latin America and the Caribbean. A horizontal view allows us to distinguish between the countries and groupings of the region, in the hope of discerning patterns of engagement with the northern hegemon or the rising power in the Far East. While the governments of some countries, such as Venezuela, have had strong ideological and geopolitical motivations to engage in a dialogue with China, others, such as Peru, have seen China's rise primarily as a strategic opportunity for support of their trade agenda and an opportunity to diversify the sources of income and investment. What is more, both the countries mentioned have regional leadership agendas, with Venezuela having co-founded the ALBA, marked by a strong anti-hegemonic and socialist rhetoric, and Peru having initiated the Pacific Alliance of neoliberal economies. Colombia, on the other hand, though part of the Pacific Alliance and strongly aligned with that organization's free-market principles, as well as being one of the largest economies in the region, has not constructively engaged with China at any level.

Mineral-rich Peru has become a major recipient of Chinese FDI in Latin America and its government has been proactively seeking to attract this through trade missions to East Asia, and by adapting its commercial, legal, and diplomatic strategies. President Humala, in office from July 2011 until mid-2016, introduced a stimulus package in 2014 designed to stabilize the national economy and bolster investor confidence. It included long-term tax restructuring intended to improve Peru's investment climate, but simultaneously attempts were made to improve the processes of prior consultation with local communities, through the International Labor Organization Convention 169 (ILO 169). This law is widely regarded as the most advanced in Latin America (Viscidi and Fargo 2015, p. 4), though it also presents significant challenges in terms of oversight and implementation, stretching authorities to the limit of their capacity ("Consulta previa" 2015). It may be said that Humala achieved some success in balancing investment priorities and corporate social responsibility, as well as obligations to the varied and fragile ecosystems of Peru. Huang Minhui, China's ambassador to Peru until July 2015, has been quoted saying that Peru is "well ahead of other countries in the region when it comes to capacity to draw Chinese investments [thanks to its] legal framework, attractive policies [and] historic cultural ties" (Ojeda 2015).

Brazil has seen an important new dynamism in agricultural and technological sectors since China's increased presence and investment. It has adjusted its westward focus to a bi-oceanic projection, embodied by the plan to build a rail link through Peru to the Pacific Ocean. There has more broadly been significant attention to expanding infrastructure development in the country.

Chile has benefited from its proactive policy toward China, beginning in 2005 with the signing of a free trade agreement. It has strongly projected its commercial and political futures toward Asia, has significantly accelerated its exporting capacities and product range, and has moved to strengthen its position as a regional financial hub by becoming a platform for trading and transactions in Renminbi.

Economic analysts at ECLAC report the growing Asian trade numbers with enthusiasm (CEPAL 2012, 2015a), and it is only in separate reports (e.g., CEPAL 2015b, quoted above) that there is evident concern over the renewed exploitation of raw materials in Latin America by the developed countries. Many analysts in both China and Latin America emphasize the complementarity of China's needs and Latin America's mineral wealth (Chai and Kong 2014), while others questions the degree of China's long-term commitment and the abilities of Latin governments to take proper advantage of the opportunity (Ferchen 2011). Still others warn that, as one puts it, "governments there have not paid proper attention to their own domestic business environments, key components to their economic health in an increasingly interconnected world economy" (Gallagher 2010b). The analyses of more alarmist commentators, especially in the media, hint at "a growing racism towards Chinese is evident in Latin America and Mexico, especially in entrepreneurial circles, [combined with] highlighting the positive sides of an authoritarian regime" (Dussel Peters 2006, 13). This is something still latent in many parts of the continent.

After weathering the global financial crisis without much difficulty and indeed reasonable GDP growth across the region, the panorama in Latin America changed during the period 2013–2016. The death of Venezuela's charismatic leader Hugo Chávez has taken some of the wind out of the sails of the Latin American socialist movement and weakened the unanimity of the ALBA countries, while the peace dialogues in Colombia have similarly reduced the appeal of extreme political tendencies. The gradual normalization of U.S. relations with Cuba can also be seen as a sign of less dogmatic times in the region, while the historic first of a Latin American pope has given the region a much-needed moral boost. China has made top leadership visits to the region an annual event, while continuing to promote and finance visits by party leaders, policymakers, and academics, alongside other, lower-level activities. Brazil further enhanced its special relationship status with China through the incremental institutionalization of the BRICS, and also became the only Latin American country to join the Asian Infrastructure Investment

Bank (AIIB), launched by China in an initiative interpreted diversely as an alternative, complementary, or competing lending institution to the U.S.-led World Bank. This is likely to further strengthen China's position as the world's leading development lender (Kynge 2016).

Concluding Reflections

It seems evident that the United States, despite its relatively low level of public attention to the countries of Latin America throughout the first decade of the twenty-first century, and its problematic reputation of flouting its own guidelines on non-intervention, has a considerable advantage over China thanks to a historically grounded affinity, enhanced by cultural and geographical proximity. China, for its part, has not succeeded in translating its strategic interests and desire to be a catalyst for change into a consistent agency in the region, despite its important overtures to individual nations and groupings (Trinkunas, 2016). It may even be true that China's traditional policy of non-interference causes greater concern among the Latin American public than the United States' politically interested stance supported by commercial action, expressions of opinion, and a history of covert or armed intervention, in what are widely perceived to be elite-driven domestic policies by feeble governments.

In terms of the views from Latin America, these are as diverse as they are discombobulated. Not even the members of regional blocs designed to facilitate flow of goods and people or coordinated dialogue have a consistent approach or response to the two major powers vying for their attention. The fear of reprimarization of the economies of Latin America is a very real concern, as is the resulting dependency on the vicissitudes of global markets and trends. But this is not a phenomenon consistent across the region, as some governments are steering more consciously toward education, research, and development alongside diversified agricultural and technological segments (Chile, Brazil, Costa Rica, Ecuador, and Peru) and others are focused on maintaining numerical growth at the cost of improved development and genuine structural changes for the benefit of the broader population (Colombia, Venezuela). The issues of unsustainable extractivism and feeble physical infrastructure, alongside social stratification and exclusion, coupled with poor education and lack of public investment in research and technology that have marked most countries of Latin America are more likely to be addressed through Chinese agency than that of the U.S., but depend upon the political will and vision of the governing elites in the region, most of whom do not appear to have the grasp or interest to convert this possibility into lasting transformation.

What is needed on the part of Latin American countries is better-informed domestic development, leaning where possible on growing Chinese development lending. Without such policies on a national level, most Latin American countries will remain the exploited reserves of natural resources they have been since the Spanish and Portuguese conquest five centuries ago. If Latin Americans consciously or unconsciously choose this route, that is ultimately their own responsibility—or possibly that of the United States, where predominant scholarly and media opinion tends to call into question the Chinese rhetoric of good intentions. Then again, even China's biggest investors in the mines and oilfields of the region are working on time scales of up to twenty-five years to recoup their investments, so the window of opportunity to pull together and learn to strategize and generate change is a limited one. Should U.S. foreign policy in the Trump administration continue to profess traditional values—democracy, market-oriented economy, peace, and prosperity—this would more likely be achieved in tandem with Chinese goals of technological advancement, the building of solid, forward-looking infrastructure, and mutually beneficial cooperation all-round.

NOTES

1   See in particular Paz's cultural historical analysis in *The Labyrinth of Solitude* (1981), first published in 1950. These themes have been picked up repeatedly, most notably by Eduardo Galeano (1973) and Jorge Larrain (2000), and resurface continually in both media and scholarly discussions of Latin America's international affairs.

2   The Caribbean countries are not discussed in detail, due in part to their fragmented political relationship with China and bearing in mind the attention they are given in Richard Bernal's chapter in the present volume. At the other end of the spectrum in terms of size, Brazil is treated only tangentially, although it presents a significant exception to the Latin American mean due to its magnitude and the distinctive relationship it has built with the People's Republic framed by the BRICS group of countries, explored in the chapters by Tony Spanakos and José Augusto Guilhon-Albuquerque.

3   This is the starting point of one of the first serious and relatively comprehensive studies of China's relations with Latin America, by Marisela Connelly and Romer

Cornejo (1992). For discussions of early trade relations via the Spanish-governed Philippines see Xu Wenyuan (1992) and Manel Ollé (2002).

4   For a separate discourse analysis research project, I selected a total of thirty-one Chinese foreign policy speeches relating to Latin America between 2004 and 2015, and found that the three papers mentioned are indeed representative of the dynamic approach Beijing has designed for Latin America.

5   Information based on interviews with representatives of each of these institutions, conducted by the author in September 2014.

BIBLIOGRAPHY

Armony, A. C., and Velásquez, N. (2015). "Anti-Chinese Sentiment in Latin America: An Analysis of Online Discourse." *Journal of Political Science 20*(3), 319–346. doi:10.1007/s11366–015–9365-z.

Carpenter, T. G. (2003). *Bad Neighbor Policy: Washington's Futile War on Drugs in Latin America*. New York: Palgrave Macmillan.

CEPAL. (2012). *China and Latin America and the Caribbean: Building a Strategic Economic and Trade Relationship*. Santiago de Chile: ECLAC, United Nations.

CEPAL. (2015a). *América Latina y el Caribe y China: Hacia una nueva era de cooperación económica*. Santiago de Chile: United Nations. www.cepal.org.

CEPAL. (2015b). *Latin America and the Caribbean in the World Economy—The Regional Trade Crisis:Aassessment and Outlook*. Santiago de Chile: CEPAL.

Chai, Y., and Kong, S. (2014). "Zhongguo yu Nanmei guojia de jingmao guanxi: xianzhuang yu tiaozhan" 中国与南美国家的经贸关系:现状与挑战 [Economic and trade relations between China and South America: status and challenges]. *Lading Meizhou Yanjiu* 拉丁美洲研究 36(1), 12–21.

Chavarro, J. S. (2016, 19 May). "*U.S. Interests and the Colombian Peace Talks.*" Council on Hemispheric Affairs.www.coha.org.

"China despidió por corrupción al encargado de vínculos con América Latina." (2015, 1 February). *Clarín*. www.clarin.com.

China's Policy Paper on Latin America and the Caribbean. Beijing: Ministry of Foreign Affairs. www.fmprc.gov.cn.

"The Chinese Chequebook." (2015, 23 May). *Economist*.

"Chinese President Calls for Greater Democracy in International Relations." (2014). *Xinhuanet*. http://news.xinhuanet.com.

Congressional Research Service. (2008). *China's Foreign Policy and "Soft Power" in South America, Asia, and Africa: A Study Prepared for the Committee on Foreign Relations*. Washington, DC: Congressional Research Service, Library of Congress. http://fas.org.

Connelly, M., & Cornejo Bustamante, R. (1992). *China—América Latina: Génesis y desarrollo de sus relaciones*. México: Colegio de México, Centro de Estudios de Asia y Africa.

"Consulta previa: un balance a cuatro años de su creación." (2015, 22 June). *El Comercio*. www.elcomercio.pe.

Crow, J. A. (1992). *The Epic of Latin America* (4th ed.). Berkeley: University of California Press.

Dussel Peters, E. (2006). "China und Lateinamerika: Hat die 'Exportorientierte Entwicklung' angesichts der Exportoffensive Chinas noch eine Chance?" *Prokla (Münster)* 36, 113–126.

Ellis, R. E. (2014, 4 August). "China Fills the Vacuum Left by the United States in Latin America." *Perspectives on the Americas* 5. https://umshare.miami.edu.

Ellis, R. E. (2015, 30 September). "Strengthening America's Adversaries, Expert Commentary." *Cipher Brief*. www.thecipherbrief.com.

Evans, M. (2009, 7 January). "Los 'falsos positivos' son una práctica vieja en el Ejército." *Semana*.

Feinberg, R., Miller, E., and Trinkunas, H. (2015). "*Better than You Think: Reframing Inter-American Relations.*" Brookings Institution. www.brookings.edu.

Fenby, J. (2012). "Does China Have a Foreign Policy? Domestic Pressures and China's Strategy." In N. Kitchen (ed.), *China's Geoeconomic Strategy* (Vol. SR012, pp. 12–18). London: LSE.

Ferchen, M. (2011). "China-Latin America Relations: Long-term Boon or Short-term Boom?" *Chinese Journal of International Politics* 4, 55–86. doi:10.1093/cjip/poq020

Galeano, E. (1973). *The Open Veins of Latin America: Five Centuries of the Pillage of a Continent* (C. Belfridge, trans.). New York: Monthly Review Press.

Gallagher, K. P. (2010a). "China and the Future of Latin American Industrialization." *Frederick S. Pardee Center for the Study of the Longer-Range Future Issues in Brief* (018).

Gallagher, K. P. (2010b). *The Dragon in the Room: China & the Future of Latin American Industrialization*. Stanford, CA: Stanford University Press.

He, K., & Feng, H. (2013). "Xi Jinping's Operational Code Beliefs and China's Foreign Policy." *Chinese Journal of International Politics* 6(3), 209–231. doi:10.1093/cjip/pot010

Horsley, S. (2015, 13 April). "With a Handshake and More, Obama Shifts U.S.-Latin America Policy." *NPR*. www.npr.org.

Kynge, J. (2016, 17 May). "China Becomes Global Leader in Development Finance." *Financial Times*. www.ft.com.

LAPOP (Latin American Public Opinion Project). (2014). "AmericasBarometer." Vanderbilt University. www.vanderbilt.edu.

Larrain, J. (2000). *Identity and Modernity in Latin America*. Cambridge, UK: Polity Press.

Lopez, A. L., and Sam, C. (2015). "China's Overseas Investments (2005–2014)." South China Morning Post. http://multimedia.scmp.com.

Lynch, D. (2016, 11 January). "The End of China's Rise: Still Powerful But Less Potent." *Foreign Affairs*. www.foreignaffairs.com.

Main, A. (2014, 19 December). "One Step Forward, One Step Back in US-Latin America Policy." *The Hill*. www.thehill.com.

McKeown, A. (2001). *Chinese Migrant Networks and Cultural Change: Peru, Chicago, and Hawaii 1900–1936*. Chicago: University of Chicago Press.

Myers, M., and Yang, Z. (2012). "¿Qué significará el 12. Plan Quinquenal de China para las relaciones sino-latinoamericanas?" *Apuntes Revista de Ciencias Sociales* 39(71), 7–32.

Noesselt, N., and Soliz-Landivar, A. (2013). "China in Latin America: Competition in the United States' 'Strategic Backyard.'" *GIGA Focus 7*. www.ssoar.info.

Obama, B. (2009). Remarks by the President at the Summit of the Americas Ceremony. www.whitehouse.gov.

Obama, B. (2012). *Remarks by President Obama at CEO Summit of the Americas.*www.whitehouse.gov.

Obama, B. (2015). Remarks by President Obama at the First Plenary Session of the Summit of the Americas. www.whitehouse.gov.

Ojeda, H. (2015, 1 June). "China Ambassador: Peru Shows Great Investment Potential." *Peru This Week*. www.peruthisweek.com.

Ollé, M. (2002). *La empresa de China: De la Armada Invencible al Galeón de Manila* (Vol. 60). Barcelona: Acantilado, Quaderns Crema S.A.

Paz, O. (1981). *El laberinto de la soledad* (5th ed.). Mexico, DF: Fondo de Cultura Económica.

Pew Research Center. (2014). *Global Opposition to U.S. Surveillance and Drones, but Limited Harm to America's Image*. www.pewglobal.org.

Ratliff, W. (2012). "China en el futuro de América Latina." In B. Creutzfeldt (ed.), *China en América Latina: Reflexiones sobre las relaciones transpacíficas* (pp. 27–59). Bogota: Universidad Externado de Colombia.

Santiso, J. (2007). *The Visible Hand of China in Latin America*. Paris: OECD Publications.

Shixue, J. (2007). In C. Arnson, M. Mohr, and R. Roett (eds.), *Enter the Dragon? China's Presence in Latin America* (pp. 43–52). Washington, DC: Woodrow Wilson Center.

Viscidi, L., and Fargo, J. (2015). "Local Conflicts and Natural Resources: A Balancing Act for Latin American Governments." *Dialogue Energy Working Paper*. www.thedialogue.org.

Wen, J. (2012). *Yongyuan zuo xianghu xinlai de hao pengyou* 永远做相互信赖的好朋友 [Trusted friends forever: address by Premier Wen Jiabao at the Economic Commission for Latin America and the Caribbean of the United Nations]. Foreign Ministry of the People's Republic of China. www.fmprc.gov.cn.

Wise, C. (2012). "The China Conundrum: Economic Development Strategies Embraced by Small States in South America." *Colombia Internacional* 75, 131–170. doi: dx.doi.org/10.7440/colombint75.2012.05

Xi, J. (2015). *Gongtong puxie zhongla quanmian hezuo huoban guanxi xinbianzhang* 共同谱写中拉全面合作伙伴关系新篇章 [Jointly write a new chapter in Latin America comprehensive cooperative partnership relations] (Beijing: First China-CELAC Forum ministerial meeting). *Xinhuanet*. http://news.xinhuanet.com.

Xu, W. (1992). "Zhongla jingji maoyi guanxi de lishi, xianzhuang he qianjing" 中拉经济贸易关系的历史 现状和前景 [Past, present, and future of China's economic and trade relations with Latin America]. *Lading Meizhou Yanjiu* 拉丁美洲研究 6, 43–48.

Zhang, S., and Zhang, S. (2012). "Xin shiqi Lamei jiegou zhuyi yu Zhongla nengyuan hezuo de qianjing" 新时期拉美结构主义与中拉能源合作的前景 [New Latin American structuralism and perspectives for China–Latin American energy resource cooperation]. *Lading Meizhou Yanjiu* 拉丁美洲研究 34(6), 18–22.

"Zhao in L. America: Seeing Is Believing." (1985). *Beijing Review* 28(47), 6–7.

Zheng, B., Sun, H., and Yue, Y. (2012). "Sesenta años de relaciones entre China y América Latina: retrospectivas y reflexiones." In B. Creutzfeldt (ed.), *China en América Latina: Reflexiones sobre las relaciones transpacíficas* (pp. 61–85). Bogota: Universidad Externado de Colombia.

PART II

Perspectives from Key Countries

5

Mexico–United States–China

Conditions and Challenges of This New Triangular Relationship from a Mexican Perspective

ENRIQUE DUSSEL PETERS

Mexico and the United States share a long—in some cases problematic—history of political, military, social, immigration, cultural, and economic relations, in part as a result of a common border of more than 3,000 kilometers. These long-lasting ties were also reflected in the signature and implementation of the North American Free Trade Agreement (NAFTA) since 1994: in the case of trade, for example, Mexico has been among the three main trading partners of the US in the last decades, while the US is the number one trading partner of Mexico since we have statistics in recent history.

In this context, the goal of this chapter is to examine the "new triangular relationship" (Dussel Peters, Hearn, and Shaiken 2013) between the US, Mexico, and China and particularly from a Mexican perspective. With the global reemergence of China since the last decade of the 20th century the historical relationship between Mexico and the US has substantially shifted from a group of perspectives, including those in the political and economic fields.

The analysis will be divided into three sections. The first will highlight the general socioeconomic triangular relationship of Mexico with the US and China, based on a literature review that specifies the main topics in this relationship; a group of issues regarding China in trade and foreign direct investments (FDI), among others, are relevant, as well as the overall relationship of Latin America and the Caribbean (LAC) with China. The second section will discuss a group of items that are currently being analyzed in Mexico in this triangular relationship, particularly regarding China. These selected topics will refer to literature that deepens this debate. Finally, the third part of the analysis concentrates on the main characteristics of this "new triangular relationship" and its resulting policy and future research issues.

1. Mexico-China in the Latin American and Caribbean Context

The LAC-China relationship has increased qualitatively since the last decade of the 20th century in terms of massive political and economic relations, but also in the field of language and culture, among other fields (Arnson, Heine, and Zaino 2014; Dussel Peters 2005a; Roett and Paz 2008; Red ALC-China 2013, 2015). In general, these documents highlight the increasing relevance of both regions in terms of trade, investments, and finance: these "seismic changes" (IADB 2012:xiii) were not only the result of market forces, but also of the strategies and active policies of respective governments. As a result, the LAC-Asia relationship—and particularly with China—proved to be one of the most dynamic and relevant in terms of trade, with an average annual growth rate (AAGR) of 20.5% between Asia and the Pacific and LAC during 2000–2011. Costs of trade (IADB 2012), including items such as tariffs, transportation, and overall transaction costs (Santiso 2006), were some of the main topics in the suggested agenda between the regions. The new trade diversification—in 2014 China accounted for 12% of LAC's trade, second only to the US.[1] Also China posed opportunities and challenges for LAC in this new "South-South" relationship and specifically in terms of trade and investment cooperation, infrastructure, competitiveness and innovation, climate change, and policy dialogue on cooperation (ECLAC 2011). Particularly relevant for the case of China—as well as for India and Asia in general—is that LAC's growing trade deficit with the region, as well as for China and India, is significant in terms of its content: LAC's exports to Asia and China include mostly raw materials with little value-added and technological content, while LAC's imports from the region are manufactured goods with increasing value-added and products of medium and high-level technological content; in the last decade only 5% of LAC exports to China were of medium and high technological level, while over 60% of Chinese exports to the region were of these types (see figure 5.1). This typical "center-periphery" productive and trade structure is also deepened by the high levels of concentration

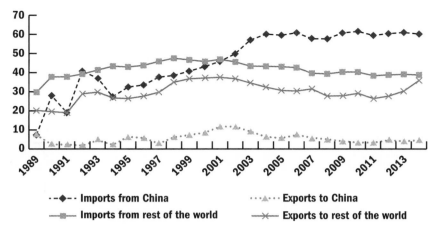

Figure 5.1. LAC: trade at medium- and high-technology level (% of total) (1989–2014)
Source: Based on data available at UN-Comtrade Database, https://comtrade.un.org.

of LAC's trade with China and in particular of its exports: the top-three export categories to China—ores, oil seed, and copper (followed by oil and wood pulp)—increased from 50% to 72% of total exports from 2000 to 2014. Over the same period, Latin America's exports to the world in these three categories fell from 42% to 32%. China's imports from Argentina and Brazil, and particularly from Venezuela, account for the highest concentration degrees—in Venezuela for levels above 99% in the last decade—while Chinese imports from Mexico have also increased substantially, but still to levels below 70% (see figure 5.2). After this first stage of the recent encounter between LAC and China in the last decade in terms of trade, three new levels and stages have been achieved.[2]

First, China started investing massively in LAC,[3] particularly since the international crisis of 2007–2008, accounting for levels above $10 billion annually for 2000–2014, but FDI is quite different from that of other countries. From 2000 to 2012, 87% of China's Latin American–bound FDI came from public-owned firms. This FDI is also highly concentrated, with 57% focused on the acquisition of raw materials (Red ALC-China 2013).

Second, China is also increasing its financing presence. From 2005 to 2014, loan commitments totaled more than $118 billion. Venezuela alone accounted for more than 50% of total loans and 42% of infrastructure projects in the region (Gallagher and Myers 2015; Gransow 2015).

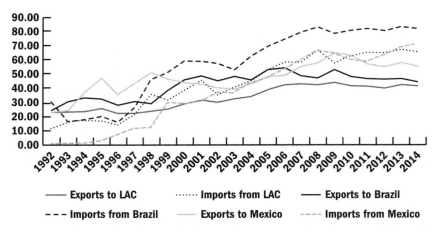

Figure 5.2. China: trade with LAC by degree of concentration (top three items' share of total respective trade) (1992–2014)
Source: Based on data available at UN-Comtrade Database, https://comtrade.un.org.

These new Chinese economic activities will likely grow substantially, given the expected increase in Chinese infrastructure projects.

Third, in addition to China's very recent and aggressive global policies to promote infrastructure projects globally under the heading of the "New Maritime Silk Road" and "One Belt–One Road Strategy" (Long 2015)—China today is able to offer turnkey projects that make it much more difficult for local and national suppliers to integrate into their processes (Dussel Peters 2014b), i.e., China offering financing, Chinese firms able to manage all parts of the project (design, logistics, construction, and many other segments), technology, and all required goods and services (Dussel Peters 2015a). These new opportunities, rather than improving existing trade and OFDI structures, might even worsen development results for LAC in its relationship with China: opportunities for LAC firms to compete and integrate to trade and OFDI from China, from this perspective, are more limited than with US or European firms.

2. The Current Socioeconomic Bilateral Relationship between Mexico and China

For the Mexican case, parallel to this regional literature, there has been an increasing analysis of the Mexico-China relationship from a general or macroeconomic perspective discussing trade and business experiences, the issue of China as an "opportunity or threat," but also in terms of cooperation and cultural and educational exchange, as well as from a historical perspective. From a general Mexican perspective, the Mexican government has continued, with few exceptions, with a consistent liberalization strategy started at the end of the 1980s and only very recently began to seriously consider Asia as an important strategic partner, particularly in terms the "diversification of its economic ties" (PND 2013:148), i.e., only until very recently Mexico considered Asia as part of a globalization process, and beyond the North American Free Trade Agreement (NAFTA) (Dussel Peters 2014a; Fernández de Castro and Díaz Leal 2007). Even more recent analysis since the 2000s (Lafourcade, Nguyen, and Giugale 2001) has not included Asia explicitly; policy makers and officials until 2013 had difficulties in integrating explicitly Asia (Acevedo and Zabludovsky 2012; Leycegui Gardoqui 2012), although the TPP (Trans-Pacific Partnership) and the Alliance for the Pacific could be functional for further reforms in Mexico (Rozenzweig 2012). Thus, while formally Mexico has been participating in a large group of Asian forums such as APEC, ASEAN (Association of Southeast Asian Nations), FOCALAE (Forum for East Asia-Latin America Cooperation), and PCEC (Pacific Council for Economic Cooperation), among others (Dussel Peters 2014a), it is only since 2013 that the Plan Nacional de Desarrollo (2013–2018) presents a group of "lines of action" (PND 2013:148) with specific goals and strategic objectives for Asia, including China and India. Mexico has also maintained important political relations with China in several multilateral groups such as the G20 and in the United Nations system.

Regarding China,[4] there has been an increasing analysis with a group of results: (a) Contrary to the increasing economic relationships of Mexico with Asia—and specifically with China—public, private, and academic institutions are weak and recent, with little capabilities of analysis, proposals, and funding of particular projects of relevance of the bilateral ties; (b) China and Mexico have developed a group of bilateral institutions since 2004—including the Binational Commission Mexico-China and at least three high-level groups (on general topics, the economy, and investments)—that have included most of the relevant bilateral issues; until 2015, rather surprisingly, most of these issues—from statistics

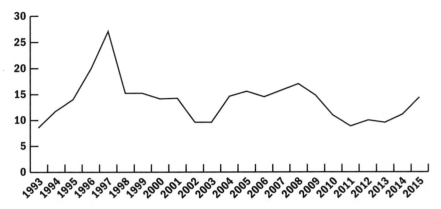

Figure 5.3. Mexico: import/export coefficient with China (1993–2015)
Source: Based on Cechimex (2016)

to education, tourism, immigration, trade, and investments—have neither been solved nor analyzed systematically and/or strategically. There are, however, important expectations that as a result of the new qualitative relationship between Mexico and China since 2013—as a result of 2 presidential meetings between Enrique Peña Nieto and Xi Jinping in 2013 and another in 2014—there will be important concrete results in this bilateral agenda;[5] (c) China has consolidated its position as Mexico's second-largest trading partner since 2003, yet accounting for a significant trade deficit (see figure 5.3) and an increasing "Latinoamericanization" of Mexico's trade with China, i.e., increasing exports in raw materials (oil and copper), while more than 60% of China's imports have medium- or high-level technological content; (d) foreign direct investment (FDI) from China accounted for less than $410 million dollars or less than 0.1% of Mexico's total FDI (in firms such as Hutchinson Ports, Sinatex, Golden Dragon, and Huawei) (see table 5.1), thus manifesting an important gap in the context of overall economic and trade intensification; (e) A group of Mexican "translatinas" have also been very active investing in China, accumulating around $320 million through 2011, including firms such as Bimbo, Nemak, Katcon, Gruma, Softek, Cemex, Interceramics, and Grupo Kuo (Dussel Peters 2013); and (f) China has made an important cultural contribution in Mexico through five Confucius Institutes, one of the largest numbers in any country in the world. Finally,

TABLE 5.1. Mexico: Realized FDI flows by country of origin (1999–2015)

	1999	2005	2010	2011	2012	2013	2014	2015	1999–2015
	(millions of dollars)								
TOTAL	13,940	25,971	26,431	23,649	20,437	45,855	25,675	30,285	436,188
Top 5 countries	10,618	17,612	18,821	17,330	14,887	38,913	14,946	20,033	265,900
China	5	15	15	28	88	25	57	30	409
	share (percentage of total)								
TOTAL	100.00	100.00	100.00	100.00	100.00	100.00	100.00	100.00	100.00
Top 5 countries	76.17	67.82	71.21	73.28	72.84	84.86	58.21	66.15	60.96
1 United States	54.24	48.25	26.61	51.66	46.94	29.98	30.17	52.16	45.80
2 Belgium	0.24	-0.08	0.14	0.69	0.00	28.98	4.91	2.84	2.73
3 Holland	7.79	16.12	34.64	10.95	8.03	11.86	6.33	2.97	3.92
4 Canada	4.95	2.66	7.65	6.05	9.05	9.86	11.61	3.60	5.94
5 Japan	8.95	0.86	2.17	3.92	8.83	4.17	5.18	4.58	2.57
25 China	0.04	0.06	0.06	0.12	0.43	0.05	0.22	0.10	0.09

Source: Based on SRE data (2016).

the current administrations of Enrique Peña Nieto and Xi Jinping have concentrated on the issue of Chinese investments in Mexico (Dussel Peters 2014b; Qiu 2014); in Mexico the Finance Ministry (Secretaría de Hacienda y Crédito Público, SHCP) has been in charge of its implementation, as part of becoming "integral strategic partners" since 2013. Thus, one of the most relevant challenges in the Mexico-China relationship involves the implementation of concrete projects in the prioritized agenda regarding investments, beyond already established formal agreements in terms of tourism, education, and culture and scientific cooperation, such as the signature of an APPRI (Agreement for the Promotion and Reciprocal Protection of Investments) in 2008.

After November 2014, however, the bilateral relationship between Mexico and China fell into a new low as a result of a group of failed Chinese investments.[6] These tensions had not been solved by the end of 2015. A group of issues stand out in explaining these increasing structural tensions beyond the diplomatic and formal "strategic integral relationship."

First, there is the Dragon Mart project—an exhibition center for Chinese goods in Cancún with links through Mexico to Central America—which started in 2007 and was presented to local and federal authorities in 2011. With an investment of around $180 million dollars— only 10% of which was Chinese capital—the project was authorized by a group of local institutions in 2013, but later cancelled by federal officials in 2014 for insufficient compliance with environmental regulations. Throughout the period the wrongly called "Chinese project" received very harsh criticism from different social, political, and business groups that went far beyond the project and made reference to China in general, but also to labor, environmental, human rights, and regional discussions in China.

Second, the high-speed train from Querétaro to Mexico City (around 200 kilometers) had a much stronger effect on the bilateral relationship. The public bidding was published in August 2014 and most participants complained that there was too little time to comply with the project's sophisticated requirements. Mexico's secretary of communication and transportation received only one proposal for the joint venture between China Railway Construction Corporation (CRCC) with other four Mexican firms, led by Grupo Higa; this group won the bidding process in early November. Three days later, just a few days before President Peña Nieto's official visit to China, he cancelled the project as a result of corruption and conflict of interest involving Grupo Higa and officials at the highest level of the Mexican executive. Public bidding was opened again in January 2015 but, as a result of international oil price fall and subsequent fiscal limitations, "definitively cancelled" two weeks later. Premier Li Keqiang openly questioned this decision in Mexico and CRCC has been requesting compensation for the costs of the project, which reflects the level of frustration of China's public sector, understanding that reimbursement of these costs is economically insignificant, but politically symbolic.

Both projects and other recent cases[7] reflect an increasing desperation from a Chinese perspective, i.e., in spite of President Peña Nieto's openness to Chinese FDI, the above analyzed cases show that Mexico is apparently not able to understand and/or host Chinese FDI. CRCC not only requests the reimbursement of the project costs, but also guarantees for future projects; the "word" of the Mexican public sector at the highest level, from this perspective, is apparently not sufficient. The experience of CRCC and other Chinese firms, on the other hand, also reflects that they have to improve their preparation and understanding to materialize their investment, not only in financial and technical terms, but also regarding social, environmental, and political topics. Large projects, particularly in infrastructure, have to include these items in detail, and improve their risk analysis and the openness and willingness to negotiate with the respective local and national groups.

3. Selected Debates on the "New Triangular Relationship" from a Mexican Perspective

China currently poses a massive challenge to Mexico's export-oriented industrialization and its long-term strategy within NAFTA: can Mexico continue to specialize in cheap labor power and cheap energy? On both terms China could reply that labor power and energy will be much cheaper in China and the Asian region—from China's rural areas to large regions further west of the coast, as well as Vietnam and other Asian countries—than in LAC for the next few decades. If China does not pursue the same development strategy as in the last two decades in LAC, what kind of room does China leave for LAC in the near future? This challenge is not only relevant for Mexico, but for the NAFTA region as a whole (Dussel Peters and Gallagher 2013) for specific value-added chains such as telecommunications, electronics, automobiles and auto parts, and yarn, textiles, and garments.

Based on this methodology, table 5.2 shows some general results regarding Chinese competition with Mexico in the US market and with the US in the Mexican market. In all cases, the competition—or "threat"—is very significant for the period 2000–2013:

1. For the Mexican market, in which the US and China compete, levels are the highest: 86.2% and 66.5% of US exports in manufactures and total to Mexico compete with China. China dramatically increased its share of total US imports during 2001–2014, from 9% to 16%. Latin America and the Caribbean's share also increased, but less dramatically—from 16% to 19%. China's share of Latin America and the Caribbean's imports increased sharply, from 3% in 2001 to 17% in 2014, while the United States' share fell from 46%

TABLE 5.2. Matrix of competitive interactions between China and other countries in export markets

		China's export market shares	
		Rising	Falling
Other countries' export market shares	Rising	A. No threat Both China and the other country have rising market shares and the latter is gaining more than China B. Partial threat Both are gaining market share but China is gaining faster than the other country	C. Reverse threat No competitive threat from China. The threat is the reverse, from the other country to China
	Falling	D. Direct threat China gains market share and the other country loses; this may indicate causal connection unless the other country was losing market share in the absence of Chinese entry	E. Mutual withdrawal: no threat Both parties lose market shares in export markets to other competitors

Source: Lall and Weiss (2005); Dussel Peters and Gallagher (2013)

to 32%. As a result, for the period 2001–2014 72.24% of the United States' exports to Latin America and the Caribbean were threatened by Chinese exports. The impact of this loss of market share in Latin America and the Caribbean on jobs in the United States is significant. It can be estimated as follows: if the US share of the region's imports had remained the same as in 2001 (46%), the value of US exports to the region would have been $145 billion higher in 2014. Based on recent estimates by the Department of Commerce (International Trade Administration) of jobs supported per billion dollars of exports, the additional $145 billion would have generated 840,000 jobs in the United States in 2014 alone, all related to manufacturing and 55% related to automobiles and auto parts.

2. In the US market, in which Mexico and China compete, 67% and 56% of Mexican exports in manufacturing and total compete with China.

a) The trade relationship of Mexico and China is economically and politically not sustainable in the short run. While China is Mexico's second-largest trading partner since 2003, the import/export ratio was 14/1 in 2015 (figure 5.3), i.e., China accounted for 16.6% of Mexican exports and only 1.5% of its exports, as well

TABLE 5.3. Percentage of "Chinese threat" in Mexican and U.S. markets (2000–2013)

U.S.	Direct	Partial	Total
percent of manufactures exports to Mexico	84.4	1.8	86.2
percent of total exports to Mexico	64.5	2	66.5
Mexico			
percent of manufactures exports to US	37.2	29.8	67
percent of all exports to US	31.6	24.4	56

Source: Based on data available at UN-Comtrade Database, https://comtrade.un.org, and on Lall and Weiss (2005)

as a $60.3 billion trade deficit in 2014; the share of trade with the US, meanwhile, declined substantially, from above 81% of total trade in 1999 to levels below 65% since 2008. While it is true that most Chinese imports are intermediate and capital goods (more than 91% of Chinese imports), so far Mexico has not been able to overcome this massive structural deficit. These structural problems might even worsen in the short run: initial information for the first half of 2015 (Banco de México 2015) reflects that imports from China increased by 8%, while exports to China fell by almost 24%.

b) In the last few decades Mexico has been able to significantly increase its technological levels in production and trade: the share of medium- and high-technology products in total exports increased from levels below 50% in the 1990s to 58% in 2013. For the case of China, however, medium- and high-technology products accounted for only 36% in exports and 74% in imports in 2013, i.e., technology in trade with China accounts for massive differences in value-added.

c) Even though the respective new administrations in Mexico and China since 2013 focused on Chinese investments in Mexico, these have not increased: Chinese FDI accounted for less than $410 million or 0.09% of Mexico's accumulated FDI during 1999–2015 and there has not been an increasing trend in the last five years (see table 5.1). As discussed in detail in the last chapter, there are good reasons to believe that this performance will not change substantially. Until the end of 2015, both presidents made a significant effort to improve the political and strategic relationship, but have so far not been successful in concrete results in terms of trade, FDI, and infrastructure projects as a result of weak and ineffective institutions and various tensions in the trade and investment areas.

d) In addition to the topic of China's challenges to NAFTA, there is an important discussion regarding the active role of Mexico in the Trans-Pacific Partnership (TPP) and the Pacific Alliance (PA) and its effects on China. While China has openly criticized and distanced itself from TPP, it is not clear if China might be more open to the PA proposal in the short and medium run.

4. Conclusions, Policy Suggestions, and Future Research

As a result of geography, history, immigration, and culture, the US is today by far the most important "partner" of Mexico. NAFTA, for example, is critical for understanding Mexico's economy and its high integration to the US economy. As a result, until very recently, Mexico's policy makers have almost exclusively focused on institutions, mechanisms, and instruments related to the US, and not to Asia and China.

As a result of not acknowledging the importance of Asia and China, Mexico today has rather weak public, private, and academic institutions regarding Asia, particularly China, with little capacity of generating knowledge, discussions, and detailed proposals. As analyzed in the first chapter, this institutional weakness in Mexico, however, is not only a "Mexican characteristic", i.e., public, private, and academic institutions are probably as weak in most of LAC and in China. Two recent experiences in 2015, the First Ministerial Meeting between China and LAC of the Community of Latin American and Caribbean States (CELAC) that took place in January in Beijing and the Latin America-China Business Summit in Guadalajara in October both reflect these structures. The Business Summit is supposed to be the major business meeting between LAC and China and the level of representation and lack of any participation of most LAC countries was surprising, while the temporary status of the secretariat of CELAC does not allow for any relevant monitoring and evaluation of its activities. Both institutions should be of strategic relevance for LAC and China.

During 2013–2014 the bilateral relationship between Mexico and China improved significantly as a result of a group of efforts of both administrations and presidents; since November 2014, however, new general tensions arose. Both governments invested substantially in their bilateral relationship and the results were disappointing. It is not clear if the bilateral relationship in the future will pick up the same dynamism as in 2013–2014, but through 2015 clearly it had not; there are good reasons for believing that it will not happen, particularly because the Mexican government is already in the second half of its administration and other enormous domestic and international pressures.

As discussed in detail concerning the economic bilateral relationship, China has become a major partner in this "new triangular relationship" for both the US and Mexico. China has not only significantly displaced US exports to Mexico, but also changed important structures of Mexico's trade (in terms of the share of medium- and high-technology products over total trade). So far, Chinese FDI has been very limited and the efforts of both administrations have not succeeded in allowing for Chinese FDI. There are good reasons for this lack of Chinese FDI. On the one hand, as a result of political tensions before 2012, China's public sector decided not to incentivize its private and public firms. In addition, the Mexican market, as part of NAFTA, is more complicated and determined by regional regulations that do not exist in other LAC and developing countries, i.e., learning processes and costs are more complex compared to other nations. Finally, based on the Chinese disappointment with the fast-speed train and other failed projects in 2014–2015, it cannot be expected that China will invest heavily in Mexico, contrary to other LAC countries.

In the last few decades, competition based on cheap wages between Mexico and China has diminished, i.e., wages in increasing parts of China have surpassed those of Mexico, in part as a result of very substantial changes in real exchange rates in both countries. It is not clear, however, if this strategy—offering cheaper wages than China—will pay off in Mexico. On the one side, China is supporting massive strategies to upgrade its productive and trade sectors, shifting in parallel from exports to services, in contrast to the rather primitive and simple value-added and technology levels in Mexico. On the other side, other countries such as Bangladesh, Pakistan, Myanmar, and Vietnam particularly, offer still much cheaper wages than most of LAC and China is increasingly transferring segments of value-added chains in which wages play an important role.

Based on the discussion on Mexico-China-US relations, in general much more detailed and specific analysis is required in order to overcome current tensions and shifts in this new triangular relationship. Surprisingly, there are rather few proposals in the fields of statistics, trade for specific sectors, tourism, visas, education, FDI in specific segments of value-added chains, etc. There are a group of public, private, and academic sectors (Agendasia 2012) that have been able to establish short, medium and long-terms goals vis-à-vis China. Surprisingly, these heterogeneous groups have focused not only on the topic of the firms interested in exporting to China, but also the issues of domestic competition and third markets, as well as achieving "reciprocal" treatment, i.e., requesting sectorial and goods-level reciprocity and respective negotiations if necessary. Skepticism, however, prevails among many social and business groups and it is not surprising that there no concrete discussion of a trade and FDI agreement with China, despite China's insistence on an FTA in the last decade.

Unless public, private, and academic institutions in Mexico and China are supported to work in this direction, there are few expectations that current tensions will decrease; the gap between economic growth and institutional development, meanwhile, has increased in the last years substantially. There has not been any effort by the NAFTA governments to update, modernize, or upgrade the North American integration process. Even in the case of the TPP, strictly from a Mexican perspective, it would make at least as much sense to participate in the TPP as to modernize and upgrade NAFTA; Mexico has FTAs with the US, Japan, and Canada, by far the most relevant TPP economies. And, of course, the TPP does not tackle the enormous challenges posed by China.

Finally, it is also surprising how little interest the US has shown in terms of these bilateral, trilateral, and regional challenges. As discussed in the paper, the US has become the main loser in the trade competition with China in Mexico and LAC, with massive impacts on job losses as a result of LAC imports increasingly shifting from the US to China.

NOTES

1 Statistics vary widely depending on sources. Based on Chinese data, Latin America has a trade surplus with China; the opposite is true if looking at numbers coming from the region. In Mexico-China trade, for example, analyses of Chinese exports versus Mexican imports differ by more than 250%. For a detailed analysis, see Dussel Peters (2005) and Morales Troncoso (2008).

2 For a full, detailed debate, see Dussel Peters (2015a, 2015b).

3 All the information on FDI in the text and tables refers to realized or effective FDI, in contrast to intended or announced FDI.

4 For a full discussion, see Cechimex (2014) and Dussel Peters (2014a, 2014b).

5 Through the end of 2015, however, there was general disappointment with the Peña Nieto administration's dealings with China. A recent document (Dussel Peters 2016), with the participation of 18 experts from the public, private, and academic sectors from China and Mexico, highlight that Mexico has not been able to establish a persuasive strategy vis-à-vis China and that Mexico lacks the required institutions to effectively overcome this shortcoming.

6 For a full analysis, see Dussel Peters 2015a; Dussel Peters and Ortiz Velásquez 2015.

7 In January 2015 Sinohydro won the public bidding for a contract worth around $400 million to construct a hydroelectric power station (Chicoasén II) in the province of Chiapas. Since then, however, the project has faced major problems with local residents as well as with trade unions and it cannot be ruled out that additional environmental problems might slow its implementation even further.

BIBLIOGRAPHY

Acevedo, Ernesto, and Jaime Zabludovsky. 2012. "Evaluación de la apertura comercial internacional (1986–2012)." In Leycegui Gardoqui, Beatriz (coord.). *Reflexiones sobre la política comercial internacional de México (2006–2012)*. ITAM, Secretaría de Economía, México, pp. 53–98.

Agendasia. 2012. Agenda estratégica México-China. Dirigido al C. Presidente Electo Enrique Peña Nieto. Agendasia, México.

Aguilar, Guillermo, and Roberto Villarreal. 2004. "El Comercio México—India." Bancomext, México.

Arnson, Cynthia, Jorge Heine, and Christine Zaino (eds.). 2014. *Reaching across the Pacific: Latin America and Asia in the New Century*. Washington, DC: Woodrow Wilson Center.

Banco de México. 2015. Database of inflation. www.banxico.org.

Cechimex (Centro de Estudios China-México). 2014 and 2016. Various studies, statistical databases, conference reports, and books. *Universidad Nacional Autónoma de México*. www.economia.unam.mx.

Chinoy, Shri Sujan R. 2014. "The India-China Relationship." Presented at the Conference at the Center for Chinese-Mexican Studies (Cechimex) at the National Autonomous University of Mexico, April 9. www.economia.unam.mx.

Dussel Peters, Enrique. 2005a. "The Implications of China's Entry into the WTO for Mexico," *Global Issue Papers* 24 (Heinrich Böll Stiftung), pp. 1–38.

Dussel Peters, Enrique. 2005b. "El caso de las estadísticas comerciales entre China y México: para empezar a sobrellevar el desconocimiento bilateral." *Economía Informa* 335, pp. 50–59.

Dussel Peters, Enrique (ed.). 2012. "40 años de la relación entre México-China. Acuerdos, desencuentros y futuro." UNAM/CECHIMEX, Cámara de Senadores y CICIR, México.

Dussel Peters, Enrique. 2013. "Recent China-LAC Trade Relations: Implications for Inequality?" Working Paper Series No. 40. Berlin: Research Network on Interdependent Inequalities in Latin America.

Dussel Peters, Enrique. 2014a. "Mexico and the Asian Challenge, 2000–2012." In Arnson, Cynthia, Jorge Heine, and Christine Zaino (eds.). *Reaching across the Pacific: Latin America and Asia in the New Century.* Woodrow Wilson Center, Washington, DC, pp. 187–252.

Dussel Peters, Enrique. 2014b. "La inversión extranjera directa de China en América Latina: 10 estudios de caso." RED ALC-CHINA, UNAM/Cechimex and UDUAL, México.

Dussel Peters, Enrique. 2015a. "China's Evolving Role in Latin America. Can It Be a Win-Win?" Atlantic Council, Washington, DC.

Dussel Peters, Enrique. 2015b. "The Omnipresent role of China's Public in its Relationship with Latin America and the Caribbean." In, Dussel Peters, Enrique, and Ariel C. Armony (coords.). *Beyond Raw Materials: Who Are the Actors in the Latin America and the Caribbean-China Relationship?* Nueva Sociedad/Friedrich Ebert Foundation, Center for Latin American Studies/Pittsburgh and Red ALC-China, México, pp. 50–72.

Dussel Peters, Enrique. 2015c. Testimony before the Joint Subcommittee Hearing Subcommittee on the Western Hemisphere and Subcommittee on Asia and the Pacific Committee on Foreign Affairs, United States House of Representatives, "Hearing on China's Advance in Latin America and the Caribbean," September 10, 2015.

Dussel Peters, Enrique (coord). 2016. "La relación México-China. Desempeño y propuestas para 2016–2018." Cechimex and Cámara de Comercio de México en China, México.

Dussel Peters, Enrique, and Kevin P. Gallagher. 2013. "NAFTA's Uninvited Guest. China and the Disintegration of North American Trade." *CEPAL Review* 110, pp. 83–108.

Dussel Peters, Enrique, Adrian H. Hearn, and Harley Shaiken. 2013. "China and the New Triangular Relationships in the Americas: China and the Future of US-Mexico Relations." CLAS-University of Miami, CLAS-UCSD and UNAM-Cechimex, México.

Dussel Peters, Enrique (coord.), Eduardo Loría, Luis Miguel Galindo Paliza, and Michael Mortimore. 2008. "Inversión extranjera directa en México: desempeño y potencial. Una perspectiva macro, meso, micro y territorial." Siglo XXI, Secretaría de Economía y UNAM/CECHIMEX, México.

Dussel Peters, Enrique, and Samuel Ortiz Velásquez. 2015. *Monitor de la Manufactura* 11. CECHIMEX-UNAM, México.

ECLAC (Economic Commission for Latin America and the Caribbean). 2011. "India and Latin America and the Caribbean: Opportunities and Challenges in Trade and Investment Relations." ECLAC, Santiago de Chile.

Fernández de Castro, Rafael, and Laura Rubio Díaz Leal. 2007. "Falsa illusión: China, el contrapeso de Estados Unidos en el Hemisferio Occidental." In Dussel Peters, Enrique, and Yolanda Trápaga Delfín (eds.). *China y México. Implicaciones de una nueva relación.* UNAM/Cechimex, ITESM y La Jornada, pp. 105–117.

Gallagher, Kevin, and Margaret Myers. 2015. China-Latin America Finance Database. IAD, Washington, DC.

Gransow, Bettina. 2015. "Chinese Investment in Latin American Infrastructure: Strategies, Actors and Risks." In Dussel Peters, Enrique and Ariel C. Armony (coords.). *Beyond Raw Materials. Who are the Actors in the Latin America and the Caribbean-China Relationship?* Nueva Sociedad/Friedrich Ebert Foundation, Center for Latin American Studies/Pittsburgh and Red ALC-China, México, pp. 86–116.

IADB (Inter-American Development Bank). 2012. "Shaping the Future of the Asia-Latin American and the Caribbean Relationship." IADB, Washington, DC.

ITA (International Trade Commission). 2015. "Jobs Supported by Exports in 2014." ITA, Washington, DC.

Lafourcade, Oliver, Vinh H. Nguyen, and Marcelo Giugale. 2001. *Mexico: A comprehensive Development Agenda for the New Era.* Washington, DC: World Bank, 2001.

Lall, Sanjaya, and John Weiss. 2005. "China's Competitive Threat to Latin America: An Analysis for 1990–2002." *Oxford Development Studies* 33(2).

Leycegui Gardoqui, Beatriz. 2012. "Capítulo 2." In Leycegui Gardoqui, Beatriz (coord.). *Reflexiones sobre la política comercial internacional de México (2006–2012).* ITAM, Secretaría de Economía, México, pp. 99–118.

Long, Guoqiang. 2015. "One Belt–One Road: A New Vision for Open, Inclusive Regional Cooperation." *Cuadernos de Trabajo del Cechimex* 4, pp. 1–12.

Millán Bojalil, Julio. 2011. "México e India: intensificar las relaciones comerciales." Consultores Internacionales, México.

Morales Troncoso, Carlos. 2008. "Triangulación del comercio China-México." *Estrategias para la competitividad. Emprendedores.* UNAM. Septiembre, pp. 41–45.

PND (Plan Nacional de Desarrollo). 2013. Plan Nacional de Desarrollo 2013–2018. PND, México.

Qiu, Xiaoqi. 2014. "China. Profundización integral de la reforma y sus relaciones con México." *Cuadernos de Trabajo del Cechimex* 3, pp. 1–8.

Red ALC-China (Red Académica de América Latina y el Caribe sobre China). 2013. América Latina y el Caribe-China. Series on economics, politics, environment, and history and culture. Red ALC-China, Mexico. www.redalc-china.org.

Red ALC-China (Red Académica de América Latina y el Caribe sobre China). 2015. América Latina y el Caribe-China. Four books on economics, politics, environment and history and culture. Red ALC-China, Mexico. www.redalc-china.org.

Roett, Riordan, and Guadalupe Paz (eds.). 2008. "China's Expansion into the Western Hemisphere: Implications for Latin America and the United States." Brookings Institution, Washington, DC.

Rosales, Osvaldo, and Mikio Kuwayama. 2007. "América Latina al encuentro de China e India: perspectivas y desafíos en comercio e inversión." *Revista de la CEPAL* 93, pp. 85–108.

Rosenzweig, Francisco. 2012. "El Acuerdo de Asociación Transpacífica: un impulse a América del Norte." In, Leycegui Gardoqui, Beatriz (coord.). *Reflexiones sobre la política comercial internacional de México (2006-2012)*. ITAM, Secretaría de Economía, México, pp. 434–445.

Santiso, Javier. 2006. "¿Realismo mágico? China e India en América Latina y África." *Economía Exterior* 38, pp. 59–69.

SRE (Secretaría de Relaciones Exteriores). 2012. "Nuevos espacios para México en Asia-Pacífico." SRE, México.

6

A Structural Explanation for
Sino-US-Venezuelan Relations

ANTHONY PETROS SPANAKOS

US-Venezuelan relations display both confrontation and cooperation. Followers of Western media should expect the expansion of Chinese relations with Venezuela to be of critical concern to the US.[1] In fact, Chinese relations with Venezuela are a most likely case for rebellion against the global governance system over which the US presides. US relations with Venezuela are a least likely case for cooperation and a most likely case for confrontation. But, as this chapter will demonstrate, there is little within Sino-Venezuelan relations to concern the US. Contrary to suggestions in news headlines, the Venezuela of 1999 to the present (dating from the first presidency of Hugo Chávez) is not the Cuba of the early 1960s, nor is the world the same as it was then. While the US and China disagree over many issues, there is no Cold War between them. China would not put missiles in Venezuela and its relations with Venezuela—however critical its government may be of the US—are not part of a strategy to challenge the leadership or security of the US.[2] Venezuela is also not Cuba (despite close relations between those two countries): the latter's value to the USSR was primarily its location as a base (and then sugar producer for the Communist world) whereas Venezuela has petroleum, a much more valuable resource, which it sells to China *and* the US.

This chapter makes a structuralist argument, arguing that the way that the three countries are positioned within global and regional governance structures conditions the underlying character of their relations with each other.[3] Simply put, the US, China, and Venezuela have very different interests and capabilities and their structural positions in South America which explains why the increased Chinese presence in Venezuela is neither a threat to the US nor does it substantially aid Venezuelan intentions toward multipolarizing the region or world.[4] To make this argument, the chapter assumes that the US foreign policy toward Venezuela is informed by its position as regional hegemon, Chinese foreign policy toward Venezuela is informed by its position as an extra-regional commercial state, and Venezuelan foreign policy toward both is informed by its position as a petrostate.

As a regional hegemon, the US has security interests (drug trafficking, political stability in the region, prevention of inter-state conflict, management of the flows of resources and people) and market interests (macroeconomic stability, a stable climate for investment and trade, places to sell its products, and so on) that extend beyond traditional notions of national security. The interest in the region as a whole, often expressed through multilateral organizations, tempers and often is more determining of foreign policy than the immediate bilateral interests of the US with each state in the region. As an extra-regional commercial state, China's concern is to maintain stable and diverse sources for key exports, support stable and good investment climates in trading partners (to benefit Chinese companies), and find markets for Chinese exports (including labor) in a country that is located in a region where it has no territorial nor immediate security interests. This does not mean that Chinese foreign policy behavior in other regions follows a similar pattern. Indeed, its activities in East Asia (Kang 2003), Central Asia (Denoon 2015), and Southeast Asia (Denoon 2017) demonstrate that key strategic issues impact Chinese foreign policy and, at times, contribute to areas of disagreement with US foreign policy actions in those regions. But in Latin America in general, and in Venezuela specifically, Chinese interests are primarily commercial and all relations follow the crest of trade flows (Sun 2014). Venezuela is a petrostate (Romero 2006). This essay assumes that a petrostate's foreign policy dynamism and willingness to challenge its primary customer and regional hegemon is directly correlated to global petroleum prices. When oil prices are higher it should assume a more confrontational attitude toward the US and pursue diversification of customers, while when oil prices collapse it should be more conciliatory and promote greater integration of its primary customer. While structural conditions encourage rebellion or obeisance, they do not necessarily predetermine how such rebellion or obeisance is expressed.

As such, the commodity boom (2003–13) led to an increasingly active Venezuelan foreign policy, recognizable for its rhetorical confrontations with the US and innovative anti-neoliberal policies. While China welcomed Venezuela as a "strategic partner" responding to the latter's policies of diversification, it has little interest in an alliance or participating in counterhegemonic activities in Latin America. As such, although China has become the second most important market for Venezuela, the US has lost ground in exports and imports, and Chinese investment is more important in financing infrastructure and other projects in Venezuela, these have little impact on the structural interests and influence of the US. If anything, Chinese activities contribute toward stabilizing the Venezuelan economy and the provision of services, which have not generated much interest among US companies, complementing US market interests without challenging any security concerns. Although China is aware that Latin America is often considered the "backyard" of the US and is cautious to not provoke US reactions, engaging in security issues in this region in general, and in Venezuela in particular, is clearly not in China's interest.[5]

1. Conceptual Elaboration

The aim in employing these three terms ("regional hegemon," "extra-regional commercial state," and "petrostate") is neither to neologize nor to argue that the terms are necessarily generalizable. If anything, the positions of the US and China are *sui generis* and are likely to remain that way. There is no other country without traditional security threats in its own region that also has such a preponderance of all forms of capability and power identifiable by scholars, nor is there any other developing country that has as large an economy, is as critical for global trade, and which has so vast a reserve of foreign currency as China (the second and third points explain why India differs). The description of Venezuela's structural position as petrostate has greater generalizability, but the claim here is not that all countries with similar structural positions will do what Venezuela has done, only that they will face very similar opportunities and constraints based on global demand for petroleum.

Power as Structural

Much of the literature examining Sino–Latin American, US–Latin American, and US-Sino–Latin American relations studies power and influence relationally. That is, it examines Sino-Venezuelan relations through relations between the Chinese government (or state-owned enterprises) and relevant Venezuelan analogues. This is true of most studies of foreign policy and international relations more generally, and it certainly makes sense as it describes much of the process through which states conduct foreign relations. Such an approach highlights the agency of the states or policy makers of the states under investigation and it recognizes changes in the capacities of each. Schell (2014), for example, compares Chinese leader Deng Xiaoping's humble presentation before then US president Jimmy Carter with current Chinese president Xi Jinping's snubbing of former president Carter in favor of Zimbabwean president Robert Mugabe. In setting up this contrast, Schell makes a very clear contrast to the relative capabilities of China to the US in 1979 and thirty-five years later. The emphasis is on the relational power between the two countries.

Similarly, one can make the argument that relations between two countries are constrained or determined by a third country. Perhaps Communist Poland's relations with the US were directed from Moscow or the trade liberalization in heavily indebted Latin American and African countries in the 1980s was promoted by some combination of the United States, the International Monetary Fund, and the World Bank (Williamson 1994, Babb 2013). This approach is also relational, though it extends the actors under study from two to three (or more). Much of the scholarship on Sino–Latin American relations is in this vein (Roett and Paz 2008, Ellis 2009). Following Zweig's (2010) work on Sino-African relations, centered on the idea of "triangular relations," these scholars note how policymakers in China consider their strategies in Latin America relative to US interests in Latin America. The introduction of the US into studies of Sino–Latin American relations adds an important set of explanatory variables, though it still tends to address power relationally—that China *does* X relative to US *desires* for Y and Venezuela's capability of producing Z or the decline in US interest and/or capabilities in Venezuela have opened a space for China that will not threaten the US. There is much of value in such accounts, but this essay takes a different approach.

Lukes (1974) famously described three forms of power—one-, two-, and three-dimensional—to describe how conflicts between parties are addressed. The one-dimensional view of power sees party A as having power if it is able to successfully pursue its interests over those of party B (and C . . .). A two-dimensional view of power sees party A as having power if it can impact decisions over which there is conflict with party B (and C . . .), suggesting that it not only achieves its objectives but is able to reduce the degree to which others can object. A three-dimensional view of power sees party A as having power when it can prevent issues of interest and areas of conflict with party B (and C . . .) from receiving any discussion or serious treatment. In this third form of power, considered structural power by Strange (1987) and others (Cox 1987, Burges 2009, Burges forthcoming), A dominates others through "legitimate" structures and bodies that disarm and handicap potential opposition without A relying on overt exercise of relational power vis-à-vis B (and C . . .). As May notes, "By controlling the agenda, the decision-making process may be presented as fair and equitable because unpalatable or unacceptable solutions for the dominant actor never reach the agenda for consideration by other actors" (May 1996, 177).

This chapter follows other works that examine international relations through structural means (see Strange 1998, Cox 1987, Buzan, Jones, and Little 1993). Such works emphasize the structural position of the countries in the regional and global constellation of economic, strategic, political, and ideational power. Strange (1987) disagreed with the overwhelming majority of analysts of the time who noted the decline in US power, influence, and economic dynamism during the 1970s. Instead, she argued that the US had not seen a decline in its structural power, which she defined as "the power to choose and to shape the structures of the global political economy within which other states, their political institutions, their economic enterprises, and (not least) their professional people have to operate. This means more than the power to set the agenda of discussion or to design (in American phraseology) the international 'regime' of rules and customs" (Strange 1987, 565). In retrospect, the 1980s may very well have been the high-water mark in terms of US global power.

It is worth keeping this in mind, as much of the literature during the commodity cycle (2003–13) emphasized not only the rise of China (and other countries and categories, such as the "Global South") but also the decline of the US. Yet following the 2008 Global Recession, widely ascribed to US economic policies and interpreted as a sign of US decline, the

US dollar has appreciated and US real estate markets have rebounded (absorbing considerable foreign money, often from previously rapidly rising economies), while other countries (the BRICS) and regions (Europe, Latin America) experienced a marked slowdown in growth. Certainly, the last few years have been difficult for China—whose move to a "new normal" of 7–8% growth has been fraught and bumpy—and Venezuela— whose economy grew by 1.3% in 2013, contracted by 4% in 2014, and may contract again by some 10% in 2015 (ECLAC 2015, 157; Neuman and Torres 2015).

Burges (forthcoming) uses a structural approach to make sense of Brazilian foreign policy, arguing that while Brazil does play (sometimes very effectively) the relational game, its foreign policy most consistently aims to change structural power. For example, Brasília has expended considerable ideational and material resources to build a notion of "South America" as opposed to "Latin America" in terms of regional security and markets as a way of reducing US influence, increasing Brazilian policy autonomy, and improving Brazilian influence with its neighbors. It has done so by often "losing out" to neighbors (not fighting Bolivia and Paraguay when the two countries renegotiated prices Brazilian companies paid for natural resources) in order to construct a sense of South American community, to improve the image of Brazil, and to cultivate regional organizations that would feature Brazil as the largest and most important actor (Burges forthcoming). Doctor (2015) uses a similar notion of power in analyzing Brazil's rise through its leadership in international political economic endeavors. She presents a ladder of influence that identifies countries as either (1) rule takers; (2) rule makers; (3) agenda setters; or (4) norm creators. Each step represents greater power and, following Lukes (1974), a more multidimensional form of power. While there is obviously overlap between these steps and some countries operate at different levels in different arenas, Doctor finds that Brazilian foreign policy makers have been very concerned not simply about relations vis-à-vis the US, Europe, China, or any single country or region, but in terms of Brazilian influence more broadly within the structure of international political economy.

What is most relevant for the present discussion is that international relations scholars, particularly those studying rising powers in Latin America, have found it profitable to separate relational and structural power and that an improvement of the latter is often a deliberate goal of developing countries' foreign-policy makers. Certainly, this has been true of the foreign policy of Hugo Chávez and, indeed, any scholarship identifying Venezuela as a security concern for the US has never made the argument that Venezuela offered any direct threat to the US but that more influence for Venezuela meant less for the US. This zero-sum reading is still largely understood in relational terms, but US influence over Latin America has been more structural in orientation (leadership in the OAS, virtual veto power in the IMF and World Bank, permanence in the UNSC, the primary foreign market for immigrants and leaders for university and graduate training, the site of production for cultural products, and so on). An increase in Venezuelan capabilities and/or a decline (or relative decline) in US capabilities does not necessitate a decline in US structural power. Knowing that, Chávez deliberately aimed to create organizations, accords, and programs that would challenge US structural power (see Toro Carnevali 2011).

Such an idea is not foreign to US or Chinese foreign policy makers. In challenging "declinist" readings of US power and overly "optimistic" readings of Chinese influence, Thomas Christensen (2015) notes the importance of US allies and multilateral organizations as mechanisms for channeling US influence even when the US is excluded from the latter. Similarly, he insists that neither he (in his time as assistant secretary of state for East Asian and Pacific affairs), nor other US officials, nor Chinese officials saw Chinese trade with Africa, for example, as zero sum, with more Chinese trade with the region automatically meaning less US influence.

An important caveat should be made in discussing structural power. This chapter suggests that while Chinese, US, and Venezuelan foreign policy makers have awareness of the interests of the others, they largely pursue policies that are consistent with the incentives created by their particular positions in the global economy and trajectories shaped by historical engagement with other countries. Such a structural argument must be offered alongside an important caveat. To emphasize the role of structures in conditioning the activities of the state actors involved does not mean that structure determines all foreign policy. Clearly, leaders, ideas, and institutions are important as well. For example, the shift from Hugo Chávez (1999–2013) to Nicolás Maduro (2013–) has been important. While Chávez was the charismatic leader of a revolutionary program, his successor is not charismatic and is only one among several leaders in a movement whose various currents were better held together under Chávez's leadership (Hetland 2016). Similarly, an increased capability to resist the influence of a regional hegemon does not determine how such resistance will manifest. In the Venezuelan case, this led to a diverse range of domestic and foreign policy experiments (see Serbín 2010).

During his first presidency (1974–79), Carlos Andrés Pérez oversaw a major boom in petroleum prices and was involved in the nonaligned movement, exercised regional leadership, and was critical of the US. But his critiques were neither as consistent nor acute nor was he as singularly influential nor as organizationally innovative as Hugo Chávez in his efforts to increase the autonomy of Venezuelan domestic policy making and the ability of the country to project its power in the region and beyond. The assertiveness of Pérez's first presidency is often neglected because his second mandate (1989–93), which terminated in his impeachment, began with his acceptance of an IMF package that he had repudiated only weeks earlier while on the campaign trail. During that presidency, constrained by weak petroleum prices, high inflation, and heavy debt, he made a major shift toward neoliberal policies, cooperated with the US and IMF, and pursued more cooperative relations with the US. Chávez entered office with low oil prices and chose to exercise more radical responses where possible (mostly in the area of domestic politics and carrying out diplomacy with US-labeled pariahs, such as Iran). His foreign policy became increasingly confrontational over time, particularly as prices rebounded and he further developed a vision for a Bolivarian revolution. While both he and Pérez increased the role of the state in the economy and rebuffed the US when they faced more favorable terms of trades, how he did so reflects opportunities offered by structural conditions and strategic choices made possible by his leadership.

Regional Hegemon

Hegemony can indicate two things, both of relevance for the argument in this chapter. In neorealist studies, "a hegemon is the only great power in the system" (Mearsheimer 2001, 40) and "[t]he United States has been a regional hegemon in the Western Hemisphere for at least the past one hundred years. No other state in the Americas has sufficient might to challenge it, which is why the United States is widely recognized as the only great power in its region" (Mearsheimer 2001, 40). On Mearsheimer's view there is no global hegemon, but there is no other power with the power of the US or the ability to dominate its own region and therefore safely intervene in the balancing games of other regions. The relative superiority of US capabilities has led scholars (Ikenberry, Mastanduno, and Wohlforth 2009) and commentators (Krauthammer 1990) to see US leadership as fundamental and ubiquitous in interstate relations within all regions of the globe. Thus whereas a great power's security concerns are likely to be limited to its region, US concerns extend beyond region to encompass the entire world. The US, for example, has some 1,100 military bases in 156 countries, and some twenty aircraft carriers patrolling the world (Agyeman 2014). The US, therefore, has a very powerful stake in the current structure of global governance as it occupies the leading position in such a system.

A second perspective, Gramscian in orientation (Cox 1987), considers hegemony to be leadership that is made effective through legitimately leading others as opposed to direct domination. Burges notes that the "role of the hegemon is thus to provide the initial impetus to start the hegemonic process and encourage other countries to participate in the formation of the hegemony" (Burges 2009, 10). Whether more individualistic or more altruistic/collectivist, this notion of hegemony leverages ideas and moral suasion, not the threat or use of material capabilities.

The US is clearly the regional hegemon in both senses. Its capabilities are unmatched, its currency a necessary reserve, its military incomparably equipped, its labor market uniquely attractive, and its market enormous and wealthy. It is also the center of practically every effective regional organization and institution, it houses the academic and policy institutes which produce the ideas that frame policy discussions and those that operate on the margins of such discussions, and the key institutions of global governance are headquartered there. The hegemony of the US in the region (and its extension of power in the world more generally) may have emerged because of its preponderance of capabilities in any dyadic pair (say, US-Russia, US-China, US–North Korea), but its maintenance owes much to its ability to transmit its power through mechanisms that are less directly tied to traditional material capabilities and are more structural in orientation. That said, Gramscian hegemony does not involve coercion when it is accepted by non-hegemons. The US intends to be hegemonic in Latin America and its hegemony receives a mixture of enthusiastic and muted acceptance and resistance by diverse sectors within each country. The leaders and supporter of Bolivarian governments in Venezuela have been among the loudest and, at times, most important segments in the region resisting US hegemony.

Extra-regional Commercial State

Perhaps the most important ongoing exercise in international relations in the past two decades has been the assessment of Chinese foreign policy capabilities, interests, and likely future trajectories. China is the world's largest economy (when adjusted for purchasing power parity) and was a powerful engine of global growth during the 2003–13 commodity cycle. Its fundamental foreign policy concerns are extensions of primary domestic policy goals of political stability and economic development. To that end, China has sought to pacify its border regions and ensure the territorial integrity of China—most notably in relation to Hong Kong, Taiwan, and–autonomous regions such as Xinjiang and Tibet. It has also sought to improve the ability of Chinese companies to compete in foreign markets and to reduce the costs of primary products imported from various parts of the world.

China's "going out" strategy has largely followed this pattern of seeking trade where its products could best compete and the local products were most necessary for Chinese production and consumption. Importantly, this going out is led by commercial activities, followed by investment and increased diplomatic relations, because it is "outside"—not part of greater China—and is not seen through the lens of territorial integrity or the stability of political rule of the Communist Party (Callahan 2004). Trade with Central Asian, Southeast Asian, and Northeast Asian countries is considered alongside security issues that may, in practice, take priority (see Denoon 2015, 2017). Although scholars may note that China is concerned about how the US may perceive its security interests affected by Chinese activity in Africa (Zweig 2010) and Latin America (Spanakos and Xiao 2013), Chinese security issues are at stake only in a rather distant manner (if US interests are threatened in region X, the US could add pressure in a region contiguous to China's territory and force China to deploy more resources to respond to this shift in US attention).

As an extra-regional (hence no territorial claims or concerns) commercial state, Chinese interests are initiated and led by trade possibilities, followed by investment and infrastructural projects to solidify such trade and to reduce transaction costs. Once a certain volume of trade and capital flows is established, the commercial state is not only interested in maintaining and increasing trade but also takes an interest in supporting trade partners facing political instability or other challenges (if, for no other reason, this guarantees the regular flow of goods and capital, and facilitates the payment of obligations). The examination of Sino-Venezuelan relations below aims to demonstrate that China's position as extra-regional commercial state indeed captures its relations with Venezuela.

Petrostate

Venezuela is clearly a petrostate (Coronil 1997, Karl 1997, Corrales and Penfold 2011, Tinker Salas 2009). It has some 297.7 billion barrels of proven crude oil reserves and oil sales are responsible for "96% of export earnings, about 40% of government revenues, and 11% of GDP" (CIA n.d.). Venezuelan GDP in 2014 is estimated at $509 billion while state-owned Petróleos de Venezuela S.A. (PDVSA, Petroleum of Venezuela) controls $231 billion of assets and receives $114 billion in revenue (Pitts 2014). Venezuela's relations with other states—its projection beyond its own borders and region—are the result of its production of petroleum and the demand for that product in industrial centers. Serbín notes that Venezuelan international activism is "based on oil resources . . . [which allow it to go] beyond the capacity of a medium-sized developing country" (2010, 15).[6]

Given the concentration of the Venezuelan economy around petroleum production (and the historic recognition of territorial borders by Venezuela and its neighbors), Venezuelan foreign policy has historically been oriented toward the primary consumer of Venezuelan oil: the US and, in the last decade, increasingly China (though the US is still the primary export market for Venezuelan oil). That orientation, determined by demand for Venezuelan exports, is strengthened by local Venezuelan demand for industrial products of that primary trade partner. As industrialization moved from the US to China, Venezuela has increasingly purchased Chinese products, but this did not occur until there was first a massive increase in Chinese purchase of Venezuelan oil.

The concentration of foreign policy around oil policy (export to and import from a particular partner) facilitates a vision that foreign policy of the petrostate is primarily (and at times) exclusively conducted with a single country. As such, it is typical to see relations with that country as zero sum. This is exacerbated by the historic volatility of global petroleum prices. When oil prices surge—often because of greater coordination by oil-producing countries—the petrostate suddenly experiences leverage vis-à-vis the more developed, diversified trade partner and is able to make hitherto impossible demands, insist on renegotiation of contracts and ownership, and display conspicuous demonstrations of policy independence, often done in solidarity with other "poor countries" (whether as a leader of Latin America and the developed world, as in the case of former president Carlos Andrés Pérez, who nationalized petroleum fields, or as a leader of the Global South and Bolivarian solidarist movements, as in the case of Hugo Chávez, who renationalized a number of critical industries; see Ellner 2009). One such act is to offer petroleum to other poor countries at discounted rates, both an act of solidarity and part of an approach to diversity markets that is especially palatable during a boom. But inasmuch as commodity booms produce acts of political independence vis-à-vis the primary trading partner, commodity collapses encourage humility, efforts toward greater integration with the primary trading partner, and a willingness to renegotiate contracts and to potentially privatize previously nationalized sectors. During such a collapse, previous efforts to diversify might be reversed and there is often greater concentration in trade partners, while the weaker price for oil leads to greater export diversification. That is, the boom-bust cycle of petroleum prices creates incentives for a petrostate to pursue a cyclical foreign policy of antagonism/independence followed by humility/interdependence with the country's primary trading partner.

2. Venezuelan Foreign Policy since 1999

Serbín (2010) argues that Venezuelan foreign policy radicalized with Chávez's assumption of the presidency in 1999. Prior to that, Venezuelan foreign policy focused on democracy promotion and thirdworldism, yet it remained clearly on the Western side in the Cold war. Since Chávez, Serbín notes, Venezuelan foreign policy has been more geopolitical and more radically ideological. However, consistent throughout has been the harnessing of oil rents to expand influence beyond what might otherwise be possible (15). There have been a number of critical components to Bolivarian foreign policy: (1) to revitalize OPEC so that higher prices can be attained (this often pitted Venezuela against Saudi Arabia, though with Iran and non-member Russia); (2) to support regional integration of states and people as a means of resisting US hegemony; (3) to diversify trade: export oil to China, Caribbean, and South American neighbors, increase weapons purchases from Russia and Belarus, expand trade and joint projects with China, Russia, India, and Iran; and (4) to support, fund, and create programs that encourage a more multipolar world (see Smilde and Gill 2013).

Chávez's foreign policy became more radical over time but particularly following the 2002 coup attempt and the three-month-long PDVSA strike (2002–3), both of which he believed was supported by the US government (see McCarthy-Jones and Turner 2011) and the rise in petroleum prices (which were at their nadir of some $9 per barrel when he entered office, but truly took off in 2003). With a return to economic growth in 2004, ample resources, and renewed incentive to resist the US, Chávez shifted from a policy oriented around preserving national sovereignty toward one that more actively challenged US hegemony in the region and world (Gónzalez Urrutia 2006). That is, while he had been critical of the need to reduce US presence in his country previously, it was primarily as part of an effort to protect policy-making autonomy; once oil prices changed dramatically he began to conceive of his critique of US foreign policy more globally and holistically.

Beginning in 2003, Chávez launched a number of social programs (*misiones*) in coordination with Cuba, based on a model of exchange of Venezuelan oil for the services of Cuban doctors. From this framework, Chávez developed Petrocaribe in 2005 (and later Petroandino and Petrosur for the Andean countries and Southern Cone, respectively), which sold petroleum at discounted rates and extended maturity to neighboring countries as part of an alternative model of trade and an effort to offer "solidarity" to other Southern countries. ALBA, the Bolivarian Alliance of the Peoples of Our Americas, brought into existence in 2006, consists of eight states (it briefly included Honduras) and is a self-styled alternative (the word "alliance" in its name was originally "alternative") to the US-led Free Trade Area of the Americas and other regional integration efforts built on liberalization of trade and transfer of commercial cases to non-national courts. Increasingly based on principles of twenty-first-century socialism, it collects radical left-wing governments that favor economic arrangements between state-owned corporations (so-called grand national corporations, as opposed to multinational corporations); it has its own development bank (the Bank of ALBA, with some $1 billion in capital) and its own currency for intra-ALBA trade (the SUCRE). In announcing the creation of the SUCRE, Chávez declared, "Enough with the dictatorship of the dollar, long live the SUCRE" (in Hirst and Sabatini 2015, 6). ALBA also sponsors cultural and sporting activities, in addition to a range of ministerial meetings. In six years it has held no fewer than sixteen "ordinary and extraordinary summits" (Hirst and Sabatini 2015, 8). All of these activities have been funded by Venezuelan oil revenues, which became increasingly under the control of the Bolivarian government following the 2002–3 strike, and have been aimed at developing regional solidarity and a mode of non-neoliberal relations between states and "peoples" in direct opposition to the "neoliberal model" "imposed" by the US.

The "New Television Company of the South," or Telesur as it is known, was created in 2005 as a Latin American CNN, a counterhegemonic project to the private media of the US, which was seen as disseminating imperialist propaganda. Telesur is a regional channel (it is financially supported by Argentina, Bolivia, Cuba, Ecuador, Nicaragua, Uruguay, and Venezuela, though more than half of its funding comes from Venezuela) that has no commercials, promotes positive images of the countries, shows documentaries about historic battles of the people against domestic elites and foreign oppressors, and supports the creation of a regional identity. One of the reasons for the creation of Telesur was the Chávez government's reaction to the coup that removed him from office for two days in 2002. During the coup, private television stations played cartoons and then later released a statement in which Chávez was quoted as resigning the presidency, something he insists he did not do. Realizing the power of the media, Chávez needed a "countermedia."

Since the coup, he has invested in community radio and television, but Telesur has been the biggest budget effort in this regard. Telesur provided important counterinformation during the 2009 coup that removed Honduran president, and Chávez ally, Manuel Zelaya from office. Importantly, it challenged the Honduran elite and US narrative that Zelaya was constitutionally removed from office. That said, the majority of the material on the Telesur television station is not anti-US propaganda but cultural and historic programming, more like National Geographic than Fox News/MSNBC. Even the webnews wing of Telesur, which includes pages on "the Empire," mostly contains short news accounts with little revolutionary critique.

In each of the cases discussed (Petrocaribe, ALBA, Telesur), the Venezuelan government used oil money to advance its foreign policies through the creation of multilateral and/or multigovernmental projects aimed at solidarity and, in the case of ALBA and Telesur, with a clear goal of weakening US influence in the region. While these projects do not make any real change in the power disparities between the US and any of the countries involved, including Venezuela, they do create new space, legitimate among some actors, for dialogue, agenda setting, and critique where the US exercises no influence. In this way, they make little change in relational power but strip away, perhaps only a little, at the structural power of the US as regional hegemon. Latin Americans will not abandon free trade, but ALBA gives more voice and space for different discussions about trade possibilities and their orientation. This makes it easier for countries to bring up new topics, such as the Summit of the Americas issue, which previously would have been prevented outright.

It is worth noting that the satellite technology (satellites *Bolívar* [2008], *Miranda* [2012], and *Sucre* [forthcoming]) that partially supports Telesur has been the result of China-Venezuelan cooperation and the satellites have been launched from China. Telesur coverage of the cooperative agreements and launches discusses how the satellites will be used to expand education and improve internet access. Accounts in Chinese official media organ Xinhua are brief and mention only cooperation and the technology transfer from China to Venezuela. In other words, both the Chinese and Venezuelan side have presented this as South-South cooperation, technology transfer, and extending internet access, not in an anti-US framework. So while Telesur may contribute to Venezuelan challenges of US structural power, Chinese participation is clearly identified as that of a Southern partner state which is transferring technology and helping to broaden and enable Venezuelan market participation, an activity that makes sense for the country's second-largest trade partner. Simply put, more internet access in Venezuela means more Venezuelans will purchase Huawei devices.

3. US-Venezuelan Relations

There is no parity between the capabilities of the United States and Venezuela. The US has a GDP of almost $18 trillion and a GDP per capita of roughly $56,000, while those of Venezuela are $545 billion and $6,000, respectively. Venezuela's combined military capabilities were ranked by Global Firepower with a score of 1.5179, 63rd out of 126 countries. This placed it behind Greece, Slovakia, and Croatia and ahead of Azerbaijan, Jordan, and Kazakhstan.[7] The US ranks first with a score of 0.1661 and the index does *not* include nuclear capabilities. On its own, Venezuela hardly constitutes a security threat to the US, though the reverse is not true. Although the US has no interest in war with Venezuela, it has been regularly accused of coup plotting and arming opposition by supporters of the Bolivarian governments (see Golinger 2007).

In their analysis of Venezuelan foreign policy toward the US, Corrales and Romero emphasize Venezuelan use of soft-balancing against the US (2012). Given the stark inequality of capabilities, soft-balancing is a rational strategy since Venezuela can hardly expect to do anything other than "rais[e] the costs of action" for the United States (Corrales and Romero 2012, 9). Implied in the discussion of soft-balancing is that the direct relational power (US-Venezuela) might be affected by projects such as ALBA, but the true efficacy of Venezuelan efforts results from challenging US structural power by acting in concert with others. While Venezuela has often been in a leading role, it is worth noting that the resources it deploys are minuscule in comparison to the potential resources deployable by the US. But due to US prioritization of other matters and regions, and its reliance on the ordinary channels of structural power (say, US cultural influences, procedures in the IMF, World Bank, and OAS), Venezuelan resources may appear significant at any particular moment. This has led to some exaggerated discussions of Venezuela outspending the US on development and aid in Latin America, alarmist comments that do not give enough attention to the fact that long-term investment of political, economic, and social resources are the fundamental basis for US leadership in the region. Again, this leadership may be exercised directly and relationally but, in its most quotidian form, it is exercised structurally and indirectly. So it is not Venezuelan spending versus US spending that matters, but how Venezuelan activities can weaken the ability of the US to coordinate and manage plural partners with divergent interests.

Emphasizing the role of soft-balancing and projects such as ALBA can be highly misleading. While political relations between the US and Venezuela have deteriorated since 1999, and especially since 2002, the US is still the primary export and import market for Venezuela, Venezuela remains in the top five oil exporters to the US, the US continues to be the most important military power in the region where Venezuela is located, and it provides considerable military support to Venezuela's neighbor, Colombia, with whom it faces recurring border problems. US oil refineries remain the closest, cheapest, and best options for Venezuelan oil. The US has significant influence in Guyana, which has been bickering with the Maduro government, to say nothing of the coordinating role of the US within the Organization of American States and Inter-American Bank, and the implied veto power of the US in the IMF and World Bank, institutions whose necessity to Latin American states has increased since commodity prices have declined.

Trade

Since 2003, as the Venezuelan government produced sharper critiques of the US in the world, Venezuela's appetite for US goods and its export of oil to the US expanded rapidly. US commodity exports to Venezuela increased 367% between 2003 and 2013 and its service exports increased by 102% from 2002 to 2012.[8] All the while, Venezuela maintained a favorable trade balance with the US ($32 billion compared to $13.2 billion, respectively).[9] At various points, especially following 2006, Chávez threatened to cut off the sale of Venezuelan oil to the US, but no interruption ever occurred (rather, sales peaked in 2008). Trade continued, though rules and protections for US corporations in Venezuela worsened. In 2006, Venezuela announced a new wave of nationalization in oil that necessitated 60% government ownership of projects previously controlled by foreign companies. This change was fought by the US's ExxonMobil in foreign courts with little result other than rhetorical victories for both sides. In 2008, the country introduced a windfall tax on all oil production in the country, further reducing the profit share for foreign companies though, by then, most US oil companies had reduced their exposure to Venezuela although, again, the flow of oil continued to move toward the US in massive quantities.

Throughout the commodity boom, the Chávez government announced multiple mechanisms that were intended to diversify purchasers of Venezuelan oil, particularly China. Certainly oil sales to China have expanded considerably (see the next section), but the US remains the primary purchaser of Venezuelan oil. In 2015, Venezuela sent some 750,000 barrels per day to the US (M. Romero 2015; though this is down from 1.5 million bpd in 2008). Indeed, in 2013, Venezuela increased its imports of refined oil from the US and still sold some 40% of its oil to the US (Ferchen 2014). That number appears to have increased to nearly 50% but "Venezuela has become less important to Washington . . . now accounting for only 9–10 percent of daily oil imports, ranking fifth . . . after Canada, Mexico, Nigeria, and Saudi Arabia" (Adams and Gunson 2015, 33).

If one accepts Venezuelan figures that some 600,000 bpd now go to China (US reports put this number closer to 260,000 bpd; Christensen 2015, 78–79), much of the decline in sales to the US has been absorbed by China. This would seem to suggest a zero-sum relation but, while this might describe US-Venezuelan relations, according to Thomas Christensen, this is not how this is seen by US and Chinese officials. If anything, he notes, the US had little influence on the Venezuelan government when it was purchasing 1.5 million bpd from the country and he wondered how much China could possibly have even if it were buying 600,000 bpd.

Representation

The persistence of trade has coexisted with not only poor relations between the two countries but substantive decreases in formal representation.

Chávez had long argued that the US gave support to and was involved in the coup that removed him from office for two days in 2002 (see Golinger 2007) and repeatedly referred to US-concocted plots to remove him from office. In 2008, in an expression of solidarity with Bolivian president Evo Morales, who expelled the US ambassador to Bolivia on suspicion of supporting a coup, Chávez expelled the US ambassador to Venezuela (and the US responded in kind). Relations were particularly heated between US president George W. Bush and Chávez as both engaged in heavy critiques of the other government. The style of President Obama, to not engage Chávez, did little to change regular critique of the US, though, to be fair, there were few substantive changes in US policy toward Venezuela under Obama (and indeed, regular references by Obama and Secretary of State John Kerry to human rights violations and lack of freedom in Venezuela rankled Chávez).

With the death of Hugo Chávez, both sides have engaged in periodic discussions of the possibility of reconciliation and an eventual exchange of ambassadors. Efforts broke off in 2013 when Samantha Power, nominee for ambassador to the United Nations, included Venezuela with Iran and Russia when speaking of "repressive regimes." Both sides returned to dialogue, but the Obama administration issued an executive order in 2015 "declaring a national emergency with respect to the unusual and extraordinary threat to the national security and foreign policy of the United States posed by the situation in Venezuela."[10] In so doing, it seized the US property of and denied entry to seven-high ranking current and former members of the Venezuelan armed forces and national guard.

The Maduro administration responded by noting that the US "systematically violates the human rights of its people and the people of the world . . . [including] violence against immigrants, against thousands of Central American children, discrimination against minorities of African descent, unpunished crimes by those in power, as in the case of the young Michael Brown, racism, the open practice of kidnapping and torture, as flagrantly occurs in the torture centers of Guantanamo, and other North American military installations around the world; and support for terrorism, bombings, and military attacks in other countries" (in Gill 2014). Maduro "also announced that figures such as former President George Bush, former Vice President Dick Cheney, and Congressmen Ileana Ros-Lehtinen, Marco Rubio, and Bob Menéndez would be prohibited entry to Venezuela 'as terrorists' who had 'abused human rights in Syria and Iraq'" (M. Romero 2015). Maduro has also made demands that the US embassy reduce its staff by some 80% since the US has some one hundred diplomatic officials in CCS, while Venezuela has only seventeen in Washington, and he has imposed more restrictions on the activities of such personnel.

Clearly, the sound and fury of a government that believes it is under siege by the US has not disappeared. But neither has the considerable reliance on the US as an export and import partner. And through 2016 the Maduro government continued to reach out to an Obama White House that was, curiously, more inviting to the Cuban government than Venezuela. What can explain this? Certainly it is not simply a matter of an anti-US revolution deepening, as this does not explain efforts toward diplomatic rapprochement *and* increased trade since 2013. Relations with the US have suffered intensification at various points and have been worst precisely when trade between the two countries expanded very rapidly. This intensification and radicalization of Venezuelan critiques of the US make more sense when one considers the role of commodity prices in creating facilitating conditions for such aggression against the country's primary export partner. That is, more access to revenue and a relative improvement vis-à-vis the primary purchaser/regional hegemon gives the petrostate more capability and incentive to establish its independence. The structural opportunities were seized by President Chávez, who saw important domestic gains to be obtained by pursuing an anti-colonial and anti-neoliberal foreign policy. At the same time, the US has not been a neutral party and it has contributed to the breakdown in talks with Venezuela by referring to and, eventually punishing, Venezuela as a repressive regime which violates human rights. Although the tone of the Bush and Obama administrations that different, the US characterization of the Bolivarian governments was fairly consistent, not surprising given its structural role as global hegemon and chief trade partner with the country. This role has become increasingly important with the collapse of commodity prices and the decline in Venezuelan growth since 2013. As such, the patience with which the US reacts to the growing governability crisis with a "wait and see" attitude—which means not intervening and allowing the crisis to deepen—places the pressure on the Maduro government (despite its rhetoric) to seek reconciliation with the US. Given the improvement of relations with Cuba—and Venezuela's inability to prevent this—there is additional pressure on the Maduro government to reach out to the regional hegemon.

4. Sino-Venezuelan Relations

Venezuela has had diplomatic relations with the People's Republic of China since 28 June 1974, though it is only in the last fifteen years that relations have deepened. In one of the most comprehensive analyses of Sino–Latin American relations, Enrique Dussel Peters writes that the Sino-Venezuelan relationship "has gone far beyond" trade from "the beginning" (2015, 20). Going beyond trade involves investment (which supports trade), as well as support for China on issues of political concern to the PRC (specifically agreement over the status of Taiwan and Tibet, China as a "full-market economy," and cooperation on UN human rights proposals that were seen as pushed by the US to punish China; Sun 2014, 651). But it is important to note just how far beyond trade the relations go: they do not reach geostrategy and geopolitics. Thus, while Venezuela and China both publicly discuss interest in a more multipolar world, they do so separately. Chinese leaders do not use relations with Venezuela to advance or divulge such interests, nor do they approve of the aggressive way in which Chávez and Maduro challenge the status quo. Indeed, as Paz has noted, despite many reciprocal visits and pledges of investment projects, "Beijing . . . kept Chávez at arm's length, but almost certainly for reasons of self-interest, including Venezuela's huge oil reserves, it has not abandoned him" (Paz 2011, 223). Additionally, while Sino-Venezuelan relations go beyond trade, it can be argued that Chinese efforts are led by trade concerns. Chinese entry into the region was motivated primarily by the search for natural resources and new markets for Chinese products (Sun 2014). The importance of oil and the openness of the Venezuelan government (which more energetically reached out earlier in the twenty-first century than did other Latin peers) led to a very quick and intense expansion of trade. Over time, however, Chinese investment in Venezuela slowed, excepting in 2014–15, largely reflecting efforts to help the government at a moment of instability and to improve transportation, both of which aim to guarantee Venezuelan capacity to repay Chinese loans.

While Chinese interest in Venezuelan oil is based on energy, Venezuelan interest has been in geostrategic reorientation and diversification, in both cases diverting resources from the US. At various points, Chávez declared a goal of exporting 1 million bpd to China by 2012. Given Venezuela's capacity (about 2.46 million bpd), the peak of US purchase (around 1.5 million bpd in 2008), and its estimated export capacity at 1.65 million bpd, the increase in sales to China (and Petrocaribe, and others) comes directly as a result of a decrease in sales to the US. The Venezuelan vision, in this sense, is zero sum: less exposure to the US means less influence of the latter. China, as an extra-regional commercial state, faces no such challenges. It has pursued Venezuelan oil as it diversifies partners, with a clear interest in safeguarding flows of oil (particularly from US partners, who might be induced to cut supplies to China in case of an eventual confrontation). But purchase of Venezuelan oil has occurred alongside investments and trade agreements in the oil sector with Brazil and Russia. That is, while Venezuela might be tempted to see in China an "alternative" great power, China sees Venezuela as one of many energy suppliers. An internal document of the Chinese Development Bank identifies its loans to other countries with two key goals: (1) internationalization of the Chinese economy, and (2) Sinicization of the global economy (Sun 2014, 658). The former is very clearly not a challenge to the US and the latter could only be considered so if economics were understood as zero sum. Thomas Christensen notes that neither the Chinese nor the US government holds that view (Christensen 2015). Such a positive-sum vision does not necessarily guide Chinese (or US) approaches to the Taiwan Straits, North Korea, or territorial issues between China and other East and Southeast Asian states. But, again, Chinese involvement in Venezuela can be characterized by both regional and commercial logics.

Trade

As late as 2000, China was Venezuela's thirty-fifth-largest export market and by 2011 it was second for exports and imports (the US was and remains first for both; Rosales 2012, 31). But, as is the case with virtually all of Chinese trade with Latin America, Sino-Venezuelan trade is highly concentrated. Rosales (2012, 35) notes that the sum of the top five export products of Venezuela account for 99.8% of its exports to China (practically all of this either in the form of petroleum and derivatives, or iron ore; see also Dussel Peters 2015).

Oil exports to China had been 50,000 barrels per day in 2006 and climbed to 540,000 bpd in 2014,[11] far short of the often promised 1 million bpd by 2012 but still significant. Venezuela runs a consistent trade surplus with China, as it does with the US, and Venezuela is among the top ten suppliers of oil to China (Sun 2014, 650). The trade arrangement is particularly attractive to Venezuela as it involves state-led negotiations between state-owned enterprises. Given Venezuelan leadership's suspicion of international courts and private enterprises, working with state-owned enterprises is more favorable because of the possibility of making non-traditional market arrangements. The Venezuelan government, for example, contracted some $40 billion in loans between 2007 and 2014 with Chinese firms and has been repaying the loans with current and future oil exports (roughly half has been repaid; Wilson 2014).

These arrangements offer a number of immediate benefits for Venezuela: (1) it can deal directly with governments instead of corporations; (2) doing so helps increase Venezuelan contact/influence in that country; (3) debt can more easily be forgiven or modified in kind and maturity by governments than corporations; (4) Venezuela receives cash immediately with few constraints (say, reforms in institutions or anti-corruption measures). Lending without conditions is common to Chinese lending in developing countries and doing so often allows Chinese firms to charge a higher-than-market interest rate, while still seeming to offer "South-South" solidarity (Bräutigam and Gallagher 2014). More critically for China, however, is that the long-term contracts with Venezuela guarantee long-term access to petroleum. Given the centrality of oil to Chinese industrial production and the potential US weapon of sanctions and/or embargo, which could be exercised through US allies or through manipulation of the oil market, the long-term contracts with Venezuela serve as an important form of insurance for China. However, this is only one form of protection as China has expanded its purchase of Russian oil, invests heavily in clean energy production, and is intentionally slowing its economy, aiming to increase the relative weight of domestic consumption. Each of these fronts helps China reduce vulnerability while also reducing the relative importance of Venezuela for China.

This is particularly important as oil sales to China seem to have pla-
teaued and, given the decline in oil prices, Venezuela is a less important
partner. Even with the decline in shipping costs resultant from oil's decline, the transportation and eventual refining of Venezuelan crude oil is
particularly expensive. It takes one ton of Venezuelan oil some three to
seven days to reach US refineries (designed for such oil) but some thirty
to forty days to reach China, which may explain why oil sales to China
have hit a ceiling and why some of the oil purchased by Chinese companies is resold (rather than shipped back to China). Thus, while there
may be some strategic gain from Sino-Venezuelan trade, the potential
gain and ways of obviating challenges are understood and addressed by
China in commercial terms (searching for other partners and developing domestic alternatives).

Sino-Venezuelan trade, although characterized by consistent Venezuelan trade surpluses and extreme export concentration, also includes a
growing and diverse range of Chinese exports to Venezuela. Total value
of imports from China expanded from $1 billion in 2006 to $9.8 billion
in 2012, declining somewhat since then, with the most important category being industrial goods used for broadcasting, air-conditioning,
and computers. The increase in Chinese goods is the result of a boom
in Venezuelan consumption (as a result of commodity-driven growth,
an overvalued exchange rate, and official policies favoring consumption
of appliances, cell phones, and computers), as well as cooperation with
China in areas of technology transfer, specifically, but not limited to, the
ongoing cooperation over Chinese-designed satellites.

Loans and Investment

Following the expansion of trade, the most noticeable increase in Chinese
presence in Latin America has been in the area of loans, and Venezuela
received more than 50% of these loans (Dussel Peters 2015, 9). According
to the Inter-American Dialogue China–Latin American Finance Database, loans from China to Venezuela totaled some $56.3 billion with loans
peaking in 2010–11 and another spike in 2013–14.

Since 1999 there have been 450 agreements (Dussel Peters 2015, 21)
for some 241 projects (Sun 2014). These agreements began with the 1999
Venezuela-China High Level Commission Joint Committee, which was

established in May 2001 when then Chinese president Jiang Zemin visited Venezuela (Paz 2011, 224). A joint Heavy Strategic Fund was established in 2007 with $6 billion, which was expanded to $12 billion in 2008, then $20 billion in 2009. The fund provided Chinese money that would be repaid with Venezuelan oil, as discussed earlier.

The agreements between the two governments have involved considerable investment, including areas outside of energy. A sample includes: in November 2005, CITC announced $940 million toward real estate construction; in July 2008, Sinomach, $140 million in agriculture; in July 2009, China Railway Engineering, $7.5 billion; in April 2010, Sinomach announced another $960 million in energy and coal; in December 2010, Gezhouba, $290 million in agriculture; in May 2011, Chery, $200 million in transportation; in February 2014, Power Construction Company invested some $480 million in transportation (López and Sam 2015). Also noteworthy is joint cooperation on the launching of a satellite from Venezuela on 29 October 2008, which has supported Telesur, the anti-colonial and pro–Latin American news channel funded by the Venezuelan government. As part of this project, China "built two control stations in Venezuela . . . and more than ninety Venezuelan engineers were trained in China to operate the satellite" (Paz 2011, 229), at a cost of $400 million. Since then a second satellite was launched in 2012 and a third is in process.

Chinese loans to Venezuela cluster between 2008 and 2010, before declining until 2014–15, when a few large new measures were announced. The decline in loans going to Venezuela in 2010–13 was matched by an increase toward Brazil. Consider that Chinese lending to Venezuela from 1990 to 2009 was some $240 million and for Brazil $225 million. Between 2010 and 2013 Venezuela received $900 million and Brazil $23.2 billion. Brazil has eight Confucius Institutes and only in 2015 did China announce the establishment of a future Confucius Institute in Venezuela. Clearly, since the formal establishment of the BRICS in 2009, Sino-Brazilian cooperation has expanded, but the $10 billion deal with PETROBRAS to send 100,000 bpd to China, as well as SINOPEC's $7.5 billion investment in Brazilian Repsol in 2010 and SINOPEC's investment of $4.8 billion in Galp Energia (among other energy deals) demonstrate an opening of Brazilian energy markets to China and a Chinese shift in preference for Brazil—not only a partner in the BRICS but a far more politically stable country. This last point is particularly important for two reasons: not all investment plans come to fruition; and the big deals of the past two years are tied to questions of governmental stability, not deepening relations between the involved countries.

The data used for this section and virtually all data publicly available of Chinese loans to Latin America are based on officially published announcements of such news. The databases are not based on actually transfers of money nor on evidence of such money being spent. Interviews with analysts of the energy sector in Venezuela reflect a cynicism about the delay between announcing loans and even the actuality of receiving such funds, while Chinese oil officials expressed private concern about the instability of property rights in Venezuela. There are also examples of incomplete programs. Simón Romero reports that Venezuela-Chinese companies "broke ground on a 290-mile-high-speed railway, part of a grandiose plan by President Hugo Chávez, to 'rebalance' the population away from the coast" by 2012. China now claims that more than half the railway is built, but Venezuelan media reported the project as "abandoned" (S. Romero 2015). Given that neither government is especially transparent in making data on this available (Venezuela's Central Bank ceased divulging inflation data in February 2015), the amount of actual cash transfers to Venezuelan entities is uncertain.

A more important concern is the timing of the reinvestment in Venezuela during 2014–15, a period when the country faced very significant anti-government protests. Ellis (2015) has argued that Chinese money has provided critical resources to an otherwise failing Bolivarian government. He explains that "the PRC provided $4 billion to Venezuela prior to the October 2012 presidential election, allowing its 'Bolivarian Socialist' government to expand spending to increase electoral performance" and a further $20 billion was promised during a Maduro visit to China in January 2015, with some $10 billion immediately "available to the embattled Maduro government during the run-up to the December 6th mid-term elections in that country" (Ellis 2015, 10). Because the money flows from state to state, rather than private corporation to corporation, money lent to PDVSA is available to the Maduro government and can be used to plug fiscal holes, expand credit prior to elections, or whatever purposes are chosen. Venezuela is not alone in receiving renewed Chinese interest in 2014 and 2015. President Xi and Premier Li visited a number of Latin American countries, and publicly announced new trade and investment goals and programs. All of these countries were suffering from a decline in commodity prices. The Venezuelan case is a bit special as its government has faced greater governability crises than other countries visited by the Chinese leadership (Brazil, Colombia, Peru) and Chinese contracts are, thus, in greater danger.

Ellis argues that the US has largely been keeping its distance, allowing Venezuela to implode, with the hope of a new type of government emerging from the rubble. While this may reflect the view of many within the US administration—better to let the country fail than risk criticism about "imperialism"—a possible collapse of the Venezuelan government would not only punish an anti-US ruling group but would have serious repercussions for the Andes and South America more generally. Though such a collapse is unlikely, maintaining governability and preventing state collapse is clearly in the interest of the US, given its deep and long-term commitments both in Venezuela and Latin America more broadly. In other words, a collapse of an anti-US government might be a victory in relational zero-sum international relations, but it would probably be far more problematic and costly for the regional hegemon in structural terms. In this sense, new Chinese investment— clearly to protect existing contracts—both helps stabilize the Venezuelan government and contributes to stabilization in the US sphere of influence. This is clearly a case of positive-sum benefits coming to the US as a result of what might otherwise seem to be Chinese support for a "failing anti-US regime." It is also worth pointing out that Chinese loans are not a bailout of an "ally," nor has the Chinese leadership couched its new offers to Venezuela in language different from its offers to other Latin American countries (including the more pro-US countries of the Pacific Alliance). That China is not engaging Venezuela (or any other country in the region, including Brazil) in a traditional sense as an ally whose support is sought to balance against the US is consistent with its structural position relative to the US and Venezuela in South America.

5. Current Issues and Concluding Remarks

In October 2015, the Venezuelan barrel of oil traded around $40, practically $100 short of its peak in 2008. Inflation in May–June 2015, no longer released by the Central Bank, was estimated at an annualized 128% (by October there were reports of 1,000%), and GDP contracted in 2015. Central Bank reserves in July were only $15.3 billion but recovered to $17 billion (probably because of a new agreement with China). The weakening economy led Maduro to take a harder-line position regarding ongoing disputes with Colombia and Guyana, both US allies, but to also keep returning to the US with efforts to improve relations. This was an important way of continuing the "war against imperialism" while being pragmatic about the worsening structural conditions facing the Venezuelan government.

The use of petro-diplomacy continues, though it is tilted at smaller projects and weaker challengers. On 10 September 2015, jailed Venezuelan opposition leader Leopoldo López was sentenced to thirteen years in prison by a Venezuelan court. A bill to criticize the decision and the Maduro government was submitted to the Uruguayan assembly, but it failed because the government's (the center-left Frente Amplio, or Broad Front) deputies refused to support it. This surprised some given the Frente Amplio's long-term defense of political freedoms and human rights (many of its leaders had their rights deprived and their colleagues' lives taken by the Uruguayan dictatorship). On 18 September, an agreement was signed between Uruguay's state energy company (Ancap) and PDVSA, which reduced Uruguayan debt to the Venezuelan state-owned company from $434 million to $267 million. The agreement also included a Venezuela pledge to buy 256,000 tons of food (worth roughly $300 million).

But the declining price of oil has made it difficult for Venezuela to maintain an ambitious foreign policy agenda. While at one point analysts may have seen Venezuela as having outsized influence on the US and/or China, the reverse seems to be the case now. The Bolivarian subsidized alternatives (Petrocaribe and ALBA, among others) to US-led projects have been scaled back considerably. Venezuela is also far less attractive to China now and its recent investments are largely part of an effort to double-down. In this way, increased Chinese presence in Venezuela is indeed giving the state critical support—providing the state more options than would be possible otherwise—but it is not part of a global rebalancing against the US. This is consistent with the long-term Venezuelan foreign policy goals of autonomy and it demonstrates that China sees Venezuela first and foremost through the lens of trade.

Clearly, Venezuelan assets are "on sale" at the moment. A challenger to the US could see this as a Leninist moment to be seized: oil prices are low (weakening the Venezuelan government), the US has been relatively disengaged in the region (weakening the role of US qua hegemon), and the US has had very little contact with the Venezuelan leadership for the past sixteen years. China could expend relatively few resources and gain influence over the Venezuelan government and exacerbate the decline of US power in its "own backyard." Such a scenario would be especially likely with the new "great power" politics of Xi Jinping, whose foreign policy orientation toward the US has been far more assertive than that of his predecessor, Hu Jintao. But no such thing has happened. Visits by Xi and Premier Li Keqing to the region have been dominated by economic issues, expanding trade and investment, and deepening economic relations. Responding to an increasing chorus of criticism that Sino–Latin American trade involves the reprimarization of Latin America (as it is too focused on the purchase of commodities and has harmed Latin American industry; see Rosales in this volume), Chinese leaders have spoken of more cooperation in areas of science, technology, and innovation (Benito 2015, "ECLAC Officials" 2015). This is not because China is uninterested in challenging the US, as its recent defense of territorial waters around the Spratly Islands suggests (Fenby 2015). Rather, China sees little value in challenging the US in this particular geopolitical space, as its interest in Venezuela is that of an extra-regional commercial state.

The US has a different historic and structural relation with Venezuela. The period studied in this chapter covered the presidencies of George W. Bush (2001–9) and Barack Obama (2009–17), fundamentally different in tone, though less so in substance (see Restrepo and Mora, as well as Sabatini, in this volume). Regardless of who won the 2016 presidential contest, Obama was going to be replaced by a president more assertive on foreign policy issues. This will mean talking tougher with China and, possibly, Venezuela, but that does not mean the US will see a greater strategic threat from Chinese relations with Venezuela. For the reasons elaborated above, it is likely to continue to separate any "threat" from China from its commercial and complementary activities in Venezuela. China is likely to express its new "great power" politics in fora and on issues relevant to its contiguous regions, and possibly global governance more generally, but not as a partner in an anti-US coalition that includes

Venezuela (it has not done this even with more realistic emerging powers, like the BRICS). As its economy worsens, Venezuela will need to reach out to both the US and China, the latter for investment, the former for sales. Its leadership cannot abandon its Bolivarian principles if it is to maintain its political support, but it must also stay in office, and this creates a need to reassess its relationship with the US.

The pressure upon the Venezuelan government increased considerably following the 6 December 2015 parliamentary elections, which delivered a massive victory to opposition candidates. Carrying 112 of 167 seats in the unicameral National Assembly, the opposition, for the first time since 1999, will control the country's legislature and does so with a supermajority. At the same time, Maduro can rely on a Supreme Court, bureaucracy, and military that are overwhelmingly led by people loyal, or at least sympathetic, to the Bolivarian revolution, as well as a reserve of activists whose numbers have decreased but remain very committed to demonstrating their support in public manifestations. The opposition is most likely to attempt to recall the president and hold fresh elections, which could bring about a reversal of much of the domestic and foreign policy orientation of the past decade and a half. Whether the opposition is successful or not and whoever occupies the government, the structural constraints will continue to eviscerate the bold legacy of foreign policy activism of the Chávez governments. Neither the opposition nor government will alter the country's relations with China. Venezuela's foreign policy continues to be conditioned by its being a petrostate.

The relative positions of each country in regional and global governance structures, more than extrapolating expectations of risk or conflict from critical statements made by officials in the governments of the three countries, best explain relations between the three. In addition to giving evidence for a structural argument, this chapter also suggests that while foreign policy between the US and Venezuela may be zero sum, Sino-Venezuelan relations and US readings of Sino-Venezuelan relations are not. This is because Chinese activities are led by commercial efforts and logics, and the core of US influence in Latin America, in general, and Venezuela, in specific, is structural, not relational. Venezuelan efforts to reduce US influence (ALBA, Petrocaribe, Telesur) aimed at US structural power and were most successful when commodity prices gave Venezuela more bargaining power and its neighbors had less need of the US.

In sum, structures conditioned the foreign policies of the three countries examined. That said, they did not wholly determine them. Previous Venezuelan presidents who experienced higher oil prices pursued more assertive foreign policies, but the leadership of Hugo Chávez was critical for shaping these more assertive policies. At the same time, the role of leadership and ideas was less important and structural factors more determining of Venezuelan foreign policy retrenchment.

NOTES

1 The author thanks Dave Denoon, Sean Burges, the other authors in this book, Amy Freedman, Riordan Roett, Ambassador Winston Lord, Alfredo Toro Carnevali, Dimitris Pantoulas, Luis San Vicente Portes, Yanran Xu, and an anonymous reviewer for their helpful comments on an earlier draft of this chapter, as well as Liana Eustacia Reyes for her excellent research assistance.

2 If there is a threat, it is to be identified in how an assertive Venezuela that has wooed China, Russia, and Iran, and supported anti-US and anti-neoliberal politicians in the region, challenges US influence in the region. But much of the decline in US influence was due to a commodity boom that weakened its relative position vis-à-vis its southern neighbors and the particular policies of George W. Bush and Barack Obama. One could argue that the increased presence of Russia in Latin America—as a primary provider of weapons to and conducting joint exercises with Venezuela—might constitute a threat. But, again, this claim relies on a potential decline in US influence, not a direct threat to the security of the US. Indeed, Venezuela provides no direct military or economic security challenge to the US and can only hope to challenge the US through "soft-balancing" (Corrales and Penfold 2011), which might stymie US efforts at times, but in no way undermines US security, even if it may weaken the legitimacy of US authority.

3 Relations are conditioned but not wholly determined by structural positions. In the case of Venezuela, the leadership of Hugo Chávez was important in explaining how the country bristled against the US when it was flush with petrodollars. The author is grateful to the anonymous reviewer for clarification on this point.

4 This does not mean that China and Venezuela do not share an interest in a more multipolar world nor that Chinese financial support of the Venezuelan government does not assist Venezuela in its foreign policy aims. Rather, China does not directly engage with Venezuela on the question of challenging US hegemony, preferring to make such comments in other fora.

5 As the region's second-largest trade partner, however, it does have interest in the macroeconomic stability of the countries in the region. Of course, the caution China has shown is not necessarily replicated by other powers with increased interest in the region, such as Russia.

6 This "international activism" long precedes Hugo Chávez and was part of Venezuelan foreign policy since the country democratized in 1958.

7   See Global Firepower at www.globalfirepower.com.

8   "Trade in Goods with Venezuela," *United States Census Bureau*, www.census.gov; Office of the United States Trade Representative, "U.S.-Venezuela Trade Facts," *Executive Office of the President*, www.ustr.gov.

9   U.S. Energy Information Administration, 2014. EIA Beta. http://www.eia.gov.

10 Office of the Press Secretary, "Fact Sheet: Venezuela Executive Order," *White House*, 9 Mar. 2015, www.whitehouse.gov.

11 As noted earlier, US accounts dispute this number and have it closer to 260,000 bpd (Christensen 2015, 78–79).

BIBLIOGRAPHY

Adams, David, and Phil Gunson. 2015. "Chávez and ALBA." In *Decline of the U.S. Hegemony: A Challenge of ALBA and a New Latin American Integration of the Twenty-First Century*, edited by Bruce M. Bagley and Magdalena Defort, 33–42. Lanham, MD: Lexington Books.

Agyeman, Opoku. 2014. *Power, Powerlessness, and Globalization: Contemporary Politics in the Global South*. Lanham, MD: Lexington Books.

Babb, Sarah. 2013. "The Washington Consensus as Transnational Policy Paradigm: Its Origins, Trajectory and Likely Successor." *Review of International Political Economy* 20 (2): 268–97.

Bagley, Bruce, and Magdalena Defort. 2015. *Decline of the U.S. Hegemony?: A Challenge of ALBA and a New Latin American Integration of the Twenty-First Century*. Lanham, MD: Lexington Books.

Benito, Daniel. 2015. "China and Latin America: A New Phase of Engagement?" *Dialogochino.net*, 15 Sept. www.dialogochino.net /.

Bräutigam, Deborah, and Kevin Gallagher. 2014. "Bartering Globalization: China's Commodity-Backed Finance in Africa and Latin America." *Global Policy* 5: 346–52.

Burges, Sean. 2009. *Brazilian Foreign Policy after the Cold War*. Gainesville: University of Florida Press.

———. 2016. *Brazil in the World*. Manchester: Manchester University Press.

Buzan, Barry, Charles Jones, and Richard Little. 1993. *The Logic of Anarchy: Neorealism to Structural Realism*. New York: Columbia University Press.

Callahan, William. 2004. *Contingent States: Greater China and Transnational Relations*. Minneapolis: University of Minnesota Press.

Christensen, Thomas J. 2015. *The China Challenge: Shaping the Choices of a Rising Power*. New York: W.W. Norton.

CIA. n.d. *CIA World Factbook*. www.cia.gov.

Coronil, Fernando. 1997. *The Magical State: Nature, Money, and Modernity in Venezuela*. Chicago: University of Chicago Press.

Corrales, Javier, and Michael Penfold. 2011. *Dragon in the Tropics: Hugo Chávez and the Political Economy of Revolution in Venezuela*. Washington, DC: Brookings Institution Press.

Corrales, Javier, and Carlos Romero. 2012. *US-Venezuela Relations since the 1990s: Coping with Midlevel Security Threats.* New York: Routledge.

Cox, Robert. 1987. *Production Power and World Order.* New York: Columbia University Press.

Denoon, David B. H. (ed.). 2015. *China, the United States, and the Future of Central Asia.* New York: New York University Press.

———. 2017. *China, the United States, and the Future of Southeast Asia.* New York: New York University Press.

Doctor, Mahrukh. 2015. "From Rule-Taker to Rule-Maker and Agenda-Setter?: Brazil's Role in Global Economic Governance." Latin American Studies Association Conference (LASA), San Juan, Puerto Rico.

Dussel Peters, Enrique. 2015. "China's Evolving Role in Latin America: Can It Be a Win-Win?" Washington, DC: Atlantic Council.

ECLAC. 2015. *Economic Survey of Latin America and the Caribbean 2015.* Santiago: United Nations Economic Commission of Latin America and the Caribbean. http://repositorio.cepal.org.

"ECLAC Officials Laud Li's Speech on China-LatAm Cooperation." 2015. *Xinhua,* 26 May. http://news.xinhuanet.com.

Ellis, R. Evan. 2009. *China in Latin America: The Whats and Wherefores.* Boulder, CO: Lynne Rienner.

———. 2015. *Testimony to the Joint Hearing of the Subcommittee to the Western Hemisphere and the Subcommittee on Asia and the Pacific.* US House of Representatives, Washington DC.

Ellner, Steve. 2009. *Rethinking Venezuelan Politics: Class, Conflict, and the Chavez Phenomenon.* Boulder, CO: Lynne Rienner.

Fenby, Jonathan. 2015. "Neither China nor the US Will Give Way in This South China Sea Showdown." *Guardian,* 29 Oct. www.theguardian.com.

Ferchen, Matt. 2014. "Crude Complications: Venezuela, China, and the United States." *Carnegie-Tsinghua Center for Global Policy,* 23 Oct. www.carnegietsinghua.org.

Gill, Timothy. 2014. "Diversity of Interests Shapes US Venezuela Policy." Washington Office on Latin America. http://venezuelablog.tumblr.com/post/97478909119/diversity-of-interests-shapes-us-venezuela-policy.

Golinger, Eva. 2007. "USAID in Bolivia and Venezuela: The Silent Subversion." Venezuelaanalysis.com. 12 Sept.

González Urrutia, Edmundo. 2006. "Las dos Etapas de la Política Exterior de Chávez (The two stages of Chávez's foreign policy)," *Nueva Sociedad* 205: 159–71.

Hetland, Gabriel. 2016. "From System Collapse to Chavista Hegemony: The Party Question in Bolivarian Venezuela." *Latin American Perspectives* 44 (1): 17–36.

Hirst, Joel D. and Christopher Sabatini. 2015. "A Guide to ALBA: What Is the Bolivarian Alternative to the Americans and What Does It Do?" in Bruce M. Bagley and Magdelena Defort (eds.) *Decline of U.S. Hegemony?: A Challenge of ALBA and a New Latin American Integration of the Twenty-First Century.* Lanham, MD: Lexington.

Ikenberry, G. John; Michael Mastanduno, and William C. Wohlforth (eds.). 2009. *International Relations Theory and the Consequences of Unipolarity*. Cambridge: Cambridge University Press.

Kang, David C. 2003. "Getting Asia Wrong: The Need for New Analytical Framework." *International Security* 27 (4): 57–85.

Karl, Terry L. 1997. *The Paradox of Plenty: Oil Booms and Petro-States*. Berkley, CA: University of California Press.

Krauthammer, Charles. 1990. "The Unipolar Moment." *Foreign Affairs* 70 (1): 23–33.

López, Alberto Lucas, and Cédric Sam. 2015. "China's Overseas Investments." *South China Morning Post*. 28 Apr.

Lukes, Steven. 1974. *Power: A Radical View*. London; New York: Macmillan.

May, Christopher. 1996. *The Rule of Law: The Common Sense of Global Politics*. Cheltenham, UK, and Northampton MA: Edward Elgar Publishing.

McCarthy-Jones, Anthea, and Mark Turner. 2011. "Explaining Radical Policy Change: The Case of Venezuelan Foreign Policy." *Policy Studies* 32 (5): 549–67.

Mearsheimer, John J. 2001. *The Tragedy of Great Power Politics*. New York: W. W. Norton.

Neuman, William, and Patricia Torres. 2015. "Few in Venezuela Want Bolívars, but No One Can Spare a Dime." *New York Times*. 18 Oct.

Paz, Gonzalo. 2011. "China and Venezuela: Oil, Technology, and Socialism." In *China Engages Latin America: Tracing the Trajectory*, Adrian H. Hearn and José Luis León-Manríquez. (eds.) Boulder, CO: Lynne Rienner. pp. 221–34.

Pitts, Pietro D. 2014. "PDVSA Profit Surges as Lower Spending Counters Oil Slide." *Bloomberg*. 20 June.

Riordan, Roett, and Guadalupe Paz. 2008. *China's Expansion into the Western Hemisphere: Implications for Latin America and the United States*. Washington, DC: Brookings Institute.

Romero, Carlos. 2006. *Jugando Con El Globo: La Política Exterior de Hugo Chávez*. Caracas: Edicions B.

Romero, María Teresa. 2015. "Maduro Loves to Hate His 'Imperialist' Cash Cow." *PanamPost*, 2 Mar. www.panampost.com.

Romero, Simon. 2015. "China's Ambitious Rail Projects Crash into Harsh Realities in Latin America." *New York Times*. 3 Oct. www.nytimes.com.

Rosales, Osvaldo. 2012. *The People's Republic of China and Latin America and the Caribbean: Dialogue and Cooperation for the New Challenges of the Global Economy*. Santiago: United Nations Economic Commission of Latin America and the Caribbean. www.repositorio.cepal.org.

Schell, Orville. 2014. "China Strikes Back!" *New York Review of Books*. 23 Oct. www.nybooks.com.

Serbín, Andrés. 2010. *Chávez, Venezuela Y La Reconfiguración Política de América Latina Y El Caribe*. Buenos Aires: Siglo XXI.

Smilde, David, and Timothy Gill. 2013. "Strategic Posture Review: Venezuela." *World Politics Review*. Sept. www.worldpoliticsreview.com.

Spanakos, Anthony P., and Yu Xiao. 2013. "It Takes Three to Samba: Sino-US-Latin American Relations." In *Treinta Años de Relaciones Colombo-Chinas: La Presencia China En Colombia Y América Latina—Reflexiones Y Perspectivas*, edited by Benjamin Cruetzfeldt. Bogotá: Universidad Externado de Colombia.

Strange, Susan. 1987. "The Persistent Myth of Lost Hegemony." *International Organization* 41 (4): 551–74.

———. 1996. *The Retreat of the State: The Diffusion of Power in the World Economy.* Cambridge, UK: Cambridge University Press.

———. 1998. *States and Markets.* 2nd Edition. London: Bloomsbury.

Sun, Hongbo. 2014. "China-Venezuelan Oil Cooperation Model." *Perspectives on Global Development and Technology* 13 (5–6): 648–69.

Tinker Salas, Miguel. 2009. *The Enduring Legacy: Oil, Culture, and Society in Venezuela.* Durham, NC: Duke University Press.

Toro Carnevali, Alfredo. 2011. "El ALBA Como Instrumento de Soft Balancing." *Pensamiento Propio* 33 (16): 159–85.

Walt, Stephen. 2005. *Taming American Power: The Global Responses to U.S. Primacy.* New York: W.W. Norton, 2006.

Williamson, John. 1994. "What Does Washington Mean by Policy Reform?" In *Latin American Adjustment: How Much Has Happened?*, edited by John Williamson. Washington: Institute of International Economics.

Wilson, Peter. 2014. "Falling Oil Prices Push Venezuela Deeper into China's Orbit." *Bloomberg.* 21 Dec.

Zweig, David. 2010. "'Resource Diplomacy' Under Hegemony: Foreign Policy 'Triangularism' and Sino-American Energy Competition in the 21st Century." In *China's Energy Rise: The U.S., and the New Geopolitics of Energy*, edited by Mikkal Herberg and David Zweig, 35–74. Los Angeles: Pacific Council on International Policy.

7

U.S., China, and Brazil

Do We Need Three to Samba?

JOSÉ AUGUSTO GUILHON-ALBUQUERQUE

This chapter is divided into four sections. The first one compares Brazil's bilateral relations with the U.S. and China. The following section discusses how China's rise might affect U.S. interests in Brazil and its region. I then analyze areas in which the competition between the U.S. and China could be positively affected by Brazilian courses of action in foreign policy. Finally, I suggest possible U.S. foreign policy orientations toward Brazil and its region.

Comparing Brazil's Bilateral Relations with China and the U.S.

Both China's and the U.S.'s relationships with Brazil are considered strategic partnerships. Brazil and the U.S. have a record of tacit and formal alliances but have also experienced periods of friction, especially during the late years of military rule in Brazil (1964–1985).[1] After a period of deepening engagement until 2003, the two countries are facing now a period of mutual misunderstanding after the incident involving the hacking of Brazilian president Dilma Rousseff's personal communications by American agents.

The election of President Lula da Silva in 2003 initiated a period of reappraisal of Brazilian foreign policy that triggered major changes in its bilateral relations with the West and particularly with the U.S. Lula had been elected by a very heterogeneous coalition, stretching from the extreme left to right-wing nationalists. His highest cabinet positions had to be distributed to accommodate the Workers' Party (Partido dos Trabalhadores, PT)'s different factions[2] and all the political parties supporting his coalition. The PT's left wing was granted a bunch of ministries and presidential secretariats dealing with social inclusion, housing, agrarian movements, and, surprisingly, foreign relations.

In his first year in office, Lula was universally acclaimed abroad as a former labor leader turned moderate world leader, who chose to continue his predecessor's market-friendly economic policies. Soon, he had to face a strong opposition, which was fueled by the PT's left wing and by the president's own desultory coalition.

On the external front, an unexpected alliance welded the new PT-appointed Itamaraty[3] leadership with the presidential inner sanctum, notably with Marco Aurélio Garcia, a former academic, with a remarkable career in the PT, including as campaign program coordinator in most of Lula's presidential bids. What was initially a successfully loaded external agenda to compensate for domestic failures became a goal in itself, aiming at providing the president with a platform to project his own persona externally as a national asset.

Lula's success abroad was such that it conferred domestic legitimacy to the shifts in Brazilian foreign policy announced in his campaign. A brand-new foreign policy, "Ativa e Altiva,"[4] was proclaimed, based on giving priority to South-South cooperation (and North-South polarization), managed trade and investment inside Mercosur, a regional focus on South America, and a commitment to a vague revisionism of the world order.[5]

Its first casualty was meant to be the country's relations with the U.S., starting with the failure of the Free Trade Area of the Americas agreement negotiations in 2003, proudly announced by President Lula.[6] As we will discuss in the final section, before Lula's election, both administrations—Cardoso's and Bush's—lacked a sense of urgency to reach an agreement in the FTAA talks. However, during the elections, the PT had sponsored a "popular" referendum against the agreement in tandem with Lula's presidential campaign, and Lula himself had promised to stop it. When the talks stalled, the newly sworn in president Lula boasted of having fulfilled his promise.

The new agenda included a number of Brazilian initiatives—and the support of initiatives taken by the Venezuela-Argentina axis—in the hemisphere, especially in South America.

The successful blockade of the FTAA inspired Itamaraty to share with China and India the leadership of the G20 faction of developing economies in order to counterbalance the OECD countries, especially the U.S. and the E.U., during the first Doha round of pre-negotiations in the WTO. Having stretched the line to the point of rupture, Lula's foreign minister, Celso Amorim, led a veto coalition that eventually sank the talks.[7] Since then, the Doha round has not advanced, but the Brazilian government keeps putting all of its chips on the WTO's global talks. The Trade Facilitation Agreement, the only step forward accomplished by the WTO, whose final wording was agreed to in July 2014, has not been signed by Brazil.

Political relations with the U.S. have also been affected by the PT's foreign policy. The official diplomatic narrative in both countries still underscored cooperation and convergence of principles and global visions, not so much Brazilian diplomatic and presidential decisions. True, Lula befriended most of his counterparts, especially the most conservative among them, such as Bush, Chirac, and Sarkozy, but his visits to countries perceived by Washington as definitely unfriendly or even rogue states, such as Libya, caused concerns, as well as Lula's attempt at circumventing the negotiations between the UNSC and Iran.[8] It did not help that Brazil had opposed the adoption of the Additional Protocol to the Non-Proliferation Treaty.[9] Other symbolic acts of disengagement with respect to the U.S. and its Western allies included Lula's initiative to call a summit between Latin American and Arab countries and frequent statements on the Israel-Palestine conflict in which Lula or his foreign minister simultaneously offered to mediate and openly sided with Ramallah.

The area of science and technology, a very sensitive theme for the Brazilian foreign service, has always been a source of tension between the two countries. The problem dates back to the end of World War II and reflects Brazilian expectations to be entitled to massive American investments in its modernization and industrialization in compensation for the country's support to the U.S. war effort.[10] Despite some serious friction during the military regime over a nuclear power plant, most conflicts remained in the background of recent Brazil-U.S. relations.

The Alcântara Satellite Launch Base is a striking example of the radical shift in the Brazilian government's relations with the U.S. It dates from 1983 and has been conceived to take advantage of its privileged location for satellite launching near the equator in the northeast of the country. The Alcântara base initially was intended to become a full-fledged space center, but due to financial and technological limitations the government opted for leasing its facilities for commercial use, in order to provide funding for future developments.

In 2001, during the Cardoso administration (1995–2003), the two governments inked a leasing agreement regulating the operations of the Alcântara facilities by the Americans. The reaction from the PT and its left-wing allies was immediate and bombastic, condemning the agreement as a violation of Brazil's sovereignty. The opposition to the ratification of the agreement was reinforced by the nationalist right wing and succeeded because of the omission of the government's coalition. Besides blaming Cardoso for giving away the country's sovereignty, a central argument against the agreement was that Washington precluded any technological transfer as a strategy to impede Brazil's development. The agreement was overturned by the Chamber of Deputies (the lower house of the Brazilian legislature).

Surprisingly, in 2003, his first year in government, Lula signed an agreement with Ukraine on the leasing of the Alcântara launch facilities, on a very similar basis as the previous Brazil-U.S. agreement, after the endorsement by the Chamber of Deputies of an agreement on technological safeguards. Despite the fact that some of the sensitive technologies included in the Ukrainian satellite launch vehicle were American, and thus subject to the same conditions, the PT's argument was that this new lease, previously negotiated in Cardoso's government in 1999, was compatible with national sovereignty and benefitted Brazilian technological development. At that time, the Ukrainian part of the investments did not take off. In 2015, in the aftermath of the conflicts in Ukraine, President Dilma Rousseff signed a new protocol giving notice of the termination of the Alcântara leasing.

The area of defense is usually depicted as a breakthrough in current Brazil-U.S. bilateral relations after the termination of the Brazil-U.S. military agreement. However, another case in point concerns the Brazilian government's tender for the purchase of jet fighters to innovate and modernize the Brazilian Air Force, dating back to 1999, during the Cardoso administration. The initial value of the deal was a modest US$700 million, involving about 20 aircraft. The American Boeing, the French Dassault, the Swedish Saab, and the Russian Sukhoi firms were in the race.[11]

Technical, economic, and political assessments by the Ministry of Defense were ready for presidential decision by the end of Cardoso's term, and it appeared that the technical and economic balances would benefit the U.S. supplier. However, Cardoso's decision would commit the next government to a sensitive deal and provide the forthcoming elections with a controversial issue. Actually, among the resolutions adopted by the PT's 2010 National Congress, one thesis clarifies the party's views about Brazil's relationship with the U.S., specifically concerning the jet fighter deal:

> Clearly, President Lula's foreign policy causes Brazil to compete with the U.S. . . . Besides, considering that [this competition] occurs in the immediate vicinity of the [U.S.], competition with Brazil has the potential to become a threat to the U.S. . . . This is what the acute debate over the renovation of the Brazilian military equipment, the nuclear submarine and the purchase of jet fighters from the French suppliers is all about.[12]

President Lula resumed the tender in 2007, early in his second term, this time involving 120 fighters for an estimated value of US$10 billion. The competitors were the same, each one offering its cutting-edge equipment. For this tender, Washington offered the latest version of its flagship fighter, the F/A-18E/F Super Hornet.[13]

In September 2009, with just one year left before the forthcoming presidential elections, the tender procedures still dragged and the final assessment by the Air Force Command had not been formally forwarded. A huge number of converging rumors pointed to a highest-level understanding between Lula and France's Sarkozy.

Unexpectedly, President Lula took advantage of a brief visit by President Sarkozy to announce an agreement with Dassault to purchase 36 Rafale jet fighters for four billion Euros.[14] However, despite the diligence of both presidents and their public commitment, the deal had not been completed before the election of Lula's successor in 2010. Question remains as to the nature of the hurdles the two close friends and colleagues have been unable to circumvent.[15]

Just one month after taking office, President Dilma Rousseff, Lula's successor and fellow party member, reopened the tender for the purchase of the same 36 aircraft, with the same bidders and for approximately the same value of US$4.7 billion. Only this time the Russian firm, Sukhoi, was supposed to be excluded.[16]

Surprisingly, despite Brazil's traditional alliance with France and the U.S., its long-time suppliers of defense equipment, and against expectations in favor of Boeing, the Swedish Gripen firm was selected in late 2013, with a prototype yet to be developed.[17] Negotiations with Gripen took two years and were completed in September 2015.[18]

In the aftermath of World War II, Brazil maintained regular diplomatic relations with the Kuomintang regime in Taiwan and did not recognize the People's Republic of China (PRC) until 1974.

In the early 1960s, Brazil's tacit alignment with American Cold War policies was very unpopular among the elites, which resented the absence of expected postwar benefits, which had been provided to Western Europe and East Asia. All the attempts to garner U.S. support to fund Brazil's industrial modernization, especially to boost the car industry, had failed.[19]

During the brief period of parliamentary government in Brazil, President João Goulart adopted an "independent foreign policy" (IFP), open to commercial and political relations with all countries.[20] Accordingly, a series of commercial offices were opened in East European, African, and Asian countries without problems, but the case of the PRC was rather special.

In 1961, Jango—as President Goulart was known—had survived an attempted military coup to impede his ascension to presidential powers, but three years later, he was ousted. In this context, a Chinese commercial mission had just arrived to establish a trade representative office in Rio de Janeiro. The new military regime arrested the Chinese diplomats, charged them for spying and subversion, and finally deported them.[21]

It was only in 1974 that General Ernesto Geisel, then president of the military regime in Brazil, decided to recognize the PRC.[22] The Brazilian domestic context was again the triggering factor. A former CEO of Petrobras, the state-owned Brazilian oil giant, Geisel was deeply concerned with the impact of the international oil crisis on the country's domestic energy supply. Accordingly, he reestablished the core objectives of the Brazilian IFP, adopting so-called responsible pragmatism (Guilhon-Albuquerque 2003).

One of his options was to diversify the country's nuclear power supply. He then decided to start a joint nuclear program with the Federal

Republic of Germany. The program consisted in developing German technology as an alternative to the American option by means of a contract with Westinghouse, which had been suspended by the U.S. government.[23]

The Carter administration then persuaded the German government to back off the sensitive clauses of the joint nuclear program. Concurrently, a U.S. Senate report on human rights, pointing out the treatment given to political prisoners, native populations, and rural leaders by the military government, provided the perfect excuse for Brazilian retaliation. Thus, the recognition and establishment of diplomatic relations with the PRC was included among other mostly symbolic retaliatory measures taken by General Geisel.

Nevertheless, bilateral relations between the Brazil and China remained lukewarm and very limited until the early 1990s. In 1993, Chinese prime minister Zhu Rongji, in a visit to Brazil, described the relationship between the two countries as a "strategic partnership."[24] Yet the content of the relationship remained rather more symbolic than real until President Lula's government (2003–2011), especially when bilateral trade increased exponentially, in the aftermath of the 2008 crisis.

China's influence in Brazil's political economy almost reversed in the first decade of this century, mostly driven by Brazil's exports of commodities. The three items comprising about 80% of Brazil's exports basket to China—soybeans, ores, and oil—underwent a dramatic increase in productivity and global competitiveness: the first, following cuts in domestic subsidies and trade barriers beginning in the early 1990s, and the other two as a result of the partial privatization of Petrobrás (oil) and Vale (iron ore) during Cardoso's administration (1995–2003).

In 2002, the year of the presidential elections, trade growth cooled down as a reaction to the risk of electing Lula, who had for a long time promised to revert Cardoso's business-friendly economic policies. In 2003, the first year of Lula's administration, bilateral trade resumed the previous growth rate due to the surprising continuity of Cardoso's policies early in Lula's first term.

In 2008, because of the international financial crisis, Brazilian exports to its traditional markets decreased significantly, but at the same time, it benefitted from the huge increase in Chinese imports of commodities, particularly those provided by Brazilian exporters.[25] Thus, exports to China doubled again in three years and its share of Brazil's total exports rose to 6.9% between 2008 and 2010. Thereafter, the country's exports growth rate to China decreased significantly from 46.6% in 2010 to -11.8% in 2014, while its share of total Brazilian exports continued to grow steadily, up to 19.02% in 2013.

Meanwhile, bilateral exchanges expanded hugely, including mostly officials and businesspersons, as well as students and fortune seekers. Most lacked both the capital and the cultural savvy to succeed in doing business in China. Exchanges at the highest level also expanded during the two PT leaders' administrations.[26] The sheer amount of high-level meetings, seminars, agreements, and bilateral forums and councils is substantial.

In spite of the huge increase in China's imports and the resulting Brazilian trade surplus (until 2013), bilateral economic relations remained tied to the commodities trade. The same three items of the Brazilian exports basket—soybeans, iron ore, and crude oil—still accounted, in 2014, for above 80% of the Chinese imports from Brazil.

Despite all the bombastic chatter about technological transfer and joint investment spurred by South-South cooperation, the same famous cases are always mentioned—the access of the Brazilian flagship aviation company, Embraer, to the Chinese market, still in abeyance; and the joint remote sensing satellite project (CEBERS), in which Brazilian participation is marginal.

The Brazilian literature and the governmental discourse about China-Brazil relations both articulate a different narrative. Most Brazilian authors[27] overvalue the so-called strategic partnership and generally endorse its relevance for a variety of reasons:

First of all, the volume of bilateral commerce as well as its exceptional growth are duly acknowledged, but it is considered by most Brazilian authors as the consequence of the special political relationship between the two countries, rather than its raison d'être. Besides, Brazil's growing dependency on its exports in commodities to China and, more recently, on Chinese investments and financial cooperation are not perceived as a liability. Joint statements and agreements between the two governments are profusely adduced, but few real improvements in the flows of trade and investment are accounted for.[28]

For both government officials and academics, Brazil-China partnership goes far beyond the economy and involves above all joint high-level diplomatic actions (mainly presidential diplomacy) in global forums—BRICS, G20, FMI, IBRD—including, more recently, the BRICS Bank and the AIIB (Asian Infrastructure Investment Bank). Besides, the scope of the relationship is considered to be based on deep socioeconomic and geopolitical identity and on the vision to create a similar social and economic development. Additionally, the priority given by both countries to South-South cooperation is supposed to provide a solid foundation for their partnership and portends a successful outcome for their strategic goals.

The same does not apply to the business community nor to Brazilian diplomats directly involved with China.[29] Besides the imbalance in trade, the characteristics of FDI inflows from China in Brazil have raised questions about the risks and opportunities they provide for the Brazilian national interest. The growth of Chinese direct investments in a small number of commodities sectors, such as oil extraction, natural gas, and minerals, has generated concerns in the Brazilian private sector and among Brazilian government authorities over the past several years. The criticism derives from the interpretation that such FDI inflows could turn the country into a raw materials provider for the Chinese economy, with uncertain benefits to the Brazilian economy.

In addition, there are concerns about economic sectors perceived as strategic by Brazilian society. China showed great interest in increasing investments in the agribusiness sector in the year 2010. In this regard, China expressed an intention to acquire directly or indirectly large agricultural properties in Brazil. This matter has been subject to intense debate and became a highly sensitive political issue in Brazil, as occurred in other countries such as Canada and Australia. This episode made clear that some sectors or activities considered sensitive to national interests could become restricted to foreign interests. A tightening of federal legislation might be required to ensure that the Brazilian government has the ability to regulate or even limit FDI inflows in activities or sectors considered strategic.

The analysis of a small sample of structured interviews with Brazilian diplomats, directly involved in Brazil-China bilateral relations, provides a narrative that differs significantly from the president's narrative. Former ambassadors and senior diplomats in charge of policy planning and decision-making, included in the sample, share a common perception of the nature, origin, and function of the strategic partnership between the two countries.

As for the concept and the origin of the partnership, the diplomats coincide in pointing out the Chinese as the party that defines the partnership according to their own criteria and interests. In exchange, the Brazilian party accepts the partnership either as a token or as an invitation to exchanging favors.

China began to appear on Itamaraty's radar as it emerged economically and politically and developed a strategy concerning Brazil, aiming to benefit from the country's position in South America, its continental dimensions, and its role in the global economy as a commodities exporter. As for the Brazilian reaction, according to the interviewees, it aims to achieve the country's immediate commercial interests and not specific strategic goals regarding China.

Thus, while China developed a clear strategy toward its South American partner, assigning Brazil a specific place in its long-term foreign and trade policies, according to Brazilian diplomats, neither the Brazilian presidency nor Itamaraty adopted any strategy to deal with the Chinese counterpart. Moreover, they also made clear that in both presidencies, the government, Itamaraty, and the business community did not manifest great commitment in outlining such strategic goals. To make it short, there is nothing strategic in Brazil's "strategic partnership" with China.

Moreover, while the presidential discourse claims that Brazil's strategic partnership with China builds on the social and economic identity between the two countries, which leverages the relevance of their bilateral commerce, the diplomats construe the Brazilian posture—including the government's, Itamaraty's, and the business community's—as purely reactive to Chinese initiatives. As for the robustness of Chinese growth and the relevance of the bilateral commerce between the countries, both the presidential and the diplomatic narratives coincide in assuming these are the key for both countries to have access to international forums—especially in the financial G20—to keep possession of a position in the global decision-making system.

Lula, however, describes bilateral cooperation in the global forums as a platform to claim an active role in the definition of global policies. Dilma does not give special relevance to the international cooperation resulting from Brazilian participation in the IMF, the World Bank, or the financial G20, but perceives the country's membership in such forums as an opportunity to reform the world system of power, while Lula seems to adopt a more conservative stance.

As for the diplomats, they attach greater strategic relevance to the G20 because Brazil's participation in that forum would permit the country to share global responsibilities, which would require a reformist perspective in order to modernize the training of new generations of diplomats.

Among Brazilian diplomats, more or less realistic ambitions, to play a larger and more central part in the global rulemaking directly concerning Brazilian trade and security interests, are not in short supply. In the presidential discourse, however—especially with regard to the accession to a permanent seat in the UN Security Council—will is power.

* * *

China and the U.S. are currently the two most important Brazilian trade partners. In terms of investments in Brazil, China is second only to the E.U. and the U.S. still holds its position as the country with the biggest stock of investments in Brazil. With both countries, Brazil is engaged in complex and intense bilateral relations in the most relevant global fora, be it in political, security-related, commercial, or financial matters. Consequently, it would be highly improbable that Brazil's relationships with each of the countries were not mutually affected.

The starting point for analyzing the mutual impact between the two bilateral relations is to understand how Lula's and Rousseff's governments perceived the so-called strategic partnerships with both the U.S. and China. For that purpose I conducted a survey on the Brazilian government perceptions of the country's special relationship with China.[30]

The general conclusion of that analysis was that the narrative of the Brazilian government in both administrations did not reflect the empirical elements of its relationship with the two countries—its commercial interests, its political objectives, the specific conditions for cooperation and conflict in both relationships. It rather reflects an idealized image of the two countries as symmetrically opposed concerning Brazil's core interests. While the U.S. is perceived as the personification of the classical imperialism, China appears as the perfect incarnation of South-South solidarity. Therefore, Brazil's bilateral relations with the U.S. are regarded as a source of conflicts and threats, while those with China are considered a source of cooperation and benefits.[31]

After having underscored the convergences between the two Brazilian leaders concerning the strategic nature of Brazil-China bilateral relations, let us give some thoughts to the differences between them. The most noteworthy feature of President Dilma's performance in foreign policy is the absence of noticeable initiatives and reactions in the international arena. In this regard there is a striking difference between the two governments, since part of the considerable success of Lula's presidential diplomacy was due to his undeniable competence to make news. Measured by Lula's standard, Dilma's ability to assert that "no news is good news" is a mediocre measure of success.

Not many of President Dilma's initiatives and/or reactions in the international arena can be referred to as evidence of her government's general foreign policy guidelines. Most of them seem to reflect symbolic, ideological, or idiosyncratic reactive attitudes rather than consistent courses of foreign policy action. Their paucity and seemingly erratic nature evoke both the lack of a broader national strategic design and of personal involvement in such matters.

Two manifestations of such attitudes caused concern and surprise among the press, one when Rousseff was president-elect and the other when she was newly sworn as president. Repeating President Bush's gesture, who invited Lula in 2002 when the latter had been freshly elected, President Obama invited president-elect Dilma in 2010, only to be rebuffed. The ubiquitous Garcia, still officially Lula's special adviser and leading figure of the transition team, cited "scheduling problems due to previous commitments with the transition government."[32]

A columnist close to the PT and a believer in the party's "Ativa e Altiva" foreign policy revealed a veiled contention among the transition team. According to him, the winning team aimed at avoiding the president-elect's first international photo opportunity showing her shaking hands with an epitome of the "North." If she accepted Obama's invitation she would have to schedule her visit for early December, before the Mercosur Summit on December 17. Instead, she had been advised to be photographed alongside Chávez and Cristina Kirchner.[33]

In her first month in office, President Dilma was expected as a global star alongside with China's Hu, at the 2011 edition of the World Economic

Forum in Davos. Due to the superb performance of the two countries' economies in the aftermath of the global financial crisis, it was expected that the presence of both leaders would offer an opportunity to compare the roadmaps followed by each country.

However, Dilma canceled her participation, again citing domestic commitments to visit housing and sports stadiums and regional venues, including the Latin American Economic Forum in Rio de Janeiro, to be held in April 2011.[34] In stark contrast, President Lula would never miss such an opportunity to further embellish his international prestige. In his time, freshly tenured, Lula not only was the focus of attention in Davos but also made sure to be present at its opposite extreme, the Forum São Paulo, known as the World Social Forum.

In other areas, still as president-elect, Dilma made a point to decouple her foreign policy from Lula's. Not by accident, she was reacting to questions in a press conference in a context still influenced by the recent elections. A question was raised about Lula's support for Tehran regarding alleged human rights violations. Lula made a demeaning allusion to an Iranian woman sentenced to death by stoning. This reference negatively affected Lula's reputation. Dilma then reacted to the issue by stating emphatically that such an execution would have been a case of barbaric treatment of women.

Despite the limited scope of the statement, focused on gender and extreme cruelty and not on human rights at large, suffice it to say that the intended evidence of a new course in foreign relations was duly registered by the press. Later, freshly tenured, Dilma returned to the subject, this time indirectly, suggesting that her priority in foreign policy would be human rights. Despite the lack of elaboration on the scope of such prioritization, the message was duly noted.

Her following steps in this regard were, in fact, toward distancing herself from any international activism in defense of human rights. Dilma's government sided with conspicuous abusers of human rights at the UN Council of Human Rights, declined to support humanitarian interventions in Libya or Syria, and abstained from even mentioning the protection of human rights in her visits to fellow developing countries. It is all about a meticulous continuity of the emphasis the PT places on South-South cooperation.

Considering similarities and differences, we might suggest that there is a clear option for continuity, but in a low key, which is more akin to her distaste for performing on the global stage or befriending world leaders. When it comes to Brazilian foreign policy after Lula, it is about continuity without panache. The question remains whether the continuity of Lula's foreign policy is possible without Lula, or if without his charisma and his passion for the stage something else should be added to his successor's foreign policy for it to be successful. No such development ever showed up to give real relevance to international relations in Dilma's personal agenda, in order to make it less erratic and mediocre.

Now, let us turn to how China's "strategic partnership" with Brazil affects the latter's relationship with the U.S.

Presently, the core interests and goals of the U.S. are arguably overdetermined by two independent but interconnected challenges: the first one is the role of the U.S. in global governance; the other is China's rise. Compared to the Cold War period, the U.S.'s role as prime guarantor of global governance involves bigger and growing costs, because its challenges are more complex. Besides, the U.S. is involved in a severe crisis of external credibility deriving both from its role in triggering the global financial crisis and its recent record of disastrous military interventions, which in turn negatively affect the country's stock of soft power, the overall result being a perception of relative decline.

China's rise poses an additional systemic challenge to the U.S.'s global leadership. Chinese global performance has proved bolder than expected in several dimensions—be it in the economic and financial field, in expanding its military clout, or even in terms of territorial claims. More importantly, China's assertiveness has been directed to all continents, causing the U.S.'s trade and investment relevance and, to some extent, its political and military leadership to be challenged.

Among U.S. strategic priorities in this new framework of international power, the search for a new domestic rebalancing of the economy and internal political decision-making is widely considered paramount. This rebalancing is particularly vital as it regards the American political system's inter-institutional relations, pointed out by many authors as a condition sine qua non for the country to keep on performing its global leadership. To achieve this rebalancing, it is imperative for the U.S. to recover its relevance (its primacy, if possible) in global trade and investment, which has been worn down by China's global progress.

Obama's initiatives to revitalize the APEC, together with relaunching trade and investment talks with the E.U. and the big boost given to the Trans-Pacific Partnership seem to converge in this direction. Concerning the TPP talks, we should note that the Obama administration tried to attract key countries in Latin America—Mexico, Peru, Colombia, Chile, and also Paraguay and Uruguay—as part of its global strategy.

Let us turn to the direct impact of China's rise on Brazil-U.S. bilateral relations. The case of Brazil is emblematic because, since 2009, China has become the country's principal trade partner. Besides, Brazil's alignment with China in the UN Security Council, as well as in other UN forums and agencies, is currently more relevant than with the U.S. or other permanent members of the Security Council. Moreover, the opportunities for a South-South cooperation between Brazil and China are manifold. The potential for such cooperation to affect, or to be affected by, U.S. interests in Brazil is significant.

When one evaluates possible areas of synergy in Brazilian bilateral relations with the two countries, some considerations appear relevant. First, let us take into account that the current trend in Brazil's foreign policy—supported by a relevant portion of international relations literature—tends to prognosticate not only the irresistible rise of China, but also the sharp decline of the U.S. Therefore, besides the natural inclination of the dominant current in the Brazilian foreign policy to align with its counterparts in South-South cooperation, sheer pragmatism would prevail in favor of a timely alignment with China.

Still, any final prognostic about the outcome of the current shift in the system of international power should be reserved. As the post–Cold War transition went through different phases, and is still far from its conclusion, any hasty exclusive alignment with one of the superpowers would be detrimental to Brazilian relations with its most traditional partners.

Secondly, can Brazil, instead of taking sides, contribute to global governance? Is it in the country's reach to positively cooperate with both the U.S. and China to concur on a peaceful transition of the international system of power?

It is in Brazil's core interests to avoid a tumultuous world order. Brazil can only achieve such a goal by avoiding an exclusive alignment with

China or the U.S. Choosing this course would require trying to reduce rivalries, avoiding taking sides in situations of conflict, and advancing in every possible arena a positive agenda.

In a number of global stages, the Brazilian contribution is becoming more relevant. In the global quest for sound global financial governance, Brazilian opportunities to participate are increasing. In this respect, Brazil should contribute more to mitigating conflicts than to spurring tensions, as it often does.

A more specific role derives from Brazil's unique ability to contribute to regional governance in Latin America. In the Western Hemisphere agenda there is a potential for conflict based in the tendency toward a dichotomous perception of the region that opposes the strategic interests of the U.S. to the rest of the region. Brazil has a clear national interest in preserving the political and economic convergence in South America. In this sense, the country might be able to gather soft power resources to act in two directions.

First, South America's political and economic stability depends in part on reversing centrifugal trends, notably in Mercosur and UNASUR, and avoiding unnecessary conflicts, especially those opposing the Bolivarian countries to Chile, Peru, Colombia, Mexico, and even Paraguay and Uruguay. A subsequent step would consist in adopting a common positive agenda, for instance in clean energy and infrastructure. Even if a common agenda is difficult to achieve, a reduction in the conflictive tendency in the region is in the best interest of Brazil, the U.S., and China.

For the same purpose of providing a common positive agenda with the U.S. and China, Brazil would have to restore the relevant role it played in international trade negotiations, since the Tokyo Round. For that purpose, it is imperative for the country to reconsider the government's current trade agenda.

Since President Lula took the decision to abort the FTAA talks, the Brazilian government bet all of its chips on the WTO Doha Round, to the detriment of Mercosur and other relevant trade negotiations. The Brazilian government's interest in keeping the Doha Round alive is reasonable, but giving it such an exclusive importance is not in the country's best interest since all relevant WTO stakeholders are currently prioritizing "minilateral" or regional negotiations.

Denying exclusivity to Doha would open the doors to a reappraisal of the most important negotiations currently available, involving Brazil's principal trade partners—the U.S., E.U., and China. In this sense, President Dilma's government proposed UNASUR apply for observer status at the Pacific Alliance, but Venezuela's Maduro scraped the proposal off the UNASUR meeting communiqué.

In a similar vein, Dilma's minister in charge of foreign trade, a former president of the Brazilian Industrial National Association (CNI), stated his interest in closely following the TPP's developments. But a formal observer status in the Trans-Pacific Partnership and the Regional Comprehensive Economic Partnership (RCEP) might be more effective. The Transatlantic Trade and Investment Partnership should be closely followed by Brazilian diplomats, as it could hugely impact the governance of international trade and profoundly affect the Latin American economy in case it ever makes progress.

Briefly, Brazil can play a more relevant regional role in facilitating convergence in the Western Hemisphere, avoiding centrifugal trends. From a global point of view, Brazil could contribute to mitigating the rivalry between the U.S. and China and concurring in a peaceful global transition resulting from a mutual accommodation between its most vital international partners, the U.S. and China.

Reengaging Latin America in the Aftermath of China's Foray

The first matters to be considered, in assessing the impact of China's presence in Latin America, are the lessons of the FTAA (Free Trade Area of the Americas), the failed Clinton initiative designed to integrate the Americas economically and politically. During the very first discussions of FTAA, it transpired that the only way to achieve a general agreement was to build upon negative rather than positive preferences.

Argentina was willing to adhere but would not do it without Brazil, while Brazil was not eager, but would do it to restrain Argentina's further alignment with the U.S. Mexico intended to be the only mediator of Latin America's integration with the North Atlantic Free Trade Agreement (NAFTA) and resented Brazil's growing influence in its own Latin American backyard. Chile had already stepped into the APEC and into the E.U. on its own. The FTAA was just another option to share with all the other Latin American countries. Similar obstacles were raised by more or less all the remaining countries. Those less industrialized would accept any clauses concerning investments, intellectual properties, and other trade-related conditions in order to escape any tariff cuts, while those willing to protect their domestic markets for goods and services would do the opposite.

You cannot have it both ways; you engage a large number of partners in minimalist terms or you raise the bar and go for a deeper commitment with fewer partners. When it sliced the FTAA into a number of differentiated regional FTAs with Latin American countries the U.S. succeeded significantly. A similar regional arrangement was signed with Mercosur (the 4+1 agreement), but both sides have never taken it seriously.

Brazil, for instance, protracted the opening of negotiations for almost eight years of the Cardoso administration, because the domestic stakeholders were divided. When it finally decided to start it, a pro-FTAA consensus had been achieved among the relevant bureaucracies, agribusiness, and a significant part of the industrial sector. The agreement was to be signed under Cardoso or be shelved definitely, for Cardoso's succession was unpredictable, and no one expected that, if elected, Lula would support it. But the U.S. negotiators lacked the sense of urgency to speed up the process.

Therefore, besides differentiating between different Latin American countries or groups of countries, one must differentiate long- from short-term goals. It is also imperative to differentiate governmental from non-governmental partners. With the exception of the PT, the leftist unions, and some minor leftist parties, the great majority of the Brazilian elite, despite showing an anti-American façade, also believes in its Western identity and would never support a one-party system. It would also be advisable to engage the government and some relevant bureaucracies differently, such as Itamaraty and the Treasury, which enjoy a relevant margin of autonomy.

Finally, there are two lessons from China's performance in Latin America. China has always directed its Latin American policy according to the three criteria: adherence to the One China policy; availability of strategic resources; no political strings attached.[35] In his tour of South America in May 2015, Prime Minister Li Keqiang reaped all but one (Argentina) of the South American crown jewels: Brazil, Chile, Colombia, and Peru. It is remarkable that the three South American members of the Pacific Alliance have been awarded a high-level visit, as they are the most pro-American countries in the region.

Applied to Brazil-China relations, this example might suggest that Brazil should be differentiated from other BRICS and emerging economies, as for instance in its request to have increased influence in the international financial agencies. Despite opposition by the Senate, the White House retains a stock of symbolic tokens to award the Brazilian government. In a certain sense, Brazil's position in the subcontinent, though not strictly comparable, is similar to that of India in South Asia.

Certainly, from the U.S. perspective, the game currently played by China and Brazil in Latin America is not over.

President Dilma's Impeachment

It came as a surprise that President Dilma was ostensibly uneasy on the very night of her reelection for a second term in October 2014. During the transitional period before her inauguration in January 2015, she had to face a number of obstacles with waning political and economic resources.

The core of her governmental coalition disagreed over the need to acknowledge the failure of her economic policy, which had driven the country to its biggest depression since 1930. Dilma was under pressure to appoint a cabinet committed to a fiscal rebalance with which she was in sharp disagreement, while at the same time her own party was divided, former President Lula remained ambivalent, and people had been protesting all over the country in huge numbers for the previous two years.

With rising expenses and falling revenues, the executive had been deprived of resources to hold together its loose coalition, which was based on the exchange of favors and provided no programmatic convergence. Dilma abandoned her ambition to form her own government, distancing herself from Lula and the PT, as well as from the PMDB (Brazilian Democratic Movement Party), her government's biggest and closest ally.

Any attempt at adopting sound fiscal legislation was blocked by the joint opposition of Dilma herself, the Workers' Party, and Lula, not to mention the general resistance to any austerity policies from her over-extended coalition. The presidency became unable to take any initiative but to defend its own survival, the inflation rate continued to run around double digits, unemployment doubled to 10%, and GDP growth was negative (-3% in 2015).

The combined effects of the government's paralysis, investigations into rampant corruption in the government, and evidence of tampering with the federal budget and public accounts led the protesters—estimated at six to nine million nationwide—to focus on Dilma, whose impeachment was initiated in the Chamber of Deputies and ultimately confirmed by the necessary two-thirds of the Senate. As of June 2016, Dilma was under investigation pending trial by the Senate by early August.[36]

NOTES

1 Guilhon-Albuquerque, "From Dependency to Globalization"; Guilhon-Albuquerque, "A Política Externa."
2 "PT" is the Portuguese initialism for Brazil's Workers' Party.
3 The Brazilian Ministry of Foreign Relations is known as Itamaraty after its former headquarters in Rio de Janeiro, the Itamaraty Palace.
4 "Ativa e altiva" roughly translates as "active and with head held high."
5 On the growing influence of the PT and the PT-leaning leadership of Itamaraty on Brazil's foreign policy, see Barbosa, *O Dissenso de Washington*.
6 Barbosa, *O Dissenso de Washington*; Lampreia, *Os Ventos do Mundo*; Amorim, *Teerã, Ramalá e Doha*.
7 "Cancún's Charming Outcome," *Economist*, 18 September 2003. Amorim named his biography *Teerã, Ramalá e Doha* (Tehran, Ramallah, and Doha) after his most salient endeavors, including the failed Doha negotiations, apparently reckoned as a victory.
8 Lampreia, *A Aposta de Teerã*.
9 As of June 2015, Brazil was not shown in the official listo g signatories.
10 Guilhon-Albuquerque,. 2005. "A Percepção da Política Externa" and "As Relações Brasil–Estados Unidos."
11 See Viktor Litovkin, "Licitação de caças para o Brasil se arrasta, mas Rússia insiste," *Gazeta Russa*, 28 February, 2011, www.gazetarussa.com.br.
12 Barbosa, *O Dissenso de Washington*.
13 See Litovkin, "Licitação de caças."
14 The whole package involved €12.5 billion: nuclear submarines (€ 6.7 billion); helicopters (€1.8 billion) and 4.0 billion Euro for the aircraft.
15 With the benefit of hindsight, taking into account the disclosures of fraud involving government procurements and contractors during the Lula and Rousseff administrations, one cannot rule out the hypothesis that the negotiations stalled because some kind of side gains were not agreed upon. Again, in January 2016, Lula was cited in a federal investigation as having supposedly favored the Swedish deal.

16 Litovkin, "Licitação de caças," citing the Russian news agency ARMS-TASS.

17 Leaks about the NSA spying on President Dilma, which had been in possession of an American journalist living in Brazil, Glenn Greenwald, since June, were published in Brazil on 1 September 2013, just one month before her planned state visit to the U.S., on 23 October 23. After trying unsuccefully that Presidente Obama apologized, President Rousseff canceled her visit on September 17 and chose the Swedish aircraft in December.

18 "F-X2: entra em vigor o acordo de transferência de tecnologia," *Poder Aéreo*, 10 September 2015, www.aereo.jor.br.

19 One example of such failed moves was the Operação Pan-Americana (Pan-American Operation), a huge international investment program to boost the industrial take of Latin American economies. For the official proposal at the 13th and 14th UN General Assemblies, see Seixas Corrêa, *Brazil in the United Nations*.

20 Guilhon-Albuquerque, "From Dependency to Globalization."

21 It is widely held that the formerly harassed Chinese diplomats were assigned to receive the Brazilian mission that came to Beijing, ten years later, to implement the new diplomatic relations between the two countries.

22 The following analysis of China's place in Brazil's international relations is based on research soon to be published as a part of a book in development.

23 Guilhon-Albuquerque, *Sessenta Anos*.

24 According to a personal interview with Brazilian diplomats, the issue was first addressed with Zhu during the flight from Beijing to Brasília. See also Oliveira, "La Asociación Estratégica."

25 Ministry of Foreign Affairs of Brazil, Business Intelligence Division (DLC), "China: Foreign Trade," 2015, www.investexportbrasil.gov.br.

26 In a press conference in 1999, Lula boasted of planning to meet President Hu nine times in different international forums that year.

27 For a brief analysis of the Brazilian literature on Brazil-China strategic partnership, see Guilhon-Albuquerque, "Business with China."

28 Oswaldo Biato Junior, *A Parceria Estratégica Sino-Brasileira. Origens, Evolução e Perspectivas (1993–2006)*. Brasília: Fundação Alexandre de Gusmão, 2010. www.funag.gov.br.

29 José Augusto Guilhon-Albuquerque and Luis Afonso Fernandes Lima, "Chinese Economic Presence in Brazil: A Relationship Still Based on Bilateral Commerce," paper submitted to *Asian Perspective*.

30 This survey is described in Guilhon-Albuquerque, "Business with China."

31 Guilhon-Albuquerque, G.A. "Brazil, China, U.S.: A Triangular Relation?," *Revista Brasileira de Política Internacional* 57 (2014): 108–120.

32 "Eleita recusa convite para ir aos EUA" [(President-)elect rebuffs invitation to visit U.S.], *Folha de São Paulo*, 26 November 2011.

33 Clóvis Rossi, "Com que foto eu vou?" [Which photo opportunity am I to be going to?], *Folha de São Paulo*, 11/20/2010. The title is a paraphrase of a traditional song,

very popular during Carnival in Rio de Janeiro: "What am I to be dressing to go to the ball you invited me to?"

34 "Davos reúne elite política e econômica mundial (menos o Brasil)" [Davos brings together the world elite (except Brazil], *BBC-Brazil*, 23 January 2013, www.bbc .com; see also "Dilma cancela apresentação no Fórum Econômico da América Latina" [Dilma cancels her presentation at the Latin American Economic Forum], *Agência Estado*, 23 April 2011, www.economia.estadao.com.br.

35 Xu, "Evolución de la Política China."

36 Editor's note: On August 31, 2016, Dilma Rousseff was formally removed from office.

BIBLIOGRAPHY

Amorim, Celso. *Teerã, Ramalá e Doha. Memórias de uma Política Externa Ativa e Altiva* [Tehran, Ramalah, Doha. Memoirs of an active and elevated foreign policy]. São Paulo: Benvirá, 2015.

Barbosa, Rubens. *O Dissenso de Washington* [The Washington dissent]. São Paulo: Saraiva, 2010.

Guilhon-Albuquerque, José Augusto. "From Dependency to Globalization: Brazilian Foreign Policy in the Cold War and Post-Cold War," in Frank O. Mora and Jeanne A. K. Hey (eds.), *Latin American and Caribbean Foreign Policy*. New York: Rowman & Littlefield, 2003.

Guilhon-Albuquerque, José Augusto. "A Percepção da Política Externa dos EUA e do Brasil por Diplomatas Brasileiros" [Brazilian diplomats' perceptions of Brazilian and U.S. foreign policies] and "As Relações Brasil–Estados Unidos na Percepção dos Militares" [Brazilian military perceptions of Brazil-U.S. relations], in Henrique A. Oliveira and José Augusto Guilhon-Albuquerque (eds.), *A Política Externa Brasileira na Percepção de seus Protagonistas*. Rio de Janeiro: Lumen Juris, 2005.

Guilhon-Albuquerque, José Augusto. "A Política Externa do governo Fernando Henrique" [Brazilian foreign policy under Cardoso], in José Augusto Guilhon-Albuquerque, Ricardo Seitenfus, and Sergio Henrique Nabuco de Castro (eds.), *Sessenta Anos de Política Externa Brasileira (1930–1990) I: Crescimento, Moderniza-ção e Política Externa* [Sixty years of Brazilian foreign policy (1930–1990) I: growth, modernization and foreign policy], 2nd ed. Rio de Janeiro: Lumen Juris, 2007.

Guilhon-Albuquerque, José Augusto. "Business with China: The Three Elements of Brazil's Strategic Relationship with China," in José Augusto Guilhon-Albuquerque and Leila da Costa Ferreira (eds), *China and Brazil: Challenges and Opportunities*. São Paulo: Annablume, 2013.

Guilhon-Albuquerque, José Augusto, Ricardo Seitenfus, and Sergio Henrique Nabuco de Castro (eds.). *Sessenta Anos de Política Externa Brasileira (1930–1990) I: Cres-cimento, Modernização e Política Externa* [Sixty years of Brazilian foreign policy (1930–1990) I: growth, modernization and foreign policy], 2nd ed. Rio de Janeiro: Lumen Juris, 2007.

Lampreia, Luiz F. *Os Ventos do Mundo* [Wordly winds]. Rio de Janeiro: Objetiva, 2010.

Lampreia, Luiz F. *A Aposta de Teerã: O Acordo entre o Brasil, Irã e Turquia* [The Teheran bid: the Brazil-Iran-Turkey agreement]. Rio de Janeiro: Objetiva, 2014.

Oliveira, Henrique A. "La Asociación Estratégica entre Brasil y China," in Jorge Ig. Matinez Cortés, *América Latina y El Caribe-China. Relaciones Políticas y Internacionales* [The strategic partnership between Brazil and China]. Ciudad de México: UDUAL/UNAM, 2014.

Seixas Corrêa, Luís F. (ed.) *Brazil in the United Nations (1946–2011)*. Brasília: Fundação Alexandre de Gusmão, 2013.

Xu, Shicheng. "Evolución de la Política China hacia América Latina" [Evolution of China's policy toward Latin America]. Keynote speech, Seminar on Latin America and Caribbean-China Relations, Universidad Nacional de México, Mexico City, 2012.

8

Argentina, the US, and China

A New Triangle in the Making?

JOSÉ LUIS MACHINEA AND LUCIO CASTRO

1. Introduction

This chapter examines the relationship between Argentina, the United States, and the People's Republic of China (PRC) in the last decade. It also puts forward some tentative ideas about the prospects of the PRC-US nexus from an Argentine perspective.

In the last decade, the PRC has turned out to be a strategic partner for Argentina. The PRC is the second-largest destination for Argentine exports and the second main source of imports. In Latin America and the Caribbean (LAC), only Venezuela and Brazil received more financial assistance from the PRC than Argentina. In 2014 and 2015, the country signed 33 comprehensive agreements with the PRC, granting preferential access to strategic sectors of its economy to Chinese companies. The PRC also became a vital source of financing for Argentina's depleted international reserves.

Contrastingly, the economic links between Argentina and the US have significantly waned in the 2000s. Between 2000 and 2014, the US share of Argentina's total trade declined by around 40%. On the financial side, Argentina's relative isolation from the global capital markets and its unfriendly policies toward foreign investment diminished the relative importance of US capital flows in the Argentine economy.

The remainder of this chapter is organized in five sections. The second section analyzes the macroeconomic performance of Argentina between 2003 and 2015 and examines some of the most relevant economic policy measures carried out by the Argentine governments over this period. The third section examines the recent history of Argentina's relations with the PRC, with particular attention to the agreements signed under the umbrella of the Strategic Partnership Treaty of 2014. The fourth section explores the trade and financial links of Argentina with the US and the PRC. The fifth section draws some parallels between Argentina's relationship with the PRC in the 2000s and the country's alliance with the United Kingdom at the outset of the 20th century. The final section concludes by discussing some tentative ideas on the likely future of the Argentina-China-US nexus, and its potential impacts on the long-term development perspectives of the Argentine economy.

2. A Glimpse into Argentina's Economy and Economic Policies at the Outset of the 21st Century

In the late 1990s and in the first decade of this century, Argentina experienced the worst economic crisis in its history. From 1998 to 2002, real gross domestic product (GDP) shrank by 18%. In the 15 days following President Fernando De la Rua's resignation on December 20, 2002, there were four governments in place and Argentina defaulted on its external debt and devaluated its currency, leading to the abandonment of the currency convertibility.

The swift recovery experienced by the Argentine economy from 2003 onward was largely driven by historically high terms of trade, a competitive real exchange rate, and a 65% relief of the external debt carried out in 2005 and 2010 (Figure 8.1).

The accelerated pace of the Argentine economy led to a rapid reduction in the unemployment rate and rising real wages. Investment also recovered promptly, reaching a high of 24% of GDP in 2008, as well as exports whose volume that year was 34% higher than in 2000. Albeit the international "Great Recession" cut short the breathtaking economic recovery in 2009—GDP contracted by 2.6%—Argentina promptly bounced back in 2010–2011 (Figure 8.1).

Abundant demand and an appreciated exchange rate served the purposes of the political alliance of the government with the trade unions and the middle class, giving rise to a steady increase in real wages up to 2011. Yet, the resulting rise in consumption proved incapable of sustaining the pace of economic growth. In 2011–2014, GDP per capita decreased by 2%, and there was a clear bottleneck in the external sector from

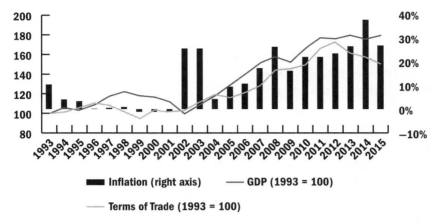

Figure 8.1. Argentina's Macroeconomic Indicators: Inflation Rate, GDP, and Terms of Trade (1993–2015)
Percent and Index 1993=100
Source: Based on Instituto Nacional de Estadísticas y Censos (2015), Universidad de Buenos Aires, Facultad de Ciencias Economicas (2015), and private estimates. Official statistics about the inflation rate and the GDP growth rate are notoriously unreliable from 2007 onward.

2011 onward. The inflation rate hovered around 38% in 2014, although it declined to around 27% in 2015, mainly as a result of a continuous appreciation of the exchange rate and the lack of adjustment of public utilities' tariffs.

In order to address these problems, the Argentine government took a wrong turn as it decided to manipulate the official inflation statistics and push forward extremely lax fiscal and monetary policies in an overheated economy. Public expenditure by the national government increased dramatically and it would have reached a historical peak of 41% of GDP in 2015, if these policies had continued. This would have led to a fiscal deficit of 6% of GDP, in spite of the extraordinary increase in tax revenues experienced in the previous decade (IMF 2015).

In turn, the fiscal unbalance is largely explained by a massive surge in subsidies—due in turn to tariff repression in the public transport and energy sectors—that amounted to 5% of GDP in 2014, and by a large jump in non-contributory pensions (Castro and Agosto 2014; Castro, Szenkman, and Lottito 2015). Regarding the external sector bottleneck, the government purportedly delayed the exchange rate adjustment and enacted restrictions on the foreign exchange market, in particular in connection to imports and international travel.

During the last decade, Argentina partly reversed the privatization and deregulation processes carried out in the 1990s. For instance, the Argentine government nationalized its flagship airline, Aerolineas Argentinas, the principal oil company, Yacimientos Petroleros Fiscales (YPF), some provincial public utilities' companies, and the private pension funds.

Perhaps more importantly, the government decided to freeze public utilities' tariffs, leading to sharp reduction in private investment in infrastructure (Castro, Szenkman, and Lotitto 2015). For instance, Argentina was of the main destinations for foreign direct investment amid developing countries in the 1990s, whereas the country ranked sixth in LAC in the last decade, behind Brazil, Mexico, Chile, Colombia, and Peru (ECLAC 2015a).

Partly as a result of the distortive policies adopted by Argentina, productivity growth was dismal in the 2000s. Total factor productivity (TFP) increased only by 0.3% per year on average between 2003 and 2014, around half of the annual TFP growth rate observed in the 1990s.[1] Labor productivity exhibited a similarly dire performance, growing at a slower rate than other Latin American countries such as Peru, Chile, Costa Rica, Ecuador, Colombia, and Mexico (Machinea 2015).

Amid these increasingly serious macroeconomic unbalances, an unexpected and peculiar ruling by a New York court in mid-2014 ordered Argentina to pay the face value of its debt to bondholders that did not accept the restructuring programs carried out in 2005 and 2010. While these "holdouts" amounted to only 7% of the bondholders of Argentina's external debt, the ruling seriously limited the country's capability to tap the global financial markets. For instance, in April 2015 Argentina issued a ten-year bond for US$1.5 billion at a 9% annual rate, twice as high as that paid by other countries in LAC by similar securities. By the end of September 2015, the discount rate on that bond reached 10%.

By mid-December 2015, the disposable international reserves of the BCRA amounted to less than US$10 billion or 2% of GDP, the lowest level in Latin America. It must be noted this estimate does not consider the US$11 billion currency swap with the People's Bank of China (PBOC) due to liquidity restriction on its use.[2]

Summing up, by the end of 2015, Argentina showed high levels of inflation, a large fiscal deficit, and a sharp distortion in relative prices, particularly in public utilities' tariffs and the exchange rate. Despite import controls, the current account deficit would amount to 2.5% of GDP. It is also estimated that by the end of 2015 delayed import and foreign companies' utilities and dividends payments would amount to approximately US$13 billion.

This bleak outlook contrasts with a public net debt—around 75% external—that would total around 30% of GDP (IMF 2015). The relatively low levels of external debt, both public and private, might allow adjusting the exchange rate without much burden on the private sector and the government's balance sheet. The main challenge for the new administration would arguably be to soften up the potential inflationary effects of adjustment of public utility tariffs and the exchange rate while dealing with a less benign international context. It is also essential to solve the problem of defaulted debt in order to access international financial markets. This will ease the necessary adjustment of public accounts and facilitate the financing of investment projects both in the private and public sectors.

In Box 8.1, the first economic measures adopted by the Macri administration are discussed and there are some additional comments on the evolution of inflation, wages, and the exchange rate. In Box 8.2, the main characteristics of the final agreement with creditors are analyzed.

Box 8.1. The First Economic Measures

After winning the November 22, 2015, runoff vote by a margin of 2.5 points, Mauricio Macri became president of Argentina on December 10. His first days in office were devoted to meeting with all the candidates he competed against in the election and the provincial governors, an attitude in sharp contrast with that of former president Cristina Kirchner, who met with neither the opposition nor the governors.

The initial economic measures are in line with what was promised in the election campaign by President Macri. The government announced that foreign exchange restrictions were lifted; that is to say, there will be a free exchange rate, although the Central Bank might intervene if it deems it necessary. This implies, as in many countries, a dirty float of the exchange rate. In order to generate a positive change in expectations and allow the Central Bank to have enough resources to intervene in the market should it be necessary, the minister of finance in his first press conference announced that the government was negotiating dollar inflows through different modalities. The figure might be around US$20 billion and it would be provided by foreign banks, grain exporters, other companies, and the use of part of the existing swap with China.* These resources would flow in over the following weeks.

The removal of restrictions on demand, which have been in place since 2011, implies that individuals or companies can freely access the exchange market. The previous import permits are reduced sharply. The remaining non-automatic import licenses will be transparent and will be vested in around 10% of the Argentine tariff lines. Likewise, restrictions on capital inflows that have prevailed over the past decade are removed.

Additionally, taxes on exports have been eliminated, with the sole exception, for fiscal reasons, of soybean exports, where the tax was reduced to 30% from 35%. The fiscal cost of these measures is around 0.5% of GDP.

Regarding the fiscal deficit, no announcements were made, except for an increase in the tariffs of public services, particularly those of electricity and gas. However, the extent of the increase, which will take into account users' economic situation, has not been specified. While it is reasonable not to make a sizeable fiscal adjustment, the government should announce how it expects to tackle the budget deficit in the coming years, considering that the current deficit, including the measures announced so far, is close to 7% of GDP.

In the first week of January 2016, the dollar on the foreign exchange market traded around 14 pesos, implying a devaluation of around 45% on the commercial market. This devaluation has been less than expected by the market, which means good news for the government, although the short time elapsed did not allow for extrapolation over the subsequent weeks.

As a matter of fact, the following months were more turbulent and the exchange rate reached a value of 16 pesos in late February. That value decreased as a result of the strong intervention of the Central Bank, which represented an increase of six points in the short-term interest rate and the sale of hundreds of millions of dollars. The sharp rise in the exchange rate in a country with a long history of inflation generated an impact on inflationary expectations and resulted in an additional effect on prices. In April and early May the trend changed due to measures taken by the monetary authority and because, seasonally, there was an important settlement of agricultural exports. At that time the concern was to avoid an excessive appreciation of the peso, which generated an intervention by the Central Bank in which it bought hundreds of million dollars in the market and very gradually reduced interest rates. It is important to mention that in recent months there was a change in the Central Bank's policy from a position of little or no market intervention to a more active stance as of March 2016.

The adjustment of the exchange rate, along with significant increases in public tariffs, especially in electricity (about 300%) and gas (around 200%) and 100% in transportation, generated a sharp increase in prices.** Inflation in the five months between December 2015 and April 2016 averaged 4.4% per month. One of the consequences of these increases was that the annual wage adjustment, expected to be less than 30%, ended up being around 35% for most sectors. It is likely that this trend will change in the second half of the year, during which it was announced that there will be no increase in tariffs for public services. Even in the most optimistic scenario of a monthly inflation rate slightly below 2% in the second half of the year, annual inflation would be around 38–40%. Therefore, as a result of the necessary correction of the distortion of relative prices and some poor economic decisions, the reduction of inflation will be slower than originally anticipated.

* The existing swap between central banks of Argentina and China is discussed in Section 4.

** As pointed out in the text, this increase has been lower than the one needed to eliminate subsidies.

Box 8.2. The Agreement with the Creditors

In 2012 half of the 7% of the creditors who did not enter the debt restructuring of 2005 and 2010 won a judgment a New York court in their favor to collect 100% of the value of their claims, plus interest and penalty payments. The ruling became final in 2014. The Argentine government decided not to accept the ruling and the American judge prevented Argentina from almost all access to international financial markets. In 2016 the new Argentine government decided to comply with the ruling. While the defaulted debt was equivalent to 0.9% of GDP, the ruling ended up generating a debt of 2.2% of GDP. The agreement was supported by a large majority of the Argentine Congress in late March.

The government agreed to a cash payment for 63% of the original debt in default that totaled US$6 billion, or about US$3.8 billion. Considering the interest and penalties, the payment made on April 22 was US$9.3 billion, accounting for an interest rate of 6.7% per annum, compounded over the 14 years of the default. About US$2.2 billion in defaulted debt is still unresolved. The Argentine government stated that much of that debt was already prescribed, but the New York court counterstated that for debt issued under its jurisdiction creditors could sue the Argentine state to claim their rights. The government hopes that when agreement with all the creditors is reached, the amount will represent US$10.5 billion. The average amount pardoned varied from 20% to 40%, depending upon the status of the creditors at the time of settlement.

The payment returns to Argentina its access to the international financial markets and puts an end to the 2001 default, now with 98% of the debt with private holders already renegotiated. So long as future rulings are complied with, this status will not be lost. For its payment, the government placed US$16.5 billion of foreign debt at an average interest rate of 7.14% for periods ranging from 3 to 30 years. The difference between this amount and the payment to creditors will be used to finance the large fiscal deficit. The government said it has no intention of issuing debt in foreign currency in international markets in 2017. The shortfall of around US$2 billion to implement the financial program is an amount that in this context could be easily achieved in the domestic market.

3. A Brief History of Argentina's Relationship with China in the 2000s

Although Argentina signed some broad cooperation agreements with the PRC in the 1990s, the Argentine-Chinese economic relationship only really flourished in the first decade of the 21st century. In 2004, during Nestor Kirchner's presidency, Argentina signed several agreements on different subjects, including railways, tourism, and space cooperation. Later that year, with the visit of China's president Hu Jintao to Argentina, a special Treaty of Strategic Partnership was signed that set forth two crucial conditions: (a) Argentina recognized the PRC as a "market economy," and (b) the PRC committed to boost imports from Argentina so that Argentine exports would amount to US$4 billion over a five-year period. In addition, Chinese businessmen accompanying the then Chinese president on an official visit to Argentina announced investments of US$20 billon over the next 20 years (Oviedo 2015; Paz 2014).

While those investment announcements never materialized, the economic ties between Argentina and the PRC henceforth blossomed, driven by increased investment and further cooperation agreements. In 2009, Argentina's Central Bank (BCRA, per its Spanish acronym) negotiated with the People's Bank of China (PBOC) a currency swap of US$10.2 billion with a three-year maturity. In 2010, the China National Offshore Oil Corporation (CNOOC) acquired 50% of one of the top local energy companies, Bridas Energy, for US$3.1 billion; and Sinopec purchased Occidental Petroleum for US$2.45 billion. The Industrial and Commercial Bank of China (ICBC), in turn, acquired one of the largest local financial institutions, the Standard Bank (Sica 2015).

In 2014, Argentina signed an international treaty establishing a "comprehensive strategic partnership" with the PRC.[3] Under this umbrella, 33 agreements were signed between the two countries. While the details of some of the commercial clauses remain unknown, the agreements constitute a tipping point in the Chinese-Argentine relationship.

The comprehensive partnership has three main objectives: putting trade on a more balanced path, diversifying Argentina's exports, and streamlining the cooperation in infrastructure. Additionally, a Joint Action Plan was signed that includes a list of goals to be met in 2014–2018 in various fields, setting forth the cooperation parameters between the parties. One of the most important agreements is the Framework of Cooperation on Economic and Investment Matters, promptly approved by the Argentine Congress in March 2015. On the basis of the treaty, two specific agreements took place: one on industrial investments and another for infrastructure. In each of them, strategic sectors were established and a five-year plan to exchange priority projects was defined.

The most outstanding agreements are those in which Argentina grants preferential access to public contracts in some strategic sectors to Chinese firms without the need for open and competitive bids in exchange for concessional financing. In particular, they allow for the construction of two hydroelectric dams in the south of Argentina. The financing will mostly come from two Chinese banks. Besides, Chinese firms will build two nuclear plants with soft financing from the PRC. The cost of the dams will total roughly US$5 billion (of which US$450 million was already disbursed in 2015) and the two nuclear plants will amount to around US$9 billion (Sica 2015). While national companies could in principle participate in the construction of the two hydroelectric dams, the agreement allows the Chinese companies to import inputs and capital goods from the PRC without limits, which has given rise to negative reactions from the local business community and opposition political parties. The second nuclear station might be built with Chinese technology, and consequently, the participation of Argentina's relatively developed industrial sector is likely to be limited. In spite of Argentina's large and increasing trade deficit with the PRC in the last seven years, the agreement does not grant preferential access to the Chinese market for Argentine exporters (Carciofi 2015; Sica 2015).

Another agreement that triggered discussions and different interpretations was that of a space center in the southern Argentine province of Neuquén funded by a PRC governmental agency under the General Armaments Department (GAD) of China's People's Liberation Army. The antecedent of this matter is the cooperation agreement signed in 2012 between the China Satellite Launch and Tracking Control General Agency and the National Commission of Space Activities (CONAE). In this agreement, it was set forth that the center would encompass "ground tracking command and data acquisition facilities, including a deep space antenna." The center's main benefit for Argentina is the effective use of 10% of the deep space antenna time per year. The three-party agreement sets forth that Neuquén will transfer 200 hectares on loan for a period of 50 years. In 2013, civil works got underway.

This is the first Chinese space center outside Chinese soil. The place was chosen on the basis of its strategic location and the absence of interference from other frequencies. Initially, it will look similar to the European Space Agency facility located in the province of Mendoza, whose antenna is also available to Argentine researchers 10% of the time. While this kind of facility can be used for different purposes, there are similar centers in other countries, such as those of the European Union in northern Chile (Ramon-Berjano, Malena, and Velloso 2015).

4. The Argentina-US-China Trade and Financial Nexus

This section presents a brief overview of the general trends and recent evolution of the trade flows between Argentina, the US, and the PRC. It then explores the main features of foreign direct investment (FDI) and financial flows from the latter two countries to Argentina.

4.1. Trade Flows with the PRC, the US, and the EU

Considering the European Union (EU) as a unified economic entity, the PRC is Argentina's third-largest trade partner, surpassed only by Brazil and the EU. In the last 20 years, the relative importance of the PRC as export destination and source of imports increased noticeably for Argentina vis-à-vis the US and the EU (Table 8.1). Other South American economies display a similar trade pattern (Dussel Peters 2015).

On the one hand, the share of the PRC in Argentina's total exports increased seven times from 1995 to 2014. The boost in exports to the PRC is largely explained by the skyrocketing Chinese demand for Argentina's main export products, like soybeans and soybean oil cakes. On the other hand, the PRC went from accounting for 3% of total imports in the mid-1990s to hovering around 15% over the last four years. In contrast, the relative importance of the EU as an export destination fell, from 18% in 2000 to around 14% in 2014. Similarly, the share of the US in Argentine total exports plummeted almost by half over the same period (Table 8.1).

Despite these recent changes, it must be noted that the US has historically been a relatively minor trade partner for Argentina. Stiff import

TABLE 8.1. Exports and Imports by Country in Selected Years (Percentage of Total)

	Exports by destination				Imports by origin			
	USA	China	EU	Brazil	USA	China	EU	Brazil
1995	8.4	1.4	21.8	26.2	20.8	3.0	30.5	20.7
2000	11.8	3.0	18.0	26.5	18.9	4.6	23.5	25.5
2005	11.1	7.9	17.3	15.7	13.9	7.8	17.0	35.5
2010	5.2	8.5	16.4	21.2	10.7	13.5	17.2	31.6
2011	5.1	7.4	16.9	20.7	10.4	14.3	15.7	29.5
2012	5.0	6.4	14.4	20.8	12.3	14.6	18.0	26.4
2013	5.6	7.5	13.0	21.4	11.0	15.4	18.4	26.0
2014	5.6	7.0	14.2	20.7	13.7	16.5	17.6	22.2

Source: Based on ECLAC (2015b)

tariffs and subsidies for US agriculture have severely restricted the participation of the highly competitive Argentine agricultural sector in the US market (Gerchunoff and Llach 2008).

In turn, while the extent of the penetration of Chinese imports in the Argentine market is similar to what has been observed in other LAC countries, a distinguishing feature of Argentina is the magnitude of its trade deficit with the PRC. While the deterioration of the trade balance with China is a widespread trend throughout the region, only Mexico exhibited in 2014 a larger commercial deficit with the Chinese economy (ECLAC 2015b).[4] Moreover, Argentina's exports to China reached their peak in 2008 and since then have decreased by 30%, whereas imports from China increased by 50% in the same period. Argentina's manufacturing producers also face fierce competition from PRC's exporters in other LAC countries, which have been important destinations for exports within the region.

While the PRC primarily exports industrial goods to LAC, a feature Argentina shares with other natural resources—abundant South American economies is the relatively low technological content of its exports to the Chinese market. Figure 8.2 classifies exports from Argentina to the PRC, Brazil, the US, and the EU by its technological intensity.

While roughly 80% of the Argentine exports to Brazil encompass manufactured products, raw materials, and natural resource–based manufactures—mostly soybean cake and soybean oil—account for

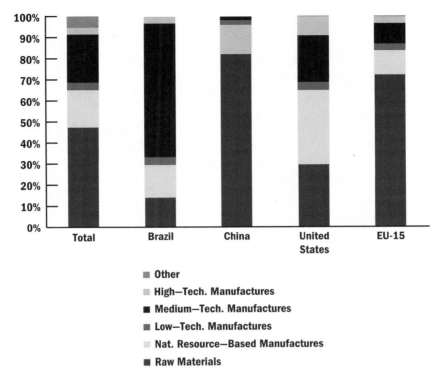

Figure 8.2. Exports from Argentina to the PRC by Technological Intensity, 2011–2013
Source: Based on ECLAC (2005c)

95.8% of the products exported to the PRC by Argentina. Moreover, just five products account for around 80% of Argentina's exports to the PRC, a similar pattern observed in other Latin American countries with the exception of Mexico (Dussel Peters 2015). In contrast, medium-technology-intensive products account for a significant share of Argentine exports to the US and to a lesser extent to the EU (Figure 8.2).[5]

Argentina's exports to the American, European, and Brazilian markets also exhibit a more diversified structure than exports to the PRC. Twenty-six and eighteen products account for around 80% of exports to the US and the EU, respectively. In turn, thirty-six products account for a similar proportion of exports to Brazil (ECLAC 2015c). Summing up, Argentina exhibits a more diversified and more industrialized export basket with all its major trade partners than with the PRC.

It is worth noticing that developed countries with abundant natural resources, like Australia and New Zealand, display a similar export structure to South American. For instance, raw materials and natural resource–based manufactures account for 80% of Australia's total exports and 94% of its exports to the PRC (own calculations based on ECLAC 2015c).[6]

However, recent evidence shows there are significant differences. Although Australia and New Zealand export similar products, they do it at higher prices, at least when they sell to developed countries and the PRC. A possible explanation of these differences is related to the higher levels of capital, marketing, services, and research and development (R&D) investment observed in both developed countries in comparison to those found in LAC (Castro 2013).

Another significant factor is the free trade agreements (FTAs) recently negotiated by Australia and New Zealand with the PRC. Despite the fact that PRC's tariff and non-tariff protection has increased over-all Chinese discrimination against value-added products, these treaties grant improved access to the Chinese market to high-value-added products and knowledge-intensive services. In contrast, only a few countries in LAC like Mexico, Chile, and Peru have signed comprehensive FTAs with the PRC.

While the hefty rise in Chinese imports is obviously related to the PRC's ascendance in global trade in the past two decades, the case of Argentina presents some particular features. For instance, the government of Argentina has utilized extensively administrative measures aimed at restricting imported products over the last decade, hindering not only Chinese imports but also products coming from other trade partners.

In 2014, a panel at the World Trade Organization (WTO) ruled against these measures and ordered Argentina to eliminate them by January 2016. In addition, Argentina has been a major user of antidumping measures, in particular against imports from the PRC.[7] In 2011, the stiffening of protectionist measures led the PRC to apply restrictions on soybean exports from Argentina. The ensuing crisis ended when the Argentine government agreed to lift restrictions on Chinese imports and to reduce the number of Chinese products subjected to antidumping measures from 17 in 2010 to 5 in 2014.

Also, the special customs and tax regime of the southern Argentine province of Tierra del Fuego subsidizes the assembly of electronic products, which are heavily dependent on components imported from the PRC and other Asian countries. Some estimates indicate Tierra del Fuego could account for around 10% of Argentina's imports (Castro 2013).

Perhaps more importantly, a bilateral agreement with the PRC approved by the Argentine Congress in 2014 arranges for trade facilities to import Chinese inputs and capital goods for the construction of energy-related infrastructure projects (see section 3). Further, the agreement expanded an ongoing reserve swap operation between the Argentine Central Bank and the People's Bank of China totaling US$11 billion.

There are some doubts on whether Argentina's new administration will partially or entirely renegotiate the 2014–2015 agreements with the PRC. For instance, the principal opposition political parties have raised serious concerns about the absence of transparent bidding procedures, the relaxation of migration procedures for Chinese citizens, and, more generally, the secrecy that surrounded the treaty's negotiations.

In spite of these concerns, it must be noted that it would be extremely difficult for the new administration to renegotiate a large part of the agreements with the PRC. Not only is the PRC a crucial export market for Argentina, but the country is also likely to continue requiring Chinese financial assistance, particularly related to the currency swap with the PBOC, in face of the potentially harsh macroeconomic and financial conditions to be faced in 2016 and beyond.

4.2. Finance and FDI Flows

Although the PRC accounted for a third of FDI inflows into Argentina in 2010–2011, Chinese investment subsided afterward. In spite of the several agreements signed during this period, presently the PRC represents only 1% of total foreign direct investment inflows.[8] As a result, the relative importance of Argentina as a destination for Chinese FDI went from accounting for more than 20% of total PRC's investments in LAC in 2010 to around 1% in 2013 (Table 8.2).

Following a similar pattern to other Latin American countries, Chinese FDI has been largely directed to the oil sector (US$5.5 billion), followed by agricultural inputs (US$2.5 billion), infrastructure (US$2.2 billion), mining (US$1 billion), and finance (US$600 million) (Sica 2015).

> **Box 8.3. Renegotiating the Agreement**
>
> In May 2016, Argentina's minister of foreign affairs met with her Chinese counterpart. Both officials emphasized the agreements for future cooperation between the two countries, which will include the program of public works Argentina has in its plans. In turn, a few changes were made regarding the size of the hydroelectric stations to be built in Southern Argentina. Instead of 11 turbines, 8 will be installed in both stations, which reduces the cost of both dams by approximately 20%, and the construction timeframe was extended. In turn, it was clearly stated that the space center in Neuquén is not to be used for military purposes.
>
> The agreement is in line with what was supposed to be the stance of the new Argentine administration: it maintains the relationship with China with only a few, relatively minor changes to what had been agreed on by the administration of former president Fernandez.

TABLE 8.2. Chinese Foreign Direct Investment (FDI) in Argentina, 2010–2013
Millions of US$ and Percentage of Total FDI inflows and Chinese FDI in LAC

	2010	2011	2012	2013
US$ in millions	3,100	2,450	600	120
Percentage of total FDI inflows	27%	23%	4%	1%
Percentage of Chinese FDI in LAC	23%	24%	7%	1%

Source: Based on ECLAC (2015a)

Looking at the stock of FDI, the minor role played by the Chinese companies in the Argentine market is even more palpable. The PRC has accounted for less than 1%of the FDI stock in Argentina. In contrast, EU investments comprised 45% of the stock of foreign direct investment, while US companies have accounted for 20% (Figure 8.3).

However, the relative importance of the EU and US noticeably diminished between 2001 and 2012, partly due to divestment by European and American firms and increased FDI inflows from Brazil and, to a lesser extent, Chile. The EU participation fell by almost four percentage points, and the share of the US declined by a similar figure (Figure 8.3).

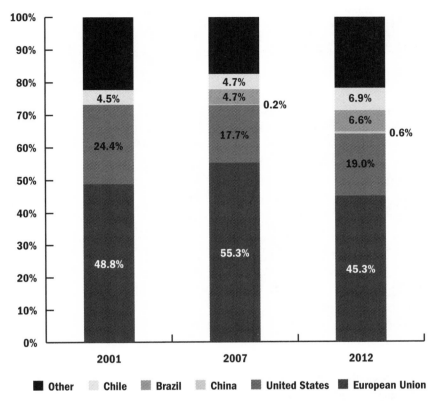

Figure 8.3. Foreign Direct Investment (FDI) Stock by Country, 2001, 2007, and 2012
Source: Based on Central Bank of Argentina (2015)

The relative decay of the PRC as a source of FDI inflows occurred in parallel to a marked rise in the importance of Chinese financing for Argentina. In 2011 to 2016, only Venezuela and Brazil received more financial assistance from Beijing in LAC. According to Gallagher and Myers (2014), between 2005 and 2013, Argentina received US$19 billion from PRC's banks and financial institutions, equivalent to around 16% of total Chinese financing to the region (Table 8.3).

A currency swap was negotiated by the BCRA with the PBOC in 2014 that was a major step to avoid a more drastic reduction in BCRA international reserves. A similar agreement was reached in 2009, but was not taken advantage of at that time by the BCRA.[9] The BCOP has signed reserve swaps with other LAC countries, including a swap with

TABLE 8.3. China's Finance to LAC (2005–2013)
Billions of US$ and Percentage of Total

	US$ billions	Percentage of total
Venezuela	56.3	47%
Brazil	22.0	19%
Argentina	19.0	16%
Ecuador	10.8	9%
Brazil	2.9	2%
México	2.4	2%
Peru	2.3	2%
Jamaica	1.4	1%
Bolivia	.611	1%
LAC	117.711	100%

Source: Based on Gallagher and Myers (2014)

Brazil for US$30 billion in 2013, and one with Chile for US$3.6 billion in 2015.

These funds played a major role in helping Argentina prevent a balance-of-payment crisis in 2015. In fact, in December 2015 it was estimated that the PBOC swap accounted for more than 40% of the BCRA's international currency reserves, although it did not increase the disposable reserves. As a matter of fact, the reason why the Argentine government did not use the renminbi to pay for imports in spite of a trade deficit with China, which exceeded US$6 billion in 2015, was an unwritten agreement that restricted the swap liquidity for that purpose. In his initial speech, the minister of finance of the new administration announced negotiations to allow some liquidity in the swap. Those negotiations will add around US$3 billion to disposable international reserves.[10]

5. Argentina, the PRC, and the US: A New Triangle in the Making?

Notwithstanding the uncertainty about the policies to be followed by Argentina after the December 2015 presidential elections, it is possible to argue that some features of the present economic relationship with the PRC resemble the situation experienced by Argentina in the 1930s. Hauled by the paralysis of international trade and a ballooning current account deficit, the Argentine government of that time signed an agreement with the United Kingdom. The treaty granted preferential access to British imports in exchange for preserving the strategic UK market for Argentina's beef exporters. In particular, the agreement led to the reduction of specific tariffs and the creation of a preferential exchange rate for UK companies (Machinea and De León 2015).

Mainly as a result of the agreement, the existing "triangular" trade scheme of Argentina with the UK and the US, where the US was the main provider of capital goods and machinery for the Argentine economy and the UK its main export destination, underwent a radical transformation. Thenceforth, the UK became not only the largest market for Argentina's exports but also Argentina's main source of imported products (Machinea and De León 2015).

More recently, the PRC offered to an again hard-currency-constrained Argentine government not only a market for agricultural products but something even more important to a government isolated from the global capital markets: soft financing. Chinese funding goes beyond trade finance as it may provide, under certain circumstances, financing for the balance of payments.

Yet, as in the 1930s with the UK, there is no such a thing as a free lunch in Argentina's "strategic partnership" with the PRC. While the agreements provide access to essential soft financing for Argentina, they also require the concession of public works to Chinese firms in strategic local markets with no open bidding process and, at least in some cases, without local provision of services and technology. The incorporation of such "Chinese-only content" clauses was one of the main impediments in Brazil's reaching a similar agreement with the PRC. The other limiting factor was that Brazil did not agree to the allocation of works without a bidding process. Besides, no progress has been made in the main objectives set forth in the comprehensive strategic partnership agreement: to achieve a more balanced path in trade and diversify Argentina's exports.

6. Conclusions and Further Comments

This chapter examines the recent evolution of the economic relations of Argentina with the PRC and the United States. We posit such a nexus must be analyzed within the broader context of the economic and international policies carried out by Argentina in the last decade. In contrast to other Latin American countries, with the exemption of Venezuela, the behavior of the Argentine government over this period was characterized by the adoption of protectionist trade policies and isolation from the international capital markets.

On the one hand, Argentina imposed stringent non-tariff restrictions on imports from its major trade partners and disallowed pursuing trade agreements with third countries, for instance, blocking FTA negotiations between MERCOSUR (the Southern Common Market) and the EU for several years. In spite of heightened restrictions, Argentina's trade with the PRC blossomed over this period, driven by historically high commodity prices. While booming exports to the PRC contributed to mitigate Argentina's recurring balance-of-payment crises, it also reinforced the country's specialization in a reduced number of primary products and destination markets. Moreover, the intensified concentration of Argentina's export basket augmented the country's vulnerability to changes in commodity prices, in a context of rapidly rising imports, stagnant exports, and limited international financing.

On the other hand, Argentina's governments were not willing, or at least not capable, to restore normal access to the international financial markets in the aftermath of the 2002 default of its external debt. Surprisingly, they continued pursuing this policy of "financial isolationism" despite worsening external conditions that led to the imposition of harsh exchange rate controls in Argentina. In turn, these isolationist policies explain, at least partly, the deterioration of the economic links of Argentina with the US, and other developed countries, observed in the last decade.

We argue that the 2014 "comprehensive strategic partnership" and the 33 agreements signed by Argentina with the PRC in 2014 and 2015 should be seen through the prism of the country's protectionist trade policies and relative isolation from the international capital markets. In particular, we contend that some of the features of the present economic relationship between the PRC and Argentina resemble the association established by the latter country with the United Kingdom in the 1930s.

Similarly, the 2014 and 2015 agreements grant preferential access to Chinese firms in the local market for the construction of strategic energy-related infrastructure projects, in return for soft-financing for Argentina's dwindling international reserves. In contrast to the 1930s treaty with the UK, however, Argentina's government was unable to improve access to the strategic Chinese market for goods with more value added than those usually exported to that destination. Perhaps more importantly, the 1930s agreement with the UK was partly a response to an exogenous shock: the collapse of the multilateral trade system and the potential loss of the then strategic British market, whereas the agreements with the PRC in 2014–2015 were largely the result of Argentina's financial isolationism, anti-export policies, and trade protectionism.

While exports to the PRC are narrowly concentrated in a reduced number of primary products, Argentina's export basket to the US and the EU includes a significant share of processed agricultural and industrial products. Despite these tendencies, and looking forward, China's growing appetite for healthy, secure, and higher-protein foodstuffs driven by the rise of the middle class potentially opens opportunities to diversify Argentina's exports to the PRC. Therefore, is a priority for Argentina to deepen its commercial and financial relations with China.

However, some of the features of the trade and financial nexus with the PRC and the US raise some questions about the long-term development implications of the current modalities of Argentina's insertion into the international economy. Among them, how might these features of the Argentina-PRC economic links affect relations with the US? Are these temporary or permanent features of Argentina's economic relationship with China? Would the 2014–2015 agreements be modified or ratified by the incoming Argentine government administration after December 2015? Would the agreement with the PRC limit the access of US firms, and those of other developed countries, to strategic sectors of the Argentine economy? How would this treaty therefore impact FDI inflows from the US to Argentina?

While finding answers to these queries is beyond the limits of this chapter, it is interesting to briefly explore the likely policies of the new administration based on the statements of President Macri during the political campaign and the measures announced during his first weeks as president.

Considering the current account deficit, the negligible level of international reserves, and the economic stagnation of the past few years, the new administration needed to promptly regain access to the international capital markets and to pursue a more aggressive trade policy with the goal of opening new export markets and diversifying the export product basket. As a matter of fact, the first announcements (Box 8.1) included new international credits and a commitment to increasing exports of agricultural goods withheld by farmers. More broadly, the removal of restrictions in the foreign exchange market and the improvement in competitiveness deriving from the peso devaluation and the elimination of taxes on exports are evidence of an attempt to achieve a more dynamic international insertion. Additionally, the new foreign affairs minister has stated the intention of strengthening MERCOSUR while improving trade and financial relations with other countries and regions.

In our view, as the minister had said, Argentina should not only consolidate MERCOSUR, but also pursue trade agreements with other regions such as the Pacific Alliance, the ASEAN, and developed countries around the globe. Given the tariff and non-tariff barriers faced by high-value-added goods, mainly based on agricultural commodities, in those latter markets, Argentina would otherwise potentially lose vital market access for local exporters of such products. Yet the presence of highly subsidized agricultural sectors in the EU and the US presents a challenge to Argentina and the rest of MERCOSUR's partners. In spite of this, at the beginning of this decade MERCOSUR was close to signing an agreement with the EU.

This more diversified financial and trade setting would potentially introduce a question mark concerning the continuity of some of the current contours of the "strategic relationship" of Argentina with the PRC, particularly in connection to the dependence on Chinese financing and the generous access to strategic domestic markets granted to Chinese firms by the local government. Decreasing the dependence on China's financing does not mean not making use of that source, as the current administration stated regarding the negotiations to renew the swap with China and provide it with more liquidity. What it does mean is reestablishing Argentina's international trade and financial balance according to the terms discussed in this document.

NOTES

1 Own calculations based on the Conference Board Total Economy Database (2015).

2 As discussed in section 4, the new authorities found the currency swap did not have liquidity; therefore it couldn't be used to pay any foreign liability, including imports from China.

3 China has signed 58 partnership agreements, 54 of them with countries and the others with the European Union, Association of Southeast Asia Nations, African Union, and Community of Latin American and Caribbean States. Twenty-one of those agreements are called "comprehensive strategic association" and among them there are five countries of Latin America (Argentina, Brazil, Mexico, Peru, and Venezuela). For a discussion of the characteristics of the different types of strategic agreements, see Ramon-Berjano, Malena, and Velloso (2015).

4 Argentina and Colombia accounted for more than 75% of the trade deficit of South American countries with China.

5 Among exports representing at least 1% of the sales to the US are products such as wines, machine and equipment parts, aluminum and aluminum alloys, chemical products, aircraft, seamless tubes and pipes, albuminoid substances, frozen and chilled fish and crustaceans, piston engines, essential oils, alcohol, and medicinal items.

6 Manufactures account for roughly a third of Australia's natural resource–based exports and 10% of New Zealand's.

7 Argentina ranks fourth, after India, the United States, and Russia, as the country that applied the most antidumping measures to China in the past 20 years (Sica 2015).

8 Besides the swap, which is discussed in the next section. There have been few capital inflows used to fund some public projects included in the treaty.

9 China needs to grant the swap with an additional agreement so as to have renminbi considered as part of the international reserves.

10 The authorization entails the use of renminbi to purchase dollars for a limited period of time, given that the purchase is conducted jointly with a forward contract that reverses the operation. The cost to use the line is tied to the LIBPR rate, depending on the country's financial conditions.

BIBLIOGRAPHY

Carciofi, R. (2015): "Argentina-China. Una Asociación Estratégica Integral." *Alquimias Económicas*, March. Buenos Aires.

Castro, L. (2013): "Variedades de primarización: Recursos naturales y diversificación productiva." El desafío de América Latina en la relación con China. Documento de Trabajo 116. CIPPEC, Buenos Aires.

Castro, L., and Agosto, W. (2014): "Cuál podría ser el espacio fiscal en el próximo período de gobierno?" Documento de Políticas Públicas 140. CIPPEC, Buenos Aires.

Castro, L., Szenkman, P., and Lotitto, E. (2015): "Como puede cerrar el próximo gobierno la brecha de infraestructura?" Documento de Políticas Públicas 145. CIPPEC, Buenos Aires.

Central Bank of Argentina (BCRA) (2015): Online database. www.bcra.gob.ar.

Dussel Peters, E. (2015): "China's Evolving Role in Latin America: Can It Be a Win-Win?" Atlantic Council of the United States, Washington, DC.

ECLAC (2015a): "Foreign Direct Investment in Latin America and the Caribbean 2015." ECLAC, June, Santiago de Chile.

ECLAC (2015b): "China y América Latina. Hacia una nueva era estratégica." ECLAC, Santiago de Chile.

ECLAC (2015c): *Comisión Económica para América Latina y el Caribe*. www.cepal.org.

Gallagher, Kevin P., and Myers, Margaret (2014): "China–Latin America Finance Database," Inter-American Dialogue. Washington, DC: Inter-American Dialogue. www.thedialogue.org.

Gerchunoff, Pablo, and Llach, Lucas (2008): "Antes y después del "corto siglo XX." Dos globalizaciones latioamericanas (1850–1914 y 1980s–2000s)," XXI *Jornadas de la Asociación Argentina de Historia Económica*, Caseros, September 2008.

IMF (2015): World Economic Outlook Database. www.imf.org.

Instituto Nacional de Estadísticas y Censos (INDEC) (2015): Online database. www.indec.gob.ar.

Machinea, J. L., and De Léon, G. (2016): "El impacto del tratado Roca-Runciman sobre las importaciones argentinas: ¿mito o realidad?" *Desarrollo Económico* 55, No. 217: 437–49.

Machinea, J. L. (2017): *América Latina: ¿el vaso está medio vacío o medio lleno?* San José, Costa Rica: PDigital S.A.

Oviedo, E. (2015): "El ascenso de China y sus efectos en la relación con Argentina." Estudios Internacionales 180. Instituto de Estudios Internacionales-Universidad de Chile, Santiago de Chile.

Paz, G. (2014): "Argentina and Asia: China's Reemergence, Argentina's Recovery." In Arson, C. and Heine, J. (Eds). *Reaching Across the Pacific: Latin America and Asia in the New Century*. Washington, DC: Wilson Center.

Ramon-Berjano, C., Malena, J., and Velloso, M. (2015): "El relacionamiento de China con América Latina y Argentina. Significado de la alianza estratégica integral y los recientes acuerdos bilaterales." CARI Documento de Trabajo, 96, October.

Sica, D. (2015): "Los vínculos entre Argentina y China: los acuerdos firmados y su impacto sobre las posibilidades de desarrollo." *Boletín Informativo Techint*, SEP/DIC, 69–86.

Universidad de Buenos Aires. Facultad de Ciencias Economicas (2015) ARKLEMS Database. www.arklems.org.

9

China and the United States in the Andes

RUBEN GONZALEZ-VICENTE

Introduction

The early 21st century has been an era of relative emancipation for Latin American countries. As the Cold War years and the lost decade under the guidance of Washington's neoliberal orthodoxy came to an end, the future of the region seemed to be more than ever in the hands of its people. In the Andean region too, electoral representative democracies became the norm after Peru's "brief foray into dictatorship in 1992" (Mainwaring 2006: 14), while free political competition has not always guaranteed better-managed countries and judicious leadership. Peoples and ideas that were once outside the political agenda shape and contest it now in powerful and imaginative ways, as proved by the emergence of activist and indigenous political leaders from outside the traditional elite circles (Cameron 2009). Without a doubt, much remains to be done with regards to the empowerment of subaltern groups, for gender, race, and economic inequalities persist. Also, while critical voices now permeate the mainstream political discourse, institutionalization often acts so as to appropriate, diffuse, and/or tame them (Laurie et al. 2005, Gonzalo Porto-carrero 2013, Oviedo Freire 2014). Yet in general this has been a decade of political ambition and imagination, with renewed attempts at tackling pressing contemporary concerns, as environmental sustainability is taken more seriously and "development" itself is debated not only in the ivory towers of academics, but in the very processes of constitutional reform.

Latin America's geopolitical landscape has also been transformed, and in some ways become more complex. Once mighty external powers have seen their influence wane. The United States can no longer under-write foreign or domestic policy agendas (Hakim 2006). Multinational corporations need to sit down with communities to discuss their action plans (Sanborn and Paredes 2014). New external actors that not long ago seemed only exotic destinations across the globe—e.g., China, Iran, India—are now playing important roles in trade, finance, and investment in the region (World Bank 2006, Mesquita Moreiro 2010). Old ones are seeing their roles reconfigured as for example the IMF is no longer a trusted lender of last resort (*Financial Times* 2013). Yet while the geopolitical context and the natural resources boom may have contributed to diminish interference in national affairs, the challenges of developing—socially and industrially—within a globalizing economy are today as acute as ever. In many ways, Latin America's attempts to "free itself from U.S. political tutelage" have not curbed the continent's dependence on external markets and reliance on primary production, which still accounts for 75% of its exports (Amin 2014), even in a period of low resource prices. In this context, China is seen as a potential challenger to the hegemonic role once played by the United States, and to the global liberal order (Paz 2012). In this chapter I show how this is a faulty assumption. The cases of Chile, Peru, Colombia, and Ecuador[1] illustrate how the market order that the United States has relentlessly tried to orchestrate in the Americas is not antagonistic to China's own pursuits.

My main argument throughout this piece is that it is too simplistic to understand the Andean region today in a dualistic fashion, as if it were a pendulum swinging between China and the United States, or any other external power for that matter. Domestic processes and global economic dynamics are today more important than international relations in shaping the future of the region. For example, the trend of primarization and the concomitant challenges to industrialization are shared throughout the region with disregard of the political sign or diplomatic predilections of individual governments (Gallagher and Porzecanski 2010, Bebbington and Bebbington 2011). In this sense, transformations in South America in general and the Andes in particular in the last decade need to be understood as a combination of variegated endogenous processes, as well as exogenous ones such as America's liberalizing endeavor, and China's direct role and indirect influence in deepening market penetration to new resource frontiers. While there are differences in China's overall approach to the region as compared to the United States—as exemplified in the disparate levels of engagement in Ecuador and Colombia—both countries also share strikingly similar interests, as well illustrated by their support for business-enabling environments in places like Peru. The Andean region is thus a good case to show that Chinese and American influences do not necessarily counterbalance each other beyond the potential competing interests of individual firms. When it comes to their impacts, they are complementary in shaping new development trajectories in tune with global pressures for marketization and competitiveness.

The chapter starts with a discussion of how United States hegemony in the form of a "marketplace society" (Agnew 2005a) created the backdrop for the emergence of China in the region, as Chinese businesses first entered Latin America following the liberalization of the mining and oil sectors in Peru. The second section explains how the impacts of Chinese businesses in the region are to a great extent complementary to those of U.S. businesses, despite their unique backgrounds and having emerged in a distinct political economy. The conclusion discusses the Andes' place in the global economy with reference to the central roles that China and the United States play in it.

Marcona 1992: Beijing Meets Washington

The rising influence of China in different regions of the world is often, and almost inevitably, studied with reference to America's global hegemony (e.g., Campbell 2007, Mearsheimer 2010). The debate typically focuses on what parameters better indicate a power transition, and on how the new geopolitical scenario would look like after the dawn of America's global liberal project. While many scholars contend that it is premature to hail China's challenge to America's hegemony, others, such

TABLE 9.1. Basic data on Andean countries

	Pop. (millions)	GDP (billion USD)	GDP per capita (USD, yearly)	HDI ranking	Primary commodity exports (% of total exports)
Chile	17	258	14528	41	87%
Colombia	47	377	7903	98	83%
Ecuador	15	100	6322	98	93%
Peru	30	202	6550	82	88%

Sources: UNDP 2015, UNCTAD 2015, World Bank 2015

as Steve Chan (2008), also add that China has little incentive to challenge a global order in which it has grown at unprecedented rates, although the sustainability of the model is today more under question than at other points in recent decades. It is thus possible to conceive a scenario where China becomes the main economic or even political partner to particular countries without necessarily defying America's liberal project or trumping the interests of American businesses. Yet in order to appreciate this possibility, we need to move on from the classical IR idea of hegemony as empire and toward an understanding of hegemony as the realization of the American dream for a globally integrated economy, or what Agnew (2005) calls the "marketplace society." This form of hegemony has opened a window of opportunity for China to emerge as a regional power without contesting existing political and economic architectures, nor mainstream ideas about modernity, prosperity, and development, as President Xi Jinping's keynote speech in defence of free trade at the 2017 World Economic Forum illustrates. Such a situation would entail a reconfiguration of the role of states in the new international division of labor along competitive lines without inevitably affecting the essence of the current model of globalization, described by Noam Chomsky as "a specific form of international economic integration . . . based on investor rights, with the interests of people incidental" (Chomsky 2002). Hence, as Agnew puts it:

> The globalizing world that the United States has done so much to realize is an emerging geographical structure that seems likely to pose serious challenges to a continuation of American hegemony in the form that it previously has taken both at home and abroad. (2005a: 71)

In this context, we are not witnessing the transition from the leadership of one nation to the hegemony of a new one. Such power-transition interpretation would require ignoring the changing role of nation-states and other actors in international politics. While states remain important actors in the era of globalization, they are today more complex, internationalized, fragmented, and multi-scalar than in the post–World War II period—when the discipline of international relations fully developed— and they share power with a plethora of other actors. We are now in a post-Westphalian age, where both effective sovereignties and power are distributed not just within increasingly complex structures of government, but also among markets and diverse social actors (Agnew 2005b, Hansen and Stepputat 2006). This is the case not only for Western developed nations but also for rising states such as China. For example, in studying China's position over territorial disputes in the South China Sea, Hameiri and Jones (2015) note how China is far from forming a unitary front, but instead there is a lack of consensus and a diversity of strategies among the Ministry of Foreign Affairs, the Navy, the national oil companies (NOCs), Hainan's provincial government, and a number of other Chinese institutions. Similarly, the International Energy Agency recognizes that Chinese NOCs have gained significant leverage versus other instances of the Chinese government and have developed their own foreign policy interests (Jiang and Sinton 2011).

It is thus difficult to talk about "China's interests," when these have grown so variegated with the internationalization of the Chinese state and the rise of entrepreneurial statehood and private interests (Gonzalez-Vicente 2011a, Breslin 2013). The sum of these trends indicates that global politics are not played only on the "inter-national" chessboard, but at different scales of governance, business, and social struggle. Local, national, and regional institutions are still immensely relevant, but their relevance resides in their capacity to navigate and regulate an increasingly globalized capitalism and to give shape to its geographical variegations (Peck and Theodore 2007). It is in these times of "deep marketization" (Carroll 2012), we cannot interpret China's emergence in the Andean region as the essential threat of a Chinese national project to a U.S.-centric system.

To demonstrate this, one can begin by observing the way in which China's investment started flowing into Latin America through Shougang's acquisition of the Marcona iron ore mine in Peru in 1992. An early example of corporatization and of business internationalization in China, Shougang arrived in Peru precisely thanks to a wave of (neo)liberalization in the Andean country (Gonzalez-Vicente 2013). Shougang, a company owned by the government of the municipality of Beijing, did not seek improbable alliances with the infamous and allegedly Maoist Communist Party of Peru—best known as Shining Path—but instead negotiated with the Fujimori regime to acquire the Marcona mine through a process of privatization. The privatization of mining concessions in

Peru was part of a wider transformation along the Washington Consensus lines. The Andean country lived in convulsive times and the Fujimori government implemented a series of structural reforms in order to gain access to loans from the International Monetary Fund, the Inter-American Development Bank, and the World Bank, and to the international legitimacy that these institutions granted (Ruiz Torres 2005). The reforms resulted in a mining sector and an economy in general that is today "dominated by the private sector, regulated by market forces, and intricately linked to the global economy" (Bury 2005: 223). Thereby, this is a Washington-inspired economy, but at the same time one that facilitated the first overseas foreign direct investment by Chinese companies in the region, and as we will see soon, one that has remained an attractive destination for Chinese investments through the early 21st century.

This is a critical point to understand China's engagement with Chile, Peru, Ecuador, and Colombia. While Chinese businesses may navigate differently the sociopolitical contexts in which they operate, they are out for profitable deals and will not shy away from the opportunities created by liberal investment regimes. In this way, they have contributed significantly to the expansion of the mining sectors in Peru and Ecuador—despite the distinct political orientations—and furthered the penetration of global markets to rural areas of the Andes in the same way as other transnational businesses. To give just a few examples, China's Andes Petroleum is a member of Ecuador's Association for Hydrocarbons Industry (AIHE in its Spanish acronym), the lobbying arm of oil companies in the country. The discourses of Chinese mining companies in Peru—staffed by locals and non-Chinese expatriates (Gonzalez-Vicente 2011a)—align neatly with those of other international mining businesses. Not surprisingly, their operations receive the same kind of backlash as other mining companies from communities and NGOs that oppose extractive activities. And in Colombia, investments by Chinese mining companies have been deterred by the same sort of risk aversion that has kept other transnationals at bay (Creutzfeldt and Gélvez 2011).

Interestingly, the Going Out policy, showcasing traits of an "outward developmental state" strategy, has succeeded in its early stage of foreign acquisitions in the region as a result of the liberalizing trends that the United States has supported through various means (e.g., structural adjustment, ideational influence, FTAs, company lobbying, etc.). Chinese companies have hence benefited from a particular historical conjunction in which the Chinese state's developmentalism and nurturing of national businesses has been combined with the liberalizing attempts of the United States and other actors.

Different Backgrounds, Similar Outcomes

At first glance, it would seem shortsighted to suggest that the impacts of Chinese companies in the Andes are similar to those of their U.S. counterparts. Chinese enterprises are in many ways different from American ones. Most Chinese companies with large investments in Latin America are state-owned, have dismal environmental and social records at home, and pursue distinct strategies of accumulation. Ching Kwan Lee argues that while Chinese companies pursue profit, they do not necessarily seek profit maximization as private capital would, but "encompassing accumulation" (Lee 2014). In the case of Chinese mining investments in Peru, for example, state-owned companies secure resources to feed into their metallurgical businesses, rather than directly making a profit by selling into the copper markets (Gonzalez-Vicente 2012). Very importantly, large Chinese companies gain access to projects in Latin America through easy credit from Chinese policy banks rather than by raising capital from private investors.[2] Another important peculiarity that I have discussed elsewhere is the difficulties experienced by transnational activists networks when trying to engage firms in China (Gonzalez-Vicente 2011b). These few characteristics set Chinese enterprises apart from traditional investors in the Andes. Yet when one focuses on their impacts—rather than on the paths that they followed to land in Latin America—the activities of Chinese companies are in many ways complementary to those of U.S. ones, contributing to deepening primarization and its associated challenges.

This section explores how three key vectors of engagement—investment, trade, and finance and infrastructural contracts—have been advanced with varying levels of success in the four countries here studied. Of the three of them, only finance and infrastructural contracts have impacts that seem to be quite eminently "Chinese." A forth vector, traditional security, remains largely inconsequential in China's engagement with the region and is not covered in this analysis. Contrary to mainstream opinion, China's vision of the Andes is chiefly guided by a geoeconomic rational, rather than geopolitics, contrasting in this way with the United States' more variegated engagement.

Foreign Direct Investment

Still adhering to the essences of neoliberal policymaking, Peru remains today the main destination for Chinese mining investment in Latin America (Gonzalez-Vicente 2012). Ecuador has become an important recipient of Chinese mining and oil FDI as well, with Tongling and China Railway Construction's Mirador project likely to become the first large-scale mine in the country. Colombia, on the other hand, hosts only a modicum amount of Chinese investments within its oil sector, whereas Chile's copper sector remains dominated by Codelco and Western corporations. Mining and oil remain the preferred sectors for Chinese investors in the region, with 90% of Chinese investment between 2010 and 2013 going into these sectors—way above the 25% that these industries attract on an average in Latin America. Among these two extractive activities, oil investment is less discriminate, for Chinese companies operate in every country in the region with oil reserves except Mexico, where the sector remains largely closed to foreign investors (CEPAL 2015: 62). While geopolitical thinking and energy security rationales may distort investment choices in the oil sector, Chinese businesses in the mining sector are more clearly attracted to profitable projects.

There are two main reasons why mining occupies such a central position in the early stage of internationalization of Chinese companies in the Andes. The first one is that mining companies in China are considered able to profitably operate internationally given their levels of technological development, and thus can easily act as the spearheads of the Going Out strategy. Few sectors of the Chinese economy can boast a similar capacity to conduct successful businesses overseas.[3] A second reason is that out of the three main FDI determinants highlighted by business literature (Dunning 1981), Chinese companies in the early 21st century have found less incentives to pursue market-seeking and cost-reduction strategies in the Andes, given greater comparative advantage elsewhere. They have instead focused on resource seeking, due to the overcrowding and limitations of China's natural resource sectors and to the demands in China's domestic market. This is a trend that may change with the slowdown of the Chinese economy—with IMF forecasts of 6 to 7% GDP growth, down from a 10% average in the three decades up to 2010 (IMF 2015)—as we observe an interesting parallel between lower growth rates and a 29% increase in overseas direct investment in the first quarter of 2015 (*China Knowledge* 2015). Yet this trend would need to consolidate for investment to diversify, and the fact remains that Chinese companies in the Andean region have so far focused chiefly on natural resources.

As outlined in the section above, the presence of Chinese firms in the Andes is very much determined by the availability of market opportunities. Enabling business environments—at times guaranteed by neoliberal regulations, on other occasions by strong leaders keen to keep cash flowing into their countries—are responsible for attracting Chinese investment, but they are not enough on their own. If Peru stands as the most successful case in luring Chinese mining investment to the region, and Ecuador is depending on Chinese investment to advance its mining sector, Chile and Colombia are the other side of the coin despite their highly liberalized economies—ranking first and second in Latin America in the Heritage Foundation's 2015 Index of Economic Freedom (Heritage Foundation 2015). Nonetheless, it is precisely China's emphasis on mining investment—due to China's commercial and strategic interests—that explains why Chile and Colombia lag behind in terms of attracting investment from the Asian country.

In the case of Colombia, Chinese investment has been deterred by the relative backwardness of the mining sector as compared to those of Peru or Chile. While Colombia is the tenth-largest producer of coal in the world and ranks number one in exports of emeralds, its mining potential has not lived up to expectations, with mining accounting for just 2.4% of GDP (*Economist* 2012). Endemic violence in some resource-rich areas, lack of institutional capacity to regulate large-scale projects, and low levels of governmental support are some of the reasons for the wide gap between potential and actual levels of investment (*Mining Markets* 2014). However, as latecomers into the region's mining sectors, and having ventured themselves into challenging and risky projects such as the development of Ecuador's first large-scale mine, Chinese companies are likely to consider projects in Colombia as long as these are deemed commercially viable. As pointed out above, a second and more diversified wave of investment could also open opportunities in other sectors of the Colombian economy, although Premier Li Keqiang's latest visit to the region in May 2015 seems to indicate that infrastructural contracts will take priority over new kinds of direct investment, in an impulse to internationalize China's efficacious construction sector as China's GDP growth and real state sector slow down (*Economist* 2015).

The case of Chile is a different one. The main factor impeding Chinese mining investments in Chile is the lack of new opportunities in a very consolidated sector. Major international companies are usually satisfied with their operations in the country and have no incentives to flee. Moreover, there have been no large projects in the market in the last few years, except for Mitsubishi's $5.39 billion purchase of a share in Anglo American's copper mining complex in 2011 (*Wall Street Journal* 2011). While appreciating the commercial motives of Chinese firms, we can nonetheless observe how their status as latecomers to the region, the impulse given by cheap credit from Chinese policy banks to acquire new greenfield projects, and the domestic structures of China's economy shape in different ways their engagement in the region.

This being said, there are also striking similarities with the investment patterns of U.S. firms or other transnationals. To start with, the acquisition of large mining projects in the Andes has not been the result of government-to-government deals, but occurred through company-to-company negotiations or in stock markets (London, New York, Toronto). The day-to-day operations of Chinese companies in the region are also highly localized, as they subcontract multiple tasks to local and international companies (including American ones such as Jacobs Engineering Group or Montgomery Watson Harza). This is to a great extent the reason why, from the perspective of activists and communities, Chinese companies are not all that different from other companies in the extractive sectors. A telling example in this sense is how Chinese mining projects see themselves involved, along with North American ones, in larger debates about extractivism in the region. For example, China Minmetals' Galeno project is awaiting the resolution of the Conga project conflict in its vicinity—run by the Colorado-based Newmont Mining Corporation—to gauge its own prospects. Both companies share identical interests in the region against local opposition to mining. Similarly,

Canada's Lunding Gold counts on the progress of the Mirador project—run by China's CRCC-Tongguan consortium—to pave the way for its Fruta del Norte mining project. The key disputes in these areas are not between North American and Chinese businesses, but between global mining and national governments, and local opposition to it.

A specific problem regarding the image of Chinese businesses is precisely that their concentration in natural resource sectors and their contribution to deepening the penetration of extractive activities into areas kept until recently pristine puts them at the center of conflicts and debates over extractivism in the Andes. In particular, the two mining projects close to the border between Ecuador and Peru (Mirador and Río Blanco) are situated in areas where local populations resist extraction due to its potentially negative environmental effects and subsequent impacts in agriculture-based livelihoods (Bebbington et al. 2007). The projects have thus met significant opposition. Ray and Gallagher also remark how the most biodiverse areas in eastern Ecuador and northern Peru "are heavily populated with Chinese-managed oilfields" (2015: 13). Research to date seems to indicate that Chinese extractive investments in the region do not perform worse than those by United States or local firms in terms of labor or environmental standards (Irwin and Gallagher 2013). Opposition to extraction is also not often directed at the nationality of Chinese firms, but is instead related to a growing disenchantment with mining in the region and with the increased leverage of dissident voices. However, the role that Chinese firms play in the geographical expansion of extraction and in transforming rural Andean economies into commodity providers for the global economy is highly problematical.

The main difference between U.S. and Chinese investments in the region has to do with the composition by sector—with the U.S. showing a more diversified portfolio of investments—rather than with strikingly dissimilar standards, strategies, or interests. This composition is not related to China's higher standing as opposed to that of other Western countries in the international division of labor, as a classical dependency analysis could suggest. Instead, in the more globalized new international division of labor, businesses expand their operations internationally and China is not yet seen as an innovation hub but an economy that stands out for relatively qualified cheap labor—kept cheap through the exploitation of a vulnerable working force—and lax environmental standards. In

TABLE 9.2. U.S. and China FDI stock by 2012 (million USD)*

	Chile	Colombia	Ecuador	Peru
China	126	346	408	753
U.S.	39870	8434	851	10918

*Note: FDI statistics have many flaws. For example, they do not acknowledge country of origin, but the last destination investment came through. Also, they do not reflect promised investment, in which case China's numbers would be higher: they would probably remain lower than those of the U.S. in Chile and Colombia, have a similar level in Peru, and perhaps surpass the U.S. in Ecuador.

Source: UNCTAD (2014)

this new globalized economy the Andean resources that travel to China contribute much more to internationalized production than those moving to the U.S., where they are much more heavily utilized to support local lifestyles (Xu, Williams, and Allenby 2010). It is actually estimated that around one-fourth of Chinese pollutants are associated to the production of goods for export—in many cases by non-Chinese companies, and among these around 21% are attributed to China-to-U.S. exports (Lin et al. 2014). The composition of investment thus tells us more about the nature of economic globalization than about intrinsic characteristics of Chinese investment. When compared within the same sector, the preferences and strategies of U.S. and Chinese firms in the Andes are in many ways similar and complementary.

Trade

If the position that China, the U.S., and the Andes occupy in increasingly globalized production networks explains many of the investment dynamics in Chile, Peru, Ecuador, and Colombia, this is even more the case when it comes to explaining their trade links. Trade statistics are quite telling in this case, with the Andean economies focused on the export of commodities to China and the U.S., China as an exporter of increasingly value-added manufactures to the Andes (while the value is not necessarily added in China), and the United States as an exporter of higher-end manufactures and services (ECLAC 2011).

Yet if one seeks to elucidate what these trends mean for social and industrial development in the Andes, one needs to further disaggregate data and understand commercial exchanges within a framework of globalized production where nation-states are no longer self-contained units. The question is hence: what does it mean for the people of Chile, Colombia, Peru, and Ecuador to live in countries whose exports are overwhelmingly focused on commodities?[4] There are many dimensions to this question, and the impacts of this economic structure are not evenly distributed, but we can summarize a few indicators here. The first point would be that despite the traditional disadvantageous position of commodity exporters, Andean economies have grown steadily through the early 21st century, in great part thanks to a global commodity boom triggered by Chinese consumption. This growth has been more pronounced in Peru (7% in the eight years up to 2013) and Ecuador (4.5% yearly from 2000 to 2014)—the two countries with closer trade ties to China, than in Chile (4% from 2001 to 2014) and Colombia (1.08% from 2001 to 2014) (*Economist* 2013, Trading Economics 2015, World Bank 2015). The three poorest countries have also made significant headway in poverty reduction, with the percentage of population living on less than $2 a day going down from 24% to 8% in Peru, 37% to 9% in Ecuador, and 31% to 11% in Colombia between 2000 and 2011 (World Bank 2015).[5] Inequality has also been slightly reduced but remains high, with the Gini coefficient of Colombia at 0.53, Chile at 0.50, Ecuador at 0.46, and Peru at 0.45 in the year 2012 (where zero represents perfect equality and 1 is perfect inequality) (World Bank 2015).

These overall positive trends need to be stressed. According to Gallagher and Porzecanski, China is outcompeting Latin American manufacturers in regional and global markets and narrowing the production niches in the region, while it is projected that Chinese demand cannot ensure high commodity prices in the long-term (Gallagher and Porzecanski 2010: 25, 56). This would be particularly troubling for the Andean region (including Venezuela), which presents the highest degrees of primarization in Latin America and the Caribbean (ECLAC 2011: 19). There is indeed a heated debate with regard to the sustainability of high commodity prices. Pessimists predict that the traditional volatility of natural resource prices will lead to a substantial decline in the aftermath of the commodity boom. More optimistic analyses suggest that key structural changes on the supply side of the industry and growing aggregate demand globally will help to avoid a drastic deterioration of prices (Humphreys 2010). With the cooling down of the Chinese economy—and the end of speculative demand for some metals in China—and seven years after the peak of the Global Financial Crisis, commodity prices have dropped but remain far from historic lows. Copper sells today at over $6,000 per ton, and a barrel of crude oil is at $50,[6] prices that are above those of previous commodity crises. Yet while these debates are still open, Andean countries would truly find themselves in a vulnerable position in case of a more serious downturn in commodity prices.

A more current and pressing concern for Andean governments is the high level of conflicts around projects of natural resource extraction in the region. Out of the 149 active conflicts registered by the Peruvian ombudsman in April 2015, 70 are related to mining activities and 19 to projects of oil extraction (Defensoría del Pueblo de Perú 2015). Resistance to resource extraction is also considerable in Colombia and Ecuador. Chile is an outlier in this case, since most of its more productive mines are located in deserted regions. Opposition in this case does not revolve around issues of livelihoods but conservationism and broader environmental concerns. The reasons for the high levels of opposition in the Andes are plenty, including the historical incapacity of extractive industries to develop the region, the high levels of inequality and exploitation associated with these sectors in rural areas, and the threats posed to environmental sustainability and to resource-based livelihoods. In many cases positions have been entrenched after decades—if not centuries—of conflict. While central governments have promoted participatory approaches to project development, processes of dialogue, and the devolution of resource wealth to producing regions, there are few indications that the end of confrontations is anywhere near. If anything, civil societies have grown stronger and more interconnected, and the visibility and incidence of conflicts is higher than ever. This strengthening of dissenting voices is by no means a negative trend, but it is symptomatic of unequal politics of resource access and brings to the fore questions about what development should mean in the Andes and how to achieve it within a globalized economy.

Therefore, in the case of trade we observe once more how the links between Andean countries and the U.S. and China are indicative of their position in the global economy. This position is certainly not static, and policy decisions matter in terms of reconfiguring a country's engagement with the global economy. Scholarship suggests that certain degrees of government intervention in the economy and protectionism may help to alleviate the negative impacts of engaging the global economy, while businesses should be disciplined and gradually encouraged to compete globally (Chang 2008). Specialists on China–Latin America relations have also called for more proactive states so that countries in the region can better leverage the benefits from China's demand for commodities (Hearn and León-Manríquez 2011). Free trade agreements such as the ones signed by China with Peru and Chile, or those signed by the U.S. with Chile and Colombia, are likely to tighten competition and reinforce asymmetries, as well as to impact more severely vulnerable groups (Garay Salamanca et al. 2009). Yet at the same time, the efforts made by the Ecuadorian government to diversify its economic base and add value locally still have yet to pay their dividends. China and the U.S., the region's two most important markets, are thus offering important revenues in the form of trade but also increasing competition and posing significant challenges to industrialization and socially and environmentally sustainable development.

Financing and Infrastructural Contracts

Financing is the area of interaction between China and the Andes where the Asian country is having a distinct impact. Whereas in terms of investment Chinese companies adapt to a variety of political environments in search for new opportunities in an otherwise crowded market, and while trade dynamics respond chiefly to comparative advantages, Chinese loans in the region can be seen to overwhelmingly gravitate toward governments that seek to cut relations with private and multilateral lenders. Of the four countries studied here, Ecuador has been the most keen to rely on Chinese finance following its default on sovereign bonds in 2008. According to the Inter-American Dialogue database (Gallagher and Myers 2014), Ecuador has received 12 loans from China for a total of $10.8 billion. Peru negotiated 4 loans for a total of $4 billion. Chile and Colombia only signed 1 loan each, for the modest amounts of $150 million and $75 million respectively. Despite some alarmism about the size of loans and potential difficulties to repay them (e.g., Oppenheimer 2015), Ecuador's debt to GDP ratio stood at a reasonable 32.6% by July 2015, and only 36.7% of the total debt was in the hands of Chinese creditors (Ministerio de Finanzas 2015, El Universo 2015).

Yet the debate runs deeper. What many question today is the effectiveness of the loans to foster industrialization, the possibility of a hegemonic shift as China expands its influence through debt dependency, and the geostrategic rationales of Chinese lending. Gallagher and Irwin (2015) have studied this last point seriously. Their detailed study indicates that the main driver behind Chinese loans in the region is profit, since all loans given by policy banks are shown to be commercially viable. As for the remaining two matters, the early stage of Chinese financial engagement in the region invites speculation. There are serious concerns about whether the loans are being used responsibly or rather fostering a "culture of complacency" (Oppenheimer 2015), as well as whether the marked preference for infrastructure and resource extraction projects underpins further primarization.

Yet the focus of Chinese finance is not strikingly dissimilar from that of other multilateral lenders. The World Bank and its International Finance Corporation (IFC) have traditionally placed emphasis on market-oriented infrastructural projects in Latin America and beyond (e.g., Calderón and Servén 2010). Gabriel Goldschmidt, head of infrastructure in Latin America and the Caribbean at the IFC, concurs that Latin America has an acute need for infrastructures, and adds that "all too often, infrastructure is seen as an expense. In reality, it is an investment that allows people to get to work quickly, children to study in the evenings with reliable electricity, and families to stay healthy with affordable water and sanitation." He goes on to contend that it is the private sector that will "help Latin America achieve its dream of greater prosperity for all" (*Financial Times* 2015). In this, his approach diverts from the Chinese formula, in which central governments play an essential role alongside markets in channeling businesses (Gonzalez-Vicente 2015). Yet inasmuch as they act as commercial lenders, Chinese policy banks do not represent state-owned finance from the perspective of the Andes. They occupy a place in the market alongside private lenders and international financial institutions(IFIs). In fact, the policy banks share more characteristics with the private bond market than with IFIs (Gallagher and Irwin 2015).

The distinctiveness of Chinese finance in the region thus arises from the way in which Chinese banks act as a lender of last resort to Latin American governments that antagonize markets and multilateral lenders. In this way, Chinese finance has allowed countries such as Ecuador to triangulate between potential lenders. Ecuador did, in fact, return to bond markets in 2014. Chinese finance in the Andes represents a different market alternative, but one that is often used to finance the same kind of projects as would have otherwise been financed through other market mechanisms. In this sense, once more, we find that China's impacts in the Andes do not differ wildly from those of the U.S.: Chinese finance accentuates a trend of market-led financialization, it facilitates infrastructural development, and it poses similar challenges of indebtedness and potential primarization.

A Place for the Andes in the Global Economy

This chapter has discussed whether China is taking the Andean region in a different developmental path than it would have otherwise followed under unequivocal U.S. influence. There is no straightforward answer to such a largely speculative question, but this piece argues that it is problematic to understand the future of the Andes as determined by its international engagement with China or the U.S. Indeed, these two countries play an important role among a wider constellation of actors that shape the region's political economy. However, neither are they the only relevant actors in the region, nor are they necessarily unitary actors, but globalized economies engaged in wider production networks. To give just a couple of examples of other relevant actors, one could point out how Spain's FDI stock in Chile in 2012 surpassed that of the United States, China, and Hong Kong put together, with a total of $32.2 billion versus the combined $31.6 billion of the three economies. This is not a rarity: Mexico invests heavily in Colombia; Peru receives significant investments from the United Kingdom, Brazil, and Chile; and Ecuador hosts an important stock of Swiss and Mexican investments (UNCTAD 2014).

Other essential actors include the WTO—whose rules still regulate much of the trade between the region and the world; transnational activist groups that help to articulate local opposition to resource extraction (and may incidentally be based in the same countries as the competing extractive business—further complicating the "inter-national" perspective); Canadian mining companies that manage more mines in the region than businesses from any other country do; Southeast Asian economies that outcompete the region's garment sector; and credit rating agencies that determine how easy it will be for a country to raise money in the private market. The idea of the Andes as a place captured in a triangular relation with two mighty empires that seek to outcompete each other seems to obscure many of the actors and real dynamics of change in the region.

This piece thus favors an understanding of the Andean political economy as led by endogenous and exogenous factors, or a conjunction of vibrant domestic politics and global economic and political trends. But this is of course not a shapeless or flat-earthed globalization where the nation-state no longer matters. And this is the last point that I wish to raise in this conclusion. If anything, the rise of China tells us that states still play an important role in processes of industrialization, and policies can be devised to create and retain value within a particular territory, and subsequently to distribute it socially in various ways. The four countries here analyzed have pursued differentiated economic strategies in the last decade, with dissimilar levels of state involvement in macro- and microeconomic management—from the rather statist approach of Ecuador to the more liberal outlook of the other three. Yet as of today, none of them seem to have escaped dependency on natural resources and become able to export a wide range of value-added products (see table 9.1 at the beginning of the chapter). The region's resource wealth offers opportunities for development, but it also carries with its promise associated environmental, industrial, and social challenges. As the early-21st-century commodities boom wanes and governmental budgets become tighter, policymakers in the region will need to become more resourceful and imaginative. Time will tell which among these countries are better positioned to upgrade their economies and transform narrower economic gains into tangible social progress.

NOTES

1   Bolivia is excluded from this review due in part to space limitations, but also to the limited relations that the country holds with China until recently (see Poveda 2010 for a review of later developments). However, other authors have argued that Bolivia's dependence on and management of natural resources puts it on par with Ecuador and Peru (Bebbington and Bebbington 2011), which suggests that this chapter's arguments would also apply to landlocked Andean country.

2   While Chinese state support of national companies cannot be easily overemphasized, one must be wary of understandings of Western businesses as pure market entities exempt from state support. Whether in the form of agricultural subsidies,

support of R&D, investment in education or military intervention in key areas, Western governments also have ways of supporting their corporations. According to the World Bank (2015), China's government expenditure was just around 13% of the country's total GDP by 2013, while that of the U.S. was around 15%, and in other European countries such as France or the Netherlands government spending was responsible for 24% and 26% of the countries' GDPs.

3 Construction and infrastructure development could also be in this category (Nolan 2012), and latest developments seem to indicate that they may take the lead in a second wave of Chinese investment and contracts in the region. However I have decided not to include construction contracts in this section for they do not comfortably fit within an orthodox definition of FDI. According to the World Bank (2015, emphasis added), "foreign direct investment are the net inflows of investment to acquire a *lasting management interest . . .* in an enterprise operating in an economy other than that of the investor." One-off contracts with a single deliverable do not indicate a lasting management interest and the establishment of a business in a given economy.

4 Conversely, one may also ask what it means for the people of China to live in the world's manufacturing hub, and for the people of the United States to live in an economy specialized in the export of services and high-end manufactures. The answer is too complex to be discussed in detail here, but we must not forget that the ostensibly privileged positions that these two countries occupy with respect to the Andes does not necessarily translate in increasingly high living standards for their citizens. Through the recent era of global economic integration, wealth inequality has risen exponentially in the US, with real wages experiencing a sluggish growth. Subsequently, "average family income for the bottom 90 percent has been flat since 1980" (*Huffington Post* 2014). While China has experienced staggering rates of economic growth and absolute poverty reduction, inequality today is at similar rates with Ecuador and Peru and the level of Human Development is comparable to that of countries in the Andean region. Also, the remarkable achievements in terms of poverty reduction and economic growth have been achieved in a context of authoritarianism and repression where exploitation, political inequality and environmental degradation are in many ways more serious than in the Andes.

5 In the same period the number of people in China living with less than $2 a day went down from 61% to 18%. The number of people living on less than $1.90 a day in Chile went down from 3.11% to 1.3%.

6 In the case of oil, lower prices are not only due to a decrease in consumption, but to the discovery of fracking technologies to recover shale oil reserves, which has significantly increased output.

BIBLIOGRAPHY
Agnew, John A. (2005a). *Hegemony: The New Shape of Global Power*. Philadelphia: Temple University Press.

Agnew, John A. (2005b). "Sovereignty regimes: territoriality and state authority in contemporary world politics," *Annals of the Association of American Geographers* 95(2): 437–461.

Amin, Samir (2014). "Latin America confronts the challenge of globalization: A burdensome inheritance," *Monthly Review* 66(7): 29–34.

Bebbington, Anthony, and Denise H. Bebbington (2011). "An Andean Avatar: Postneoliberal and neoliberal strategies for securing the unobtainable," *New Political Economy* 16(1): 131–145.

Bebbington, Anthony, Michael Connarty, Wendy Coxshall, Hugh O'Shaughnessy, and Mark Williams (2007). *Mining and Development in Peru, with Special Reference to the Río Blanco Project, Piura.* London: Peru Support Group.

Breslin, Shaun (2013). "China and the South: Objectives, actors and interactions," *Development and Change* 44(6): 1273–1294.

Bury, Jeff (2005). "Mining mountains: neoliberalism, land tenure, livelihoods, and the new Peruvian mining industry in Cajamarca," *Environment and Planning A* 37(2): 221–239.

Calderón, César and Luis Servén (2010). "Infrastructure in Latin America," World Bank Policy Research Working Paper Series 5317.

Cameron, Maxwell A. (2009). "Latin America's left turns: Beyond good and bad," *Third World Quarterly* 30(2): 331–348.

Campbell, Horace (2007). "China in Africa: Challenging US global hegemony," *Third World Quarterly* 29(1): 89–105.

Carroll, Toby (2012). "Working on, through and around the state: The deep marketization of development in the Asia-Pacific," *Journal of Contemporary Asia* 42(3): 378–404.

CEPAL (Comision Economica para America Latina y de Caribe). (2015). *América Latina y el Caribe y China: hacia una nueva era de cooperación económica.* Santiago: Comision Economica para America Latina y de Caribe.

Chan, Steve (2008). *China, the U.S., and the Power-Transition Theory.* Abingdon: Routledge.

Chang, Ha-Joon (2008). *Bad Samaritans: The Myth of Free Trade and the Secret History of Capitalism.* New York: Bloomsbury Press.

China Knowledge (2015) "China's non-financial ODI up 29% in H1," www.chinaknowledge.com.

Chomsky, Noam (2002). "On escalation of violence in the Middle East—Noam Chomsky interviewed by Toni Gabric," *Croatian Feral Tribune*, 7 May, www.chomsky.info.

Creutzfeldt, Benjamin, and Tatiana Gélvez (2011). "Un dragon en Colombia: realidad o cuento chino?," *Revista Zero* 26: 110–115.

Defensoría del Pueblo de Perú (2015). "Reporte de conflictos sociales número 134: Abril 2015," www.defensoria.gob.pe.

Dunning, John H. (1981). *International Production and the Multinational Enterprise.* London: Allen & Unwin.

ECLAC (2011). *The United States and Latin America and the Caribbean: Highlights of Economics and Trade*. Santiago de Chile: United Nations, http://repositorio.cepal.org.

Economist (2012). "Mining in Colombia: Digging deeper," 4 August, www.economist .com.

Economist (2013). "Peru's roaring economy: Hold on tight," 2 February, www.economist .com.

Economist (2015). "China's economy: A slower slowdown," 13 May, www.economist.com.

El Universo (2015). "Deuda externa de Ecuador subió 31,6% y alcanza los $16.913 millones," 12 January, www.eluniverso.com.

Financial Times (2013). "Latin American countries rail against IMF over Greek bailout," 31 July 2013, www.ft.com.

Financial Times (2015). 'Infrastructure: The road to greater prosperity in Latin America," 6 October, www.ft.com.

Gallagher, Kevin P., and Amos Irwin (2015). "China's economic statecraft in Latin America: Evidence from China's policy banks," *Pacific Affairs* 88(1): 99–121.

Gallagher, Kevin P., and Margaret Myers (2014). *China-Latin America Finance Database*. Washington, DC: Inter-American Dialogue.

Gallagher, Kevin P., and Roberto Porzecanski, (2010). *The Dragon in the Room: China and the Future of Latin American Industrialization*. Stanford, CA: Stanford University Press.

Garay Salamanca, Luis Jorge, Fernando Barberi Gómez, and Iván Cardona Landínez (2009). *Impact of the US-Colombia FTA on Small Farm Economy in Colombia*. Bogotá: Oxfam International.

Gonzalez-Vicente, Ruben (2011a). "The internationalization of the Chinese state," *Political Geography* 30(7): 402–411.

Gonzalez-Vicente, Ruben (2011b). "China's engagement in South America and Africa's extractive sectors: New perspectives for resource curse theories," *Pacific Review* 24(1): 65–87.

Gonzalez-Vicente, Ruben (2012). "Mapping Chinese investment in Latin America: Politics or market?," *China Quarterly* 209: 35–58.

Gonzalez-Vicente, Ruben (2013). "Development dynamics of Chinese resource-based investment in Peru and Ecuador," *Latin American Politics and Society* 55(1): 46–72.

Gonzalez-Vicente, Ruben (2015). "The limits to China's non-interference foreign policy: Pro-state interventionism and the rescaling of economic governance," *Australian Journal of International Affairs* 69(2): 205–223.

Hakim, Peter (2006). "Is Washington losing Latin America," *Foreign Affairs* 85(1): 39–53.

Hameiri, Shahar, and Lee Jones (2015). "Rising powers and state transformation: The case of China," *European Journal of International Relations*, http://journals.sagepub .com.

Hansen, Thomas Blom, and Flinn Stepputat, (2006). "Sovereignty revisited," *Annual Review of Anthropology* 35: 295–315.

Hearn, Adrian H., and José Luis León-Manríquez (2011). "China and Latin America: A new era of an old exchange," in Adrian H. Hearn and José Luis León-Manríquez (eds.), *China Engages Latin America: Tracing the Trajectory*. Boulder, CO: Lynne Rienner.

Heritage Foundation (2015). *2015 Index of Economic Freedom—Country Rankings*, www.heritage.org.

Huffington Post (2014). "The rising costs of U.S. income inequality," 12 January, www.huffingtonpost.com.

Humphreys, David (2010). "The great metals boom: A retrospective," *Resources Policy* 35(1): 1–13.

IMF (2015). *World Economic Outlook—April 2015: Uneven Growth, Short- and Long-Term Factors*, www.imf.org.

Irwin, Amos, and Kevin P. Gallagher (2013). "Chinese mining in Latin America: A comparative perspective," *Journal of Environment Development* 22(2): 207–234.

Jiang, Julie, and Jonathan Sinton, (2011). *Overseas Investments by Chinese National Oil Companies*. Paris: International Energy Agency.

Landry, Pierre (2008). *Decentralized Authoritarianism in China: The Communist Party's Control of Local Elites in the Post-Mao Era*. Cambridge, UK: Cambridge University Press.

Laurie, Nina, Robert Andolina, and Sarah Radcliffe (2005). "Ethnodevelopment: Social movements, creating experts, and professionalising indigenous knowledge in Ecuador," *Antipode* 37(3): 470–496.

Lee, Ching Kwan (2014). "The spectre of global China," *New Left Review* 89 (September/October): 29–65.

Lin, Jintai, Da Pan, Steven J. Davis, Qiang Zhang, Kebin He, Can Wang, David G. Streets, Donald J. Wuebbles, and Dabo Guan (2014). "China's international trade and air pollution in the United States," *Proceedings of the National Academy of Sciences of the United States of America* 111(5): 1736–41.

Mainwaring, Scott (2006). "The crisis of representation in the Andes," *Journal of Democracy* 17(3): 13–27.

Mearsheimer, John J. (2010). "The gathering storm: China's challenge to US power in Asia," *Chinese Journal of International Politics* 3(4): 381–396.

Mesquita Moreiro, Mauricio (ed.) (2010). *India: Latin America's Next Big Thing?* Washington, DC: Inter-American Development Bank.

Mining Markets (2014) "Why Colombia's mining sector hasn't lived up to its promise," 6 August, www.miningmarkets.ca.

Ministerio de Finanzas (2015). *Deuda Pública del Sector Público del Ecuador*, 31 July, www.finanzas.gob.ec.

Nolan, Peter (2012). *Is China Buying the World?* Cambridge, UK: Polity Press.

Oppenheimer, Andres (2015). "Chinese loans to Latin America causing alarm," 28 February, www.miamiherald.com.

Oviedo Freire, Atawalpa (ed.) (2014). *Bifurcación del Buen Vivir y el Sumak Kawsay*. Quito: Ediciones SUMAK.

Paz, Gonzalo Sebastián (2012). "China, United States and hegemonic challenge in Latin America: An overview and some lessons from previous instances of hegemonic challenge in the region," *China Quarterly* 209: 18–34.

Peck, Jamie, and Nick Theodore (2007). "Variegated capitalism," *Progress in Human Geography* 31(6): 731–772.

Portocarrero, Gonzalo (ed.) (2013). *Sombras Coloniales y Globalización en el Perú de Hoy.* Lima: Red para el Desarrollo de las Ciencias Sociales en Perú.

Poveda, Pablo (2010). "Bolivia and China: indirect relations in a global market," in Alex E. Fernández Jilberto and Barbara Hogenboom (eds.), *Latin America Facing China: South-South Relations Beyond the Washington Consensus.* New York: Berghahn Books.

Ray, Rebecca, and Kevin Gallagher (2015). *China-Latin America Economic Bulletin 2015 Edition*, Boston University Economic Governance Initiative, Working Group on Development and Environment in the Americas, Discussion Paper 2015–9.

Ruiz Torres, Guillermo (2005). "Neoliberalism under crossfire in Peru: Fujimori's implementation of the Washington Consensus," in Susanne Soederberg, Georg Menz, and Philip G. Cerny (eds.), *Internalizing Globalization: The Rise of Neoliberalism and the Decline of National Varieties of Capitalism.* New York: Palgrave Macmillan.

Sanborn, Cynthia, and Álvaro Paredes (2014). "Consulta previa: Perú," *Americas Quarterly* (Spring).

Wall Street Journal (2011) "Anglo American sells stake in Chile Sur complex to Mitsubishi for $5.39 billion," 10 November, www.wsj.com.

Trading Economics (2015) "Colombia and Ecuador's GDP annual growth rates," www.tradingeconomics.com.

UNCTAD (2014). "Bilateral FDI statistics," www.unctad.org.

UNCTAD (2015). "State of commodity dependence 2014," www.unctad.org.

UNDP (2015). "Human Development Reports," hdr.undp.org.

World Bank (2006). *Latin America and the Caribbean's Response to the Growth of China and India: Overview of Research Findings and Policy Implications.* Washington, DC: World Bank.

World Bank (2015). *Data Catalog,* available at datacatalog.worldbank.org.

Xu, Ming, Eric Williams, and Braden Allenby (2010). "Assessing environmental impacts embodied in manufacturing and labor input for the China-U.S. trade," *Environmental Science and Technology* 44(2): 567–573.

10

Central America and the Caribbean's Relations with China and the United States

Contrasting Experiences! Converging Prospects?

RICHARD L. BERNAL

The Issue

The United States has been and continues to be the dominant and unchallenged global power in Central America and the Caribbean. American suzerainty has not been seriously challenged although there was U.S. concern over Soviet encroachment during the Cold War as manifested in the Cuban Missile Crisis and later on with the Sandinista regime in Nicaragua leading to U.S. support for the Contras. There was the perception of Cuban influence with the Bishop regime in Grenada eventually leading to a U.S. invasion of the island in 1983. The U.S. has at times not been comfortable with left-leaning governments such as Manley's in Jamaica in the late 1970s and the self-style "cooperative socialism" of Burnham in Guyana. China's economic, diplomatic, and psychological presence in the Caribbean and to a lesser extent in Costa Rica has increased during the last decade. This new development, termed "Dragon in the Caribbean,"[1] is concomitant with the economic rise of China and its growing involvement in international affairs. This has prompted a discussion about whether China's growing presence in the Caribbean is a trend about which the U.S. should be concerned and whether it portends a challenge by China given the way that it is jousting with the U.S. over influence in the Pacific Ocean and Asia. How this question is answered in Washington will determine U.S. reaction and how that response will be reflected in U.S. foreign policy. There are those who see China as a global competitor with the U.S. and see the Latin America as just another arena of rivalry. The media is prone to stories of China's displacement of the U.S.

as the largest trading partner of Latin America.[2] More nuanced observers such as Farnsworth have suggested that the U.S. is being complacent
about China's economic activities in the hemisphere[3] and Ellis argues that
there are security -related implications beyond the economic realm.[4] Paz
has characterized China as a "hegemonic challenge"[5] to the U.S in Latin
America but the U.S. does not see China as a threat in Latin America.
Roberta Jacobson, assistant secretary of state for Western Hemisphere
affairs, at the Sixth China-U.S. Sub-Dialogue on Latin America in 2013
stated clearly: "We do not in any way see China as a threat. What we do
see is the potential for greater partnership."[6]

China in Central America and the Caribbean

Relations between Central America and the Caribbean and the United
States and between these counties and China are a story of contrasts.
Given the countries' small size and limited strategic importance to the
U.S. and China the triangular conception for analysis of the interrela-
tionships is not as useful as is when it is applied to Mexico or Brazil,[7]
which are much more important to both the U.S. and China. The direction of influence runs from the U.S. and China to Central America and
the Caribbean, whereas what happens in the region, including shifting
diplomatic allegiances, is not likely to have much impact on either the
U.S. or China and is unlikely to affect the bilateral relationship between
Washington and Beijing. What occurs between the U.S. and China
elsewhere in the world could, however, have serious repercussions in
Central America and the Caribbean.

First, these relations differ significantly and in a variety of ways
from those between the U.S. and South America and China and South
America, and hence must be treated separately. This regional specificity
is often subsumed or overlooked in the literature on Latin America.[8]
The former weakness is particularly the case for the literature on Latin
America and China and the latter condition is characteristic of much
of the literature on U.S.–Latin America relations. Both failures of omission are to be found even in the publications of institutions whose mandates encompass Latin America (inclusive of Central America) and the
Caribbean. As egregious is that the general conclusions based on the
China–South America experience are misleadingly applied to Central

America and the Caribbean. For example, exports of agricultural products from South America to China have grown dramatically in recent
years, but exports of agricultural commodities are not significant for
Central America and the Caribbean. Given this lacuna in the existing
literature, it is necessary to separate Central America and the Caribbean
for examination. (This book recognizes this and remedies it by commis-
sioning a paper on Central American and the Caribbean.)

Second, while the U.S. has been the hegemonic power in Central
America and the Caribbean and its dominance has not been challenged
within this commonality, the history and modalities have diverged. This
divergence arises because many English-speaking Caribbean countries
remained colonies of Britain until 1962 when democratization proceeded apace. They gained political independence, and indeed some
islands in the Caribbean remain part of France. Even after the start of
decolonization, the British with the tacit agreement of the U.S., retained
a residual, yet diminishing governing role. Adding to the variety of interactions between the U.S. and the Caribbean is the special place and
differentiated treatment of Cuba and Haiti. This is in contrast to Central
America, where the colonial experience ended for some countries as
early as the 1830s,[9] and the U.S. has been the dominant power ever since.

A third point of importance is that relations with China are a relatively recent development in the Caribbean: relations commenced in the
early 1970s starting with Barbados, Guyana, Jamaica, and Trinidad and
Tobago. There has been a noticeable intensification of China's relations
with the Caribbean during the last decade and to a lesser extent with
Central America.

Fourth and of paramount importance is that relations with China
exist only with those countries that give diplomatic recognition to the
People's Republic of China (China). Central American countries other
than Costa Rica continue to recognize the so-called Republic of China
(Taiwan) as the government of mainland China. The diplomatic allegiances of Central American and Caribbean countries are shown in
table 10.1. This is not a major issue in South America, where only Paraguay recognizes Taiwan. The contestation of diplomatic recognition is
the basis of a vigorous rivalry between China and Taiwan. China finds it
an intolerable embarrassment and is prepared to invest high-level diplomatic engagement and development aid in the quest to eliminate this

TABLE 10.1. Embassies of China and United States and Overseas Offices of Taiwan in the Caribbean and Central America

Country	Embassy of China	Overseas Office of Taiwan	Embassy of the U.S.
Antigua and Barbuda	X		Serviced from Barbados
Bahamas	X		X
Barbados	X		X
Belize		X	X
Costa Rica	X		X
Cuba	X		X
Dominica	X		Serviced from Barbados
Dominican Republic		X	X
El Salvador		X	X
Guatemala		X	X
Guyana	X		X
Grenada	X		Serviced from Barbados
Haiti		X	X
Honduras		X	X
Jamaica	X		X
Nicaragua		X	X
Panama		X	X
St. Kitts and Nevis		X	Serviced from Barbados
St. Lucia		X	Serviced from Barbados
St. Vincent		X	Serviced from Barbados
Suriname	X		X
Trinidad and Tobago	X		X

diplomatic ambiguity. Taiwan's independence has never been accepted by China and Taiwan's desire to remain separate impels Taiwan to spend a considerable sum on maintaining, through generous aid, "friendships" with countries increasingly tempted by China's larger pool of aid and the obvious long-term strategic benefits of an alliance with China. Indeed, Costa Rica's switch from Taiwan to China is an example of this dilemma. Maintaining relations with both Taiwan and China is not acceptable to China, as St. Lucia found out when they sought such an option.[10] China applies this "One China" policy strictly and without exception.

Global Re-Dimensioning of China

China has the largest population, it is the second-largest economy, and it is the fourth-largest country in land area. It has nuclear weapons and the largest standing army. It is not merely a country, it is a civilization whose culture has been known from antiquity. The world is not changing; China has changed and changed profoundly. This change has, in recent decades, been driven by a sustained period of economic growth of over 10 percent per annum over an unprecedented duration. China's presence and its role in the world continue to experience a re-dimensioning in economic and political terms. This has inevitably brought China into competition with the U.S. in the economic sphere. As its share of global trade and financial flows have grown, it has invariably asserted, albeit gradually and subtly, a political presence through a worldwide diplomatic campaign that reinforces its expanded economic and strategic interests. The U.S. has taken the approach to China's rise of encouraging China to take an increased role in global affairs with a concomitant share of the cost of global multilateral governance while not challenging the dominance in the final instance of U.S. power. This could be styled as enlightened participation in a schema of cooperation designed and supervised by the U.S. The U.S. design of limited and gradually phased devolution of global power acquiesces to yielding some economic ground while holding a firm line on security. The objective of the U.S. approach is—as Robert Zoellick, deputy secretary of state, explained in 2005—that China would become a "responsible stakeholder" in the international system, working cooperatively to resolve global issues.[11]

How this template is operationalized varies from issue to issue, and from region to region. For example, Asia is a region in which the U.S. is prepared to tolerate the shifting of gravity of economic growth but, in some circumstances, to resist an enlargement of China's role in security issues. Perhaps what President Theodore Roosevelt said in June 1905, "Our future will be more determined by our position on the Pacific facing China than by our position on the Atlantic facing Europe," is symptomatic of today's mindset. The response in Asia is in stark contrast to that in Africa, which has done little to hinder or channel China's growing involvement in financing projects in oil and gas.

The United States has expressed concern about China's policy in Asia and has taken steps to reassert the security role of the U.S. in the Asian arena. While China has become an important trade partner in Latin America and the Caribbean, the U.S. does not regard this economic presence as portending increased political influence, as U.S. dominance in the region has been unchallenged since World War II. The Western Hemisphere is certainly not a region in which the U.S. and China could come into conflict over security issues.

Enhanced Presence of China

During the last decade, China has been expanding its economic and political relations with developing countries, including small island developing states, as it expands its involvement in the global economy and its engagement in international affairs. Apart from the desire for a presence everywhere in the world evinced by superpowers, relations with small states are a usually low priority for superpowers preoccupied with global perspectives. It may appear strange that these small, strategically unimportant countries would be on the agenda of China's global outreach. China's motives for enhancing and intensifying its diplomatic relations in the Caribbean emanated from the rivalry with Taiwan for diplomatic recognition. Most of the countries that still grant recognition to Taiwan as the government of China are in Central America and the Caribbean. China wants to eliminate that diplomatic recognition and to prevent any country from switching allegiance to Taiwan. The steady and calculated escalation of China's presence in the Caribbean is most clearly evident in the significant increase in the flow of economic aid (loans, grants, and technical assistance) to the countries of this region. There has been a concomitant increase in diplomatic interaction between China and the Caribbean states and rising fealty.

China's presence in the Caribbean has increased significantly in scope and intensity in contrast to its presence in Central America, where it only established diplomatic relations with Costa Rica on June 1, 2007. Imports of manufactured goods from China are increasing in all the countries of Central America and the Caribbean, although unevenly. Exports from the region have not kept pace with imports, resulting in an expanding trade deficit. China's development aid is concentrated in those countries with which it has diplomatic relations. Costa Rica has sought to expand trade with the conclusion of a free trade agreement with China that entered into force on August 1, 2011. When phased implementation is completed, approximately 90 percent of goods will trade at zero tariff and some service sectors will be liberalized. The FTA also includes intellectual property rights, trade remedies, customs procedures, technical barriers to trade, and rules of origin.

China's rise to being a global superpower inevitably affects its relations with the United States. How these relations develop and are managed has implications for China and the Caribbean states. Of paramount importance is where in the multidimensional dynamics of China-U.S. relations does the increasing presence of China in Central America and the Caribbean fit. In raising its profile, China has trespassed into a region that is traditionally the preserve of U.S. hegemony. Enigmatic as its motives seem, China regards its engagement as vital. It is because relations with Taiwan are viewed as an insult to the prestige of a global power which China now feels itself to be. The growing presence of China in the Caribbean has been proceeding apace, but has elicited little attention and no discernable foreign policy response from the United States who has traditionally regarded this part of the globe as the proverbial "U.S. backyard." In the case of the Caribbean, in spite of being designated as the "third border" of the U.S., China's expanded trade and its diplomatic rivalry with Taiwan are not contentious issues. In fact, Washington may well welcome the increase in Chinese aid, as reducing demands for U.S. aid at a time when the U.S. is trying to wind down costly and extended engagements elsewhere in the world and when the political atmosphere in Congress is not propitious for economic aid. Narcotics trafficking, illegal migrants, and the associated transnational crime do not constitute a sufficient threat in a region of mostly middle-income democratic countries to warrant greater U.S. attention.

Global U.S.-China Relations

How the U.S. will respond to China in the Central America and the Caribbean has to be contextualized against the backdrop of the global U.S.-China relations. The U.S. has not exhibited animosity or even concern about the intensification of relations between China and Latin America centered on a rapid expansion of trade, particularly with Argentina, Brazil, Chile, and Peru. In contrast, the U.S. has "upped its game" in Asia, as manifested in a reassertion of a security presence, although it is not clear how far either China and the U.S. would go in maintaining their security interests. The accepted limits to engagement are continually shifting, consequent to China's activities in the South China Sea.

Future U.S. policy toward China will depend on which school of thought prevails in U.S. foreign policy. Fareed Zakaria opines: "Conflict and competition—particularly in the economic realm—between China and the United States is inevitable. But whether this turns ugly depends largely on policy choices that will be made in Washington and Beijing."[12] Several analysts are of the view that the U.S. and the rising powers, including China and India, have a vested interest in a stable world order and would avoid a frontal conflict with the U.S. while asserting increased influence in world affairs. The Obama administration opted to pursue a policy of engagement and dialogue with China, emphasizing interdependence and cooperation. This approach is premised on the assumption articulated by Ikenberry[13] that China's rise will end the United States' unipolar moment, but the U.S. can remain dominant in the international order while integrating China. Combative approaches would portend dangerous scenarios.

The degree, pace, and modalities of China's assertiveness in international affairs are still debated in Beijing, including the extent to which China would go to prevent Taiwan's independence. There are a variety of currents of thinking in China, prompting Jiang's observation that in the conduct of foreign policy "a consensus has never been reached on the balance between keeping a low profile and taking action."[14] As China's profile and tangible presence increases, it will have to work assiduously through its foreign policy to prevent resentment and ensure harmonious trading relationships. It will avoid head-on confrontations with the U.S., but pursue careful diplomacy aimed at not clashing with the U.S. while probing and contesting for political space in the international arena. This mode of diplomacy with the U.S. has been described as: "China has always played the weak hand brilliantly."[15] While not challenging U.S. dominance, China's increased economic and diplomatic involvement in Central America and the Caribbean, a region that the U.S. regards as its exclusive preserve, has not gone unnoticed in Washington. The U.S. was sanguine about China's deployment of 143 peacekeepers in Haiti in 2007, which constituted a precedent in the Western Hemisphere. The willingness to allow China's gradually more assertive approach has aroused calls for action both in regard to Chinese economic encroachment and steadily growing diplomatic presence. Nick Lardy of the Institute for International Economics has characterized the U.S. attitude as "China is just pushing through an open door across the globe—and in the U.S. backyard."[16]

Obama's China Policy

It is difficult for any U.S. administration to maintain a nonconfrontational policy of cooperation toward China because the foreign policy environment is one where many insist on conceiving of China as a protagonist motivated by nefarious goals of overtaking or undermining U.S. security across the world. This portrayal is very much a continuation of the Cold War prism of competition as head-on confrontation. In the United States, there is concern about the rise of China in world affairs, and in some quarters this gives way to thinking that borders on the paranoid.[17] This state of mind is perpetuated and propagated by an embattled view of security, of "us versus them," heightened since the events of 9/11 and subsequent U.S. "War on Terror."[18] Public receptivity to the view that China is an antagonistic rival is fostered by sensationalist journalism. Emblematic of such journalism is an article in *Time* magazine on August 31, 2015, which reported that "many outsiders see China as a country where dark forces may one day ignite a sudden conflagration inflicting massive damage-for reasons that are murky."[19] The Bush and Obama administrations pursued a policy of constructive engagement with the intent of inducing China to be a compatible multilateral player with a vested interest in the stability of the current American-designed and -managed international order. The policy was a pragmatic blend of accommodating assertive but reasonable Chinese positions and resisting revision of the existing security parameters and geographic deployment. Where, how, and when to yield and pushback were a continuously recalibrated multidimensional mix within the overall spectrum of global policy priorities and deployment. Among the most pressing issues was to reassure Asian allies that the U.S. will be resolute in resisting and even blocking China's rapidly escalation of assertiveness in the Pacific. Jeffrey Bader, who served in the National Security Council of the Obama administration, makes the profound observation that "the problems in U.S. leadership in Asia were not the consequence of Asia-specific policy errors, but rather of the spill-over effect of misguided policies elsewhere in the world that had consequences everywhere."[20]

China's Diplomatic Presence

At present, the People's Republic of China is recognized by Antigua and Barbuda, the Bahamas, Barbados, Costa Rica, Dominica, Grenada, Guyana, Jamaica, Suriname, and Trinidad and Tobago. Belize, the Dominican Republic, El Salvador, Haiti, Honduras, Nicaragua, Panama, St. Kitts and Nevis, St. Lucia, and St. Vincent and the Grenadines have relations with Taiwan. Costa Rica and Dominica have switched diplomatic allegiance from Taiwan to China. Costa Rica is the first and only Central American country to do so. St. Lucia switched from Taiwan to China and back to Taiwan.

Formal diplomatic relations between the People's Republic of China and Caribbean states began with the establishment of diplomatic ties with Guyana and Jamaica in the latter half of 1972, and shortly thereafter with Barbados and Trinidad and Tobago. China and those Caribbean countries have signed a variety of agreements aimed at enhancing economic cooperation. They have established institutionalized arrangements to expand trade and investment, as well as to operate meetings on a regular schedule between China and the Caribbean governments as a group. These include the China-Caribbean Economic and Trade Cooperation Forum, which met in February 2005, July 2007, and September 2011. The institutional vehicle for fostering business cooperation is the China-Caribbean Joint Business Council; it includes Antigua and Barbuda, the Bahamas, Barbados, Dominica, the Dominican Republic, Cuba, Grenada, Guyana, Haiti, Jamaica, Suriname, and Trinidad and Tobago. These institutional arrangements are supplemented and complemented by high-level visits to the region, including a visit by President Xi Jinping in June 2013 to Trinidad and the reception of several Caribbean heads of government in Beijing.

The United States has diplomatic relations with all the countries of Central America and the Caribbean. With embassies in all of these countries, the U.S. has comprehensive coverage, whereas China has only partial coverage of the region. The U.S. is a powerful member of important hemispheric organizations such as the Organization of American States, and the largest shareholder in the Inter-American Development Bank. In multilateral and international organizations such as the United Nations, the U.S. has the possibility of having the support of all the countries of the region, a situation that is ruled out for China by the split diplomatic recognition.

China has significantly increased its engagement in the Caribbean, and this is evident in the substantial increase in development assistance and the construction of projects of political importance to Caribbean governments such as the prime minister's office complex in Port of Spain. The Chinese have courted these small states through numerous visits of high-level delegations, i.e., at the presidential, vice presidential, and ministerial levels. The president of China, Xi Jinping, visited Trinidad and Costa Rica in June 2013. Obama visited Jamaica in April 2015. The heads of government in the Central American and Caribbean countries with diplomatic relations have without exception traveled to Beijing, and in some cases more than once.

China has built goodwill and consolidated relations with the Caribbean countries and Costa Rica by what has been called "stadium diplomacy,"[21] i.e., the construction of sports stadiums that are highly visible symbols of China's assistance and a lasting source of pride for the beneficiary country. Chinese firms are beginning to complement government-to-government goodwill through donations to sport and education to reinforce the campaign of their government. China Harbour, in September 2012, made a very substantial financial contribution to bolster the professional soccer league in Jamaica.[22]

Tensions and Possible Flashpoints

China's increased presence in the Caribbean and, to a lesser extent, in Central America does not worry the U.S., but there are issues outside of the region that could prompt countermoves in the Caribbean. The issue of China-Taiwan relations is one that could cause a spillover in the Western

Hemisphere. The China-Taiwan rivalry will continue because China is committed to the view of the People's Republic of China as a single holistic state and regards Taiwan as a breakaway province. Taiwan will continue to mobilize diplomatic support because recognition by other states is a plausible way of claiming that it is an independent country. Meanwhile a "greater China economy" involving China, Hong Kong, and Taiwan has been emerging. The already significant and deepening catenation of the two economies is likely to have an ameliorating effect on the intensity of the diplomatic maneuvering. China and Taiwan could both devote less attention to the Caribbean and Central America if there was a standstill agreement on competing for diplomatic recognition. This is not farfetched because of the high level of economic integration between Taiwan and China, amounting to 40 percent of Taiwan's trade, and the fact that the prohibition of Chinese investment in Taiwan has been lifted.[23]

There have been recent signs of rapprochement.[24] In 2015, President Xi Jinping of China and then-President Ma Ying-jeou of Taiwan agreed to meet in neutral territory, Singapore. This historic meeting is the first in the 66 years since the takeover of China by Communists in 1949.[25] The meeting took place just before elections in Taiwan and therefore could be China's way of bolstering support for the political party in Taiwan that is favorably disposed to peaceful coexistence, euphemistically described as "consolidat[ing] cross-strait peace and maintain[ing] the status quo."[26] The issue of relations with Beijing is a controversial election issue[27] and the announcement of the meeting sparked protests.[28] On the Chinese side feelings on this issue are still strong. For instance, in 1997 China vetoed sending United Nations peacekeepers to Guatemala. The justification for the action was Guatemala's relations with Taiwan.[29] The U.S. has welcomed the historic meeting, but some have opined that there is already a process of "Finlandization" underway that will see Taiwan drift away from the U.S. and into the orbit of China.[30]

To China, the South China Sea is what the Caribbean Sea is to the United States.[31] China has been building or enlarging an island in the South China Sea by enlarging submerged reefs. The United States and several Asian countries have expressed concern about China's construction of airstrips and naval fortifications on artificial islands built on reefs in the South China Sea. Admiral Harry Harris Jr., head of the U.S.

Pacific Command, defended the decision to sail a U.S. naval destroyer within 12 miles of the Chinese-occupied Subi Reef in the disputed waters of the South China Sea. He stated: "Our military will continue to fly, sail and operate whenever and wherever international law allows. The South China Sea is not—and will not—be an exception. I truly believe that these routine operations should never be construed as a threat to any nation."[32] While criticizing the U.S. action as "hegemony and hypocrisy,"[33] China has signaled that what the U.S. sees as the right of navigation of international waters as allowed by international law[34] will not be allowed to impair the relationship with the U.S.[35] This posturing and joisting could inadvertently lead to an incident that could heighten tensions, as both sides have to show resolve. Chinese and American naval vessels have come dangerously close to collision on several occasions, for example in the South China Sea in December 2013.[36]

China's closeness to Venezuela was motivated by locking in long-term supplies of oil rather than by a political alliance, such as the way that China has consolidated its relationship with Brazil. For Venezuela, relations with China are a combination of an export opportunity and a strategic alliance not susceptible to U.S. pressure. The decline in the price of oil and the financial and fiscal difficulties of the Maduro government in Venezuela have reduced the capacity to support the PetroCarib facility. The Dominican Republic and Jamaica have repaid a large share of their debt to Venezuela at a substantially discounted rate.

The normalization of relations between the U.S. and Cuba could have implications for U.S.-China relations. Both American and Chinese investors (both state enterprises and private firms) will move with increased alacrity to seize investment and trade opportunities. In this regard Chinese is somewhat ahead, and has the advantage of possible affinity of political philosophy and the residue of anti-Americanism in the Cuban leadership born of a long and difficult history. China's economic relations with Cuba began in 1961 following Ernesto "Che" Guevara's visit to China, which resulted in the first bilateral Economic and Technological Cooperation Agreement and a $40 million line of credit for the purchase of goods from China. During the first two decades after the Cuban Revolution, China accounted for 9 percent of Cuba's trade, with sugar constituting three-quarters of Cuba's exports to China. By 2013, trade with China accounted for some US$1.8 billion, making the People's

Republic of China Cuba's second-largest trade partner, with the largest being Venezuela. Xi Jinping and Raul Castro signed new agreements in July 2014 that should give impetus to further trade and investment.

If China were to build and control a transoceanic canal across Nicaragua it could raise geopolitical and security concerns in the U.S.[37] At this time, the status of the planned Nicaragua Grand Canal is not clear. The idea of a canal across Nicaragua predates the Panama Canal, which was seen as the less difficult engineering task of the two alternatives. A Chinese company, the Hong Kong Nicaragua Canal Development Investment Group (HKND Group), has signed an agreement with the government of Nicaragua to construct the canal by 2020 at an estimated cost of $50 billion. The Nicaragua Grand Canal is to be able to accommodate ships with capacities up to 23,000 TEUs (twenty-foot equivalent units), which exceeds the 13,000 TEUs that the Panama Canal will be able to accommodate after its expansion. Projected freight does not appear to support the commercial viability of tow canals. As of August 2015, no significant construction work had started[38] on the largest earthmoving operation in the history of mankind. The government of China has denied financial involvement.[39]

A new aspect of China's aid to the Caribbean has been the provision of funds to the Jamaica Defense Force (JDF), which since its formation has relied on assistance from the United States, the United Kingdom, and Canada. In August 2011, China committed to providing military aid worth 8 million RMB (US$1.1 million), the specific uses of which are yet to be defined.[40] This step is in keeping with China's expansion of cooperation with the military in Latin America, and is related to furthering its diplomatic, political, and commercial interests rather than being motivated by security concerns.[41] In October 2004, China provided 125 police officers as part of a UN Security Council mandated peacekeeping contingent in Haiti, an unprecedented event because it involved Chinese security personnel for the first time in the Western Hemisphere.

China's Economic Presence

During the past decade, China's economic presence in the Caribbean countries has increased, but has varied from country to country. Imports of Chinese goods have grown in all Caribbean countries, even though some countries have chosen to maintain diplomatic relations with Taiwan. Development assistance from China has increased significantly in those countries that have diplomatic relations with China or have changed their diplomatic allegiance. The differentiation in the pattern of economic interaction reflects the fact that some countries recognize the People's Republic of China (China) while others have chosen to maintain diplomatic relations with Taiwan.

Trade

Imports from China into the Caribbean have grown substantially and rapidly—$577.8 million in 2003 to $4.8 billion in 2012[42]—because of their very competitive prices and improving quality. Imports from China are mainly manufactured consumer goods, however, in recent years, imports of capital goods have begun to increase. Most Chinese exports to the Caribbean compete with local production and could displace local production notably including a range of processed food, tilapia fillets, cement, apparel, furniture, and paper and plastic products. It is estimated that "in the Caribbean, 96 percent of manufacturers were losing export competitiveness to China, 86 percent in Central America and Mexico, and 79 percent from South America."[43] For several consumer products, such as footwear, electronics, and T-shirts, the region has come to depend predominantly on imports from China. Despite the steady growth in imports, there are some Chinese products that have not yet appeared in Caribbean markets, such as motor vehicles and medicines. In Central America imports from China have grown but have been inhibited by the lack of diplomatic relations with China. However, by 2012, China (including Hong Kong and Macao) had become Guatemala's fourth-largest trade partner, after the rest of Central America, the U.S., and Mexico.[44] Guatemalan exports to China are highly concentrated in select products, e.g., sugar and plastics, whereas Chinese exports to Guatemala are much more diverse and value added, e.g., electronics and auto parts.[45]

Exports from the Caribbean countries to China's large and rapidly growing market have not grown significantly. Exports increased from $120.6 million in 2003 to $705.3 million in 2012, with the Dominican

Republic accounting for over 50 percent of the region's total exports to China. This makes the Dominican Republic the largest Caribbean trading partner of China, although it does not have diplomatic relations with China. During the period 2003–2012, most countries exported less than US$10 million per annum; exports average less than $1 million for Antigua and Barbuda, St. Kitts and Nevis, St. Lucia, and St. Vincent and the Grenadines. Exports from Guyana, Jamaica, Haiti, Suriname, and Trinidad and Tobago have slowly increased. Among the most important exports are bauxite and alumina, lumber, asphalt, and scrap metal. The entire Caribbean represents less than 0.001 percent of China's total imports. Exports from Central America to China as with the Caribbean have remained small, amounting to less than 5 percent of the region's total exports during the period 2000–2011.[46] In addition, exports from Central America and the Caribbean to China are largely raw materials, food, agricultural products, and scrap metal. All the countries of the region would like to diversify the composition of their exports to China to manufactured goods and products higher up the value chain. Costa Rica in particular has been frustrated by what has been described as the "reprimarization" of exports.[47]

The trade deficit between China and the Caribbean has increased very substantially, from $457.2 million in 2003 to $4.1 billion in 2012. The increase in the trade deficit has occurred because the growth of imports from China has far outpaced the expansion of exports from the region. Goods from China have proven very attractive to Caribbean importers because of their price and quality, consequently they have increasingly substituted Chinese goods for those from traditional trading partners such as the United States. The Caribbean countries other than the Dominican Republic and Haiti are not important markets for the U.S., and the Chinese share of the market is small but is likely to grow particularly in certain manufactured goods, and the encroachment could involve capital goods, which have traditionally been the preserve of the U.S., e.g., motor vehicles. China's exports to Central America have grown steadily, but exports from the region to China have not increased noticeably and, with the exception of Costa Rica, consist of primary products or products destined for the recycling industry.[48] Exports from the region have not kept pace, resulting in a huge trade deficit with China with 94 percent of the total trade consisting of Chinese products entering the region.[49] In addition to the trade deficit with China, there is further aggravation caused by Chinese exports competing against Central American exports of apparel and textiles to the U.S. market.[50]

Imports from China have outpaced exports, leading to a growing adverse trade balance. China's trade with Central America has not grown rapidly. The main trade partner is Costa Rica, reflecting the commencement of diplomatic relations and the stimulus of the free trade agreement. Since the FTA has come into effect Costa Rica's exports to China have increased from $195 million in 2011 to $371 million in 2013. Costa Rica is the only country that has an FTA with China. The Dominican Republic and Central American countries other than Costa Rica have free trade agreements with Taiwan. The Dominican Republic–Central America FTA (CAFTA-DR), which came into force in 2005, is a free trade agreement between the United States and Costa Rica, El Salvador, Guatemala, Honduras, Nicaragua, and the Dominican Republic. Belize and Panama are not members of CAFTA-DR. On October 31, 2012, the United States–Panama Trade Promotion Agreement entered into force. Collectively these countries constitute the third-largest U.S. export market in Latin America, exceeded by Mexico and Brazil. Total trade in 2013 amounted to $60 billion with U.S. exports totaling $30 billion.[51]

None of the Caribbean countries have FTAs with either China or Taiwan, although the Caribbean does have an FTA with the European Union, the CARIFORUM-EU Economic Partnership Agreement signed in 2008.[52] There has been no interest in the Caribbean in negotiating an FTA with China. The Caribbean countries other than the Dominican Republic conduct trade with the U.S. under the Caribbean Basin Economic Recovery Act (CBERA),operative since January 1, 1984, which provides for duty-free entry of goods into the United States from designated beneficiary countries, and the Caribbean Basin Trade Partnership Act (CBTPA) of October 2000. The CBTPA expanded preferential treatment for apparel made in the Caribbean region. The Caribbean countries as a group were ranked 19th among U.S. export destinations in 2012, accounting for $19 billion or 1.4 percent of total U.S. exports.[53] Central America and the Caribbean together represent an export market of almost $50 billion although many of the individual national markets are very small.

Development Finance

China's development finance consists of aid and loans to finance construction and infrastructure projects executed by Chinese companies. China provides aid to over 123 developing countries, and over 30 international and regional organizations. China's development assistance takes the form of grants, loans, lines of credit, technical assistance, and donations in kind. Loans from China carry terms similar to those from multilateral development institutions, but are attractive because they are dispensed with less conditionality than assistance from Western bilateral agencies and multilateral development institutions. The increase in Chinese aid to the Caribbean region and Costa Rica is consistent with a substantial escalation of development aid to developing countries. The *Financial Times* calculates that China's lending to developing countries in the two years 2009 and 2010 was more than that of the World Bank.[54]

Development assistance is the principal means of influence employed by China in its foreign policy in the Caribbean. The amount and allocation are related to the rivalry with Taiwan for diplomatic recognition. Chinese government is also willing to extend generous aid to those countries that switch diplomatic allegiance from Taiwan. For example, when Dominica switched its diplomatic recognition from Taiwan to China, it benefited from the construction of a $17 million cricket stadium and a promise of $122 million in economic assistance.[55] Those countries that have chosen to recognize Taiwan have done so for pecuniary motives rather than ideological reasons. Dr. Denzil Douglas, prime minister of St. Kitts and Nevis, explained: "We took an informed position that we would prefer to support Taiwan because Taiwan at the moment can bring the greater support in the advancing of the economic, social and political development of the people."[56]

The construction of critical infrastructure, such as bridges, and important and highly visible buildings, such as hospitals, has earned the gratitude of several Caribbean governments. Chinese aid has prompted Antigua and Barbuda's prime minister, Baldwin Spencer, to declare, "China has time and time proven that it is a true friend of Antigua and Barbuda and is prepared to assist us as we develop this country. For this we are eternally grateful."[57] Such laudatory comments are no surprise, given China's agreement to construct a new terminal at the airport at a cost of $45 million. The increase in Chinese aid is taking place at a time when aid from traditional sources such as the United States has declined, prompting one observer to state, "China has filled a void left by the United States and other Western nations."[58] In 2007, China promised to provide the Caribbean economic assistance of 4 billion yuan in low-interest loans and for training related to the promotion of trade.[59]

Throughout its relationship with the Caribbean countries, China has provided some development assistance, starting on a small scale with projects enabled by technical assistance, e.g., shrimp farming and bamboo weaving in Trinidad and Tobago.[60] Later, China increased its development assistance to Caribbean countries, focusing resources on large, highly visible infrastructure projects such as the construction of national stadiums in Dominica, Grenada, and St. Lucia, and a community-based stadium in Jamaica. Schools have been built in several countries, a hospital in St. Lucia, a multipurpose sports arena in Barbados, and a cricket stadium in Jamaica (US$30 million). The Chinese government also provided funding for the Montego Bay Convention Centre in Jamaica in the amount of US$45.2 million at a concessionary rate of interest, through the Export-Import Bank of China. Jamaica also benefited from a loan of US$400 million for road construction and repair. In Suriname, Chinese companies plan to undertake US$600 million worth of construction projects, including a new deep-sea harbor, a railway from Paramaribo to Brazil, an east-west sea wall, a new highway to the airport, and 8,000 low-cost houses.[61]

The growth of China's economy and its foreign policy outreach offers opportunities for Chinese foreign direct investment (FDI). FDI will provide Chinese firms with a production platform for exporting to the European Community, the United States, and Canada, where CARICOM has preferential trade arrangements. As these trade and investment interests grow, China, cognizant of Taiwan's aggressive competition in the region, will increase its foreign aid to Caribbean countries. Governments in the Caribbean are likely to be receptive to offers of development aid including loans and lines of credit, even if these are tied to procurement in China and to execution by Chinese firms and workers. Interest in financial assistance from China will be high, given the fiscal situation and debt profile of several Caribbean governments[62] and Costa Rica. When diplomatic arrangements were set up with China, Costa

Rica sold bonds to China and in September 2015, approaching China as a potential source of finance to address a widening fiscal deficit.[63]

The generous concessionary terms of loans from China have generated opportunities for Chinese firms and workers. Activities in Dominica provide a lucid illustration of the nexus between Chinese development aid and construction projects. On signing a framework agreement, the government of Dominica and the government of China were able to finalize loan arrangements with the Export-Import Bank of China. The loan of up to US$40 million has an interest rate of 2 percent per annum, with a repayment period of 20 years, including a grace period of 5 years. It will be used for the construction of the Dominica State College, the State House, the office building of the Electoral Commission, and the rehabilitation of major roads.[64] Critics have complained that while the interest rate on loans from China is lower than the rates offered by international development institutions, these loans are tied to employment of Chinese workers, ignore environmental standards, and deliver shoddy construction. Beneficiary governments have not expressed these concerns and have been pleased with the speed with which urgently needed facilities have been completed.

During the last decade, China has supplied construction services to Central American and Caribbean governments financed by development aid from China and loans from the China Development Bank. The provision of aid to Costa Rica has not been as successful as in the Caribbean countries. During his visit to Costa Rica in June 2013, President Xi Jinping signed 13 agreements worth $2 billion for projects including upgrading the Moin oil refinery and construction Route 32, a major highway. These projects are stalled for a variety of reasons including mistrust,[65] public protests, and disagreements over design and implementation. China donated 350 motor cars to the national police, but they did not prove to be very durable, with a large number in need of repair and spare parts.[66]

Apart from bilateral development assistance, China has become a development partner in regional and multilateral development finance institutions that service the Caribbean. China is a non-regional member of the Caribbean Development Bank (CDB), with US$56 million in shares and US$33 million in the CDB's Special Development Fund.[67] All borrowing members of the CDB are eligible for these resources regardless of whether their diplomatic relations are with China or Taiwan. The Central American countries, Cuba, and the Dominican Republic are not members of the CDB. In 2008, China also became a member of the Inter-American Development Bank (IDB) with a contribution of $350 million and all borrowing members of the IDB are eligible to draw on these funds, regardless of their diplomatic affiliation.

Taiwan is very conscious of China's enormous capacity for development aid, and has kept up its aid to those Central American and Caribbean governments that have diplomatic relations with Taipei. Taiwan's International Cooperation and Development Fund (ICDF) financed 48 active projects across the region in 2013, with ICDF approving more than US$120 million in new loans for the regionwide social development, education, and technological training in the coming years.[68] Taiwan provides financial support to the Central American Economic Integration System (SIECA in Spanish), and is a member of the Central American Economic Integration Bank (BCIE in Spanish), contributing over US$150 million.[69]

Foreign Direct Investment

Outward FDI from China was authorized in 1979, when the first joint venture law was passed, and particularly after the 16th Congress of the Chinese Communist Party promulgated the "Go Global Strategy." Starting from a low level, FDI grew slowly throughout the 1980s and 1990s, increasing rapidly during the last decade. The impetus for FDI emanates from both the state and the enterprises, and the state and large enterprises are either in tandem or at least in alignment.[70] While the state has an overarching role, it is not possible to control all FDI given the number of firms involved. Based on a survey of executives of Chinese companies, it was reported that "[t]he first primary push factor propelling the internationalization of Chinese SOEs (state-owned enterprises) is the central government's 'Go Global' policy and related incentives, while the second relates to the business strategies adopted by enterprise leaders."[71] In 2013 China with $101 billion was the third-largest source of foreign direct investment after the U.S. and Japan.[72] The stock of Chinese FDI has increased dramatically during that period from $90.6 billion to $531.9

billion.[73] In 2012, China's outward FDI accounted for 6.3% of global FDI and 2.3% of global stock of FDI, which put China third, behind the United States and Japan, in global FDI and 13th in the stock of global FDI.[74] This trend is likely to continue, as President Xi Jinping in November 2014 proclaimed that Chinese "offshore" investment would reach $1.25 trillion over the next decade.[75] As China's FDI continues to expand on a global scale, it will scrutinize investment opportunities in Central America and the Caribbean. Chinese delegations and investment missions with participation by the China Development Bank (CDB) have made several trips to the region to identify projects.

Chinese FDI in Central America is very small, totaling under $500 million, nearly all of which is in Panama, amounting in 2013 to $479 million.[76] Surprisingly, given all the many projects that have been mooted, FDI from China was only $3.26 million in 2013.[77] China and Costa Rica have signed an agreement to create five Special Economic Zones with the objective of attracting Chinese investment; however, after many years, they have not actually been established. Elsewhere in Central America, there has been little Chinese FDI but the proposed transoceanic canal through Nicaragua could change this paucity. In those Central American countries that do not have diplomatic ties with China, there is a lack of awareness about the region among Chinese firms, and this has been a limitation on trade and, more so, FDI.[78] Although China has become a large and expanding source of FDI, little has found its way into Central America. The flow of Chinese FDI is unimportant, representing only 2.5 percent of the total FDI in Panama in 2011, and less than 1 percent in Costa Rica and Guatemala.[79] FDI flows from Central America into China are virtually nonexistent, totaling less than $15 million during the entire period 2006–2012.[80] This could change, if the investment in a transoceanic canal in Nicaragua by the Hong Kong Nicaragua Canal Development Investment Group, a Hong Kong–based consortium, were to materialize. The initial estimate is $50 billion for construction.

Foreign direct investment from China in the Caribbean countries is very small,[81] both as a share of China's FDI and as a share of the stock of FDI in the Caribbean. Data for the period 2003–2011 reveals: (a) By 2011 the largest recipients were Cuba with $146.4 million and Guyana with $135.1 million. (b) There are some unexplained changes in the value of the stock of investment, for example, Chinese FDI in the Bahamas was $56.5 million in 2007 but $0.6 million a year later. In Cuba, Chinese FDI declined from $85.32 million in 2009 to $68.98 million in 2010 only to jump to $146.4 million in 2011. (c) Cuba accounts for over one-quarter of Chinese FDI and the figure for the rest of the Caribbean is $322.5 million. (d) The data does not appear to include the largest investment by a Chinese firm in the Caribbean: the $2.6 billion port facility in Freeport, Bahamas, built and operated since 2000 by the Hong Kong–owned Hutchison Whampoa.[82] The stock of Chinese FDI amounted to $88.3 million in 2003 but by 2011 it had grown to $468.9 million. The stock thus increased by over 500 percent in less than a decade. Chinese companies have initiated ventures in several Caribbean countries, with the Bahamas (tourism), Cuba (agriculture), Guyana (mining, agriculture), Suriname (agriculture), and Jamaica (agriculture, infrastructure) standing out as the most important destinations for investment. Cuba and Guyana are the countries with the largest amount of investment with $146.4 million and $135.1 million, respectively. The FDI flows from the Caribbean to China are almost unidentifiable, with $2.38 million from Jamaica being recorded.[83]

Chinese FDI in the Caribbean is beginning to pick up,[84] mainly in tourism, for example in the Bahamas where the China State Construction Engineering Corporation, a state enterprise, purchased the British Colonial Hilton. Other hotel projects are planned for Jamaica and Antigua. Chinese FDI projects have occurred in agriculture and mining, i.e., sugar in Jamaica, palm oil in Suriname, and bauxite in Guyana. A number of projects have not come to fruition in Costa Rica and Trinidad and Tobago.

The drivers of Chinese FDI in Central America and the Caribbean are the same as those operative in the global spread, and hence the region does have prospects for garnering FDI from China in tourism, agriculture, energy, and mining. Some of the opportunities in the small developing economies of the region are not unique, and Chinese investors will have alternatives elsewhere in the world. Caribbean and Central American governments should identify factors beyond those common to all investment venues, such as the attractiveness of the policy environment and the ease of doing business, that would influence Chinese decisions about FDI in the region.

Tourism

The rising standard of living and the rapid expansion of the middle class in China has set off a boom in foreign travel. The number of travelers is forecast to climb to 53 million in the next decade, with an anticipated expenditure by 2020 of $120 billion annually.[85] This type of opportunity is not likely to escape the attention of Chinese investors willing to buy into hotels and cruise shipping. With some planning and marketing, the Caribbean could be early in capitalizing on these new trends, especially if the opportunities were designed specifically for the taste of Chinese tourists, e.g., shopping.[86] All Caribbean states have recognized the potential of the Chinese travel market,[87] but only those that have established diplomatic ties with China have received "approved destination status." Most aspects of tourism by Chinese are at a fledgling stage, for example cruise travel. It was not until April 2015 that the first cruise ship from China docked in the Caribbean, when 1,000 plus Chinese tourists arrived in Jamaica as part of an 86-day round-the-world cruise.[88]

China's Psychological Presence

The Chinese understand the importance of "soft power" in the execution of foreign policy[89] and this is hardly a new development. As Sun Tzu in the *Art of War* advised that "the supreme art of war is to subdue the enemy without fighting." China has developed an increasingly sophisticated approach to the use of soft power in international relations since the mid-2000s[90] and is spending significant sums on propagation of its history and culture. Shen Ding regards this "cultural proselytization" as the core of China's use of "cultural soft power."[91] Kurlantzick speaks of China mounting "a systematic, coherent soft power strategy," which he describes as a "charm offensive."[92] China has established Confucius Institutes since 2004 in 64 countries[93] to teach its language and expose its history and culture. China has also significantly increased the number of scholarships to allow foreign students to study in China. As a direct result, enrollment of foreign students in China numbered 240,000 in 2011, compared to just 36,000 a decade earlier. The soft power outreach has been effectively extended into the Caribbean, illustrated in Jamaica with the establishment of 600,000-square-foot, "feng shui"–based Chinese garden in the Hope Botanical Gardens in Kingston in August 2015.[94]

By the end of 2015, there were 27 Jamaicans studying in China under full Chinese government scholarship, bringing the total to date to 70. Six Chinese coaches have received training in Jamaica, and four students are currently studying sports management at the G.C. Foster College.[95] By 2014, over 50 Barbadians had studied in China.[96] There were 6 Grenadian students in China in 2005, and that number increased to 35 by 2015.[97] Over the ten years since Grenada established diplomatic ties with the PRC, 96 Grenadians have studied in China and 424 received short-term training courses in various fields. There are 5 Chinese lecturers based in Grenada and 650 students have taken the basic Chinese course. In addition, 11 cultural groups and 28 business delegations visited China.[98] Starting in 1993, the Chinese government sent more than 100 Chinese doctors and experts to assist Guyana's health sector, and 20 Guyanese are currently studying medicine in China.[99] An interesting development is that some 3,800 Chinese students from China have studied (including medicine) in Cuba since 2006 under a bilateral government education exchange program.[100]

China also provides training in the Caribbean. In February 2009, during the official visit of then vice president Xi Jinping to Jamaica, he inaugurated the Confucius Institute at the Mona campus of the University of the West Indies, the first of its kind in the English-speaking Caribbean. The Confucius Institute began operating on July 19, 2010, with the objectives of teaching Mandarin and promoting Chinese culture. It currently offers courses in Mandarin, Chinese calligraphy, and tai chi, and screens a Chinese film series.[101] Also in 2009, a Confucius Institute was opened at the University of Costa Rica with four Chinese language professors.[102] A Confucius Institute was established at the College of the Bahamas in November 2013.[103] A Confucius Institute co-founded by the University of Guyana (UG) and Dalian University of Foreign Languages (DUFL) was officially inaugurated on May 19, 2014.[104] A Confucius Institute was officially launched at the Cave Hill campus of the University of the West Indies in Barbados in April 2015.[105] There is a Confucius Institute in Cuba at the University of Havana serving 500 students that was inaugurated on November 30, 2009, with the objectives of teaching Mandarin and promoting Chinese culture in Cuba.[106]

The people-to-people exchange has occurred in a number of ways. There are the ubiquitous friendship associations in Antigua, the Bahamas, Barbados, Guyana, Jamaica, Suriname, and St. Lucia, which now has diplomatic ties with Taiwan. These associations are open to both citizens of Chinese descent and newly arrived migrants. The friendship association in Jamaica is illustrative of the activities of these associations in the Caribbean. Established in August 1976, the Jamaica China Friendship Association (JCFA) was an expression of elite support of the One China policy being pursued by the PRC. At that time, the One China policy was controversial. Jamaica was an early supporter of the One China policy and the application by the People's Republic of China for admission to the United Nations. The PRC officially established diplomatic relations with Jamaica in 1972 and China opened an embassy in Kingston the following year. The JCFA was immediately embraced by the Chinese People's Association for Friendship with Foreign Countries (CPAFFC), whose mission is to promote relations between China's people-to-people outreach to people of Chinese origin across the world. The goal of the JCFA is the deepening of friendship between Jamaica and China through people-to-people contact, the facilitation of cultural exchange, and increasing understanding of Chinese history and achievements. Activities in furtherance of these objectives have included organizing visits to China in collaboration with CPAFFC, disseminating information about China's history, culture, etiquette, and topical issues through lectures, newspaper articles, and films, celebrating the Chinese New Year, and hosting the annual gala banquet celebrating the National Day of China, attended by the governor general, the minister of foreign affairs, and the ambassador of China. Its most notable achievement was organizing and hosting the first regional conference of the friendship associations in the Caribbean and Central and South America in 1998. This event marked the first time, in the Caribbean, that a friendship association established regional and international linkages among its counterparts. In 2012, the JCFA held a successful forum on "Doing Business with China" with over 400 attendees.[107]

The role of friendship associations in keeping alive the Chinese culture and traditions is a task that has been made easier by the increasingly available Chinese news channel in English, which is in the cable television packages in several Caribbean countries. In 2009–2010, Beijing invested

$8.9 billion in external publicity, including China Central Television (CCTV) 24-hour news channels and ensuring that China Radio International broadcasts in English (the most widely spoken language in the world) 24 hours a day.[108] This is at the same time that the U.S. has downscaled resources in this area, continuing a trend started after the end of the Cold War.[109] News from China is available in many cable television packages throughout the Caribbean as it is in the United States. In addition to their availability, China's news sources are becoming increasingly credible and their coverage is much more global than U.S. networks, which tend to focus on a few places and issues that are the priorities for the U.S. The more global coverage is attracting an increasing share of global audiences to CCTV, and more and more, like the BBC which is seen as a credible global source.

Future

The following developments are likely to assume prominence in the future of China, the U.S., Central America, and the Caribbean.

1. Looking ahead to the immediate future, it appears that the Central America–Caribbean region is not going to be a region where U.S.-China rivalry will become contentious, as security issues are not a primary concern. The U.S. is likely to welcome Chinese development aid and loans as a form of burden sharing.

2. The pressure to eliminate Taiwanese diplomatic relations could ease as the China-Taiwan situation is ameliorated by enhanced economic integration. This would result in a diminution of Chinese interest and reduced development aid and loans. This could deprive the region of a flow of capital that has come to assume some significance. Chinese capital will become even more important if, as is likely, Venezuela's economic difficulties prevent it from continuing the PetroCaribe on the existing scale and on the current terms.

3. The escalation in China's diplomatic engagement may prompt the U.S. and other traditional developed countries—e.g., the U.K., Canada, and Japan—to give more attention to Central America and the Caribbean. Such a response would be indicative more of

pride and political interests than the perception of vital interests, as these countries are likely to remain complacent about the erosion of their share in the small markets of the region.

4. The Caribbean is not a region where China and the United States confront each other on security issues or vital raw materials such as oil, and hence the U.S. is not worried by a growing Chinese presence, as it is understood that China's actions are still largely driven by the unresolved rivalry with Taiwan. U.S. policy will be one of peaceful coexistence with a new but subsidiary partner. Such arrangements will not pertain in other regions of the world, e.g., Asia.

5. In the future, Chinese motivations in Central America and the Caribbean will inevitably become more varied as its private sector-become more active in trade and the execution of infrastructure and construction projects. Foreign direct investment is likely to expand rapidly from its nascent beginnings. This will be the outgrowth of China having become a major source of FDI. China, as of 2013, is the third-largest source of FDI. It will also mirror the global expansion of Chinese corporations and the expanded role of the private sector in the Chinese economy.

6. At some point, the competition for markets will become more vigorous, because imports from China will continue to grow and even encroach on product categories now supplied by American firms.

7. In 2008, nearly 46 million Chinese travelled abroad and spent approximately US$30 billion.[110] These numbers have increased significantly as incomes rise and as the middle class continues to grow. China's middle class is predicted to reach 361 million by 2030.[111] According to the World Tourism Organization,[112] China is expected to become the world's fourth-largest source of tourists by 2020, generating 100 million outbound touristswith an anticipated expenditure of US$120 billion annually.[113] The demand for tropical vacations has yet to be developed in China, and in this regard the Caribbean and Central America may benefit as Chinese tourism expands.

8. There is certainly significant unexploited potential for exports, given China's need for food, seafood, primary products, raw materials, natural gas, asphalt, and some manufactured products

such as rum. There is also potential in cultural and entertainment services. Central American and Caribbean firms will seek to export to the vast Chinese market, and in this regard the expatriate Chinese community in the region, which has been bolstered by new migrants, could play a constructive role.

Conclusions

China's increased presence in the Caribbean and Central America in the last decade and the deepening of its relations with some of these countries do represent a challenge to the position and traditional role of the United States in this region. The U.S. has not been displaced in the Caribbean and Central America in the economic, security, and diplomatic spheres. The U.S. remains the largest trading partner; although imports from China have increased, they do not represent a significant share of total imports. Exports to China remain small and have not grown significantly in the last decade, and therefore the U.S. is still the main market for the export of goods from the region. The U.S. remains the largest source of tourists traversing the region, in which several economies are highly dependent on tourism. There are virtually no Chinese tourists, although there is potential for growth as China becomes the second-largest source of tourists on a global scale. The U.S. has traditionally been the biggest source of FDI inflows while Chinese FDI is at an embryonic stage of emergence. Development assistance, particularly loans to finance construction projects carried out by Chinese firms, has assumed considerable importance, even in countries that have diplomatic relations with Taiwan. The execution of these infrastructure projects has generated goodwill for China in a region in which there is some unease with Chinese investors and traders. The U.S. has accepted if not explicitly welcomed China's deployment of development finance and aid at a time when U.S. aid in real terms has not been as much as the governments in the region would like. All of this has made for a relationship between China and the U.S. that is not encumbered by potentially volatile issues, but this comfort level could be disturbed by repercussions from contentious issues outside Central America and the Caribbean.

NOTES

1 Richard L. Bernal, *Dragon in the Caribbean: China's Global Re-Positioning: Challenges and Opportunities for the Caribbean* (Kingston: Ian Randle Publishers, 2014).

2 Michele Fumento, "As the U.S. Sleeps, China Conquers Latin America," *Forbes*, October 15, 2015, www.forbes.com.

3 Eric Farnsworth, "Memo to Washington: China's Growing Presence in Latin America," *Americas Quarterly*, Winter 2012, www.americasquarterly.org.

4 R. Evan Ellis, *U.S. National Security Implications of Chinese Involvement in Latin America* (Carlisle, PA: Strategic Studies Institute, 2014); R. Evan Ellis, *China on the Ground in Latin America: Challenges for the Chinese and Impacts on the Region* (New York: Palgrave Macmillan, 2014).

5 Gonzalo Sebastian Paz, "China, United States and Hegemonic Challenge in Latin America: An Overview and Some Lessons from Previous Instances of Hegemonic Challenge in the Region," *China Quarterly*, Vol. 209 (March 2012): 18–34.

6 "China's Latin America Presence Not a Threat: U.S. Official," *Xinhua*, November 13, 2013, www.news.xinhuanet.com.

7 Adrian H. Ahearn, "The Mexico-China-U.S. Triangle: An Ethnographic Perspective," in Enrique Dussel Peters, Adrian H. Ahearn, and Harley Shaiken (eds.), *China and the New Triangular Relationships in the Americas: China and the Future of US-Mexico Relations* (Miami: Center for Latin American Studies; Mexico City: Centro de Estudios China-México, Universidad Nacional Autonomía de México, 2013), 59–65.

8 Robert Devlin, Antoni Estevadeordal, and A. Rodriguez-Clare (eds.), *The Emergence of China: Opportunities and Challenges for Latin America and the Caribbean* (Washington, DC: Inter-American Development Bank, 2005); Claudio M. Loser, *The Growing Economic Presence of China in Latin America* (Miami: Center for Hemispheric Policy, University of Miami, 2006); Osvaldo Rosales and Mikio Kuwayama, "Latin America Meets China and India: Prospects and Challenges for Trade and Investment," *CEPAL Review*, No. 93 (December 2007): 81–103; Rhys Jenkins, Enrique Dussel Peters, and Mauricio Mesquita Moreira, "The Impact of China on Latin America and the Caribbean," *World Development*, Vol. 36, No. 2 (2008): 235–253; Daniel Lederman, Marcelo Olarreaga, and Guillermo E. Perry, "Latin America's Response to China and India: Overview of the Research Findings and Policy Implications," in Daniel Lederman, Marcelo Olarreaga, and Guillermo E. Perry (eds.), *China's and India's Challenge to Latin America: Opportunity or Threat* (Washington, DC: World Bank, 2009); Cynthia J. Arnson and Jeffrey Davidow, *China, Latin America and the United States: The New Triangle* (Washington, DC: Woodrow Wilson International Center for Scholars, 2011): Osvaldo Rosales and Mikio Kuwayama, *China and Latin America and the Caribbean: Building a Strategic Economic and Trade Relationship* (Santiago: Economic Commission for Latin America and the Caribbean, 2012); Cynthia J. Arnson

and Jorge Heine with Christine Zaino (eds.), *Reaching Across the Pacific: Latin America and Asia in the New Century* (Washington, DC: Woodrow Wilson Center for International Scholars, 2014); CEPAL, *Latin America and the Caribbean and China: Towards a New Era in Economic Cooperation* (Santiago: United Nations Economic Commission for Latin America and the Caribbean, 2015).

9 Political independence dates from 1838 for Nicaragua, Honduras, Costa Rica, and Guatemala; 1841 for El Salvador; 1903 for Panama; and 1981 for Belize.

10 Bernal, *Dragon in the Caribbean*, 84–86.

11 Robert B. Zoelick, "Whither China: From Membership to Responsibility? Remarks to the National Committee on U.S.-China Relations," *NBR Analysis*, Vol. 16, No. 4 (December 2005): 5–14.

12 Fareed Zakaria, "The Rise of a Fierce yet Fragile Superpower," *Newsweek*, December 31, 2007/January 7, 2008: 12–13.

13 John G. Ikenberry, "The Rise of China and the Future of the West," *Foreign Affairs*, Vol. 87, No. 2 (January–February 2008): 22–37.

14 Shixue Jiang, "The Chinese Foreign Policy Perspective," in Riordan Roett and Guadalupe Paz (eds.), *China's Expansion into the Western Hemisphere: Implications for Latin America and the United States* (Washington, DC: Brookings Institution Press, 2008): 111–147.

15 Fareed Zakaria, "China Is Not the World's Other Superpower," *Washington Post*, June 6, 2013: A15.

16 Doreen Hemlock, "Ready for China's Approach: Caribbean Wants to Enhance Its Contacts," *Sun-Sentinel*, January 30, 2005, articles.sun-sentinel.com.

17 Ross Terrill, *The New Chinese Empire and What It Means for the United States* (New York: Basic Books, 2004); Richard Bernstein and Ross H. Munro, *The Coming Conflict with China* (New York: Vintage, 1998); John Bolton, "America Is Far Too Doft in Its Dealings with Beijing," *Financial Times*, January 19, 2011: 11.

18 Bernstein and Munro, *The Coming Conflict*; Ted Galen Carpenter, *America's Coming War with China: A Collision Course over Taiwan* (New York: Palgrave Macmillan, 2006); Hugo deBurgh, *China: Friend or Foe* (Flint, MI: Totem Books, 2003); Qiao Liang and Wang Xiangsui, *Unrestricted Warfare. China's Master Plan to Destroy America* (Los Angeles: Pan American Publishing Company, 2002); Jed Babbin, *Showdown: Why China Wants War with the United States* (Washington, DC: Regnery Publishing, 2006).

19 "The China Decade," *Time*, August 31, 2015: 39–42. See page 40.

20 Jeffrey A. Bader, *Obama and China's Rise: An Insider's Account of America's Asia Strategy* (Washington, DC: Brookings Institution, 2012), xvii.

21 Rachel Will, "China's Stadium Diplomacy," *World Policy Journal*, Vol. 29, No.2 (Summer 2012): 36–43.

22 Kwesi Mugisa, "PLCA Scores with $22m China Harbour Deal," *Jamaica Gleaner*, September 19, 2012, jamaica-gleaner.com.

23 Martin Jacques, *When China Rules the World: The End of the Western World and the Birth of a New Global Order*, 2nd ed. (New York: Penguin, 2012), 391.

24 Editor's note: The cross-strait relations have deteriorated from those of a decade ago, because China has demanded Taiwan reaffirm the "1992 Consensus" which President Tsai Ing-wen is unwilling to do.

25 Jane Perlez and Austin Ramzynov, "China, Taiwan and a Meeting after 66 Years," *New York Times*, November 3, 2015: A1, A12; Jeremy Page, "China, Taiwan Set for Historic Meeting," *Wall Street Journal*, November 4, 2015: A10.

26 "Hands across the Water," *Economist*, November 7, 2015, www.economist.com.

27 Ben Bland, "Taiwan and China Leaders to Hold Historic Summit," *Financial Times*, November 4, 2015.

28 "Protests in Taiwan ahead of Key Meeting with China," *Al Jazeera*, November 4, 2015, www.aljazeera.com.

29 "'Guatemala cannot expect on the one hand to do something that harms the sovereignty and territorial integrity of China while on the other hand requesting China to cooperate in peacekeeping,' said Shen Guofang, the Chinese Government spokesman." Patrick Tyler, "China Asserts Taiwan's Ties to Guatemala Led to Veto," *New York Times*, January 12, 1997.

30 Bruce Gilley, "Not So Dire Straits. How Finlandization of Taiwan Benefits U.S. Security," *Foreign Affairs*, Vol. 89, No. 1 (January/February 2010): 44–60.

31 Robert D. Kaplan, *Asia's Cauldron: The South China Sea and the End of a Stable Pacific* (New York: Random House, 2014), 32–50.

32 Simon Denyer, "China Claims Hypocrisy as U.S. Admiral Affirms South China Sea Patrols," *Washington Post*, November 4, 2015: A8.

33 Ibid.

34 Geoff Dyer, "US Tells China Naval Missions Will Stay," *Financial Times*, November 4, 2015: 2.

35 Gordon Lubold and Jeremy Page, "U.S., Beijing Tussle over Maritime Disputes in Asia," *Wall Street Journal*, November 4, 2015: A11.

36 Sui-Lee Wee, "China Confirms Near Miss with U.S. Ship in South China Sea," *Reuters*, December 18, 2013, www.reuters.com.

37 Daniel Runde, "Should the U.S. Worry About China's Canal in Nicaragua", *Foreign Policy*, May 26, 215. www.foreignpolicy.com; Eric Hannis, "Building a Canal to Power", *U.S. News and World Report*, October 22, 2013. www.usnews .com.

38 Michael D McDonald, "China's Building a Huge Canal in Nicaragua, But We Couldn't Find It", *Bloomberg*, August 19, 2015.

39 "Has Beijing backed a US$50 bn canal project in Nicaragua? Funding mystery continues". *South China Morning Post*, December 28, 2014.

40 "JDF gets military aid from China", *Jamaica Observer*, August 23, 2011.

41 R. Evan Ellis, *China-Latin America Military Engagement: Good Will, Good Business, and Strategic Position* (Strategic Studies Institute, 2011).

42 IMF, Direction of Trade Statistics (DOTS), 2015, data.imf.org.

43 Kevin Gallagher, *The China Triangle: Latin America's China Boom and the Fate of the Washington Consensus* (New York: Oxford University Press, 2016), 97.

44 Enrique Dussel Peters, *Politica economica-comercio e innversiones-de Guatemala hacia la Republica Popular China. Hacia una estaategia en el corto, mediano y largo plazo* (Mexico DF: Comision Economica para America Latina y de Caribe, 2014), 17–22.

45 Ibid., 23–24.

46 Antoni Estevadeordal and Theodore Kahn, *Pathways to China: The Story of Latin American Firms in the Chinese Market* (Washington, DC: Inter-American Development Bank, 2012), 4.

47 CEPAL, *América Latina y el Caribe y China: hacia una nueva era de cooperación económica* (Santiago: Comision Economica para America Latina y de Caribe, 2015), 6.

48 "Trade and Investments between Central America and China," Centro Latinoamericano para la Competitividad y el Desarrollo Sostenible, August 2014.

49 Ibid., 39.

50 Dussel Peters, *Politica economica-comercio e innversiones.*

51 Tenth Report to Congress on the Operation of the Caribbean Basin Economic Recovery Act, December 31, 2013 (Washington, DC: U.S. Trade Representative).

52 Richard L. Bernal, *Globalization, Trade and Economic Development: A Study of the CARIFORM-EU Economic Partnership Agreement* (New York: Palgrave Macmillan, 2013).

53 CBERA annual report.

54 Geoff Dyer, Jamil Anderlini and Henry Sender, "China's Lending Hits New Heights," *Financial Times*, January 18, 2011: 1.

55 Ezra Fieser, "Why Is China Spending Billions in the Caribbean?," *Global Post of Canada*, April 22, 2011.

56 "Nevis prime minister says support for Taiwan will continue," *Caribbean360*, January 23,2008.

57 Bernal, *Dragon in the Caribbean*, 80.

58 Ronald Sanders, "China's presence in Dominica", *Carribean360*, April 28, 2011, www.caribbean360.com.

59 MOFCOM, "Joint Declaration of the 2nd China-Caribbean Economic and Trade Cooperation Forum," September 10, 2007, bb2.mofcom.gov.cn.

60 Sahadeo Basdeo and Graeme Mount, *The Foreign Relations of Trinidad and Tobago: The Case of a Small State in the Global Arena* (Port of Spain: Lexicon Trinidad Ltd., 2001), 178–179.

61 David Jessop, "China-Caribbean Ties Offer Alternative Development Model," *Jamaica Gleaner*, February 20, 2011.

62 Damian King and David Tennant, *Debt and Development in Small Island Developing States* (New York: Palgrave Macmillan, 2014).

63 Michael D. McDonald, "Costa Rica Looks to China for Bond Sale as Budget Deficit Widens," *Bloomberg*, September 18, 2015, www.bloomberg.com; "Eight Years Later, Costa Rica Looks to China for Bond Sale," *Q Costa Rica*, September 19, 2015, www.qcostarica.com.

64 "Dominica Signs Framework Agreement with China," *Dominica Central.* May 13, 2010, www.dominicacentral.com.

65 Ignorance and fear regarding the Chinese is not confined to Costa Rica for example it remains strong in Mexico in the media and the private sector. See Ahearn, "The Mexico-China-U.S. Triangle."

66 R. Evan Ellis, "China and Costa Rica. A New Beginning?," *Foreign Area Office Association Journal of International Affairs*, Vol. XVIII, No. 1 (Spring 2015): 39–41.

67 Richard L. Bernal, "The Growing Economic Presence of China in the Caribbean," *World Economy*, Vol. 38, Issue 9 (September 2015): 1425.

68 Paul Shortell, "Growing Chinese Presence Challenges Taiwan's Influence," *China and Latin America* [blog], August 27, 2014, www.chinaandlatinamerica.com.

69 "Trade and Investments between Central America and China," *Centro Latinoamericano para la Competitividad y el Desarrollo Sostenible*, August 2014: 4.

70 FDI by Chinese companies that are mostly state owned is "in alignment" with the plans of the state. See P. J. Buckley, L. J. Clegg, A. Cross, X. Liu, H. Voss, and P. Zhong, "The Determinants of Chinese Outward Foreign Direct Investment," *Journal of International Business Studies*, Vol. 38, No. 4 (2007): 499–518; Gaston Fornes and Alan Butt Philip, *The China-Latin America Axis: Emerging Markets and the Future* (London: Palgrave Macmillan, 2012), 84.

71 Ilan Alon, "The Globalization of Chinese Capital," *East Asian Forum Quarterly*, Vol. 4, No.2 (April–June 2012): 6.

72 UNCTAD, *World Investment Report 2014* (Geneva: United Nations Conference on Trade and Development, 2014), xv.

73 MOFCOM, *2012 Statistical Bulletin of China's Outward Foreign Direct Investment* (Beijing: Ministry of Commerce of the People's Republic of China, 2013), 77.

74 UNCTAD, *World Investment Report 2013* (Geneva: United Nations Conference on Trade and Development, 2013).

75 Jamil Anderlini, "China Foresees $1.25tn in Outbound Investment," *Financial Times*, November 10, 2014: 4.

76 *2013 Statistical Bulletin of China's Outward Foreign Direct Investment*, 135–136.

77 Ibid.

78 "Trade and Investments between Central America and China," Centro Latin-American para la Competitividad y el Desarrollo Sostenible, August 2014, 36.

79 Ibid., 39.

80 Estevadeordal and Kahn, *Pathways to China*, 6.

81 Richard L. Bernal, *Chinese Foreign Direct Investment in the Caribbean: Potential and Prospects* (Washington, DC: Inter-American Development Bank, 2016).

82 J. Collins, "China's Whampoa Ltd. Opens Port in Bahamas," *Washington Times*, November 20, 2001.

83 Estevadeordal and Kahn, *Pathways to China*, 6.

84 This paragraph draws on Richard L. Bernal, *Chinese Foreign Direct Investment in the Caribbean: Potential and Prospects, October 2015* (forthcoming).

85 Michael J. Silverstein and Abheek Singhi, *The $10 Trillion Prize. Captivating the Newly Affluent in China and India* (Cambridge, MA: Harvard Business Review Press, 2012), 45.

86 Ibid.; Elizabeth Becker, *Overbooked: The Exploding Business of Travel and Tourism* (New York: Simon & Schuster, 2013), 309.

87 Roland Sanders, "Get a Slice of the Chinese Tourism Cake," *Caribbean Net News*, March 20, 2006; "Barbados: Caribbean Urged to Pursue Chinese Tourists," *The Voice*, August 17, 2009; "Dominican Rep. Has What Chinese Tourists Look For," *Dominican Today*, June 19, 2015, www.dominicantoday.com.

88 "Jamaica: Cruise Ship Brings 'Record' of Chinese Tourists," *Philippine Star*, April 23, 2015, www.philstar.com.

89 Joseph S. Nye. Jr., *Soft Power: The Means To Success In World Politics* (New York: PublicAffairs, 2005); Joseph S. Nye. Jr., *The Future of Power* (New York: Public-Affairs, 2011), 81–112.

90 Michael Barr, *Who's Afraid of China? The Challenge of Chinese Soft Power* (London: Zed Books, 2011), 27.

91 Sheng Ding, *The Dragon's Hidden Wings* (Lanham, MD: Lexington Books, 2008), 16–17.

92 Joshua Kurlantzick, *Charm Offensive: How China's Soft Power is Transforming the World* (New Haven, CT: Yale University Press, 2008).

93 For the goals and mission of the Confucius Institutes, see Ding, *The Dragon's Hidden Wings*, 117–123.

94 Chad Bryan, "Prime Minister Thanks China for Enjoyment Garden," *Jamaica Information Service*, August 20, 2015, http://jis.gov.jm.

95 "China's Role in Jamaica: No Strings Attached," *Jamaica Gleaner*, May 3, 2015: 1.

96 "Ten to Study in China," *Barbados Today*, August 21, 2014, www.barbadostoday.bb.

97 "China, Grenada Celebrate 10th Anniversary of Ties Resumption," *State Council–People's Republic of China*, January 21, 2015, http://english.gov.cn.

98 "Grenada China Relation Is Stronger than Ever," *Grenadian Buzz*, 22 Jan 2015. http://on.grenadianbuzz.com.

99 "China Offers Eight More Scholarships in Medicine," *Kaieteur News*, July 5, 2011, www.kaieteurnewsonline.com.

100 "Chinese Students Fall for Cuba," *China Daily*, July 22, 2014, http://usa.chinadaily.com.cn.

101 "Confucius Institute—University of the West Indies," *University of the West Indies*, November 19, 2008, www.mona.uwi.edu.

102 "Costa Rica Gets Confucius Institute", *China Internet Information Center*, November 5, 2015, www.china.org.cn.

103 "New Confucius Institute Location Officially Opens," *College of the Bahamas*, November 12, 2013, www.cob.edu.bs.

104 "Confucius Institute at the University of Guyana Officially Inaugurated," *Embassy of the People's Republic of China in the Cooperative Republic of Guyana*, May 22, 2014, http://gy.chineseembassy.org.

105 "Confucius Institute O‚fficial," *Barbados Advocate*, April 21, 2015, www.barbados advocate.com.

106 "Learning Chinese in Cuba," *Cuba Headlines*, September 29, 2010, www.cuba headlines.com.

107 Chinese Embassy in Jamaica, "Doing Business with China Forum an Astounding Success," July 18, 2012, jm.china-embassy.org.

108 Joseph S. Nye. Jr, "China's Soft Power", *Wall Street Journal*, May 8, 2012;Barr, *Who's Afraid of China?*, 45–46.

109 Adam Clayton Powell III, "Many Voices: Is Anyone Listening?," in William P. Kiehl (ed.), *America's Dialogue with the World* (Washington, DC: Public Diplomacy Council, 2006), 115–128.

110 W. Arlt, *China as a New Tourism Source Market for Jamaica* (Heide, Germany: China Outbound Tourism Research Institute, 2008).

111 Kishore Mahbubani, *The New Asian Hemisphere: The Irresistible Shift of Global Power to the East* (New York: PublicAffairs, 2008), 57.

112 World Tourism Organization, *Chinese Outbound Tourism Market: Madrid* (Geneva: World Tourism Organization, 2006).

113 Silverstein and Singhi, *The $10 Trillion Prize*, 45.

PART III

Outside Powers

11

China's Rise in Latin America

Myths and Realities

HE LI

China's growing presence in Latin America is one of the most visible trends in the Western Hemisphere.[1] With growing trade and investment, China has reshaped the economy of several countries in the region. This development is raising doubts and concerns both in Latin America and in the United States. This study examines the Chinese economic involvement in Latin America, focusing on trade, direct investment, and finance. The chapter makes five arguments. First, due to weaker growth in both China and Latin America, China's economic expansion will slow down in the years to come. Second, China is keen to forge closer ties with Latin America, but the idea that Latin America has become the major target of the Chinese expansion abroad is delusional. Third, Beijing talks a lot about South-South cooperation. With the country's rapid rise, South-South cooperation has been more of a principle than actual practice. In other words, China no longer belongs to the periphery; like other Asian emerging economies such as South Korea and Taiwan, it has become part of a semi-periphery in the global system. Fourth, some argue that emerging economic ties are detrimental to Latin America. This is another myth. In fact, the rise of China presents both challenges and opportunities for the development of Latin America. Fifth, the perception of China as a direct and emerging threat to U.S. interests in Latin America is a false fear, creating a wall of worry. At this time, there is little evidence that Beijing is seeking to upend the U.S. dominance in Latin America.

With China's record growth figure, its trade with Latin America grew from $10 billion in 2000 to $257 billion in 2013. From 2000 to 2014 bilateral trade between Latin America and the Caribbean and China expanded 22 times. If this trend continues, China might surpass the U.S. as Latin America's largest trading partner. China pledged 6,000 government scholarships and 6,000 training opportunities, and invited 1,000 party leaders to visit China, as well as setting up a "Bridge for the Future" training program that will involve 1,000 young leaders. China has already eclipsed the U.S. as the top destination for South American exports.[2]

The 2016 edition of the *Latin American Economic Outlook* explores how the region could deepen and improve its partnership with China as part of its development agenda. Despite the end of the "Golden Decade" of the commodities boom, China will continue to be a game changer for the region. The report states that the world's economic center of gravity is moving away from the Organization for Economic Cooperation and Development (OECD) countries toward emerging economies, a phenomenon called "shifting wealth." Ties between Latin America and China are evolving well beyond trade and challenge the region to adopt modern reforms and policies to build a mutually beneficial partnership with China.[3]

China's growing presence in Latin America is one of the most visible trends in the Western Hemisphere. With growing trade, direct investment, and finance, China has reshaped the economy of several countries in the region. This development is raising doubts and concerns both in Latin America and in the United States. China's rise in the region is a mixed blessing for Latin America. It is often misunderstood. To help us have a clearer picture of the complex interactions between China and Latin America, this chapter assesses the myths and realities in Sino–Latin American ties.

I. Sino–Latin American Economic Relations

Booming Trade

Trade is central to growing ties between China and Latin America and the Caribbean. China has become the second-largest economic partner of Latin America, driven largely by the Chinese demand for commodities such as crude oil, ore minerals, and soybeans; it has replaced the United States as the biggest buyer of crude oil in the world. Chen Rui, a senior researcher at the China National Petroleum Corporation (CNPC) Economics and Technology Research Institute, forecasts that, by 2020,

China's reliance on oil imports will rise from the current 60 percent to 67.1 percent in 2020 and 70.6 percent in 2030.[4] In addition to crude oil, China is also the largest buyer of coal and iron ore. Along with the turmoil in the Middle East, Latin America has emerged as a strategic region to meet China's growing consumption for oil. China possesses large reserves of natural gas, yet it needs technology and resources to get the gas out.

China is already the largest trading partner of Brazil, Chile, and Peru, and the second-largest trading partner of Argentina. Latin America is well-placed to meet many of Chinese commodity needs in the years ahead. Much of Chile's exports are copper, and Peru is another significant provider. Latin America is also an important food producer. Brazil is the world's largest producer of coffee and sugar, and one of the largest in soybeans. Chile is well-known for its wines, fish, and especially fresh fruits and vegetables; its exports to China have tripled in the past decade. Latin America, with a population of more than 580 million and an economy of over $9.5 trillion (measured by purchasing power parity) is an attractive market for Chinese products. China's balance of trade with Latin America has been in China's favor in the past few years.

China's trade relations with Latin America have not affected all countries in the same way. South American countries benefited from the rise in Chinese demand for the commodities they produce. In the case of Brazil the rise of a new middle class has even been seen as due to Chinese commodity demand.[5] China's exports to those counties are dominated by machinery and electrical products, especially those with high value added, like automobiles, tractors, motorcycles, computers, home appliance, and so on. Compared with Russian–Latin American relations, Sino–Latin American economic exchange is complementary, since Russia also depends on export of resources.

It should be noted that Mexico and Central America have suffered from a growing trade deficit with China. Chinese trade with Mexico is growing, but China runs a huge trade surplus with Mexico. Mexico tends to see China as a formidable competitor, because of its ability to lure investment away from the low-cost manufacturing plants just south of the U.S. border. In the global market, China competes intensively with many Latin American manufacturers. Several Latin American countries have also been severely hurt by Chinese competition in the U.S.

market, despite their greater proximity to the U.S. and the benefits they receive from the North American Free Trade Agreement (NAFTA) and the Dominican Republic–Central America Free Trade Agreement, commonly known as the DR-CAFTA.

The People's Republic of China (PRC) hopes that free trade agreements (FTAs) can further stimulate the growth of its export-led economy. China has signed free trade agreements with Chile (2005), Costa Rica (2010), and Peru (2009). All these three already have free trade agreements with the United States. China and Columbia are conducting the feasibility study of a FTA. FTAs could potentially provide China with a dynamic channel to the American market.

Bourgeoning Direct Investment

Whereas for many years, China's development policy relied almost exclusively on a strategy called "welcome in" (*yinjinlai*), i.e., attracting foreign capital, technology, and managerial skills, today it also pursues a strategy of "going out" (*zouchuqu*). This has led China to become a major source of foreign direct investment (FDI) in the region. According to statistics from the United Nations Conference on Trade and Investment (UNCTAD), China ranked third behind Japan and the U.S. in terms of total outward investment flows in 2013. The next wave of Chinese interest in the region might show the tide increasingly turning from trade to investment. As can be seen in Table 11.1, by the end of 2013, China's total stock of investment in Latin America and the Caribbean stood at $86 billion and its investment in Latin America was heavily concentrated in the tax havens of the Cayman Islands ($42 billion) and the British Virgin Islands ($34 billion), which are considered to be "stopping off" points, rather than final destinations for many investments. This practice of "stopping off" obscures the true destination of a large part of China's outbound investment. While China's Ministry of Commerce (MOFCOM) statistics give the impression that China had a huge FDI in Latin America in recent years, in reality this figure is likely to be much lower. The MOFCOM's statistics are based on information submitted by Chinese companies during the registration and approval process. This information often reports the initial destination of investment, rather than the final destination.[6] The data from MOFCOM (Table 11.2)

TABLE 11.1. Chinese Investment in Latin America and the Caribbean: 2011–2013 (US$ million)

	2011	2012	2013
Argentina	405.25	897.19	1,658.2
Bolivia	66.320	156.19	118.92
Brazil	1,071.79	1,449.51	1,733.58
Cayman Islands	21,692.32	30,072.00	42,324.06
Chile	97.94	126.28	179.04
Colombia	59.80	3,461.5	3,686.9
Cuba	146.37	135.69	111.34
Ecuador	95.24	407.63	1,008.79
Guyana	135.13	151.88	225.18
Mexico	263.88	368.48	409.87
Panama	330.78	196.62	478.64
Peru	802.24	752.87	867.78
St. Vincent and Grenadines	36.20	36.20	36.20
Surinam	78.84	45.61	111.93
Uruguay	8.15	17.65	25.93
Venezuela	501.00	2,042.76	2,363.38
British Virgin Islands	29,261.41	30,850.95	33,902.98
Total	55,171.75	68,211.63	86,095.93

Source: Ministry of Commerce, *2013 Statistical Bulletin of China's Outward Foreign Direct Investment*, China Statistics Press, 2014

TABLE 11.2. Chinese Investments in Tax Havens in the Caribbean: 2011–2013 (US$ million)

	2011	2012	2013
Cayman Islands	21,692.32	30,072.00	42,324.06
British Virgin Islands	29,261.41	30,850.95	33,902.98
Total	50,953.73	60,922.95	76,227.04

Source: Ministry of Commerce, *2013 Statistical Bulletin of China's Outward Foreign Direct Investment*, China Statistics Press, 2014

suggest that China invest much less than commonly assumed as most China investment in the region concentrate in the above-mentioned tax havens.

In the past three decades, the Chinese economy expanded rapidly. But keeping capital bottled inside the country risks asset bubbles and offers little means of diversification. It is therefore in China's interest to seek investment opportunities abroad. Latin America offers growing opportunities for China. "Going out" could also contribute to more balanced and sustainable development and allow China to relocate some of its labor-intensive and low-value-added manufacturing facilities overseas.

Though Chinese investment in the region includes manufacturing assembly, telecommunications, and textiles, it has been mostly in the extractive sectors, concentrating on oil, gas, and mineral extraction, and soybeans. In recent years, infrastructure projects have become a major target of Chinese investment. The Pacific-Atlantic Railroad, across the Amazon, from Brazil's Atlantic coast to Peru, is one of the major infrastructure projects that China is offering to finance in Latin America. Li Keqiang, China's prime minister, signed an agreement for a feasibility study for the railway during an eight-day trip to South America in May 2015.

China's overseas investment has historically been dominated by state-owned enterprises (SOEs), but the role of private actors is now becoming increasingly important. Giant SOEs are major players in the Chinese investment in the region. With strong state support, they could compete with powerful MNCs from the West. On the other hand, MNCs from North America and Europe have an advantage over Chinese companies, possessing stronger networks with local elites built on decades of mutual knowledge. Few Chinese firms have the global reach of their counterparts in the North. Chinese private enterprises do not always have the same access to incentives and state support as SOEs, but they are often seen as being more dynamic and quicker to adjust to market conditions.[7]

In 2014, China relaxed regulations for the management of outbound investment. Since the adoption of these new rules, except for those valued over $1 billion and in sensitive areas or industries require approval; overseas investments simply require registration at the appropriate level. With the relaxation of outbound investment rules, China's outbound investment is likely to continue to rise over the coming years.[8]

Loans

Flushed with the world largest foreign reserve, since 2005, China has provided more than $100 billion in loan commitments to Latin American countries and firms. China's loan commitments of $37 billion in 2010 were more than those of the World Bank, the Inter-American Development Bank, and the U.S. Export-Import Bank combined. China is now Latin America's biggest annual creditor.[9] In addition, the Chinese loans are more in line with what Latin America nations want, rather than what Western development institutions say they need.

China is an increasing source of finance for those countries in the region with weaker access to global capital markets, such as Argentina, Ecuador, and Venezuela.[10] Since 2007, China has provided over $50 billion in loans to Venezuela in so-called oil-for-loan deals. It means that the loan is repaid in the form of oil and gas shipments from Venezuela to China, ensuring Beijing a steady supply. China, however, is moving away from a model of international financing that accepts high-risk projects. According to a recent study by the Inter-American Dialogue, most of China's overseas lending is issued by the China Development Bank ($83 billion since 2005) and China Export-Import Bank ($20.9 billion). Both were created as "policy banks" to support the Chinese government's policy objectives.[11]

Chinese scholars Li Xue and Yanzhou Xu recommend that "China's investments in Latin America can be low-profit or even zero-profit, but should not result in big losses." When it comes to Venezuela specifically, Xue and Xu argue that China should cut off funding altogether: "China's investment and loans in that country amount to more than $70 billion. Considering the state's political and economic situation, it is inappropriate to further increase the amount of investments and loans."[12] In contrast, quite a few Chinese scholars feel that the price of crude oil might hit bottom, and they think the loans could be paid back in the long run.[13] Beijing claims that Chinese loans to the developing countries don't have any political conditions; still, like financial institutions in the West, Chinese banks set a number of financial "conditions" to ensure that loans will be paid back. Given the current political and business environment, the risks of the Chinese current investment in Venezuela are extremely high.

II. Myths and Realities

China's expansion and growing influence in Latin America is arguably one of the most remarkable global political and economic developments in the 21st century. China's foray into Latin America started in the late 1990s, propelled by its desire to obtain new sources of raw materials and energy for its economic growth, as well as new markets for its manufactured goods. While China's "no political strings attached" policy proves attractive to a number of Latin American leaders, China has been criticized as interested mainly in stripping Latin America of its mineral wealth without proper environmental or social precautions. In recent years, there has been a robust market for books and articles on China's rise in Latin America. Against this backdrop, there have been enduring myths about China's engagement with the region. The following section examines some myths that have molded the perceptions of the rise of China in Latin America.

Myth 1: Chinese Trade and Investment Will Continue to Expand Rapidly

In his remarks at the opening ceremony of the China-CELAC Forum in January 2015, Xi Jinping, the president of China, set the goal for bilateral trade to reach $500 billion in the coming 10 years.[14] He also pledged that the Chinese direct investment in Latin America would reach $250 billion over the next decade. Many Chinese Latin American specialists share the view that the goals that Xi raised will be achieved.[15] They stressed the point that strong demand and plentiful investment from China could fuel growth and expand opportunities in Latin America. Cardenal and Araújo posit that China's conquest of the rest of the world is now entering a phase of the penetration of Western markets, armed with cash, diplomacy, tireless entrepreneurs, and a massive, varied flood of products that are becoming progressively more difficult to compete with. They see China's expansion as an unstoppable force.[16]

This perspective on China's engagement with Latin America and its future trajectory is wrong. Since 2011, three major factors that fueled the stellar growth of Sino–Latin American relations have all reversed. First of all, Latin American nations that have relied on exports of natural resources are reeling from a slump in commodity prices. Second, growth in China—the main driver of such relationships—has dropped precipitously. The world's second-largest economy is now at risk of stalling as authorities try to transform the country's export- and credit-gassed economy into a more sustainable model relying on domestic consumption. China's growth rate remains high but it has fallen to a 25-year low. Its economy is in need of major structural reform. In addition, China's rising wages and modest currency appreciation are making its goods relatively less competitive in the world. Given the softer growth of the Chinese economy and declining prices of commodities, it could be a challenge for China to reach the $500 billion target.[17] That trend isn't likely to reverse in the short term. To reach Xi's goal, bilateral trade needs to grow 7 percent per year over the next ten years; given the current economic environment in both China and Latin America, trade volume does not have such tremendous upside potential until economic trends on both sides accelerate.

The last decade has seen an attempted shift toward the domestic market and higher-level technological goods and processes along with an interest in financing global infrastructure projects. The Chinese economy has been undergoing a historic and underappreciated shift. The major economic centers of Beijing, Shanghai, Shenzhen, and Guangzhou have long since ended their zealous promotion of further manufacturing and industrialization. Indeed, to meet high-technology and environmental protection goals, these regions have been actively pushing out polluting factories. Their economic development programs emphasize the promotion of high-value-added services. Services are now the leading force in the economy. The service industry nationwide now accounts for 48.2 percent of China's GDP (versus 42.6 percent for manufacturing, construction, and other industries). It is also the engine of growth, rising at 8.1 percent in 2014 (versus only 7.3 percent for industry). Services use less energy by far, and consume few resource inputs. Accordingly, the economy may still grow strongly—even more healthily—even without the usual hallmarks of growth.[18] As the Chinese economy slows and transforms, its demand for Latin American products is likely to drop. Commodity-led growth is not sustainable in the long run.

Third, Latin America is witnessing the end of the so-called "left turn" and a comeback of the right. Corruption scandals, rampant inflation, the fall of commodity prices, and weaker economic growth have contributed to the decline of the left throughout Latin America. Argentina's November 2015 election overturned the ruling Peronist coalition, bringing the center-right pragmatist Mauricio Macri to power. In Venezuela, the result of the parliamentary election in 2015 was a decisive defeat for the left-wing United Socialist Party of Venezuela (PSUV), which lost control of the Assembly for the first time since 1999. In Brazil, revelations in the massive Petrobras corruption scandal contributed to the impeachment of President Dilma Rousseff of the Workers' Party. These left-wing regimes were keen to accelerate economic relations with China.

International rail contracts are a political priority for Beijing, which sees exports as a solution to China's burdensome overcapacity in steel, rail, construction, and engineering services as the economy slows.[19] In spite of rapid growth, China suffered some major setbacks in 2015 including the Mexico City–Querétaro high-speed rail, a $3.75 billion project. With increasing investment in the region, how to manage the risk of doing business in the region is a major task that Beijing faces.[20] With a few exceptions, such as Huawei and Chery, at present most of the Chinese firms are not making money in Latin America, and many of them have left the region disappointed. This is largely because Chinese businesspersons are not well prepared when they come to invest in Latin America. Many of them have little understanding of how the market in the region works, and only a few could communicate in Spanish.[21]

Development and application of better production technologies can allow for continued industrial output with fewer commodity or energy inputs. Accordingly, we should expect to see a slowing or even decline in energy and input consumption, even without a decline in output. Outside heavy industry, innovation and improved efficiency are both major government and major corporate goals. China's increased innovation capabilities make it only logical that there should be declining resource intensity. This means economic growth can continue—even without growth of consumption resources. Therefore, it is reasonable to expect that China will have relatively stable or slower corporate growth in Latin America.

Myth 2: China Is Pivoting to Latin America

It is widely believed that Latin America is critical to the foreign policy of China. In his keynote speech at the United Nations Economic Commission for Latin America and the Caribbean (ECLAC) headquarters in Santiago, Chile on May 25, 2015, premier Li Keqiang made it clear

that Latin America is a high-priority region for China. China has proposed the "Silk Road Economic Belt" and the "21st-Century Maritime
Silk Road," or "One Belt, One Road" (OBOR), an even broader and more
ambitious initiative that focuses on cooperation and economic integration of countries. Essentially, the "belt" includes countries situated on
the original Silk Road through Central Asia, West Asia, the Middle East,
and Europe. The maritime "road" is designed to link the South China Sea
to the Indian Ocean, east Africa, the Red Sea, and the Mediterranean.
Clearly, the OBOR is primarily connected to Eurasia and Africa. China
is not in an economic or political position to extend the OBOR to Latin
America in the foreseeable future.

Though China's relations with Latin America have important political
and security aspects, the most prominent dimension is economic. The
region exhibits many features that complement Chinese needs and strategy: Latin America has an abundance of raw materials and agricultural
products, and the region is in a good position to supply China with services such as tourism. It has the potential to consume Chinese exports
and thereby to encourage their diversification. China has four major
goals: (a) to gain recognition of full market status;[22] (b) to secure the
raw materials it needs and to diversify the sources in order to reduce the
country's vulnerability; (c) to maintain a high level of access to the market in order to assure the exports of its manufactured products; (d) to
contain Taiwan in Central America and the Caribbean. Latin America
plays a role in satisfying each of these goals.[23] Presently, Beijing is not
pivoting to Latin America. In other words, China is not strategically rebalancing away its focus on major powers and its neighboring countries
to Latin America. The Chinese investment flows have begun to shift
more toward Latin America, but the bulk of China's FDI outflows still
go to its Asian neighbors. Latin America still ranks very low in China's
diplomatic priorities. In the past few years, the focus of China's foreign
policy has changed from *Daguo Waijiao* (great powers diplomacy) to the
"One Belt, One Road" strategy. Simply put, that is meant to be a strategic
"rebalancing" of Chinese interests from major powers, toward China's
neighboring countries in Asia and Eurasia. In short, the main thrust of
Beijing's foreign policy is to cultivate "good-neighborly relations" with
countries on its periphery and closer political and economic ties with
countries afar. There is little doubt that that a large number of Chinese

academics and policy makers worry about the potential trade war and renewal of protectionism under the Trump administration and some of them wish to counterbalance the U.S. efforts in its "pivot to Asia" in the "backyard" of the United States. But at this point, Beijing does not have the capacity to achieve that goal. China is keen to forge closer ties with Latin America, but the idea that Latin America has become the major target of the Chinese expansion abroad is delusional.

Myth 3: South-South Cooperation

Until the late 1970s, China's economy was insular. In the first three decades of the PRC (1949–1978), Chinese exports relied on raw materials. In that sense, China and Latin America were tied together. Those days ended long ago. Today, the Chinese leaders want China to be seen as a developing country and its relations with other developing countries as South-South and win-win cooperation rather than a Sinicized version of hegemonic North-South win-lose relations, which the PRC explicitly and repeatedly repudiates. In this connection, China has been taking a leading role in the BRICS coalition (Brazil, Russia, India, China, and South Africa) to advance its strategy of changing the existing international order and promoting the development of the developing countries.[24]

From China's perspective, its trade and investment in Latin America mutually complement and reinforce each other; China and Latin America could set a good example for South-South cooperation in which everyone wins. Latin America has a major infrastructure gap. Chinese banks can provide for major infrastructure projects, and have many companies that are fit to do the job. As a country that was invaded by Western powers repeatedly after the 1840s and suffered from Western hostility during much of the Cold War era, China, like Latin American countries, treasures and is particularly sensitive about state sovereignty including judicial sovereignty, and it does not endorse the concept of "human rights above sovereignty."

Beijing believes that as a developing country with a semi-colonial and semi-feudal past, China shares a common cause with Latin America: both wish to diversify their trade, lessen their dependence on the West, and reform the existing global order dominated by the rich countries. For this reason, Brazil and China have become active participants in the BRICS group. In 2014, the Sixth BRICS summit, held in Brazil, had the presence of the Union of South American States (UNASUR) leaders, which includes all the South American countries. By providing project loans to developing countries, the BRICS Bank could extend China's reach and diminish the U.S.'s negotiating leverage. In 2015, Brazil joined the Asian Infrastructure Investment Bank (AIIB) as a non-regional member, the only one from Latin America. Brazil's share in the AIIB is about 3.24%, with a 3.02% vote.[25] The AIIB is regarded by some as a rival to the IMF and the World Bank, which are regarded as dominated by developed countries like the United States.

Politically, China stands behind Latin American countries that oppose American interference into the domestic affairs of other countries such as Cuba and Venezuela. However, the idea that China is part of the developing world is just another myth. In the 1970s, when Deng Xiaoping spoke of South-South cooperation, China was as poor as some of the world's poorest countries in the world today, while Latin America was considered a region of middle-income countries. Nowadays, China is a global economic giant boasting the second-largest economy, a large aid donor, and a provider of FDI and other financial resources. It has become fashionable to point out that China is exploiting Latin America and it has become increasingly difficult for the countries in the region to find common ground with China.

At present, a large part of the exports of Costa Rica and Mexico to China are manufactured goods. Under "Made in China 2025," a new government initiative put forward by Beijing in 2015, this might change soon.[26] "Made in China 2025" is a ten-year plan for upgrading China's manufacturing capacity so it can catch up with production powerhouses like Germany and fend off competition from other developing countries. In fact, like the "Asian Tigers" before it, China has been pushing into higher-end manufacturing and innovation. Chinese scholar Yiping Huang maintains that China is a special developing country.[27] Nevertheless, with China's rise as the second-largest economy in the world, and some even calling it an emerging superpower, it is more and more difficult for the developing world to acknowledge that China remains a developing country.

It is true that Chinese engagement with Latin America is reshaping the external economic relations of the continent. Trade between China and Latin America, for example, has grown dramatically. China has become an important source of foreign direct investments in the region. Chinese government officials emphasized that the Chinese relationship with Latin America is not about neo-colonialism but "win-win South-South cooperation." Nonetheless, some of their counterparts from Latin America argue that the emerging relationship is a kind of "new dependency."[28] Apparently, the Chinese trade and investment in the region resembles the relationships that Latin America has had with the West, which is extractive in nature. A large number of Chinese scholars hold the view that Latin America needs to change its economic strategy from export of commodities to export of processed goods, for instance, not just export of soybeans and crude oil, but processed products. Rising demand for commodities and funds for infrastructure was driving Latin America closer to China in the past two decades, but the relationship is far from equal. Commodity exports could drive up growth in the short run, but they could make Latin America less competitive as an exporter of manufacturing goods. Raúl Prebisch, a well-known Argentine economist, finds that terms of trade are unfavorable to the developing world in the long run.

A number of countries in the region have embraced the Chinese dragon as a welcome alternative to the United States and the conditions imposed by the IMF and the World Bank. They are seeking to diversify their trade partners and take advantage of the economic opportunities presented by China. Commodity exports are likely to remain a main driver of the economies of quite a few Latin American countries. Beijing talks a lot about South-South cooperation. In reality, China has a theory, but the proof is patchy. With China's rapid rise from a backward agrarian society to an industrial powerhouse in the past three decades, South-South cooperation has been more of a principle than actual practice.

Myth 4: Emerging Economic Ties Are Detrimental to Latin America

Latin America has a huge market and possesses raw materials that China needs and China has capital that the region lacks. It looks as if there is a win-win situation. Beijing has been trying to promote co-prosperity and win-win cooperation, yet its economic ties have not proven to be quite the panacea Beijing hoped. These expressions appear to arouse doubt rather than trust in China's intentions. There are concerns about Chinese resource extraction from and market expansion in Latin America. From Beijing's perspective, however, Chinese economic ties with Latin America are mutually beneficial and sustainable. One recent study implies that such win-win cooperation might turn into win-lose condition.[29]

Three factors make the win-win difficult to achieve. First of all, since its entry into the WTO, China has moved up the value chain and re-defined its competitive advantage in the global marketplace. In other words, China no longer belongs to the periphery, like other Asian emerging economies such as South Korea and Taiwan; it has become part of a semi-periphery in the global system. The Chinese companies are innovating furiously, producing all kinds of devices. They want to be trend-setters rather than trend followers. Second, it is important to remember that China has abandoned the planned economy model. Like other market economies, China is composed of companies seeking to maximize their profits. In other words, like the Western multinationals (MNCs), Chinese firms' interest in developing Latin America's infra-structure is not altruistic.

Third, a growing number in Latin America are suspicious of Chinese business activities, worrying about unfair deals and environmental damage. Opposition is fueled by Latin America's thriving civil society, which demands more transparency and environmental protection. This can be an unfamiliar challenge for the PRC, whose foreign policy is heav-ily based on state-to-state relations, with little appreciation of the gulf between rulers and their people. During his visit to the United Nations in September 2015, Xi declared China will provide $2 billion dollars in assistance to developing countries and forgive debt to the least devel-oped nations. In spite of tremendous efforts, trade, labor, and environ-mental disputes between China and many Latin American countries have been on the rise.[30]

Latin American countries need foreign capital, and China holds the largest foreign reserve in the world. A few recipient countries in Latin America have poor credit, which means many projects may sound promising at the beginning but will be hard to pursue. Agreement and consensus are typically reached at the top governmental level but imple-mentation occurs at the local level. Local governments may not care about the central government's policies and do not always cooperate with foreign investors.[31] The key is how to turn good intentions into actions of cooperation. Some bumpy roads lie ahead for Beijing's ambitious new initiatives.

China faces a major challenge in terms of creating jobs for rural workers. According to the National Bureau of Statistics, the number of rural migrant workers increased to 262.61 million by the end of 2012. Nearly one in every five Chinese people were rural migrant workers, those from rural areas working in cities.[32] If "socialist" China is behaving like the United States in Latin America, it is largely because it is being driven by market forces while being simultaneously starved of resources. Undoubtedly, China and Latin America can benefit from the evolving relationship, but both competition and cooperation exist at the same time. There is evidence to suggest that China's strong demand for resources has significantly contributed to Latin American economic development. Yet past success is no guarantee of future stable growth. Both sides need to pay close attention to nurturing their close and growing economic and political ties.

Some argue that emerging economic ties are detrimental to Latin America. This is another myth. In fact, there is a thin line between the positive and negative implications of growing economic relations between China and the region. Rather than blaming China for their economic woes, the countries in the region need to have an honest conversation about what must be done to strengthen their economies. Kevin Gallagher finds that Latin American governments mishandled the windfall of revenue spurred by trade with China and therefore face tough years ahead.[33] What is more, Latin America needs to increase savings, invest more in innovation, and pursue technological changes. [34]

The lack of adequate infrastructure is a bottleneck for economic growth in Latin America. By engaging in close trade relations with China, South American countries, Ecuador and Peru, for example, have tried to address this lacuna. They have been able to do so as a result of the state's capacity to facilitate foreign investment in infrastructure. A number of interest groups in the region embrace the liberalization of trade with China, since it brings along benefits such as an increase of investment in infrastructure, telecommunications, and information-technology sectors. Others support the increase in trade with China even if it has a negative impact on import-competing sectors of the economy.[35] When China's economy was booming, commodity-exporting countries of South America such as Argentina, Brazil, Chile, and Peru largely benefited from the rise in Chinese demand for the commodities they produce, especially soybeans, iron ore, and copper.

China is still urbanizing. At present, about 50 percent people live in cities. Its capital stock per capita—factories, locomotives, bridges, and so on—is only a fraction of the U.S.'s, which means that demand for basic industrial goods will not fade out. China has a 2030 goal to create ten urban centers, clusters of cities linked by infrastructure. Taken together, these plans would call for ten new airports, tens of thousands of miles of additional roads and railroads, bridges, ports, and of course, schools, housing, and power and communication infrastructure. Chinese purchases of food have been resilient and may even increase as a result of lower food prices. Food consumption is likely to increase. Under such circumstances, in the long run, Chinese demand for commodities will continue.

On the other hand, after three decades of extraordinary economic growth, the Chinese economy is cooling down. Slower growth has become a "new normal."[36] Meanwhile, Beijing has called for efforts to shift the world's second-largest economy from an export-led growth model fueled by government investment to one driven by higher domestic consumption and a larger services sector. With less robust economic growth, China's appetite for commodities is slowing down in the short run.

China's investment, like its trade, is potentially a boon. But both have pitfalls.[37] There are of course many concerning environmental impacts related to the huge increase in extractive industries and agriculture by Chinese companies in Latin America, including pollution and deforestation. In several countries there have been protests against the rising inflow of Chinese manufactured goods and local Chinese businesses, and the perceived loss of manufacturing jobs to China. Furthermore, a few believe that China has served to reinforce Latin America's specialization in commodities.

Growing Chinese economic clout is stirring local resentment. Shut out from international capital markets, Argentina has to borrow heavily from China, reciprocating with no-bid infrastructure projects and looser visa requirements for Chinese workers. Latin America badly needs infrastructure. The Pacific-Atlantic Railroad, one of the major projects that

Beijing is proposing in the region, is also in China's interest, because ship-
pers would be able to ferry soybeans and other goods from Brazil to ports
in Peru for export to China and Chinese goods in the other direction.
That would bypass the expensive and congested Panama Canal.

Latin America needs foreign investments, including those from
China, but not Chinese laborers. Labor is an abundant production factor
in both China and Latin America. Given that many Chinese investment
projects assume the use of Chinese workers and equipment, the net gain
to Latin American countries is less than similar investment from higher
income countries. On the one hand, economic performance is one of the
major dimensions of regime legitimacy in China. It is hard to imagine
central and local governments in China could just see Chinese business
idle plants and lay off large number of workers. It is not surprising that
the groups associated with labor have been very reluctant to liberalize
trade and investment. On the other hand, Latin American manufacturers in countries that also rely on labor-intensive exports, particularly the
Central American nations and Mexico, have been severely hurt by Chinese competition in the U.S. market, despite their greater proximity to
it. Brazil and Argentina share the same pain as well. There is clearly a
competitive dynamic here.

In spite of growing competition, China's cooperation with Latin America promises great benefits for the continent. As Antonio Hsiang, a long-
time Latin America watcher in Taiwan, put it rightly, China's emergence
in the region is peaceful and constructive. China's rise in Latin America
provides more opportunities than challenges for both Latin America and
the United States. China behaves as a "responsible stake-holder" in Latin
America. Compared with Russia's "security and military-technical cooperation" with Latin America, China's engagements have been more
constructive. Indeed, China's purchase of commodities has been the
main factor in Latin America's economic growth in the last decade.[38]
In the words of Kevin Gallagher, one of the closest watchers of China in
Latin America, "Latin America rode the coattails of the boom in China,
growing at an annual rate of 3.6 percent from 2003 to 2013. This stands
in stark contrast to the previous two decades dominated by the Washington Consensus. Under Washington Consensus growth was a much
slower 2.4 percent and inequality increased."[39]

In brief, although the strategy of China toward Latin American development seems to be muddled with selfish national interests, the emerging Sino–Latin American economic link is both complementary and competitive.

Myth 5: China's New Alliance with Latin America Is a Threat to the U.S.

There is a grave concern in the Western Hemisphere that the robust economic ties between China and Latin American countries will enhance China's political influence and encourage political cooperation between China and those countries. One recent study finds that the combined success of authoritarianism and economic growth, a core characteristic of the "China model," is potentially very attractive to the ruling classes of Latin America.[40] Yet Wang notes that thus far China's expanding economic relations with the region have not had a significant spillover effect into political systems.[41] In spite of growing economic ties with Latin America, Beijing still faces a lot of challenges. For instance, one Chinese scholar acknowledges that China lacks appealing soft power and has few instruments to protect its interests in the region in the context of its insistence on its respect for the internal affairs of its partners as sovereign countries.[42] In the words of Andrew Nathan, China does not have the economic, military, or soft-power resources to exert substantial influence over the domestic political systems of faraway countries. It has not been able even to prevent a democratic transition in its close neighbor Burma or to persuade its only formal ally, North Korea, to adopt liberalizing economic reforms.[43]

Unlike in the early period of the PRC, China does not intend to export its political system, ideology, or model of development to the region. As Xi Jinping indicated in Mexico City in 2009, "Some foreigners with full bellies and nothing better to do engage in finger-pointing at us." He went on: "First, China does not export revolution; second, it does not export famine and poverty; and third, it does not mess around with you. So what else is there to say?"[44] Instead, China, as a rising power, is likely to continue to use aid, investment, and loans to protect and enhance the country's economic and political interests.

At present, China has few political ambitions in the "backyard" of the United States. It cooperates with democracies as much as with authoritarian regimes. China is likely to maintain its support of left-wing regimes such as Cuba and Venezuela, though it is important to note that Havana and Washington are in the process of normalizing their relations. Actually, for a long time Beijing has wished Havana would follow China's model of reform and open its doors to private business and foreign investment.

China has broad interests in Latin America, but the economic interest is of the most importance and its engagement with Latin America is pragmatic. For instance, China maintains close relationship with both left-wing regimes such as Cuba and the Bolivarian Alliance (Venezuela and Bolivia) and the free-trade and market-oriented Pacific Alliance (including Colombia, Peru, and Chile). Peru and Chile are important trading partners of China, and they had agreed to join TPP if it went ahead.

The Cold War and its ideologically driven battle for hearts and minds are over. But there is a contest for influence between the two very different political and economic systems, one that prevails will set the standards and write the rules for international trade and investment in the coming years. The competition for economic influence continues. Beijing leadership realizes that it has a large stake in fostering stability and economic development. Unlike in the first three decades of the PRC, since the late 1970s, Beijing has quietly recognized the dominant position of the United States in the region. China has important reasons not to challenge U.S. interests in the region. In an interdependent world, China increasingly needs the United States for various benefits. In dealing with Latin American countries, China's current concern is not with global geopolitical competition but more with potential mutual gains from growing interactions.

The top geopolitical priority of China is to avoid a direct contest with the U.S. Beijing understands China's growing role in Latin America is considered a strategic challenge to the Monroe Doctrine and thus a serious threat to U.S. interests. Chinese leaders have been very sensitive to U.S. perceptions and interests. There are several forces propelling China's engagement in the region: its dependency on natural resources, its thirst to open new markets for its manufactured products, and its desire to create a strong alliance. At this time, there is little evidence that China is seeking to upend U.S. dominance in Latin America. To sum up, the belief that China poses a direct and emerging threat to U.S. interests in Latin America is a false fear. The Chinese support of Latin American economic development is not simply charity; it is based on anticipated gains in finance, investment, and trade. Its economic engagement with the region has been a key driver of economic growth since the turn of this century. There is little doubt that the increasing Sino–Latin American economic tie is in the long-term interests of the United States.

Conclusion

China's involvement in Latin America is expanding in a spectacular way. In a time frame of less than two decades, China has gone from having virtually no presence in Latin America to being a major actor in the region's economic arena. China's presence in Latin America is part of a more general policy of "going out" (*zou chuqu*). In the wake of the global financial crisis, many Chinese scholars share the view that Europe and the U.S. are on the wane and there are more opportunities in the developing world. China's involvement in Latin America is likely to deepen and intensify in the years to come. Through a mixture of FTA, direct investment, development aid, and high-level political exchange, China has become an increasingly important player in Latin America. Overall, China largely plays a constructive role, mainly involving itself in regional affairs with the aim of promoting trade and investment.

Chinese growth looks more or less in line with that of other emerging economies, which all experienced slowdowns following high growth. Subsequently, the growth in Chinese demand for commodities is slowing. That said, put in a longer-term context, China's hunger for agricultural goods, and perhaps for farm land, may grow as China's population expands and the middle class becomes richer. Mao Zedong once said, "The future is bright, but the road is tortuous." This saying can be used to appropriately describe the Sino–Latin American economic exchange. In spite of a rocky path, China, now Latin America's second-biggest trade partner and major provider of financial resources, is likely to maintain its presence in the region in the foreseeable future.

NOTES

1 This study is supported by a Fulbright research grant and a Faculty Development Grant from Merrimack College. I would like to express my appreciation to Institute of Latin American Studies at the Chinese Academy of Social Sciences that provided me with excellent facilities during my field trip to China. The views in the paper are entirely mine and should not be ascribed to the institutions acknowledged above. An earlier version of the paper was presented at the conference held in New York University in June 2015. The author would like to thank Dr. David Denoon and participants of the conference for their thoughtful feedback.

2 Editorial Board, "China's Pivot."

3 OECD, CAF and ECLAC, *Latin American Economic Outlook 2016.*

4 "China Crude Oil Output Rises 4.9% in August," China Daily, http://usa.china daily.com.cn.

5 Zamora, "China's Double-edged Trade."

6 Rosen and Hanemann, *China's Changing Outbound Foreign Direct Investment.*

7 "China's Outward Foreign Direct Investment in 2013," *Greenovation Hub*, October 11, 2014, www.ghub.org.

8 Ibid.

9 Editorial Board, "China's Pivot."

10 "Zhongguo ziben 'niliu ershan' touzi lamei xucong zhengcexing guodu dao shangyexing" [Against the odds, Chinese investment in Latin America; transformation is needed from policy banks to commercial banks], August 8, 2015, EastMoney.com, http://finance.eastmoney.com.

11 IAD and GEGI, "Chinese Lending to LAC in 2014."

12 Xue and Xu, "Why China Shouldn't Get Too Invested."

13 Personal interview in Beijing, China, in October 2015.

14 Premier Li Keqiang's keynote speech at CEPAL's headquarters in Santiago, Chile, on May 25, 2015 is the most recent example of China's official state rhetoric toward Latin America, reaffirming China's strategy of engagement with the region, which dates back to the earliest days of the People's Republic and was expressly established in *China's Policy Paper on Latin America and the Caribbean.*

15 Personal interview in Beijing, China, in October 2015.

16 Cardenal and Araújo, *China's Silent Army.*

17 Zhang, "Zhongla guanxi."

18 Murphree and Breznitz, "The Sky Is Not Falling."

19 Hornby and Schipani, "China Tilts."

20 For detail, see Tian, "Zhongguo qiyejia."

21 Tian, "Zhongguo yaozou."

22 When joining the World Trade Organization in 2001, China agreed that it would be recognized as a non-market economy within 15 years of its entry. Owing to this status, many countries have turned anti-dumping measures into a means of

trade protectionism against China; the PRC has become the world's largest anti-dumping target. Consequently, China has made the market economy status issue one of the highest priorities on its economic agenda. In recent years, the PRC has secured market economy status from a number of Latin American countries, including Argentina, Brazil, Chile, Peru, and Venezuela.

23 Li, "China's Growing Interests."
24 Mishra, "China Is Driving."
25 "Georgia, Denmark, Brazil, Netherlands, Finland Join China's AIIB Bank," *Sputnik International*, April 12, 2015, available at https://sputniknews.com.
26 In May 2015, China's State Council (China's cabinet) unveiled a ten-year plan for upgrading the nation's manufacturing capacity so it can catch up with production powerhouses like Germany and fend off competition from other developing countries.
27 Huang, "China Is a Special Developing Country."
28 Gonzalez-Vicente, "Political Economy of Sino-Peruvian Relations."
29 Zhang, "Zhongla guanxi."
30 Ray et al., *China in Latin America*.
31 Romero, "China's Ambitious Rail Projects."
32 "Rural Migrant Workers Top 262 Million," *China Daily*, February 2, 2013, www.chinadaily.com.cn.
33 Gallagher, *China Triangle*, 8–9.
34 Ibid., 112–116.
35 Coral, Creutzfeldt, and Leiteritz, "The Impact of China."
36 For detail, see Hu, "Embracing China's 'New Normal.'"
37 "The Chinese Chequebook," *Economist*, May 23, 2015, p. 29.
38 Hsiang, "China Rising in Latin America."
39 Gallagher, *China Triangle*, 8.
40 Minglu Chen and David S. G. Goodman, "The China Model: One Country, Six Authors," *Journal of Contemporary China* 21, no. 73 (2012): 169–185.
41 Wang, "The Missing Link."
42 For a Chinese perspective on China's soft power in Latin America, see Guo, "Keguan kandai."
43 Nathan, "China's Challenge," 157.
44 Sim Chi Yin, "Chinese V-P Blasts Meddlesome Foreigners," *Straits Times*, February 14, 2009, http://news.asiaone.com.

BIBLIOGRAPHY

Aranson, Cynthia, Mark Mohr, and Riordan Roett, eds. (2008). *Enter the Dragon: China's Presence in Latin America* (Washington, DC: Woodrow Wilson International Center for Scholars).

Cardenal, J. P., and & Araújo. (2014). *China's Silent Army: The Pioneers, Traders, Fixers and Workers Who Are Remaking the World in Beijing's Image, trans. Catherine*

Mansfield (London: Penguin Books). (First published in Spanish as *La sclenciosa conquista China*, 2011.)

Cheng, Yinghong. (2007). "Fidel Castro and China's Lesson for Cuba: A Chinese Perspective," *China Quarterly* 189 (March): 24–42.

Cheng, Yinghong. (2012). "The 'Socialist Other': Cuba in Chinese Ideological Debates since the 1990s," *China Quarterly* 209 (March): 198–216.

Coral, Horacio, Benjamin Creutzfeldt, and Ralf J. Leiteritz. (2015). "The Impact of China on the Domestic Political Economy of Colombia, Ecuador and Peru: Getting to Grips with Divergence," paper presented at New Directions in International Political Economy, Warwick University, UK, May 13–15.

Deng, Yong, and Fei-ling Wang, eds. (2004). *China Rising: Power and Motivation in Chinese Foreign Policy* (Lanham, MD: Rowman & Littlefield).

Devlin, Robert, Antoni Estevadeoradal, and Andrés Rodríguez-Clare. (2006). *The Emergence of China: Opportunities and Challenges for Latin America and the Caribbean* (Cambridge, MA: Harvard University Press).

Dussel Peters, Enrique. (2015). "China's Evolving Role in Latin America. Can It Be a Win-Win?," *DusselPeters.com*, www.dusselpeters.com/88.pdf.

Editorial Board. (2015). "China's Pivot to Latin America," *Bloomberg View*, May 25, www.bloombergview.com.

Ellis, Evan. (2014). *Chinese Companies on the Ground in Latin America* (London: Palgrave Macmillan).

———. (2013). *The Strategic Dimension of Chinese Engagement with Latin America* (Washington, DC: Perry Center for Hemispheric Defense Studies).

Ferchen, Matt. (2014). "China's Shaky Latin American Liabilities," *National Interest*, www.nationalinterest.org.

Fernández Jilberto, Alex E., and Barbara Hogenboom, eds. (2010). *Latin America Facing China: South-South Relations beyond the Washington Consensus* (New York: Berghahn Books).

Fornés, Gastón, and Alan Butt Philip. (2012). *The China-Latin America Axis: Emerging Markets and the Future of Globalisation* (London: Palgrave Macmillan).

Fravel, Taylor, Sun Xuefeng, and Matt Ferchen, eds. (2012). *China's Rise and International Norms: A CJIP Reader* (Oxford: Oxford University Press, 2012).

Gallagher, Kevin P. *The China Triangle: Latin America's China Boom and the Fate of the Washington Consensus* (London: Oxford University Press).

Gallagher, Kevin P., and Roberto Porzecanski. (2010). *The Dragon in the Room: China and the Future of Latin American Industrialization* (Stanford, CA: Stanford University Press).

Gonzalez-Vicente, Ruben. (2012). "The Political Economy of Sino-Peruvian Relations: A New Dependency?" *Journal of Current Chinese Affairs* 4, no. 1: 97–131.

Guo Cunhai. (2015). "Keguan kandai zhongguo zai lamei de ruanshili" [We should study China's soft power in Latin America objectively], Institute of Latin American Studies ILAS-CASS, http://ilas.cass.cn.

Han, Qi, ed. (2012). *Shijie xiandaihua jinchen: ladingmeizhou* [History of world modernization: Latin America volume] (Nanjing, Jiangsu: Jiangsu People's Publishing).

Hearn, Adrian H., and José Luis León-Manríquez, eds. (2011). *China Engages Latin America: Tracing the Trajectory* (Boulder, CO: Lynne Rienner).

Hornby, Lucy, and Andres Schipani. (2015). "China Tilts towards Liberal Latin American Economies," *Financial Times*, www.ft.com.

Hsiang, Antonio C. (2009). "China Rising in Latin America: More Opportunities than Challenges," *Journal of Emerging Knowledge on Emerging Markets* 1: 33–47.

Hu, Angang. (2015). "Embracing China's 'New Normal': Why the Economy Is Still on Track," *Foreign Affairs* 94, no. 3 (May/June): 8–12.

Huang, Yiping. (2015). "China Is a Special Developing Country," *New York Times*, www.nytimes.com.

IAD (Inter-American Dialogue) and GEGI (Boston University's Global Economic Governance Initiative). (2015). "Chinese Lending to LAC in 2014," www.thedialogue.org.

Jiang, Shixue. (2011). "Ten Key Questions about the China-Latin America Relationship," in Adrian H. Hearn and José Luis León-Manríquez, eds., *China Engages Latin America: Tracing the Trajectory* (Boulder, CO: Lynne Rienner).

Li, He. (2007). "China's Growing Interests in Latin America and Its Implications," *Journal of Strategic Studies* 30, nos. 4/5 (August–October): 833–862.

———. (1991). *Sino-Latin American Economic Relations* (New York: Praeger).

Long, Guoqiang. (2015). "'One Belt, One Road': A New Vision for Open, Inclusive Regional Cooperation," *DusselPeters.com*,www.dusselpeters.com.

Mishra, Pankaj. (2014). "China Is Driving the BRICS Train." BloombergView, July 20, www.bloombergview.com.

Mora, Frank O. (2009). "Strategic Implications of China's Evolving Relationship with Latin America," *Security and Defense Studies Review*, 9, nos. 1 & 2.

Murphree, Michael, and Dan Breznitz. (2015). "The Sky Is Not Falling—the Truth about China's Economy," *Yale Books Unbound*, http://blog.yupnet.org.

Nathan, Andrew J. (2015). "China's Challenge," *Journal of Democracy* 26, no. 1 (January): 156–170.

National Bureau of Statistics of the People's Republic of China. (2015). *China Statistical Yearbook, 2014*, http://www.stats.gov.cn/tjsj/.

OECD, CAF, and ECLAC. (2015). *Latin American Economic Outlook 2016: Towards a New Partnership with China* (Paris: OECD Publishing).

Oppenheimer, Andres. (2014). "China Is Flexing Its Muscle in Latin America," *Miami Herald*, www.miamiherald.com.

Ray, Rebecca, Kevin P. Gallagher, Andres Lopez, and Cynthia Sanborn. (2014). *China in Latin America: Lessons for South-South Cooperation and Sustainable Development*, Boston University, www.bu.edu.

Romero, Simon. (2015). "China's Ambitious Rail Projects Crash into Harsh Realities in Latin America," *New York Times*, October 3,, www.nytimes.com.

Rosen, Daniel H., and Thilo Hanemann. (2009). *China's Changing Outbound Foreign Direct Investment Profile: Drivers and Policy Implications* (Washington, DC: Peterson Institute for International Economics).

Shen, Simon. (2012). "Online Chinese Perceptions of Latin America: How They Differ from the Official View," *China Quarterly* 209 (March): 157–177.

Sutter, Robert. (2008). *Chinese Foreign Relations: Power and Policy since the Cold War* (Lanham, MD: Rowman & Littlefield).

Tian Zhi. (2015a). "*Zhongguo yaozou lamei "dongtian li de yibahuo*" [Chinese firms must work actively in Latin America], *Sina.com*, http://finance.sina.com.cn.

———. (2015b). "*Zhongguo qiyejia ruohe kandai lamei shichang de qianjing*" [Chinese entrepreneurs' perspectives on the future of the Latin American market], *Aiweibang.com*, www.aiweibang.com.

Wang, Hongying. (2015). "The Missing Link in Sino-Latin American Relations," *Journal of Contemporary China* 24, no. 94: 922–942.

Wu, Baiyi, ed. (2013). *Zhuanxin zhongde jiyu: Zhongla hezuo qianjin de duoshijiao fenxi* [Opportunity during the transition period: analysis of prospect of Sino–Latin American cooperation] (Beijing: Jingji guanli chupanshe).

Yue, Yunxia. (2008). "Zhongmo jingmao jinzhengli yanju" [Economic and trading competitiveness: a comparison of China and Mexico], *Lamei Yanju* [Latin American studies] 30, no. 3.

Xue Li and Xu Yanzhuo. (2015). "Why China Shouldn't Get Too Invested in Latin America," *Diplomat*, March, http://thediplomat.com.

Zamora, Jordi. (2014). "China's Double-edged Trade with Latin America," Agence France-Presse, September 11.

Zhang, Sengen. (2015) "Zhongla guanxi zhengzai buru yige kunnan shiqi" [Sino–Latin American relationship is entering into a difficult period], *Caijing.com.cn*, http://comments.caijing.com.cn.

12

Strategic Aspects of the China–Latin America Interaction

HAIBIN NIU

Compared with the advanced western countries, and Africa, Latin America occupied a relatively marginal priority in China's foreign strategy in the last century. However, the importance of Latin America in China's international relations has been increasing because of the impressive economic engagement since the beginning of this century. Chinese President Xi's two visits to Latin America in his first two years in office raised the profile of Latin America in China's diplomacy. The China-CELAC Forum was established during his last visit in 2014. A comprehensive partnership between China and the region is emerging with the deepening economic ties and a broader cooperation agenda set by the first ministerial meeting of China-CELAC Forum in Beijing. Coincidentally, the United States declared the end of the Monroe Doctrine era in 2013, which will provide more space for China and Latin American to build a comprehensive relationship.[1] Against this backdrop, there is more and more curiosity and even suspicion about the political and strategic implications of China-Latin America relations.[2]

In contrast with the view that China is going to Latin America to check the US strategy of rebalancing in Asia, it is important to understand the emerging China–Latin America interaction as a part of China's efforts to be a global player. The same logic applies to Latin America's newfound interest in China, since both Latin America and China are working hard to benefit from an increasingly integrated and globalized world. By strengthening their relationship, Latin America can build a diversified relationship beyond the US and Europe, while China can build a global tie beyond its periphery and the developed world. To make it clearer, China's approach to Latin America is not based on geopolitical calculations of sphere of influence, but based on win-win cooperation in a globalized world. China aims at building a comprehensive partnership with Latin America since China no longer act as if Latin America is the backyard of the United States.

Geopolitical thinking has a long tradition in Western IR theory based on the Western powers' experiences in world politics, and it is gaining new influence because of China's rise as a global player. The rise of populism in Latin America since the beginning of the 21st century and the willingness of Latin American regimes led by left politicians to build strong relationships with China also increased the geopolitical concerns of the established powers. The rise of China and its economic ties across the globe changed the world economic landscape, and it will definitely have some geopolitical and strategic implications around the world. China's increasing tie with Latin America is a natural reflection of China's rise as an important world economy and an important global player in dealing with challenges such as global security and climate change, etc. Both China and Latin America might enjoy larger autonomy and enhance their influence in the international system if they cooperated directly. It is extremely important for China, as a rising global power, to build a good relationship by helping the world to better understand and accept China's peaceful rise.

Latin America's historical interaction with the US and Europe makes it clear that it is not easy for any external player to build a strong, sustainable, and equal relationship with the region. Building such a relationship is a long and zigzag process that requires calculations of prestige, interests, and values. In Latin America, there is a growing concern that the economic relationships with China may be unbalanced. Between China and Latin America the honeymoon seems to be ending and both sides need to explore new dynamics for their economic ties in a slowing world economy. With the deepening interaction with Latin America, there is an expanding academic community in China on Latin American studies, which is helpful for China to understand the region better and to design reasonable policy toward the region. In general, China's engagement with Latin America is mutually beneficial in nature, which might influence other major powers as they develop their relationships with the region.

A Shifting Chinese View on Latin America

After the establishment of the People's Republic of China in 1949, China was isolated by the western world for almost three decades. In order to get international support, China built closer ties with the Soviet Union and its allies across the world, including in Latin America. From that point of view, some scholars argue that China's foreign policy toward Latin America has been primarily driven by a one-dimensional concern: global geopolitics from a historical perspective.[3] During the Cold War, maintaining relationships with more neutral countries rather than with countries that belonged to either camp was in China's national interest. During that period, China's relationship with Cuba was negatively influenced by China's relationship with the United States and the Soviet Union.

It was noteworthy that after the rapprochement of the United States and China in 1970s, China maintained a good political relationship with all types of regimes in Latin America except the countries maintained diplomatic ties with Taiwan. To a large extent, China's independent diplomacy is to be credited for achieving this kind of good relationship with Latin American countries. After the September 11 terrorist attack in 2001, Latin American countries' economic ties with China became closer since the priority of United States foreign policy moved to Middle East and Central Asia. Since that time, leaders from both China and Latin American countries have been looking to each other for new opportunities to achieve growth. Clearly, whether China has a fully designed geopolitical strategy toward Latin America, global geopolitical situations, especially major power relations, do have a structural impact on the Sino–Latin American relationship. It is naïve to overlook both the global and regional geopolitical situations where China does overseas investment, even though the country doesn't have geopolitical ambitions in the region.

Geopolitical logic is not a very strong way to explain China's recent engagement with Latin America. The continued geopolitical challenge to China has been located on its borders. China lacks the capacity and willingness to impose a strategy on Latin America. From China's domestic point of view, the priority of developing its economy requires a peaceful and stable international environment. The economic agenda has taken a high profile in the Sino–Latin American relationship since the establishment of the China-Brazil strategic partnership in 1993. The most visible achievements of the strategic partnership are economic in nature. For example, China surpassed the United States as Brazil's largest trade partner in 2009, both China and Brazil are founding members of the newly established multilateral investment banks such as the New Development Bank (NDB) and Asian Infrastructure Investment Bank (AIIB), etc. China's FTAs with Chile, Peru, and Costa Rica show clearly the primacy of the economic agenda in the relationship. China's economic growth strategy is to integrate itself into the world economy, and Latin America is an increasingly important partner for China.

In economic terms, the strategic importance of Latin America for China has mainly been interpreted as Latin America serving as a market and raw material supplier for China.[4] However, things go beyond that perception. As a relatively advanced region in the developing world, Latin America is important for China not only as a potentially sizeable market but also an alternative development model for China to study. As a revolutionary party, the Chinese Communist Party (CPC) pays much attention to others' development experiences. Models of the Soviet Union, Singapore, and the United States have been highly discussed in the academic world and shed some light on the China's development path. The exchange of ideas on state governance and political management is a popular topic when the Chinese media reports on meetings between Chinese leaders and their counterparts. For instance, the International Liaison Department Central Committee of CPC took the loss of power by the Mexican Institutional Revolutionary Party (which had controlled the government for more than 70 years) as a development with important political implications. The Chinese academic world has also been studying Latin America's political and economic development experiences to avoid the middle-income trap and achieve political stability in China.

From the perspective of international strategy, the discussion in China is whether China should defer to the US because Latin America is so close to US borders. Traditionally, when Chinese scholars explain China doesn't have the intention of being a threat in the "backyard" of the United States, they defend China's intentions in Latin America while taking the notion of treating Latin America as the backyard (or sphere of influence) of the United States for granted.[5] This kind of thinking reflects a strategic consensus that the Sino-US relationship is more important than the Sino–Latin American relationship. However, Latin American countries have moved far away from it. South America has become more independent from the US than before under the leadership of Brazil, in dealing with regional issues and rejecting the FTAA proposal. Mexico, integrated into the American economy in the framework of NAFTA, is starting to come back to Latin America by initiating the Pacific Alliance and the Community of Latin American and Caribbean States (CELAC). Chinese scholars gradually realized the increasing autonomy of Latin American countries on the world stage, which should be the new context in which to observe the emerging Sino-Latin American relationship.

China highly values Latin America's overall importance in the international system. In 1988, Deng Xiaoping stated that the 21st century should be the century of both the Pacific and Latin America. Strategically speaking, Latin America enjoys a much higher status in China's foreign strategy than as merely a raw materials supplier. There are three Latin American members of the G20 states. Against the backdrop of the 2008 financial crisis, both China and Latin America reinforced their bilateral financial cooperation and joined hands to make the current international financial architecture more accountable by promoting reforms. In implementing peacekeeping works, both China and Brazil have a major say in UN tasks in Haiti. Latin America is also a key partner in dealing with global climate change and other international development challenges for China.

Therefore, China increasingly values the strategic importance of Latin America as a partner in global governance. The first China Policy Paper on Latin America and the Caribbean was published in 2008 to draw a roadmap for building a comprehensive and cooperative partnership. Latin America's development experiences were well studied by the OECD as well as in China. Considering the importance of the region, China aims to build a strategic, sustainable, and institutionalized tie with Latin America and the Caribbean states.[6] China has engaged with almost all multilateral institutions in the region at different levels from OAS to Mercosur to build consensus and provide public goods beyond pursuing economic interests. China also keeps a politically neutral attitude toward regional affairs in Latin America besides being increasingly involved in the regional institutional arrangements. "Despite its disagreements with the United States about many issues, Beijing has adopted a low-key approach and managed to avoid any public confrontation with the United States in the Western Hemisphere."[7] Despite this kind of political neutrality, China has started to upgrade its cooperation with selected states in the region to include issues of high politics such as the space program.[8]

Geopolitical Implications of China's Presence in the Region

a) Different Views among Scholars

Some scholars have raised the question of the geopolitical implications of China's economic ties with Latin America by arguing that, as one put it, "China is performing the traditional roles played by the United States in trade and the Europeans in investment. This is potentially a ground-shifting change in the geopolitics of the Western Hemisphere, and by assuming this new role, China must also bear the geopolitical consequences and responsibilities that come with it."[9] The United States has formally abandoned the Monroe Doctrine, the FTAA was rejected by Brazil under the Lula presidency, and rapprochement between Cuba and the United States was gradually coming true. It was a surprise if you followed the zero-sum geopolitical thinking based on China's deepening and broadening economic ties with Latin American countries. The new situation in Latin America shows that there is no easy answer to the geopolitical implications of China's presence in the region.

Though former US secretary of state Hillary Clinton criticized China, claiming China pursues a so-called neo-colonial way in Africa, there has been no similar formal criticism of Chinese policy in Latin America. In fact, both the United States and China are world powers that object to colonialism based on their painful histories. In reality, China doesn't have any official plans to export its citizens to Latin America. On the contrary, China abandoned its one-child policy to increase its available labor. There are real concerns about the environmental implications of Chinese investment in the extractive sectors in Latin America. In addressing these concerns, the Chinese government has been educating

Chinese companies to pay more attention to corporate social responsibilities. It is noteworthy that even companies from the advanced economies don't have good records in Latin America, as shown by BP's 2010 Gulf of Mexico oil spill. The situation is getting better as Chinese firms are making efforts to strengthen their environmental standards.

China's investment in infrastructure is, different from the Europeans', with a priority on railway systems and continental transportation projects. The private firm–proposed Nicaragua Canal and government-proposed Bi-Ocean Railway projects recently are positive responses to the enhanced economic ties between Latin America and China.[10] China's experience shows that infrastructure building must be accompanied by trade flows and investment, otherwise it will be unprofitable and unsustainable. If they come to pass, both continental projects will have a huge impact on the Panama Canal, which has been a sign of American hegemony for a long time. It is hard to say that the original purpose of these huge infrastructure projects is to achieve geopolitical goals, but they do have geopolitical implications. The Nicaragua Canal will reduce the business of the Panama Canal while the Bi-Ocean Railway will strengthen the Panama Canal's importance. Good infrastructure might also enhance the ties between China and Latin America from a geo-economics perspective. In fact, the shortage of infrastructure in Latin America is a handicap to the region's growth, which is well recognized by multilateral financial institutions and countries in the region.

One of the Latin American concerns regarding the China–Latin American trade pattern is how its character is similar to the North-South relationship when the North was exporting manufactured goods in exchange for raw materials from the South. Deindustrialization or recommodification has increasingly become a concern for some Latin American countries. The financial crisis of 2008 was a turning point. The United States was eager to revitalize its industrial sector by encouraging its manufacturers to come back, which was bad news for Latin America. The positive development is that both investment and financial cooperation were given more emphasis by the Chinese side so as to enhance its economic ties with the region. A prominent feature of Chinese investment is its scope and quality beyond raw materials and the extractive sector.[11] China aims to address the concern of deindustrialization by increasing its investment in the region's manufacturing sector and innovation by building partnerships with its Latin American counterparts.

Whether China is a threat in Latin America is a question being discussed by many American scholars. This reflects a strong geopolitical approach in the United States in thinking about Sino–Latin American relations. Closer Sino–Latin American ties have resulted in mixed reactions in US policy circles. Most analysts think that China's primary interest in the region is to gain access to resources and markets by means of trade and investment. They are confident in America's cultural, economic, and geographical advantages over China. Meanwhile, some analysts argue that China's involvement in the region could pose a future threat to US influence. They further argue that some regional countries look to China as an economic and political alternative to the Washington Consensus and US hegemony. China's close ties to those countries ruled by left-leaning politicians with anti-American characteristics have also been criticized. These mixed US reactions toward China's presence in Latin America reflect both cooperative and competing perspectives of globalization and geopolitics.

b) Diplomatic Positions of the US and China

The formal abandonment of the Monroe Doctrine might signal that the United States no longer views the presence of external power as a threat in the Western Hemisphere. While making such a judgment, it would be naïve to argue that there will not be strategic competition between China and the United States at all. At the bilateral level, the United States and China have held several strategic dialogues on Latin American affairs since 2006. The purpose of these dialogues is to enhance mutual trust and prevent misunderstanding of each side's strategy toward the region. These institutionalized dialogues help the US government to keep a positive attitude toward China's increasing presence in Latin America. There are, however, some critical voices from American conservative think tanks and the military sector.[12] The American support of both China's permanent observer status in the Organization of American States and China's membership in the Inter-American Development Bank are positive signals from the US side toward China's engagement with the region.

One interesting thing is that Latin America and the Caribbean have gradually been gaining priority in the foreign policy of both the US and China, even though for different reasons. President Obama's enhanced engagements with the region at the end of his second term were largely to deal with the resistance of Latin American countries to the Summit of the Americas because of the Cuba issue as well as to build his diplomatic legacy. Chinese president Xi Jinping's repeated visits to the region during his first two years were unprecedented, largely because of the attention that the Chinese leadership paid to the region. Chinese high-level attendance of the BRICS 2014 summit in Brazil and the 2016 APEC summit in Peru are examples of Chinese visibility and support of multilateral institutions. Chinese premier Li Keqiang also paid a visit to the region in 2015 with a very impressive economic agenda and the priority of China's international industrial capacity cooperation. This round of diplomacy, initiated by the US and China, focuses on soft power and economic engagement rather than geopolitical matters.

c) Political and Economic Implications

One strategic concern from the American side is China's enhanced ties with left-wing countries in Latin America. The concerns are about the implications for the character of Latin American democracy, the future of anti-Americanism, and US efforts to deal with non-traditional security issues such as illegal immigration and money laundering, etc. Some scholars have argued that although the earlier manifestations of Latin American populism involved heavy doses of nationalism, contemporary radical populists have anti-globalization, anti-liberal, and, to varying degrees, anti-US postures at the core of their foreign policy rhetoric and strategies.[13] It should be noted that even the left-leaning governments in Latin America are divided into two groups, "right left" and "wrong left," as a number of US scholars have identified them.[14] Therefore, the geopolitical concern is whether China's relationship with so-called "wrong left" countries like Venezuela will undermine American influence in the region.

It is fair to say that Venezuela as led by Chávez and Maduro is more anti–United States than Brazil's more neutral Lula and Dilma governments. Whatever their attitudes toward the United States, all left politicians in Latin America are cosmopolitan in nature, and their international vision goes beyond the Americas. Brazil's approach to China under the Lula government was mainly to create a partner for broader political and strategic objectives, such as the pursuit of a multipolar international order.[15] Against this background, China is the important partner these countries were looking for to build a diversified external profile. China's economic relationship with Venezuela and Brazil doesn't undermine their economic ties with the United States since China has a economic comparative advantage very different from the US's. It is also noteworthy that China didn't show the intention to support any anti-American agenda from those Latin American countries under populist leaders in the past decade.

The turn to the center or the left since the beginning of the 21st century was a remarkable political development in the region. There was also an important background of development model debates in Latin America. In the 1990s, most countries in the region adopted the Washington Consensus as a free-market recipe for restructuring their debt-crisis-hit economies, which helped them to improve efficiency but exacerbated many social problems, such as poverty, inequality, and public safety. The widely cited "turn to the left" in Latin American elections in 2005–2007 reflected the economic realities and social concerns of the voters. Latin American voters need both democracies to achieve their political rights, and strong and effective governments to address social issues including unemployment, public safety, education, and quality of life. Some left governments tried to achieve these goals by nationalizing the energy sectors, which posed a threat to foreign investors including China. However, the left governments are willing to expand their external relations, which was good news for China.

In these circumstances, the participants in the World Economic Forum on Latin America in 2007 reemphasized the Santiago Consensus, which was originally introduced in 1998. They aimed at achieving and sustaining higher productivity and growth with equity by agreeing on five priorities for the region: education, the environment, R&D investment, efficient taxation, and infrastructure. These priorities are intended to improve income distribution as economies grow and to take full advantage of the opportunities and innovation potential created by globalization. The Santiago Consensus represents a new policy para-

digm shift in the region. While Latin America has achieved rapid economic growth during the raw material boom period, it has still been
slower than Asian countries in terms of GDP growth. In this context,
China has become an attractive model for Latin American countries to
discuss and learn from. It is clear that there was a regional commitment
to democracy while what they can learn from China is to put priority on
infrastructure, the role of the public sector, etc.

China gradually realized that it is necessary to build knowledge of
all parties in Latin American countries because of their possibility to
come to power through regularly held elections. The CPC's new strategy
downplayed ideological differences and focused on mutual respect and
overall state diplomacy, which helped it to build a strong relationship
with all major parties across the region.[16] It is obvious that China did
not support these countries' anti-US strategy while it kept a low profile in building relationships with them. This is similar to the pragmatic
model of the United States when it continues to import oil from a country while criticizing the country's human rights record. China invests
heavily in the oil sector of Venezuela as well as other sectors despite
Venezuela's conflictual relationship with the United States. At the same
time, both the United States and China have concerns regarding the economic management of Venezuela.

Though there is some competition between American and Chinese
companies in the oil refinery sector, the energy-security dynamics have
changed a lot with the domestic energy revolution of shale gas in the United
States, which makes the US an oil exporter. The low price of energy
also makes it difficult for Latin American countries to attract foreign
investment in their oil sectors. NSA contractor Edward Snowden's revelations that Brazilian president Dilma Rousseff's phone and Petrobras
were spied on by the NSA stirred outrage in Brazil and resulted in the
cancellation of a state visit by Dilma to the White House in 2014. She
rescheduled the visit and it came about without incident in June 2015.
Furthermore, the spying scandal created more space for Chinese companies like Baidu to explore the Brazilian cyber market as well as other
regional countries such as Cuba, which is gradually building its domestic internet infrastructure. The importance of sovereignty in cyberspace
is a shared value for China and most of its Latin American peers. To
some extent, China is a more relevant partner than the United States for

the economic agenda of Latin American countries. At the same time, a closer economic tie between China and Latin America will stimulate the US effort to improve its economic ties with the region.

It is too early to identify China as a threat to the United States in Latin America. Bandwagoning is a cooperative strategy adopted by countries to get benefits from both sides of a competition. The United Kingdom has led the way by joining the AIIB and declaring the future decade as the golden age for Sino-Britain relations. There is similar thinking to the UK's in Latin America. However, Brazil, as a founding member of the AIIB as well as the NDB, is the only country in the Americas with the capability and willingness to act on that thinking. Latin American countries with strong trade ties with China, like Chile, take a very positive attitude toward the internationalization of the renminbi, which was thought of as a challenge to the hegemony of the US dollar. Countries across the region are looking for loans from the NDB as an additional financial resource to the IMF and World Bank. How to run these newly established multilateral financial institutions has been a great concern not only for the United States, but also Latin American countries. In terms of the international economic order, Latin American countries are expecting a more diversified one that can offer more options for them to achieve domestic growth.

There is concern that, with the development of President Obama's rebalance strategy in the Asia-Pacific region, China was adopting a similar one in the Western Hemisphere.[17] American observers closely examine China's strategic impact on the Latin America's military capabilities, and power structure. However, it is natural for both the US and China as world powers to have diplomatic interactions globally. Latin America is definitely a diplomatic space for China to reach, which does not necessarily mean that China will challenge US hegemony or influence in the region. China attaches importance to the principle of non-interference in others' domestic politics. So, when it engages with Latin American countries, China's strategic partnership building is based on development potential, regional influence, and global capacity of the partners, rather than the ideology or anti-US attitude of the governments.

After the rapprochement in the US-Cuba relationship, the US is regaining influence in its engagement with the region, while China is building a regional approach with the establishment of the China-

CELAC Forum. Comparing platforms between the OAS summit and China-CELAC Forum, the OAS summit is more institutionalized and broader in terms of its agenda, while the Forum focuses more on economic cooperation. Different from the emphasis on a commitment to democratic values by the summit, mutual respect of each other's political systems is the main value at the Forum. The United States openly expressed its concerns about the political and economic statecraft of some Latin American countries such as Venezuela, while China took a cautious approach in influencing domestic politics of Latin American countries in which China has huge investment. To safeguard China's economic interests in Venezuela, China prefers to help the country to improve its industrial capacity rather than purely provide financial liquidity. In dealing with relations with left-wing governments in Latin America, it seems that China focuses more on its long-term economic interests while the United States emphasizes its political interests. Whether China's economic approach to Venezuela is sustainable is being debated in Chinese academic circles.

The other case to test China's strategy in Latin America is to examine China's attitude toward the rapprochement in US-Cuba relations. Most Chinese scholars highly value the rapprochement's positive implications for the US–Latin American relationship as well as Cuba's future.[18] China highly cherished its relationship with Cuba based on socialism and good political relations despite difficulties due to the ideological struggle between China and the Soviet Union during the Cold War. Cuba has learnt some lessons from China on how to rebuild relations with the United States and how to build a market economy gradually. Generally speaking, China expects to benefit from a more open and stable environment in Cuba for Chinese FDI, while it keeps cautious in evaluating the political implications of the rapprochement for the future of Cuba's socialist system. There are different expectations of Cuba's future political arrangements for obvious reasons, however China clearly leaves Cuba's people to determine the country's institutional arrangements.

With increasing awareness of the knowledge gap between China and Latin America, China has strengthened its cultural ties with the region. To strengthen mutual understanding by doing more cultural exchanges has been an integral part of China's public diplomacy toward Latin America. Chinese public diplomacy to the region focuses on cultural exchanges such as building sister cities, organizing cultural exhibitions, hosting various Latin American delegations in China, and offering numerous government scholarships and training opportunities for young Latin Americans.

Confucius Institutes and Confucius classrooms have been established in many universities across the region to offer professional Chinese-language studies and opportunities to learn Chinese culture. During Chinese premier Li Keqiang's visit to Colombia in 2015, one sign of the increased cultural interaction was that the Chinese Nobel laureate Mo Yan was invited as a member of Li's delegation to attend a cultural seminar with Li's Colombian counterpart.

Looking Ahead

When talking about the world order, Dr. Kissinger argued that a reconstruction of the international system is the ultimate challenge to statesmanship in our time.[19] Both established powers and rising powers need to pay attention to the future of the international system. Rather than being a destructive power, China increasingly identifies itself as a beneficiary and constructive reformer of the current international system. In shaping regional order in Latin America, it is necessary to respect regional countries' creativity, wisdom, and vision. It is important to respect the growing autonomy of Latin American countries as both the US and China enhance their engagements with the region. Perhaps it is necessary to integrate some representatives from Latin America into the US-China strategic dialogue on Latin American affairs.

To build a more positive and constructive interaction among the US, China, and Latin America, the key is to pursue a mutually beneficial and win-win approach. Both the US and China should build partnerships with Latin American countries to help them achieve sustainable development. It is also critical to keep healthy Sino-US relations in key regions. China needs to learn how to be a major power among others, while the United States needs to learn how to sustainably interact with a rising state which embraces a distinctly different domestic political model.[20] Although Latin America was rarely mentioned when talking about the future world order in academics, the interaction between the

US and China in Latin America will have implications for the future international system.

Despite their different development stages, it is fair to say all sides—the United States, China, and Latin American countries—are in the midst of a transitional phase. All three societies face the challenge of minimizing income gaps, developing greengrowth paths, and building sustainable financial sectors. All need to redesign their domestic growth models in a post-liberal period and external strategies in a post-hegemonic world. Brazil's case tells a lot about the complexity of the world order. Brazil rejected the American initiative of the FTAA, and joined the BRICS group with China. So, while all the concerned countries are key players in established multilateral institutions such as the United Nations, WTO, World Bank, IMF, G20, and the Inter-American Development Bank. Against this backdrop, a strong China–Latin America tie will help China to adapt to a world in transition.

Under the framework of South-South cooperation, China's economic ties with Latin America are becoming more and more substantial and expanding to high-technological cooperation. From the Latin American perspective, it is apparent that the structural dependency of peripheral regions is fading away and China is helping the region to gain greater autonomy with respect to the United States.[21] The United States has brought the Washington Consensus to the region with a mixed result. China's influence on the region's growth paradigm is still not clear. Some Latin American scholars argue that China's presence provides an alternative model for the structure of the countries' internal political processes.[22] Different from the above-mentioned optimistic views on China's influence in Latin America, I would say China is closely watching its peers in the Americas with an intention to learn from their lessons rather than exporting its development experiences. China's joint space programs with Brazil, Venezuela, Bolivia, and Argentina are not aimed against a third party militarily but are meant to achieve development path featuring technological innovation and cooperation.

In the near future, China is highly likely to keep silent on Latin America's domestic politics and regional geopolitical affairs, and prefers exchanging ideas about each other's domestic governance practices to offering prescriptions. By following this strategy, China enjoys broad trust across the region, while the United States has been less trusted by countries in ALBA and Mercosur than countries in Central America and the Pacific Alliance.[23] China is trying to keep a comfortable distance from the region's major players while deepening its overall ties with the region. Considering the influence of the United States and a rising Brazil in the region, it is better for China to avoid the task of regional security, thus limiting power competition. Even the US is rethinking Latin American policy, placing more emphasis on foreign policy rather than development efforts. This recognizes that Washington's direct influence on region's domestic affairs has diminished.[24] The economic agenda will be dominating, while China is building an increasingly comprehensive partnership with the region.

The daunting bidding process for the Mexico City–Querétaro high-speed railway project and current political-economic deadlock in both Brazil and Venezuela show that the biggest challenge to China's interests in Latin America is not rivalry among big powers but domestic governance of Latin American countries. All sides are looking for a model in which the relations between state and market in achieving growth can reach a healthy, legitimate, and dynamic balance. Besides economic interaction, both China and Latin America need to build their confidence in the other's development model and enhance their commitment to a closer relationship. China noticed that the recent leadership changes in both Brazil and Argentina didn't affect those countries' cooperation with China very much, even though both countries are working to reinforce their traditional relationships with the advanced economies. China understands the new efforts by Brazil and Argentina well, and will be confident that the China–Latin America relationship is an increasingly interdependent one. Despite the changed priorities or approaches of some Latin American countries, China continues to attach importance to cooperation with them in dealing with a globalized world.

Besides the increasing economic ties, Taiwan issue, and other interests, the role of partnership between China and Latin America will be emphasized during China's rise. China needs support from Latin America to deal with global challenges including climate change, SDGs, world economic governance, and cyberspace governance. The legitimacy of China's rise and the rise of China per se will be enhanced if there is a well-designed global governance system. China also needs political support from Latin America regarding China's views on regional and global order. When many western leaders have stayed away, Venezuela president Maduro's attendance of the military parade in Beijing marking the 70th anniversary of the end of World War II on September 3, 2015, is important for China. It is safe to say China appreciates the international support from Latin America in a world of transition and uncertainty.

NOTES

1 John Kerry, "Remarks on U.S. Policy in the Western Hemisphere," November 18, 2013, U.S. Dept. of State, www.state.gov.

2 See R. Evan Ellis, "China's Growing Relationship with Latin America and the Caribbean in the Context of US Policy toward the Region," *Air & Space Power* [Chinese journal], 2nd Semester 2014, pp. 79–93; R. Evan Ellis, "China's Strategy in Latin America Demonstrates Boldness of President Xi," *Manzella Report*, February 19, 2014; Isabel Rodríguez Aranda, "An Assessment of Relations between China and the Americas: Foreign Policy Under Xi Jinping," in Soria and García, eds., *Latin America, the Caribbean and China*.

3 Xiang Lanxin, "An Alternative Chinese View," in Riordan Roett and Guadalupe Paz, eds., *China's Expansion into the Western Hemisphere*, Brookings Institution Press, 2008, pp. 44–58.

4 Kerry Dumbaugh and Mark P. Sullivan, "China's Growing Interest in Latin America," *CRS Report for Congress*, April 20, 2005.

5 Jiang, "China's New Leadership"; Wu Hongying, "On 'China Posing a Threat to America's Backyard,'" *Contemporary International Relations* [Chinese journal], Vol. 194, No. 12, 2015, pp. 8–13.

6 Haibin Niu, "On Strategic Significances of the Current Chinese-Latin American Relations," *Journal of Latin American Studies* [Chinese journal], Vol. 35, No. 3, 2013, pp. 49–52.

7 He Li, "China's Growing Interest in Latin America and Its Implications," *Journal of Strategic Studies*, Vol. 30, August/October 2007, p. 833.

8 Noesselt and Soliz-Landivar, "China in Latin America."

9 Xiang Lanxin, "An Alternative Chinese View," in Riordan Roett and Guadalupe Paz, eds., *China's Expansion into the Western Hemisphere*, Brookings institution Press, 2008, p. 57.

10 A Chinese company invested in the Nicaragua canal, and the governments of Peru, Brazil, and China proposed the Bi-Ocean Railway project to link Brazilian Atlantic ports with their Peruvian counterparts.

11 See Peters and Armony, *Beyond Raw Materials*.

12 Examples of hose suspicious voices in America regarding China's intentions in Latin America include Andres Oppenheimer, "China Is Flexing Its Muscle in Latin America," *Miami Herald*, July 19, 2014; Mary Anastasia O'Grady, "The Middle Kingdom in Latin America," *Wall Street Journal*, September 3, 2004.

13 Carlos de la Torre and Cynthia J Arnson, "Introduction: The Evolution of Latin American Populism and the Debates over Its Meaning," in Torre and Cynthia J. Arnson, *Latin American Populism*, p. 13.

14 Jorge G. Castaneda, "Latin America's Left Turn," *Foreign Affairs*, Vol. 85, No. 3, May/June 2006, pp. 28–43.

15 Institute of the Americas, Woodrow Wilson Center, and China Institute of Contemporary International Relations, *Latin America and China: What Do They Mean for Each Other?*, October 2011, pp. 17–22.

16 Haibin Niu, "Party Diplomacy with Chinese Characteristics," in Yang Jiemian, ed., *China's Diplomacy: Theory and Practice*, World Scientific Publishing Corporation, 2014, pp. 415–476.

17 See Daniel Morgan, "Expanding the Rebalance: Confronting China in Latin America," *Parameters*, Vol. 45, No. 3, Autumn 2015, pp. 103–114.

18 Jiang Shixue, "Reasons and Implications of Improved US-Cuba Relations," *Studies on International Affairs* [Chinese journal], No. 2, 2015, p. 47.

19 Kissinger, *World Order*, p. 371.

20 Ibid., p. 226.

21 Soria and García, eds., *Latin America, the Caribbean and China*, pp. 11–13.

22 Ibid., p. 12.

23 Nashira Chávez, "Latin America, United States and China: Strategic Continental Relations," in Soria and García, *Latin America, the Caribbean and China*, pp. 88–89.

24 Sabatini, "Rethinking Latin America."

BIBLIOGRAPHY

Adrián Bonilla Soria and Paz Milet García, eds., *Latin America, the Caribbean and China: Sub-Regional Strategic Scenarios*, FLACSO, 2014.

Maxwell A. Cameron and Eric Hershberg, eds., *Latin America's Left Turns*, Lynne Rienner Publishers, 2010.

Carlos de la Torre and Cynthia J. Arnson, eds., *Latin American Populism in the Twenty-first Century*, Woodrow Wilson International Center for Scholars, 2013.

Juan de Onis, "China's Latin Connection: Eclipsing the US?," *World Affairs*, January/February 2014, pp. 62–68.

Enrique Dussel Peters, "Recent China-LAC Trade Relations: Implications for Inequality?," *Geopolitics, History, and International Relations*, Vol. 5, No. 2, 2013, pp. 44–71.

Enrique Dussel Peters and Ariel C. Armony, eds., *Beyond Raw Materials: Who Are the Actors in the Latin America and Caribbean-China Relationship?*, University of Pittsburgh, 2015.

R. Evan Ellis, *China in Latin America: The Whats and Wherefores*, Lynne Rienner Publishers, 2009.

R. Evan Ellis, *China–Latin America Military Engagement*, Independent Publishing Platform, 2012.

Alex E. Fernández Jilberto and Barbara Hogenboom, *Latin America Facing China: South-South Relations beyond the Washington Consensus*, Berghahn Books, 2010.

Kevin P. Gallagher, "What's Left for Latin America to Do with China?," *NACLA Report on the Americas*, May/June 2010.

Francis Fukuyama, ed., *Falling Behind: Explaining the development Gap Between Latin America and the United States*, Oxford University Press, 2008.

Peter Hakim, "Is Washington Losing Latin America?," *Foreign Affairs*, Vol. 85, No. 1, 2006.

Adrian Hearn, "China and Latin America: Economy and Society," *Latin American Policy*, Vol. 4, No. 1, 2013, pp. 24–35.

Jiang Shixue, "China's New Leadership and the New Development of China–Latin America Relations," *China Quarterly of International Strategic Studies*, Vol. 1, No. 1, 2015, pp. 133–153.

Henry Kissinger, *World Order*, Penguin Press, 2014.

Iacob Koch-Weser, "Chinese Energy Engagement with Latin America: A Review of Recent Findings," *Inter-American Dialogue Report*, January 2015.

Nele Noesselt and Ana Soliz-Landivar, "China in Latin America: Competition in the United States' 'Strategic Backyard,'" *GIGA Focus*, No. 7, 2013.

Gonzalo S. Paz, "Rising China's 'Offensive' in Latin America and the U.S. Reaction," *Asian Perspective*, Vol. 30, No. 4, 2006.

William E. Ratliff, "In Search of a Balanced Relationship: China, Latin America, and the United States," *Asian Politics & Policy*, Vol. 1, No. 1, 2009, pp. 1–30.

Riordan Roett, *The New Brazil*, Brookings Institution Press, 2011.

Riordan Roett and Guadalupe Paz, eds., *China's Expansion into the Western Hemisphere*, Brookings Institution Press, 2008.

Christopher Sabatini, "Rethinking Latin America: Foreign Policy Is More than Development," *Foreign Affairs*, Vol. 91, No. 2, 2012, pp. 8–13.

Michael D. Swaine, "Xi Jinping's Trip to Latin America," *China Leadership Monitor*, No. 45, Fall 2014.

Vigevani Tullo, *Brazilian Foreign Policy in Changing Times*, Lexington Books, 2012.

Cynthia Watson, "China's Use of the Military Instrument in Latin America: Not Yet the Biggest Stick," *Journal of International Affairs*, Vol. 66, No. 2, 2013, pp. 101–111.

Yang Jiemian, ed., *China's Diplomacy: Theory and Practice*, World Scientific Publishing Corporation, 2014.

Fareed Zakaria, *The Post-American World*, W. W. Norton, 2011.

13

The United States, China, and Latin America

Taking Advantage of Globalization and Moving beyond a Threat Matrix

DANIEL A. RESTREPO AND FRANK O. MORA

Introduction

Ever since China's economic and diplomatic engagement in Latin America and the Caribbean (LAC) began to "take off" more than a decade ago, some analysts and policymakers alike began to warn of an extra-hemispheric challenge threatening the U.S. sphere of influence in the Americas. The default approach for many in Washington regarding China's growing presence seems[1] to be a return to the familiar zero-sum international politics that largely characterized U.S. policy during much of the Cold War. In the end, this threat narrative, though a minority view, seems to dominate the discussion regarding China's presence or "inroads" in LAC.[2] At a minimum, some scholars perceived "Chinese presence in the Western Hemisphere as a sign of erosion of both power and geopolitical position of the United States in the region."[3]

There is no question that, in its effort to feed and fuel its massive industrial growth of the last 15 years, China's aggressive search for markets and commodities has led to an exponential growth in economic ties with LAC. Bilateral trade expanded 22 times between 2000 and 2014 resulting in China becoming the largest trading partner of Brazil, Chile, and Peru while second or third most important for much of the rest of LAC. Meanwhile, in the area of financing, China has provided more than $119 billion in loans to governments and firms since 2005 (more than 80% to Venezuela, Brazil, and Argentina), and in terms of investments, PRC FDI has averaged $10 billion a year since 2010.[4]

China's growing presence in LAC is also apparent in the cultural, educational, military, and political spheres. Many analysts, for example, point to the 20 visits by Chinese premiers or presidents since 2008 as an indicator of Beijing's focus on expanding ties with the region. More recently, China hosted the first-ever ministerial-level forum between the PRC and the nations of the Community of Latin America and Caribbean States (CELAC) where a five-year roadmap for strengthening relations, particularly in the area of technical cooperation and financing, was approved. Also, technical and military cooperation and ministerial dialogue are features of the relationship in many countries as are a growing number of Confucius Institutes.

China's growing activity in the Americas is not, however, an isolated phenomenon. The Americas today are more global and independent than ever. Political stability and steady economic performance have increased the region's confidence and expanded its global economic and diplomatic ties. Differences remain as to the degree and speed to which LAC countries have globalized, but the region is no longer inward-looking. In fact, it is increasingly diversifying its trade and investment patterns, while establishing or expanding diplomatic and societal ties with governments and entities outside of the region. Regional foreign policies show greater independence and willingness, notwithstanding differences in performance, to join and collaborate in regional groupings, such as the Union of South American States (UNASUR) and the Pacific Alliance. The countries of the Americas are not passive actors waiting to play the United States against an extra-hemispheric power. They are increasingly engaging the world on their own terms, offering opportunities for the United States and others to interact as partners.

At the same time, U.S.-LAC relations are strong, and more importantly, built on a broad base of sophisticated, organic relationships that extend well beyond state-to-state engagements. Furthermore, U.S.-LAC relations encompass far more than what is often covered by the commentariat—like the number of presidential visits, the emergence of extra-hemispheric actors, problems related to drugs and immigration—or when compared to the visibility of U.S. engagements in others parts of the world. These outdated measures fail to truly appreciate the complexity and depth of U.S.-LAC relations today, all of which are the result of persistent and deliberate engagement with the Americas. Despite its impressive engagement across multiple areas, China has yet to come close to reaching the depth, breadth, and complexity that characterizes U.S.-LAC relations today. As a result, the United States, regardless of administration, does not see China posing a threat to its interests in the region. This chapter examines Obama administration policy toward LAC in the context of China's growing presence in the region.

Key Elements of U.S. Policy

Although core U.S. national security interests in the Americas have not changed during Barack Obama's presidency, the means to promote those interests have shifted markedly. The United States remains deeply interested in "a Western Hemisphere that is prosperous, secure, democratic, and plays a greater global role."[5] President Obama, however, has broken with past U.S. policy approaches in pursuit of those goals. At its core, Obama's shift has been one from an ownership mentality to a partnership mentality that endeavors to leave behind ideological differences of the past and to focus on common interests and challenges in an increasingly interconnected hemisphere. U.S. policy has further sought to leverage that interconnection as well as the globalization of key LAC countries to advance U.S. economic, political, and security interests well beyond the Americas.

a) Partnership Agenda

Partnership grounded in today's reality rather than yesterday's ideology has been the touchstone of President Obama's approach to the Americas—manifest in rhetoric, affirmative policy initiatives, and crisis response. President Obama firmly established partnership as the defining characteristic of his regional approach at the Fifth Summit of the Americas in Port of Spain, Trinidad, less than 100 days into his presidency, when he stated:

> While the United States has done much to promote peace and prosperity
> in the hemisphere, we have at times been disengaged, and at times we've
> sought to dictate our terms. But I pledge to you that we seek an equal

partnership. There is no senior partner and junior partner in our relations; there is simply engagement based on mutual respect and common interests and shared values.[6]

Secretary of State John Kerry, in his first extended remarks on the Americas as secretary, made the break with the past most explicit when he declared that "[t]he era of the Monroe Doctrine is over."[7]

The Obama administration's policy of discarding antiquated paradigms has gone well beyond rhetoric. Nowhere is this truer than the December 17, 2014, historic announcement of a change in U.S.-Cuba relations. The move toward greater engagement with the Cuban people beginning in 2009, coupled with the normalization of diplomatic relations have underscored President Obama's commitment to breaking with the past. As he declared in his speech to the Cuban people during his historic March 2016 visit to Havana:

I have come here to bury the last remnant of the Cold War in the Americas. . . . What the United States was doing was not working. We have to have courage to acknowledge that truth. A policy of isolation designed for the Cold War made little sense in the 21st Century.[8]

The Obama administration's support of the peace talks between the government of Colombia (GOC) and the Revolutionary Armed Forces of Colombia (FARC) also highlighted a future-oriented embrace of partnership. The willingness to support the GOC even as some of its negotiating positions contradicted long-standing tenets of U.S. policy underscores a commitment to true partnership. The administration, for example, ultimately accepted a GOC decision to end aerial coca eradication in the context of the FARC talks despite having publicly expressed misgivings on the issue.[9] It similarly highlighted its respect for GOC decisions on the issue of the potential extradition of FARC leaders long wanted on drug trafficking and other charges in the United States.[10]

The break from old paradigms has not been limited to new approaches to Cold War relics. The Obama administration's key citizen security initiatives—Merida 2.0 and the Alliance for Prosperity in the Northern Triangle—have prioritized an integrated approach to regional security that understands that U.S. national security depends on citizen security in the Americas. In contrast with the "War on Drugs" approach to regional security that predominated during the preceding 20 years, the administration's approach appreciates that U.S. national security begins on street corners across the region. It prioritizes helping control crime and violence in key countries and regions and understands that citizen security cannot be separated from economic development and the rule of law.[11]

The Obama administration, in response to calls from partners (and critics) throughout the Americas, has also demonstrated a willingness to engage in a meaningful reexamination of counter-drug efforts even while opposing wide-scale decriminalization. In addition to dropping traditional "War on Drugs" rhetoric, the United States has also engaged in a regionwide assessment of existing counter-drug efforts by the Organization of American States and supported regional consensus on conclusions and next steps thereto.[12]

Partnership has also been the order of the day as U.S. policy has sought to seize the opportunities presented by the energy revolution unfolding across the Western Hemisphere. At the Fifth Summit of the Americas, President Obama proposed addressing the pressing, interrelated issues of climate change and energy security by working in differentiated partnerships based on countries' needs, interests, and capabilities through the Energy and Climate Partnership of the Americas. An emphasis on public-private cooperation and working in differing combinations also marked the U.S. energy-related agenda at the Sixth Summit of the Americas in April 2012 giving rise to the Connect 2022 initiative, aimed at achieving hemisphere-wide electricity interconnection by 2022. Reacting to the potential energy-related spillover effects in the broader Caribbean Basin created by the deteriorating situation in Venezuela, Vice President Joe Biden continued the administration's approach of working on energy issues in partnership by bringing together key governments, international financial institutions, and private sector actors to formulate and execute the 2015 Caribbean Energy Security Initiative, holding regional summits on the issue in both 2015 and 2016.

The Obama administration's response to regional crisis has also emphasized partnership. In the wake of the 2009 coup in Honduras, for example, the administration, while taking some unilateral actions,[13] worked through the Organization of American States and various ad hoc country groups to help fashion a negotiated solution to Honduras's political crisis.[14] The massive U.S. response to the devastating January 2010 earthquake in Port au Prince quickly transitioned to a multilateral effort to preserve stability in Haiti (an effort led by Brazil and reliant on key contributions from others across the Americas) and to promote economic recovery and development. Although some unilateral actions were again taken, the Obama administration's reaction to the major influx of unaccompanied child migrants in the summer of 2014 also quickly became a multilateral partnership with close coordination not only with the countries of the Northern Triangle of Central America— the point of origin of the migrants—but also Mexico, the key transit country.

Partnership, of course, requires partners and the regional response to President Obama's shift has been mixed. Across the Americas, the notion of the United States as a "good partner" has been met with a variety of responses: acceptance (most notably from Mexico, Colombia, Peru, Chile, and the countries of Central America), rejection (by the countries of the Bolivarian Alliance of the Americas [ALBA]), and ambivalence (most notably from Brazil), with Argentina notably passing through all three in response to changing domestic political dynamics. The absence of willing partners on some of the thornier issues facing the region has affected U.S. policy responses. Nowhere was this more so than in the face of the rapidly deteriorating state of Venezuela's democracy. Until OAS secretary general Luis Almagro began urging the region to action, the United States lacked regional partners willing to engage Venezuela on issues of human rights and democratic governance, leaving the Obama administration hamstrung and reliant on unilateral efforts like the March 2014 sanctions against seven Venezuelans that created a regional uproar.[15]

b) People Matter

The effect of policy on people and of people on policy has been another central tenet of Barack Obama's approach to the Americas since before he was elected. In a May 2008 speech, candidate Obama declared that his policy in the region would be guided by the simple, but powerful, proposition that "[w]hat is good for the people of the Americas is good for the United States."[16] His approach as president has been largely true to that pronouncement.

The United States is home to more than 54 million Hispanics—almost a fifth of its total population—who trace their heritage to countries across the Americas.[17] As laid out in the president's 2010 National Security Strategy, the Obama administration has sought to enhance and leverage the unique connectivity the United States has as a function of "our deep historical, familial, and cultural ties."[18]

One of President Obama's centerpiece LAC initiatives, for example, has been 100,000 Strong in the Americas, which aims to double the number of U.S. students studying in the Americas and double the number of students from the Americas studying in the United States to deepen ties and enhance the hemisphere's economic competitiveness.[19] To underscore its importance, the president has personally engaged with 100,000 Strong on multiple occasions: rolling the initiative out in in his principal first-term address on the Americas;[20] highlighting it in a 2013 speech in Mexico;[21] and personally hosting roundtable discussions on it at the White House and at the April 2015 Summit of the Americas. It has also become an important component of key bilateral relationships with Mexico, Brazil, Colombia, Peru, and others.

People, of course, have also been at the center of the Obama administration's approach to Cuba, where empowering the Cuban people has been a guiding principle and to citizen security initiatives where its programs have emphasized fostering resilient communities. Although not motivated by regional dynamics, U.S. executive actions on immigration—both record levels of deportations[22] and 2012's and 2014's administrative relief for undocumented immigrants[23]—have had a profound impact on people across the Americas and on relations with LAC.

c) Embracing the Global Americas

The opening decade-plus of the 21st century has been marked by far greater global interaction by Latin American and Caribbean countries than in previous periods. Latin American trade with the rest of the world, and particularly with China, skyrocketed, fueled by that country's appetite for agricultural commodities, minerals, petroleum, and other raw materials. China, however, is by no means the only trade partner for LAC, as the region has increasingly diversified its trading partners. Chile, for example, has the world's largest number of formal free trade agreements—56.[24] In 2014, LAC was also the third-largest destination for FDI in the world, trailing only developing Asia and Europe and ahead of North America.[25] Latin countries emerged as key players in changing global architecture: Brazil's participation in the BRICS provided a Latin American accent to the voice of an increasingly assertive Global South; Argentina, Brazil, and Mexico played important roles in international economic policy making as the G20 became the preeminent forum for addressing the 2008–2009 global financial crisis. LAC also reached out politically to the rest of the world through forums like the CELAC-China Summit in January 2015; the 2005, 2009, and 2012 summits between members of the UNASUR and members of the Arab League; and the 2013 and 2015 summits between CELAC and the European Union.

Although some see the Americas' increasing global integration as a threat to U.S. influence, the Obama administration has instead seen LAC's going global as an opportunity to advance U.S. global interests. In his most recent National Security Strategy, for example, President Obama highlighted the desire to "continue to advance a Western Hemisphere that . . . plays a greater global role."[26] Then deputy secretary of state William Burns captured both the growing global importance of the Americas to U.S. interests and the need to compete in the region in remarks before the World Affairs Council in November 2011:

> Our partnerships in the Western Hemisphere are vital to the United States in their own right. They are vital to our economic recovery and competitiveness; vital to our ability to solve the transnational challenges that no country can solve on its own; and vital to our efforts to promote and consolidate democracy and human rights globally. Just as we start from a position of strength in the new Asia, our multifaceted ties with our friends closer to home give us an edge in encouraging and benefiting from a growing and increasingly integrated Americas. But we cannot be passive. We need to continue to actively strengthen our hemispheric ties with mutual respect and as partners—not junior partners or senior partners, but equal partners.[27]

Engagement with key countries in the Americas has put these sentiments into action. Mexico, for example, has been engaged not only on security, migration, and energy issues, but on a range of global issues—climate change, U.N. peacekeeping, and nuclear non-proliferation. At the United States' behest, Mexico was added to the Trans-Pacific Partnership negotiations in 2012 to modernize North American economic integration and to enhance North America's global competitiveness. On those issues and others, President Obama has repeatedly emphasized the global component of U.S.-Mexico relations and how Mexico's global emergence benefits the United States.[28]

In recognition of its foray into the ranks of first-tier global players, similar engagement with Brazil persisted despite ups and downs in the bilateral relationship and political turbulence in Brazil. Among countries of the Americas, for example, Brazil alone was singled out in President Obama's first National Security Strategy with an emphasis on its role in the G20 in dealing with the 2008–2009 global financial crisis and the looming challenge of global climate change.[29] President Obama underscored Brazil's global importance with his March 2011 trip to Brasília, where he became the first U.S. president ever to travel to Brazil for an initial meeting with his Brazilian counterpart and declared:

> As President. I have pursued engagement based on mutual interest and mutual respect. And a key part of this engagement is forging deeper cooperation with 21st Century centers of influence, including Brazil. Put simply, the United States doesn't simply recognize Brazil's rise, we support it enthusiastically.[30]

Each of President Obama's formal bilateral meetings with his Brazilian counterparts have been replete with global issues as captured in the various statements and declarations emanating therefrom.[31] Beyond declarations, the United States and Brazil, for example, joined together in 2011 to launch the Open Government Partnership to promote transparent and accountable governance around the world and have launched trilateral assistance programs in Africa.

Latin American countries have also been featured prominently in the diplomatic efforts to address one of President Obama's highest domestic and international priorities—confronting global climate change. The lead-up to COP 21 in Paris in December 2015, for example, was marked by key presidential bilateral engagements with his counterparts in Mexico[32] and Brazil[33] as well as Secretary Kerry's participation in an oceans conference in Santiago, Chile.

Perhaps nowhere has the leveraging of the Americas going global been more thorough than the Obama administration's embrace and elevation of the Trans-Pacific Partnership (TPP). The TPP's humble origins stem from the globalization of a key country in the Americas as it began as an agreement among Chile, Brunei, New Zealand, and Singapore. After the Obama administration entered and embraced the negotiation, it expanded the TPP to include 11 countries, including 5 in the Americas (the United States, Canada, Mexico, Chile, and Peru), constituting 40% of the world's gross domestic product. The TPP has also become the economic centerpiece of the Obama administration's much-touted "pivot to Asia."

d) Beyond State-State Relations

Although in world politics the state remains the most important actor, the true measure of U.S. impact in LAC (or of any country, for that matter) must go beyond state-to-state relations and policies. Nevertheless, analysts have yet to truly appreciate the impact of non-state actors beyond often-mentioned terrorist and transnational criminal organizations. In so doing, many miss the most significant (and likely the most persistent) advantage the United States enjoys compared to China in terms of exerting lasting influence in the Americas. Since 1946, total U.S. assistance to the LAC region has been more than $160 billion (in constant 2013 dollars). The current level of assistance to the region is now roughly $2 billion a year.[34]

In terms of U.S.-LAC relations, dense interactions among non-state actors have become the true determinants of hemispheric relations. In fact, the complex network of inter-American non-state relations, particularly in the social and commercial spheres, has grown exponentially in the last few decades. Chris Sabatini argues that these interactions and exchanges "have often outstripped formal state relations and helped move governments in directions that state bureaucracies would not normally steer themselves."[35] In the area of economic ties, U.S. business continues to be a significant partner in the region, despite regional trade and investment diversification. The United States remains the first or second most important trading partner for most countries; total U.S. trade with the region amounted to $846 billion in 2013, more than three times that of China.[36] Furthermore, U.S. FDI in LAC is twice as high as it was a decade ago, making the United States the most important investor in the region. A recent report from the Inter-American Dialogue (2014) notes, that "from 2000–2012, U.S. FDI in LAC increased by 83 percent, while LAC FDI in the U.S. rose by 43 percent."[37]

Beyond economic ties, U.S.-LAC societal networks are deepening. It is important to note, for example, the multiple ways in which societal and individual relationships have intensified during the last couple of decades as a result of remittances. It is estimated that about 90% of the $65.5 billion (2014) remittance income destined to the Americas comes from immigrant communities in the United States helping to expand and sustain U.S.-LAC societal links.[38] Moreover, from 2006 to2012 U.S. non-government organizations, such as churches, think tanks, and universities increased the number of partnerships with their regional cohorts by a factor of four.[39] Other areas such as travel, migration, and tourism have experienced similar exponential growth rates, contributing to a dense web of cross-national relationships that defines the true nature of U.S.-LAC relations today.

U.S. Perceptions of China's Role in LAC

There are a range of views regarding the meaning and significance of China's growing activity in LAC. Gonzalo Paz, for example, refers to concepts of international relations theory to analyze approaches in the United States to China's engagement in the Americas.[40] One position, argued by offensive realism, suggests that challenges to U.S. hegemonic power in its sphere of influence (i.e., LAC) is bound to lead to conflict with China. The counter-position argues the United States cannot thwart China's rise or expanding ties in LAC but it can avoid conflict by integrating Beijing into a framework of international institutions while maintaining robust ties in the Americas.[41] The Obama administration focus is on the latter argument, while some outside analysts and Congressional Republicans take the former view.

a) The Obama Administration's View of China in LAC

Although China's growing interest and activity in the Americas has been commented upon by top-level Obama administration officials, including the president, China's policies and actions in LAC have had no discernible effect on U.S. policy in the Americas in recent years. The Obama administration, much like its predecessors, has not perceived China's presence in Latin America as representing a serious challenge. Instead, China's activity in the Americas has been understood not as a threat, but as a reality that underscores the need for the United States to compete in the Americas and not take hemispheric relationships for granted. When asked if China was economically displacing the United States in the Americas, President Obama, for example, has said:

> U.S. exports to Latin America are growing at a healthy rate and I am confident the United States will remain Latin America's preferred partner when it comes to trade and development. . . . The United States needs to compete in the Americas and that is precisely what we are doing. That is why we worked so hard to approve the Colombia and Panama free trade agreements and why we are advancing with the Trans-Pacific Partnership that includes Chile and Peru as founding members.[42]

The president's confidence appears borne out by the facts. For example, "low-value added and low-technology goods dominate LAC exports to China amounting to approximately 60% of total Chinese imports from the region," while 57% of Beijing's investments are focused on acquiring raw materials. United States imports and investments, however, are largely high-technology, value-added manufactured goods that generate higher-paying, more sustainable jobs.[43]

Like its immediate predecessor, the Obama administration has formally acknowledged China's relevance in the Americas through the inclusion of a Latin America subdialogue in the U.S.-China Strategic and Economic Dialogue. But it has done so in terms that do not cast China as a threat. As summarized by Roberta Jacobson, former U.S. assistant secretary of state for Western Hemisphere affairs, following the fifth such subdialogue in 2013, "we see China's increasing engagement in this hemisphere—in both trade relationship and investment relationship—as extremely positive . . . we don't see it as a zero-sum game."[44] Frank O. Mora, former deputy assistant secretary of defense for the Western Hemisphere, delivered one of the administration's first remarks (November 2009) on China's evolving relationship with LAC. He highlighted some of the positive contributions that China can make to the region's development if done with greater transparency:

> It is my view that China's deepening engagement in the Hemisphere can, in cooperation with others, play a productive role in ameliorating some of the regional challenges . . . addressing problems related to under-governed and ungoverned territories, the region's lack of economic opportunity, and the causal link between economic hardship and illicit trafficking. . . . We therefore welcome China's economic engagement in the region as a natural by-product of the global economy in the hope that it fosters greater socioeconomic equality.[45]

The notion that China's increased presence in the Americas is not a threat, but does raise the need for the United States to compete and not simply rely on proximity and habit to maintain its influence in the Americas is evident in the March 2015 Force Posture Statement by Gen. John F. Kelly, United States Southern Command. Testifying before Congress, Gen. Kelly observed:

> As in other regions around the world, China has growing influence in Latin America and the Caribbean. . . . Although cultural differences often preclude close cooperation, Chinese engagement with regional militaries is gradually expanding, especially with Cuba and Venezuela. This outreach, while not a threat to U.S. interests at this time, does underscore the importance of continued engagement by the U.S. military to maintain our valued security partnerships.[46]

That the administration does not view China's increased activity in the Americas as a threat has been further manifest in its muted response to the unfolding effort of a Chinese development company to build a canal in Nicaragua to rival the Panama Canal. To date, official comment has been limited to statements regarding concerns for property rights of land holders along the proposed canal route and a lack of transparency in the process.[47]

b) Alternative Views of China's Current Role in LAC

The Obama administration's approach to China's growing activity in LAC, of course, is not the only U.S. perspective. Others see China's rise in LAC in much more traditional hegemonic power-relation terms, portraying it as a threat to core U.S. interests. There are three basic arguments advanced by those who portray China's rise as a threat to the United States. The first is the blanket assertion that China is gaining influence at the expense of the United States, and particularly as a result of perceived U.S. neglect of the region. Fears about China becoming a military rival to the United States in LAC began in 2007/2008. The title of an article by Loro Horta in *Military Review* warned of China challenging "Uncle Sam's Backyard: China's Military Influence in Latin America."[48] Subsequent publications and congressional hearings reflected this argument. For example, during the course of a September 2015 hearing in the U.S. House of Representatives on "China's Advance in Latin America and the Caribbean," several Republican members of Congress assailed purported U.S. neglect of the region and called for the explicit revival of the Monroe Doctrine in light of China's perceived intrusion in a U.S. sphere of influence. Representative Ted Yoho of Florida summarized this basic critique in the following terms:

> And I think we need to restate the Monroe Doctrine. I think that is something we need to stand for what the Western Hemisphere stands for. Because [what] we have seen over the course of the last 20 years is a slip or a slide into socialism. They are lining up with Iran. They are lining up with Russia and China. And we are losing that influence.[49]

It is, of course, not at all clear what a 21st-century reassertion of the Monroe Doctrine would look like, given that Chinese (or other "outside") influence cannot be deterred by gunboats in today's globalized world.

Several non-governmental analysts have presented slightly more sophisticated and nuanced takes on the nature of China's growing influence in the Americas and how that poses a threat to U.S. interests. One of their lines of analysis suggests that China is doing the most significant damage to U.S. regional interests by supporting anti-American populist regimes. These regimes get Chinese financial support and would have, by now, given way to changes driven by natural political and economic cycles.[50] Although Venezuela is perhaps the only populist government that has been arguably propped up in this manner, the analysts advancing this line of argument generally lump in other ALBA countries, as well as Argentina. As such their argument falls victim to ALBA's rhetoric and propaganda by accepting the notion that ALBA presents an effective counter to core U.S. regional interests. With the possible exception of Venezuela, whose economic relevance for the United States wanes by the day due to the U.S. shale revolution, it is difficult to discern how the populist agendas of any ALBA leader has had any meaningful effect on important U.S. interests.

A second argument advanced by those outside analysts who view China as a threat to U.S. interests in LAC again focuses on the indirect effects of Chinese economic and commercial activities in the Americas. China as a lender and investor, according to this line of argument, undercuts environmental and development standards advanced by Western-oriented institutions and actors.[51] Those who see China in the Americas as a threat also link Chinese activity to nearly every malady in the Americas, including many that long predate China's rise in the Americas. R. Evan Ellis, for example, testified before Congress in September 2015:

> While Chinese loans, purchases of Latin American primary products and foodstuffs, investments, and sales of products and services benefit a limited number of sectors and economic interests, they also indirectly contribute to inequality, corruption, violence, and environmental problems, while undermining democracy and the rule of law in the region.[52]

Finally, those who view China's activity in the Americas as a threat to the United States point to the possible military implications of China's presence.[53] The integration of the Chinese and U.S. economies and the severe costs associated with conflict make such an outcome unlikely, though not impossible. Furthermore, China has made few inroads in

Mexico—the strategically most significant LAC country for the United States—greatly limiting any strategic consequence to China's LAC engagement even in a doomsday scenario.

Patterns in Latin American Responses to Chinese and U.S. Actions

China's deepening and accelerated economic and diplomatic engagement in the Americas during the last two decades was most welcomed by governments in the region. Not much thought was given to this surge of Chinese economic activity in the Americas as it offered immediate benefits—trade diversification, expanding market for its commodities, foreign direct investments, and low-cost imports—helping to lessen dependence on the United States and Europe. In the diplomatic realm, intensifying engagement with China provided LAC with an opportunity to enhance its profile in the international system, particularly via multilateral fora. Moreover, for some, particularly the more anti-American governments in the region like those of ALBA, ties with China offered an opportunity to counter U.S. influence in the region and in multilateral institutions, forging greater South-South solidarity—a slogan often used by Beijing to explain its motivations in the region. In some cases, a few governments even sought to return to the binary Cold War framework of playing one side off the other, arguing to U.S. officials that "if you keep reducing the level of assistance, we would have no other option than to go with the Chinese."[54]

The challenge, however, from this rapid economic-diplomatic surge from China, is that Latin America, as David Shambaugh has noted, "lacked both an overall strategy and the domestic expertise to cope effectively with China's growing influence."[55] It does not seem LAC was ready for this surge in Chinese activity. As Enrique Dussel Peters also underscored, "the region's institutions, business chambers, general publics and academic institutions are ill prepared to engage in genuinely symbiotic partnerships with the emerging superpower."[56]

While China certainly has a strategy for LAC, most in the region do not have a strategy for managing relations with China. Latin America's ad hoc approach and overall deficit in expertise concerning Chinese culture, language, and economy is limiting its ability to compete and cooperate effectively with Beijing. Cultural and political differences and overall lack of understanding on both sides have created diplomatic complications and, most problematic, economic imbalances for Latin America. For example, LAC has so far been unable to articulate a response to the growing, already vast trade deficits and troubling economic vulnerabilities caused by a trade structure in which China imports raw materials from LAC while exporting low-cost manufactured goods, reinforcing overdependence on traditional production structures and downgrading developments in the manufacturing sector brought on by the import substitution policies of the 1950s and 1960s.

In May 2015, the editorial board of Bloomberg noted that closer economic ties with China had begun to take a toll on Latin America development.[57] In that same month, a World Bank report concluded that China had reinforced LAC's role as a commodity exporter while diminishing the weight of its manufactured exports, which had been growing since 1990 but reversed in 2000 thanks to trade with China.[58] Today, China imports less than 2% of LAC's manufactured goods. These vulnerabilities have come to light with the recent slowdown of the Chinese economy, which has led to a dramatic decline in commodity prices and, consequently, economic stagnation in the region.

Other challenges in the economic relationship are emerging. A recent study of the physical presence of Chinese companies in LAC highlights not only the operational challenges facing the Chinese in dealing with rules, cultures, and politics of the region, but also the growing backlash from governments and societal groups at the heavy-handedness of Chinese corporations, most glaring being importing workers from China to work on infrastructure projects.[59] Unfulfilled commitments of Chinese investments are also creating greater frustration among some of China's most important economic partners. In the end, despite all the South-South rhetoric, China's trade pattern with the region, in fact, resembles a North-South model. This and other economic and diplomatic complications will likely continue unless LAC develops a strategy for dealing with the imbalances caused by the torrent of Chinese activities.

With regard to LAC responses to U.S. actions, there has not been much, because Washington has refused to engage the issue of China in zero-sum terms. In fact, as noted above, senior policymakers have publicly welcomed Chinese economic activities. For example, former assistant secretary of state for the Western Hemisphere Roberta Jacobson believed China's engagement in the region, under the right circumstances, is "absolutely and definitely a good thing."[60] In short, constructive views from Washington have prevented governments from using binary Cold War rhetoric to either extract additional benefits from China and the United States or heighten anti-Americanism in the region in reaction to hostile U.S. views of China's growing presence.

A U.S.-China-LAC Triangle?

Against the backdrop of surging Chinese activity in LAC, nearly a decade ago, scholars developed the concept of a triangular relationship, in one case going so far as to argue that there was "a real opportunity to construct a three-way, cooperative geopolitics between Beijing, Washington, and Latin America."[61] Most have dismissed this notion of geopolitical cooperation as all three often pursue different, though not necessarily, competing interests. Barbara Stallings refined the concept a bit, suggesting that neither conflict nor cooperation is probable among the three, but that positive bilateral ties were likely to have a positive impact on links with the third.[62] In the end, as Evan Ellis describes, the triangular concept is not a "well analyzed academic construct" as it masked other important external actors and it encouraged a false view of Latin America as a unitary actor.[63] More importantly, the concept assumes the China–Latin America–U.S. triangle to be of strategic importance to all three, an argument that is not well grounded in evidence.

There is, however, one area in which triangular dynamics, if not triangular intent, are clearly at play with significant implications for the United States, China, and LAC. Born at least in part by a desire to constrain China's global rise, the Trans-Pacific Partnership concept has had significant implications for U.S.-LAC relations and could have even more profound effects going forward. If successful, the TPP could not only provide a road map for the U.S.-China commercial relationship, it could also serve as a framework for greater commercial integration with other U.S. trade partners in the Americas as nearly all U.S. FTA partners are Pacific-facing countries. Even short of such a result, the

TPP could reinforce a Pacific-Atlantic divide with respect to economic approaches to globalization that already exists in LAC, as manifested by the contrast between the approach to market liberalization and access among countries of the Pacific Alliance (Mexico, Colombia, Peru, and Chile) and those of Mercosur(Argentina, Brazil, Uruguay, Paraguay, and Venezuela).

Conclusion

Notwithstanding alarmist rhetoric from Congress and pundits alike, the United States has yet to demonstrate a belief that China represents a threat to its interest in LAC. In fact, it is difficult to point to any U.S. policy decision or action in recent years that resulted from or was a response to Chinese actions in the Americas. The United States, as Daniel Erikson describes, "has tacitly accepted that China's evolving role in Latin America reflects the increasingly complex mosaic of international relationships that is a product of a more globalized world."[64] So far, the United States has heeded Juan Gabriel Tokatlian's strategic warning that "it would be counterproductive to return to an apocalyptic geopolitics approach based on needs is a new zero-sum game."[65]

As a result, the United States is likely to continue looking favorably upon China's trade and investments in LAC because of its economic benefit to the region and its contribution to stability, as long as it is transparent and does not seek to directly undermine U.S. relationships in the region. Latin America will seek to continue benefiting from trade and investments with Beijing, but economic slowdown in China and lack of follow-up with investment projects will likely place additional strains on the relationship, already under some stress as a result of some Chinese pressure and mutual misunderstandings.

Whether China's presence in the Americas is surging, in decline, or in a holding pattern, the potential policy responses to increased Chinese commercial, and even modest military activities in the Americas, are the same. The days of the United States being somehow able to prevent "outside actors" from being present in the Americas is over and that has been swept aside by the realities of globalization. U.S. priorities must be finding ways to generate more and higher-quality commercial engagement in the Americas, to foster political influence, and to leverage the comparative advantages created by deep interconnections with the region based on geography, history, and migration that no other country can rival to advance U.S. national interests.

NOTES

1 Editor's note: This chapter was written during the Obama administration, and we have left the verb tenses in the present, even though we are now, of course, in the Trump administration.

2 The literature on China's challenge to US interests includes Ellis, *U.S. National Security Implications*; Roett and Paz, *China's Expansion*; Americas Quarterly, "China's Global Rise."

3 Nolte, "The Dragon in the Backyard," 589.

4 Dussel Peters, "China's Evolving Role"; Inter-American Dialogue, "China-Latin America Finance Database," www.thedialogue.org.

5 Obama, *National Security Strategy* (2015), p. 27.

6 Obama, *Remarks by the President at the Summit of the Americas Opening Ceremony*.

7 Kerry, *Remarks on U.S. Policy in the Western Hemisphere*.

8 Obama, *Remarks by President Obama to the People of Cuba*.

9 See Neuman, "Defying U.S."

10 See Alsema, "US Support."

11 See, e.g., Biden, "Plan for Central America."

12 See Speck, "OAS Position on Drugs"; "OAS Secretary General Presents Report on Drug Problem in the Americas," *Organization of American States*, May 17, 2013, www.oas.org.

13 See Wilkinson, "U.S. Pulls Visas."

14 See Meyer, "Honduran Political Crisis."

15 See Neuman, "Obama Hands Venezuelan Leader a Cause."

16 Obama, *Renewing U.S. Leadership in the Americas*.

17 Of the country's 54 million Latinos, 34 million (63%) self-identify as having a connection to Mexico; Puerto Ricans comprise the next largest group at 9% of the Hispanic population; Salvadorans and Cubans follow at approximately 4% each and Dominicans at 3%. All others make up approximately 16% of the population. See Pew Hispanic Center, "Hispanic Population Trends."

18 Obama, *National Security Strategy* (2010), p. 44.

19 See *100,000 Strong in the Americas*, www.100kstrongamericas.org.

20 See Obama, *Remarks by President Obama on Latin America*.

21 See Obama, *Remarks by the President to the People of Mexico*.

22 See, e.g., Gonzalez-Barrera and Krogstad, "U.S. Deportations."

23 See, e.g., "Executive Action on Immigration: A Resource Page," *American Immigration Council*, 2015, www.immigrationpolicy.org.

24 See *Latin America Goes Global*.

25 See UNCTAD, *Global Investment Trends Monitor*.

26 Obama, *National Security Strategy* (2015), p. 27.

27 Burns, *State's Burns at World Affairs Councils*.

28 See, e.g., Obama, *Remarks by the President to the People of Mexico*; White House, *Remarks by President Obama and President Calderon*.

29 Obama, *National Security Strategy* (2010), p. 44.

30 White House, *Remarks by President Obama and President Rousseff*.

31 See White House, *Remarks by President Obama and President Lula Da Silva*; White House, *Joint Statement by President Obama and President Rousseff* (2011); White House, *Joint Statement by President Obama and President Rousseff* (2012); White House, *Joint Communique by President Obama and President Rousseff*.

32 See White House, *Joint Statement on U.S.-Mexico Climate Policy Cooperation*.

33 See White House, *U.S.-Brazil Joint Statement on Climate Change*.

34 For an extended discussion of aid level, see Peter Meyer, "U.S. Foreign Assistance to the Latin America and the Caribbean: Recent Trends and FY2016 Appropriations," Congressional Research Service, R4413, January 2016.

35 Sabatini, "New and Not-So-New Foreign Policies."

36 Sullivan, *Latin America and the Caribbean*.

37 Hornbeck, "US–Latin American Trade."

38 Maldonado and Hayem, *Remittances to Latin America*.

39 Duddy and Mora, "Latin America."

40 Gonzalo Paz, "China, United States and Hegemonic Challenge."

41 See also Nolte, "Dragon in the Backyard."

42 Gomez, "'Colombia muestra.'"

43 Dussel Peters, 2015, 9.

44 "China's Latin America Presence."

45 Mora, "Remarks Delivered November 6, 2009."

46 Kelly, *Posture Statement*.

47 See U.S. Department of State, *2015 Investment Climate Statement—Nicaragua*.

48 Horta, "Uncle Sam's Backyard."

49 U.S. House of Representatives Subcommittee on Western Hemisphere Affairs and Subcommittee on Asia and the Pacific, *China's Advance*.

50 Ellis, *Testimony to the Joint Hearing*.

51 See, e.g., Hilton, *China in Latin America*.

52 Ellis, *Testimony to the Joint Hearing*.

53 Ibid. ("[T]hose responsible for future planning at NORTHCOM, SOUTHCOM, and other relevant U.S. government organizations, should regularly, and thoroughly evaluate how, in the event of major conflict, actors such as the PRC could leverage commercial assets and political and military relationships in the Western Hemisphere, to act against the U.S. in the region.")

54 This was a refrain that one of the authors heard on more than one occasion from senior government/military officials.

55 Shambaugh, "Foreword," xvii.

56 Dussel Peters, "China's Challenge," 212.
57 Editorial Board, "China's Pivot."
58 "Latin America's Economies."
59 Ellis, *China on the Ground.*
60 "China's Latin America Presence."
61 Tokatlian, "Latin America, China and the United States."
62 Stallings, "US-China–Latin America Triangle."
63 Ellis, *The United States, Latin America and China.*
64 Erikson, "Conflicting US Perceptions."
65 Tokatlian, "View from Latin America."

BIBLIOGRAPHY

100,000 Strong in the Americas, www.100kstrongamericas.org.

Alsema, Adriaan. "US Support for FARC Extradition Ban 'Helps Colombia Reach for Peace,'" *Colombia Reports*, October 14, 2015, www.colombiareports.com.

American Immigration Council. *Executive Action on Immigration: A Resource Page*, 2015, www.immigrationpolicy.org.

Americas Quarterly. "China's Global Rise: Implications for the Americas," special issue (Winter 2012).

Biden, Joseph P., Jr. "Joe Biden: A Plan for Central America," *New York Times*, January 29, 2015, www.nytimes.com.

Burns, William J. *State's Burns at World Affairs Councils on U.S. Foreign Policy*, Washington, DC, November 4, 2011, http://iipdigital.usembassy.gov.

"China's Latin America Presence Not a Threat," *China Daily*, November 13, 2013, http://usa.chinadaily.com.cn.

Duddy, Patrick, and Frank O. Mora, "Latin America: Is U.S. Influence Waning?," *Miami Herald*, May 1, 2013.

Dussel Peters, Enrique. "China's Challenge to Latin American Development," in Adrain H. Hearn and José Luis León Manriquez, eds., *China Engages Latin America: Tracing the Trajectory* (Boulder, CO: Lynne Rienner Publishers, 2011).

Dussel Peters, Enrique. "China's Evolving Role in Latin America: Can It Be a Win-Win?," *Atlantic Council, Andrienne Arsht Latin America Center*, September 2015.

Editorial Board, "China's Pivot to Latin America," *Bloomberg View*, May 25, 2015, www.bloombergview.com.

Ellis, R. Evan. *China on the Ground in Lain America: Challenges for the Chinese and Impacts on the Region* (New York: Palgrave MacMillan, 2014).

Ellis, R. Evan. *Testimony to the Joint Hearing of the Subcommittee on Western Hemisphere Affairs and the Subcommittee on Asia and the Pacific: "China's Activities in the Americas,"* September 10, 2015, www.foreignaffairs.house.gov.

Ellis, R. Evan. *The United States, Latin America and China: "A Triangular Relationship?,"* Inter-American Dialogue Working Paper (May 2012).

Ellis, R. Evan. *U.S. National Security Implications of Chinese Involvement in Latin America*, Strategic Studies Institute (June 2005).

Erikson, Dan. "Conflicting US Perceptions of China's Inroads in Latin America," in Adrain H. Hearn and José Luis León Manriquez, eds., *China Engages Latin America: Tracing the Trajectory*, (Boulder, CO: Lynne Rienner Publishers, 2011).

Gomez, Sergio. "'Colombia muestra que el éxito es posible': Barack Obama," *El Tiempo*, April 13, 2012, www.eltiempo.com.

Gonzalez-Barrera, Ana, and Jens Manuel Krogstad. "U.S. Deportations of Immigrants Each Record High in 2013," *Pew Research Center*, October 2, 2014, www.pewresearch.org.

Hilton, Isabel. "China in Latin America: Hegemonic Challenge?," Norwegian Peacebuilding Resource Centre, February 2013, www.peacebuilding.no.

Hornbeck, J. F. "US-Latin American Trade and Investment in the 21st Century: What's Next for Deepening Integration?," *Inter-American Dialogue*, 2014, www10.iadb.org.

Horta, Loro. "Uncle Sam's Backyard: China's Military Influence in Latin America," *Military Review* (September-October 2008), 47–55.

Kelly, John F. *Posture Statement of General John F. Kelly, United States Marine Corps, Commander, United States Southern Command*, 114th Congress, Senate Armed Services Committee, March 12, 2015, www.armed-services.senate.gov.

Kerry, John. *Remarks on U.S. Policy in the Western Hemisphere*, Organization of American States, November 18, 2013, www.state.gov.

Latin America Goes Global: By the Numbers, November 21, 2015,www.latinamericagoesglobal.org.

"Latin America's Economies: Learning the Lessons of Stagnation," *Economist*, June 27, 2015.

Maldonado, R., and M. Hayem, *Remittances to Latin America and the Caribbean Set a New Record High in 2014*. Multilateral Investment Fund, Inter-American Development Bank (Washington, DC: IDB, 2015).

Meyer, Peter J. "Honduran Political Crisis: June 2009–January 2010," *Congressional Research Service*, February 1, 2010, www.fas.org.

Mora, Frank O. "Remarks Delivered November 6, 2009, at Center for Hemispheric Studies and Brookings Institution Conference: 'Strategic Implications of China's Evolving Relationship with Latin America,'" *Security and Defense Studies Review* 9, nos. 1/2 (2009).

Neuman, William. "Defying U.S., Colombia Halts Aerial Spraying of Crops Used to Make Cocaine," *New York Times*, May 14, 2015, www.nytimes.com.

Neuman, William. "Obama Hands Venezuelan Leader a Cause to Stir Support," *New York Times*, March 11, 2015, www.nytimes.com.

Nolte, Detlef. "The Dragon in the Backyard: US Visions of China's Relations toward Latin America," *Pap Politica* 18, no. 2 (July–December 2013).

Obama, Barack H. *National Security Strategy*, May 2010, www.whitehouse.gov.

Obama, Barack H. *National Security Strategy*, February 2015,www.whitehouse.gov.

Obama, Barack H. *Remarks by President Obama on Latin America in Santiago, Chile*, White House, Office of the Press Secretary, March 21, 2011, at www.whitehouse.gov.

Obama, Barack. *Remarks by President Obama to the People of Cuba,* White House, Office of the Press Secretary, March 22, 2016, www.whitehouse.gov.

Obama, Barack H. *Remarks by the President to the People of Mexico,* White House, Office of the Press Secretary, May 3, 2013, www.whitehouse.gov.

Obama, Barack H. *Remarks by President Obama and President Calderon of Mexico at Joint Press Availability,* White House, Office of the Press Secretary, May 19, 2010, www.whitehouse.gov.

Obama, Barack H. *Remarks by President Obama and President Rousseff of Brazil in Brasilia, Brazil,* White House, Office of the Press Secretary, March 19, 2011, www .whitehouse.gov.

Obama, Barack H. *Remarks by the President at the Summit of the Americas Opening Ceremony, Port of Spain,* White House, Office of the Press Secretary, April 17, 2009, www.whitehouse.gov.

Obama, Barack H. *Renewing U.S. Leadership in the Americas* (Remarks of Senator Barack Obama, Cuban American National Foundation), *Chicago Sun-Times,* May 23, 2008 http://blogs.suntimes.com.

Paz, Gonzalo. "China, United States and Hegemonic Challenge in Latin America: An Overview and Some Lessons from Previous Instances of Hegemonic Challenge in the Region," *China Quarterly* 29 (March 2012), 18–34.

Pew Hispanic Center, "Hispanic Population Trends," 2013, www.pewhispanic.org.

Roett, Riordan, and Guadalupe Paz, eds. *China's Expansion into the Western Hemisphere: Implications for Latin America and the United States* (Washington, DC: Brookings Institution, 2008).

Sabatini, Christopher. "The New and Not-So-New Foreign Policies in the America," *Latin America Goes Global,* June 9, 2015, www.latinamericagoesglobal.org.

Shambaugh, David. "Foreword," in Adrain H. Hearn and Jose Luis Leon-Manriquez, eds. *China Engages Latin America: Tracing the Trajectory* (Boulder, CO: Lynne Rienner Publishers, 2011).

Speck, Mary. "The OAS Position on Drugs: A (Gradual) New Approach," *Crisis Group,* June 21, 2013, available at http://blog.crisisgroup.org.

Speck, Mary. "OAS Secretary General Presents Report on Drug Problem in the Americas," *Organization of American States,* May 17, 2013, www.oas.org.

Stallings. Barbara. "The US-China–Latin America Triangle: Implications for the Future," in Riordan Roett and Guadalupe Paz, eds., *China's Expansion into the Western Hemisphere,* (Washington, DC; Brookings Institution, 2008).

Sullivan, Mark P. *Latin America and the Caribbean: Key Issues for the 114th Congress.* (Washington, DC: Congressional Research Service, January 2015).

Tokatlian, Juan G. "Latin America, China and the United States: A Hopeful Triangle," *Open Democracy,* February 2007, www.opendemocracy.net.Tokatlian, Juan G. "A View from Latin America," in Riordan Roett and Guadalupe Paz, eds., *China's Expansion into the Western Hemisphere: Implications for Latin America and the United States* (Washington, DC: Brookings Institution, 2008).

UNCTAD. *Global Investment Trends Monitor,* January 29, 2015, www.unctad.org.

U.S. Department of State, Bureau of Economic and Business Affairs. *2015 Investment Climate Statement—Nicaragua,* May 2015, www.state.gov.

U.S. House of Representatives Subcommittee on Western Hemisphere Affairs and Subcommittee on Asia and the Pacific, Committee on Foreign Affairs. *China's Advance in Latin America and the Caribbean,* September 10, 2015, pp. 78–79, foreignaffairs.house.gov.

White House, Office of the Press Secretary. *Joint Communique by President Obama and President Rousseff,* June 30, 2015, www.whitehouse.gov.

White House, Office of the Press Secretary. *Joint Statement by President Obama and President Rousseff,* March 19, 2011, www.whitehouse.gov.

White House. Office of the Press Secretary. *Joint Statement by President Obama and President Rousseff,* April 9, 2012, www.whitehouse.gov.

White House, Office of the Press Secretary. *Joint Statement on U.S.-Mexico Climate Policy Cooperation,* March 27, 2015, www.whitehouse.gov.

White House, Office of the Press Secretary. *Remarks by President Obama and President Lula Da Silva of Brazil,* March 14, 2009, www.whitehouse.gov.

White House, Office of the Press Secretary. *U.S.-Brazil Joint Statement on Climate Change,* June 30, 2015, www.whitehouse.gov.

Wilkinson, Tracy. "U.S. Pulls Visas of Top Honduran Officials over Coup," *Los Angeles Times,* September 13, 2009, articles.latimes.com.

14

China's Security Challenge to the United States in Latin America and the Caribbean

R. EVAN ELLIS

Introduction

The national security challenge presented by the People's Republic of China (P.R.C.) to the United States in the Western Hemisphere is principally long-term and indirect.[1] It is a challenge that is widely misunderstood, and only partly related to the growing activities of P.R.C. armed forces in the hemisphere. The severity of the challenge, and its potential to transform from a difficult to define erosion of U.S. global position and long-term prosperity to an acute military threat, will depend, in part, on the adeptness of U.S. policymakers in navigating the landscape of threats and opportunities stemming from the rise of China as a dominant global actor. Whether U.S. policymakers are successful or not, China's presence in the Western Hemisphere will likely continue to be a defining consideration for U.S. national security in the mid-21st century.

The purpose of this chapter is to discuss that security challenge and the response of the U.S. to date, and to offer recommendations for U.S. policymakers.

Although the P.R.C. has arguably been less than transparent regarding the way in which it engages with Latin America and the Caribbean and its underlying intentions, it has consistently been very open regarding the types of activities it seeks to conduct with the region. China's 2008 white paper on its policy toward Latin America and the Caribbean, for example, explicitly mentions its desire to expand and deepen interactions with Latin America and the Caribbean in 35 areas, including science and technology and military interactions.[2] Similarly, China's roadmap for developing its relationship with the region over the next five years, released in conjunction with the January 2015 summit with the nations of the Community of Latin American and Caribbean States (CELAC) in Beijing,[3] highlights six priority areas for cooperation that closely correspond to the sectors in which Chinese companies, and the P.R.C. government, have focused the majority of their efforts to date: "energy and resources, infrastructure construction, agriculture, manufacturing, scientific and technological innovation, and information technologies."[4]

P.R.C. Objectives toward Latin America and the Caribbean

China's objectives in Latin America are principally economic in nature, yet nonetheless strategic, in that they are closely tied to the continued development of the power and prosperity of the Chinese state and people. This also means a continued role for the Chinese Communist Party.

The imperatives underlying Chinese pursuits are a product of the choice by the Chinese government, since the nation's economic opening in 1978, of an export-oriented model to achieve economic growth and national development. These include: (1) obtaining a reliable source of primary products, such as petroleum to serve China's expanding transportation and energy needs, as well as metals and minerals to serve as factor inputs for Chinese industrial production, capital formation, and urbanization; (2) access to agricultural products (and particularly animal fodders), to produce the food required to sustain China's 1.35 billion people as their diet evolves to demand ever greater quantities of animal protein; (3) markets for goods and services, as Chinese companies move up the value-added chain, pursuing foreign sales in sectors such as autos, heavy machinery, consumer electronics, and telecommunications; and (4) technology, to support the capabilities of Chinese firms in sectors of military and economic importance, and by extension, a diverse modern economy and strong state.[5]

P.R.C. security-related activities in Latin America arguably center on four major areas in support of, or tangential to, these imperatives: (1) political and economic activities that support their realization; (2) long-term military activities that advance Chinese commercial interests or protect its operations and personnel abroad; (3) diplomatic and economic activities to advance the incorporation of Taiwan and Tibet as part of the Chinese state; and (4) strategic positioning for a conflict with the United States, the government of which, many in the P.R.C. believe, will not accept (and will try to block) the continuing expansion of Chinese economic and political power.

In the political-economic realm, Chinese diplomacy, supported by loans, investment, and other economic activities, expressly seeks to advance a "multipolar world" favorably disposed to the P.R.C., and open to doing business with Chinese companies on Chinese terms.[6] While the P.R.C. has gone to great lengths to avoid defining its pursuits in Latin America and other parts of the world in an anti-U.S. manner, it benefits from, and works to support, a region devoid of a consensus in support of U.S. economic and political practices. By extension, the P.R.C. welcomes a region in which voices such as the regimes of the Bolivarian Alliance, Argentina, and Brazil resist such a U.S.-led consensus.

In the military domain, the People's Liberation Army (PLA) is increasingly moving toward a posture of global engagement in support of its economic interests. This strategy, espoused in China's first defense strategy white paper, released in May 2015, specifically embraces increased operations with foreign militaries, as well as use of the PLA to advance and protect China's increasingly global commercial interests as strategic objectives.[7] China's expanding use of the PLA Navy to evacuate its citizens from global trouble spots such as Libya[8] and Yemen[9] illustrates the PLA's cautious but expanding embrace of a role for the military in advancing such commercial objectives.

While Chinese military operations in Latin America, to date, have been limited, China's pursuit of a capability to operate in the "far seas" as a strategic goal within its official doctrine,[10] coupled with its ongoing expansion of capabilities to sustain operations far from the P.R.C., such as the establishment of a dual commercial-military port in Djibouti in March 2016,[11] demonstrates a commitment to expand its military capabilities to eventually support (however incompletely) the global flows and commercial operations on which the health of the Chinese economy and feeding of the Chinese people depends. Indeed, over the long run, China's development of capabilities such as aircraft carrier battle groups[12] is consistent with the concept of using military assets for global power projection in support of commercial interests, particularly short of a war with a major power such as the United States, in which the survivability of such assets would be questionable.

With respect to Taiwan, in 2008, then P.R.C. leader Hu Jintao and his Republic of China (R.O.C.) counterpart, Ma Ying-jeou, agreed to suspend their war of "checkbook diplomacy," by which each had used economic incentives to convince states diplomatically recognizing the other to change their position. This informal "truce" effectively left 12 states in the region continuing to recognize the R.O.C., including Paraguay in South America; Belize, El Salvador, Guatemala, Honduras, Nicaragua, and Panama in Central America; and the Dominican Republic, Haiti, Saint Kitts and Nevis, Saint Lucia, and Saint Vincent and the Grenadines in the Caribbean.

Since 2008, both the P.R.C. and the R.O.C. appear to have honored this agreement, although the continuing importance to the P.R.C. of its claims to sovereignty over Taiwan, as well as over Tibet, is illustrated by its inclusion of language supporting this position in virtually every diplomatic communiqué with those countries with whom it maintains relations.

Moreover, although there have been no changes in the region's diplomatic posture toward Taiwan since Costa Rica changed its position to recognize the P.R.C. in May 2008, a broad group of past and present leaders in countries recognizing Taiwan, including Fernando Lugo (Paraguay),[13] Ricardo Martinelli (Panama),[14] Porfirio Lobo (Honduras),[15] and Mauricio Funes (El Salvador),[16] have expressed an interest in recognizing the P.R.C. Moreover, Chinese businesses such as Sinohydro and China Harbour have won important contracts in the region, while the Chinese investment and trade promotion organization CCIPT has set up multiple offices in states recognizing Taiwan.

Collectively, such actions suggest that, while the P.R.C. is not actively working to seek to strip Taiwan of those states which continue to recognize it diplomatically, it is maintaining a credible option for those states to change their posture in the future, thus allowing the P.R.C. to hold Taiwan's international diplomatic legitimacy at risk if the ongoing P.R.C.-R.O.C. rapprochement breaks down, and a future Taiwanese government pursues a policy of independence.[17] Indeed, the victory of Democratic People's Party candidate Tsai Ing-wen in the January 2016 Taiwanese presidential election has raised concern over such a possible course,[18] while the P.R.C.'s March 2016 acceptance of Gambia's unsolicited change in diplomatic posture[19] may be a warning from Beijing about a possible return to the diplomatic struggle.

Finally, although there is no compelling evidence that the P.R.C. seeks a military conflict with the United States, it likely considers the use of its commercial assets in Latin America and the Caribbean as part of fighting a global conflict with the United States if it must do so.

While, as noted previously, the principal objective of Chinese commercial ventures is most likely, economic operations by Chinese companies in areas such as commercial logistics provide the PLA access to detailed understanding of ports, airports, and other facilities that could be leveraged to support Chinese military operations if required. Similarly, industries such as telecommunications and space support services provide opportunities for the collection of intelligence, or the conduct of network attacks against military, political, or economic targets in the hemisphere. Other Chinese commercial operations potentially facilitate the introduction and sustainment of Chinese personnel into the region to conduct operations against the U.S. or regional targets.

Even short of the use of Chinese companies for intelligence, sabotage, or other explicitly military purposes, the role of those companies in the region as employers, sources of capital, and purchasers of the region's goods would be an asset in the run-up to a conflict, dissuading countries of the region from providing political support, military or economic aid, intelligence, or other forms of assistance to a U.S.-led coalition against the P.R.C.

While China's pursuit of these objectives in the Western Hemisphere presents a serious, multidimensional, long-term challenge to U.S. national security, it is important to emphasize that none implies the inherent rejection by the P.R.C. of coexistence with the United States, nor a disposition to act against it, beyond encouragement of the gradual weakening of the U.S., vis-à-vis the P.R.C., as a potential political, economic, and military challenger.

Chinese Advances in Pursuing Its Security Goals in the Region

Consistent with P.R.C. security-related strategic goals in Latin America and the Caribbean presented in the prior section, observable Chinese activities in support of such goals generally fall into four areas: (1) sales and donations of arms and strategic technologies to the region; (2) the conduct of military operations in and military personnel contacts there; (3) political, economic, and military support to anti-U.S. countries to sustain Chinese access to the region while denying the consolidation of U.S. influence there; and (4) building an economic presence in the region in strategically high-value sectors and geographic locations, as well as advancing strategically valuable infrastructure projects.

Arms and Strategic Technologies

With respect to sales and donations of arms and strategic technologies, during the past 15 years, Chinese companies have significantly expanded the quality and sophistication of their product and services offering and their client base. They have evolved from largely competing on the basis of low prices to sell relatively unsophisticated products to a handful of politically sympathetic client states with limited alternatives, to selling much more sophisticated equipment to a far broader array of clients. Outsiders who take comfort in the number of difficulties that the Chinese have had with these recent contracts sometimes dismiss the significant overall advances that Chinese companies have achieved in this regard.

In Venezuela, Chinese companies have advanced from the sale of JYL-1 radars in 2005[20] and modest capability K-8 fighters in 2008,[21] to Y-8 and Y-12 military transport aircraft, more capable L-15 fighters,[22] SM-4 self-propelled grenade launchers, SR-5 multiple-launch rocket system vehicles,[23] and VN-1 armored personnel carriers,[24] as well as additional radars and control stations,[25] among others. In March 2016, Venezuela took delivery on the first of six additional K-8 fighters to replace three that had crashed since the first Chinese fighters were delivered in 2010.[26]

Building on a growing base of sales of sophisticated end items in Venezuela, Chinese arms companies branched out to win contracts to supply similar military goods to the similarly politically sympathetic regimes of Ecuador and Bolivia. Following Venezuela's example, Ecuador acquired four Chinese radar units, and negotiated with the Chinese for the purchase of MA-60 military transport aircraft.[27] Although Ecuador had difficulty finding the money for the MA-60 purchase, and while the acquisition of the Chinese radars ultimately terminated in a contract dispute, in

2011 the Ecuadoran government went on to contract with the Chinese electronics company CEIEC to build the nation's $240 million national emergency response and security system, ECU-911,[28] then later signed a follow-on contract for additional equipment.[29]

Bolivia was one of the first Latin American states to buy Chinese arms, purchasing Chinese-made AK-47s,[30] then, in 1997, acquiring Chinese HN-5 man-portable anti-aircraft missiles.[31] In the mid-2000s, the Bolivian military acquired Chinese military trucks and busses,[32] although due to breakdowns, none of the vehicles were in service as of 2016.[33] Beyond such vehicles, in 2009, Bolivia also followed Venezuela's lead to purchase Chinese K-8 aircraft for use in an air-defense role.[34] In 2014, Bolivia expanded the relationship even further, acquiring six Harbin H-425/Z-9 military helicopters,[35] and expressed interest in acquiring $80 million in Chinese radars.[36]

In recent years, Chinese defense companies have also begun to advance beyond the ALBA regimes in their military sales to the region.

With respect to Peru, even more than in Bolivia, Chinese arms companies have sold more capable military goods to the country for a number of years, although such sales have been fraught with difficulties. In December 2009, the Peruvian Ministry of Defense exhibited five Chinese MBT-2000 tanks in a military parade in Lima, and later publicly confirmed plans to acquire more of the tanks, only to cancel the deal four months later.[37] Also beginning in 2009, Peru purchased at least 150 military trucks from the Chinese manufacturers Beiben, Dong Feng, and Shaanxi, but has reportedly encountered significant mechanical problems with them.[38] Separately the Peruvian military was forced to prohibit the use of Chinese ammunition that it had purchased, because defects in the shell casings caused jams in the automatic weapons that used them.[39]

Despite such setbacks, Chinese arms manufacturers continue to make progress in Peru, including beating out Russian and other competitors to sell the Type 90B multiple launch rocket system to the Peruvian armed forces,[40] of which the first 27 were delivered in July 2015.[41]

In Argentina, a 2009 Chinese sale of WMZ-551 armored personnel carriers to equip its Cruz del Sur armored battalion was cancelled after the delivery of only four units, and the sale of X-11 helicopters was blocked by the objections of the French government, who claimed that it incorporated technology stolen from the French contractor Aerospatiale.[42] Despite such problems, in February 2015, Chinese companies went on to secure commitments for the purchase of 100 armored personnel carriers and 5 P-18 ocean patrol vessels (OPVs),[43] the first sale in quantity of Chinese combat ships to the region, as well as advanced JC-1/JF-17 fighter aircraft. While seemingly a breakthrough for Chinese arms vendors in the region, the aircraft sale was suspended for not meeting the requirements of the Argentine military,[44] while the other purchases were not completed prior to the departure of the government of Cristina Fernández de Kirchner, and were not further pursued by the incoming government of Mauricio Macri.

Beyond the five countries mentioned in the preceding paragraphs, other significant sales or donations of Chinese military arms to the region include the delivery of an OPV to Trinidad and Tobago in March 2014,[45] the donation of seven mobile bridge vehicles, valued at $3 million, to Colombia in October 2013,[46] and the donation of $1.1 million in military equipment to the Jamaica Defense Force (JDF) in 2011.[47] The later, although not involving large quantities nor sophisticated material, was a symbolically valuable demonstration of support at a time in which the JDF had come under substantial international criticism for its handling of a military operation against narcotics dealer Dudus Coke and his supporters in the Tivoli Gardens suburbs of Kingston.[48]

In almost none of these cases did the Chinese systems sold significantly change the military-strategic balance in the region, although the unsuccessful attempt to sell Argentina JC-1/JF-17 fighters arguably would have impacted Great Britain's defense of the Falkland Islands.[49] The more important strategic impact of such sales is arguably on advancing Chinese military relationships in the region, and undercutting the position of other arms vendors pursuing sales there, including Russia, Brazil, and the United States, as well as benefitting the P.R.C.'s own defense industry, as discussed later.

In addition to sales of traditional military items, the P.R.C. has also made progress in providing satellites, space launch services, and space facilities for itself, and for Latin American clients in the region.

Since 2008, China has launched two satellites for Venezuela, one for Bolivia, four for Brazil, and a microsat for Ecuador. It has announced further satellites to be developed and launched for Venezuela, Bolivia, and Brazil, as well as the possible development and launch of a first satellite for Nicaragua.[50]

China has also built supporting ground station facilities for Bolivia and Venezuela, and has trained the majority of key technical personnel for the space programs of those two nations within the P.R.C.

Although China failed in its attempt to participate in the ARSAT program to develop and launch a satellite for Argentina,[51] the P.R.C. has successfully secured agreements to build and operate space observation and tracking facilities in the country. This appeals to China because of Argentina's location in the Southern Hemisphere. Examples include Chinese participation in the satellite laser ranging facility in Argentina's San Juan observatory,[52] and most recently, construction of a deep-space radar tracking facility in the province of Neuquén that some analysts believe could be used for military purposes.[53]

In each of the cases of military and space goods and services discussed above, the transaction provided the P.R.C. benefits from a national security perspective. On one hand, it helped the Chinese to improve their defense technology and industrial base, including the quality and sophistication of its military equipment and supporting logistics and maintenance infrastructures, including benefits from learning and technical collaboration with Latin American and Caribbean partners during design, production, and fielding. It also potentially strengthened the relationship between the PLA and the partner militaries supported by that equipment, through expanding Chinese knowledge of Latin American military and technical institutions, as well as the personnel brought to the P.R.C. for training in the operation and maintenance of the Chinese equipment purchased.

Military Operations in and Personnel Contacts with the Region

During the past decade, consistent with P.R.C. intentions, announced in China's 2008 Policy White Paper toward Latin America and the Caribbean,[54] the PLA has expanded the size and nature of military activities in the region.[55]

With respect to military operations, the PLA has evolved from conducting multilateral activities in the region to bilateral ones, and from humanitarian activities to combat exercises. For eight years, beginning in 2004, the PLA contributed military police and other military members to the United Nations mission in Haiti, MINUSTAH. Although it withdrew the last of its forces from Haiti in October 2012,[56] it began to expand its bilateral activities in the region toward the end of the same period, conducting a humanitarian exercise with Peru in November 2010, involving the use of a mobile field hospital that it had just donated to the country.[57] In December 2011, the PLA Navy deployed its newly commissioned hospital ship *Peace Ark* to the Caribbean, with port calls in Jamaica, Cuba, Costa Rica, and Trinidad and Tobago to provide medical care to local residents.[58]

In November 2013, while the U.S. government was distracted by the impasse in approving a new federal budget, two Chinese guided missile frigates crossed the Pacific and, for the first time in the contemporary history of Chinese engagement with Latin America, conducted combat exercises in the region, with Chile,[59] before passing through the Straits of Magellan to do military engagements with Argentina and Brazil as well.[60]

In October 2015, Chinese media announced plans for the PLA 20th Naval Escort Task Force to visit Cuba, as well as the return of *Peace Ark* to the region, with port calls in Grenada, Barbados, and Peru as part of its "Harmony 2015" medical relief mission.[61]

Beyond such operations, the PLA also regularly sends military officers to Latin America and the Caribbean for training, professional military education, and other activities.[62] PLA military officers attend training courses at the Tolemaida military base in Colombia and at the jungle warfare school in Manaus, Brazil, among other sites.[63]

Reciprocally, the PLA regularly hosts Latin American and Caribbean military officers for professional military education courses in its Institute of Defense Studies at the PLA National Defense University in Beijing, and at other sites, including command and general staff schools for Army and Navy officers in Nanjing, as well as in other locations such as Shijiazhuang.[64]

As with military sales, such interactions not only strengthen the bond between Chinese and Latin American military personnel and their respective institutions, but also help the P.R.C. better understand those personnel and institutions, in order to work with them in their countries, or elsewhere, if called upon to do so in the future.

Sustaining Chinese Access and Undermining U.S. Control through Multipolarity

The interest in a "multipolar world," frequently expressed by China's leadership,[65] reflects a strategic interest that is more important to the country than is commonly recognized. A Latin America in which the United States does not dominate key trade structures and multilateral political and economic institutions, which are populated by viable regimes actively resisting U.S. policy objectives, also implies a region with ample openings for China in its pursuit of strategic economic objectives, such as obtaining reliable access to resources, foodstuffs, technology, and markets.

While the P.R.C. has been cautious not to associate itself with the anti-U.S. rhetoric and activities of the ALBA regimes and, at times, Argentina and Brazil, it has actively engaged those regimes with senior-level diplomacy while concentrating its economic activities there in a way that sustains those regimes pursuing a course independent of the United States, and encouraging the region's use of multilateral forums that exclude the U.S.

With respect to presidential-level attention, departing from the more balanced and cautious approach pursued by his predecessor Hu Jintao, P.R.C. president Xi Jinping focused his July 2014 trip to the Western Hemisphere on four countries, each of which has had difficult relations with the U.S.—Cuba, Venezuela, Brazil, and Argentina,[66]—leaving engagement with the more pro-U.S. regimes of Colombia, Peru, and Chile for his premier, Li Keqiang.

For economically sustaining regimes pursuing courses independent from the U.S., Chinese policy banks loaned $125 billion to the region between 2005 and 2015. Approximately 78% went to the countries of ALBA and Argentina.[67]

In virtually all of these countries, P.R.C.-based companies have faced enormous difficulties with stalled projects, dysfunctional bureaucracies and security challenges for their operations, in return for a portfolio of politically high-risk loans, modest quantities of Venezuelan oil, and products such as Argentine soy that the P.R.C. could have purchased from more reliable partners in the hemisphere. Yet a strict evaluation of whether China has "gotten its money worth" in its strategic choice to focus its economic engagement on these regimes overlooks how the survival of such regimes, in and of itself, has benefitted China's strategic position globally.

Much of China's money has arrived at critical points in the lives of Argentina and the ALBA regimes. The P.R.C. committed an estimated $1.4 billion to Ecuador in the run-up to that nation's March 2013 presidential election,[68] although the funds did not arrive until after the election, the expectation of receiving them arguably allowed the Ecuadoran government to expand spending in the months prior.

In a similar fashion, the P.R.C. provided a $4 billion loan to the government of Venezuela during the months prior to that nation's 2012 presidential election, allowing its Bolivarian socialist regime to purchase Chinese Haier appliances and other goods to resell at subsidized prices to impoverished Venezuelans tending to support the government.[69]

The P.R.C. has continued to provide funds to such regimes at moments when their future appeared at risk.

In the months leading up to the October 2015 elections in Argentina, the P.R.C. moved forward with multiple loan-based construction projects committed to by president Xi during his July 2014 visit to the country,[70] and on September 28, 2015, just before the election, the P.R.C. committed to a $2 billion increase in the $11 billion line of credit that it had provided to the nation's international reserves, helping it to maintain its financial stability,[71] thus indirectly bolstering the candidacy of the pro-administration candidate Daniel Scioli.

During the same period, the P.R.C. committed $5 billion to the Bolivarian government of Venezuela, helping to mitigate a growing fiscal crisis in the months prior to that nation's December 6 midterm elections.[72]

Beyond Argentina and Venezuela, although the P.R.C. does not currently have diplomatic relations with the Sandinista government of Nicaragua, Chinese financial backing will determine the future of the Nicaragua Canal project. The canal, spearheaded by Hong Kong–based developer Wang Jing, requires an estimated $50–70 billion in funding, yet is marred by questions of transparency,[73] financial viability, environmental concerns,[74] and other issues,[75] making it questionable that the funds will come from Western investors or governments.[76] Significant funding from such sources became increasingly unlikely during 2015, with the resignation of the canal's spokesman, Ronald McLean,[77] secrecy surrounding the key environmental impact study for the canal, the delayed release of a study by McKinsey and Co. regarding the canal's financial viability,[78] and a lack of progress on activities specified in the initial project plan.[79] Yet the government of Nicaragua has continued to assert its commitment to the project.[80] Moreover, the feasibility of the canal's construction, while ambitious, remains plausible. Thus the future of the Sandinista regime (which has bet its credibility on the project) is in the hands of the P.R.C. government.

With respect to promoting a regional multilateralism that is exclusive of the U.S., the P.R.C. has chosen CELAC (a forum in which the U.S. and Canada are not welcome) as its primary vehicle for multilateral diplomatic engagement with the region. Indeed, President Xi convened a meeting of the newly created China-CELAC Forum during his July 2014 trip to Latin America, and again in Beijing in February 2015. Little of substance emerged from the China-CELAC summits aside from as-of-yet unrealized Chinese offers of infrastructure projects and loan funds, predictions of future trade and investment,[81] and the previously mentioned "roadmap" of those areas in which the P.R.C. would like to focus its relationship. Yet the summits themselves strengthen the identity of CELAC as a symbolically useful institution, and create opportunities for sidebar conversations and memorandums of understanding to take individual projects forward. [82]

P.R.C. Economic Presence in Key Sectors, Infrastructure, and Geography

While P.R.C. investments in the region are principally driven by commercial considerations, the Chinese state plays a strong role in approving and/or promoting projects. Moreover, their utility in time of war as sources of political leverage, cover for introducing and sustaining clandestine Chinese operatives in the region, and a vehicle for facilitating Chinese military operations there, makes relevant the discussion of the growing P.R.C. economic presence in key sectors, infrastructure projects, and geographic locations.

In the event of a war with the P.R.C., the knowledge of the region's ports and airfields possessed by Chinese logistics companies operating in the region, including water depth, refueling capabilities, supporting consolidation areas for containerized freight, and the technical details of port and airfield operations would decrease the time, and increase the effectiveness of PLA use of such facilities. The PLA could get authorization to use the facilities or it could impose its will on the host country.[83]

Chinese commercial activities that potentially contribute to this knowledge include the operation of seven container ports in the region by the Hong Kong firm Hutchison Port Holdings (HPH)—Veracruz, Ensenada, Manzanillo, Lazaro Cardenas, Cristobal, Balboa, and Buenos Aires—and an intermodal land terminal in Hidalgo, Mexico.[84] Indeed, the ability to leverage the knowledge of these ports could be strengthened by the proposed sale of HPH by its parent company, Hutchison-Whampoa, to mainland Chinese investors.[85] Chinese shipping companies that regularly service Latin America's ports, including China Shipping and COSCO, arguably could also contribute to such knowledge.

On the aviation side, the position of Chinese companies is more modest, but includes China Airport Holdings, which operates six regional airports in the vicinity of Medellin, Colombia,[86] as well as a commitment from the government of Bolivia to use a Chinese company to modernize and operate the Viru Viru airport serving the city of Santa Cruz.[87] It also includes the presence of Chinese airlines that operate from and maintain ground operations at the region's airports, such as Air China's operations in São Paulo, Brazil.

With respect to key sectors, the expanding presence of Chinese companies in the region's telecommunications industry creates strategic opportunities for the Chinese. Chinese companies Huawei and ZTE have won contracts for building the region's 3-G and 4-G infrastructure, and sell increasing quantities of smartphones, routers, and other devices.[88] The associated supply of hardware and servicing of networks creates opportunities to capture data potentially useful in a conflict, from military and technical information to sensitive personal information. Indeed, the latter, while seemingly innocuous, could be used to compromise governmental, military, or other functionaries, as well as to introduce viruses to debilitate vulnerable Latin American systems from military communications to physical infrastructure to national economies. Concern over such possibilities was arguably a key reason why the U.S. Congress voted to block access to the U.S. market by Huawei and ZTE in 2013.[89]

With respect to infrastructure, the strategic value of projects built by Chinese companies, including highways, ports, and railways, is principally economic, albeit multifaceted. Such infrastructure facilitates Chinese access to the region's resources and market, while also providing work for the Chinese companies contracted to build them.

Consistent with this logic, the principal strategic value of the Nicaragua Canal is its role in reducing maritime transportation costs and times, as well as possible leverage over shipping companies and governments of the region if a Chinese firm is awarded the license to operate the canal once built. Although the canal might also facilitate the movement of PLA naval vessels and support ships between the Atlantic and Pacific in time of war, such explicit military value would arguably be minimal, since the canal would probably be relatively easy to monitor and shut down.

Finally, with respect to geography, the concentration of Chinese investment projects and commercial operations in the Caribbean arguably also has potential military and intelligence value for the P.R.C. in times of conflict. The Hutchison-operated port of Freeport[90] is less than 90 miles from the U.S. coast, and in close proximity to strategically important U.S. ports and military embarkation points. While the level of Chinese loans given to the Caribbean may be explained in part by the willingness of small Caribbean governments to accommodate Chinese preferences for government-to-government deals, the amount of political attention and the investment funds promised for the region, including a $3 billion Caribbean fund promised by Xi Jinping during his first trip to the region as president in June 2013,[91] seem to exceed that justified by a pursuit of access to the small and fragmented Caribbean markets and their modest natural resources and agricultural offering.

Other Impacts of Chinese Engagement on the Security Dynamics of the Region

In addition to P.R.C. advances in pursuing its security goals in the region, Chinese activities in pursuit of strategic economic objectives have impacted the security of the region in indirect ways, with consequences for the region itself, including the U.S., as well as China's own future role. These include (1) the expansion of trans-Pacific organized crime,

(2) enabling the activities of other extra-hemispheric actors in the region, and (3) increasing crime and ethnic conflict, which motivates the P.R.C. government to lobby for the well-being of ethnic Chinese in the region.

Trans-Pacific Organized Crime

The growth in the flows of goods, financial transactions, and business contacts between Asia and Latin America has, as a byproduct, facilitated trans-Pacific criminal activities, including the distribution of contraband goods, drugs, and precursor chemicals, illegal mining, trafficking in arms, trafficking in persons, and money laundering.[92]

Chinese smuggling groups frequently use Latin American and Caribbean transit routes in smuggling persons to the United States and Canada, in the process interfacing with Latin American criminal groups such as Los Zetas in Mexico, which influence the routes over which the groups move their cargo.[93]

With respect to narcotics, the P.R.C. and India are currently key suppliers for the manufacture of synthetic drugs for Latin American criminal organizations such as Mexico's Sinaloa cartel,[94] and reciprocally, Latin American criminal groups are increasingly seeking markets in Asia.[95] Similarly, Chinese companies are key purchasers of metals obtained through informal, and often illegal, mining activities controlled by Latin American criminal groups, including the extraction of metals from Madre de Dios, Peru, and Michoacán, Mexico.[96]

With respect to arms, Chinese weapons have been fraudulently supplied to the FARC rebels in Colombia,[97] and in May 2015, a shipment of munitions chemicals from the P.R.C. being smuggled into Cuba, labeled as other cargo, was seized during a stop by the ship in the port of Cartagena, Colombia.[98]

Criminal organizations also increasingly use trans-Pacific commerce and institutions in both Asia and Latin America for their money laundering activities, and to conceal wealth. Notable recent examples including the conviction of Hong Kong Shanghai Bank of China (HSBC) for laundering money for the Sinaloa cartel,[99] use of Chinese banks by the Brazilian criminal organization First Capital Command (PCC),[100] and the use of Chinese casinos and merchandise acquired in the P.R.C. by Colombian criminals to launder money.[101] Indeed, based on a high-profile case involving Colombian agents, the increasing use of China for money laundering by criminal organizations in Latin America was highlighted in a series of mainstream media reports in March 2016.[102]

Enabling Other Extra-hemispheric Actors

While there is no evidence that the P.R.C. has directly collaborated with other extra-hemispheric actors such as Russia and Iran in Latin America, Chinese funds have bolstered regimes with anti-U.S. intentions, such as Venezuela and Nicaragua, which have, in turn, collaborated with the Russians and Iranians in ways that undermine U.S. security in the hemisphere. Examples include the 2014 Russian expression of interest in military base access in Nicaragua, Venezuela, and Cuba,[103] and Venezuelan collaboration with Iran to bring Qods Force agents into the region through Venezuela[104] and construct Iranian auto and tractor factories on Venezuelan territory,[105] which may have served as a front for collaboratively conducting nuclear and missile proliferation activities outside of Iranian territory.[106]

Chinese Interest in Latin American Politics through Domestic Projects

While the P.R.C. has long proclaimed its principle of non-interference in the domestic politics of other countries,[107] its growing commercial activities in Latin America increasingly give it a vested interest in the region's internal affairs. Evidence of such interest has included investment of time by senior Chinese leaders to get major projects moving forward, such as the modernization of Argentina's Belgrano-Cargas railroad.[108] It also increasingly includes protection of Chinese nationals and commercial operations in the face of violent criminals and radical protesters in the frequently dangerous and contested areas where Chinese firms conduct activities such as construction, mining, and oilfield operations. Examples include attacks in 2011 against Emerald Energy petroleum operations in Caquetá, Colombia;[109] as well as attacks against Sinohydro's efforts to construct the Patuca III dam in Olancho, Honduras;[110] attacks against petroleum operations in Tarapoa[111] and Orellana in Ecuador;[112] and attacks against Chinese mining operations in Potosi,

Bolivia;[113] and in 2012, even against the Lupe mine in Puebla, Mexico.[114] The most recent major example, at the time of this writing, occurred at the end of September 2015, when protests against China Minmetals' development of the Las Bambas mine in Peru gave rise to riots in which three persons were killed and the Peruvian government was forced to declare a state of emergency in parts of the Apurímac and Cusco regions.[115]

In addition, the growth of Chinese populations in Latin America and, particularly, in the Caribbean Basin, through expanded migration, business, and construction projects has fomented tension with local populations, including violent actions against Chinese communities in Papitam and Maripaston (Suriname) in 2009 and 2011,[116] as well as protests in July 2013 against the Chinese community in Santo Domingo, Dominican Republic.[117] This has pushed an increasingly powerful and self-confident P.R.C. government to involve itself in Latin American security affairs, advocating for the rights and enhanced protection of ethnic Chinese. In August 2013, for example, when Jamaican prime minister Portia Simpson Miller traveled to the P.R.C. seeking Chinese investment in her country, her host, premier Li Keqiang unexpected raised the issue of crime against Chinese Jamaicans, forcing the prime minister to promise to expand efforts by the Jamaica Constabulary Force to protect the interests of ethnic Chinese living in the country.[118]

In the future, the expanding presence of Chinese businesses in the region, and the expanding size and visibility of the ethnic Chinese community there, will only create further imperatives to which the government must react, even as its confidence and economic leverage for doing so continue to expand. However sincere P.R.C. intentions not to interfere in the internal affairs of Latin American and Caribbean states, it will be arguably tempted to use its influence in an ever more intrusive fashion to promote its interests and protect its people, creating growing discomfort not only in the region, but also in the United States.

U.S. Policy in the Context of Chinese Advances in the Hemisphere

Since the end of the Cold War, and even before, Latin America and the Caribbean have received a relatively modest portion of the resources of the U.S. government, and the attention of U.S. presidents, compared to other parts of the world. Yet it is not clear whether more U.S. government attention to and resources for the region would have prevented the remarkable advances by the P.R.C. that have occurred in the hemisphere in recent years.

Such advances have also been facilitated by the dynamics of globalization, which have expanded the flows of goods, money, information, and, to a lesser extent, people between Latin America and all parts of the world; the expanding global flows of technology and corresponding physical, financial, and informational infrastructures have made such global interactions cheaper, easier, and more manageable. Latin American and Caribbean businessmen and political leaders have increasingly reached out beyond the region to construct global ties, even as physically distant actors such as the Chinese have approached the region in search of goods, markets, and technologies. In short, U.S. "neglect" of Latin America and the Caribbean may have contributed to the rapid growth of China's commercial, political, and military position in the region, but does not explain it.

As P.R.C. engagement in Latin America and the Caribbean has expanded since China's opening to the global economy in 1978, and particularly in the post–Cold War period during the past 15 years, Republican and Democratic administrations have maintained a remarkably consistent posture of not explicitly opposing such interactions, or the rights of the nations of the hemisphere to engage with the partners with whom they wished.[119] While some U.S. leaders (such as Hillary Clinton,then secretary of state)[120] have expressed concern over Chinese activities in the hemisphere, most, including policymakers responsible for Western Hemisphere affairs, from Republican assistant secretary of state Roger Noriega[121] to Democratic assistant secretary Arturo Valenzuela,[122] have avoided explicitly speaking out against such engagement. Indeed some, such as Assistant Secretary Jacobson, have suggested that it could be positive. [123]

Such underlying drivers notwithstanding, there are a number of areas in which U.S. policy has encouraged or facilitated the P.R.C. advance in the hemisphere, or augmented challenges that it presents.

As the P.R.C. has expanded its engagement in the hemisphere, both the Chinese government and academics in institutions have consistently signaled Chinese sensitivity to the U.S. response.[124] Such sensitivity, to a degree, is arguably genuine, given the importance of Chinese markets and technology in sustaining continued P.R.C. growth, as well as because of significant Chinese holdings of U.S. government debt and dependence on international trading and financial systems denominated in U.S. dollars and dominated by the U.S. and Western institutions.

In this context, the relative absence of signals from U.S. administrations to the Chinese regarding its advances in the region, including Secretary of State John Kerry's November 2013 pronouncement before the Organization of American States that it was no longer "applying" the 1823 Monroe Doctrine, resisting the advance of extra-hemispheric actors in the region,[125] arguably gave the Chinese encouragement to expand their political, economic, and military activities in the hemisphere.[126]

In addition, the focus of U.S. government international engagement resources on the Middle East and Asia, and deep mandatory cuts to the budgets of the Defense Department as part of "sequestration,"[127] arguably deeply undercut the ability of the U.S. to maintain significant, effective engagement programs in the region, and thus to help the U.S. to maintain its position as "partner of choice" in the face of the Chinese commercial, political, and military advance.

The growing engagement by and influence of the P.R.C. in the region was also complicated by the unwillingness of the U.S. to invest presidential-level attention and significant diplomatic and other resources to address the dysfunctional features of the Organization of American States (OAS). The imposition of costs on those actors (including not only the ALBA regimes, but also countries such as Brazil) has repeatedly blocked attempts to involve the OAS in hemispheric security affairs, and has led to attempts to replace the OAS with organizations that exclude the U.S., such as UNASUR and CELAC. Thus China's ability to use CELAC as its principal multilateral engagement vehicle for with the hemisphere (without the OAS) was a strategic loss for the United States.

Ironically, while the Obama administration's decision to diplomatically reengage with Cuba may, to some degree, revitalize the U.S. position in the region, the likely eventual abandonment of sanctions on Cuba, and the island nation's associated reemergence as a regional tourism and commerce hub, is also likely to have the unintended by-product of strengthening the P.R.C. position in the Caribbean. Chinese companies will be well-positioned to finance and perform much of the work to grow and modernize the island nation's tourism and logistics infrastructure, in the process making Chinese companies key commercial actors in other sectors of a revitalized Cuban economy as well, including telecommunications, export-oriented manufacturing, and retail.

Conclusion

Although Chinese activities in Latin America and the Caribbean present serious national security challenges for the United States, it would be ineffective, and probably counterproductive, for the U.S. to attempt to block China's engagement in the hemisphere. Rather, the U.S. must adapt its posture toward the region to be a more attentive, respectful, and effective partner, working with the states of Latin America and the Caribbean to help them best realize the potential benefits from economic engagement with the P.R.C., while avoiding its pitfalls. At the same time, the U.S. has striven to work with partners who share its values in Latin America, as well as Asia, to build an open-trade regime that connects the two continents across the Pacific. The formal signing of the Trans-Pacific Partnership agreement in February 2016 in Auckland, New Zealand, was a step in this direction.[128]

There are a number of concrete steps that the U.S. could take to ensure that the fact of Chinese engagement is most beneficial to the region and most compatible with U.S. and hemispheric security:[129] (1) working with U.S. partners in Latin America and the Caribbean to strengthen their government institutions for engaging the P.R.C. so that both China and the nations with which it is engaging get a fair and constructive deal; (2) ratifying an effective Trans-Pacific Partnership, open to the P.R.C. in the future, as one step in constructing a multilateral, rule-of-law-based regime across the Pacific, in which all nations, businesses, and individuals have an equal opportunity to profit from their policies and efforts; (3) facilitating ties between the Western Hemisphere and partners in Asia that share U.S. values, including, but not limited to, Japan, South Korea, Australia and India. Such facilitation could include contacts through business forums, as well as U.S. university programs, helping Asian partners expand their ties with and ability to do business in Latin

America and the Caribbean, and helping Latin American partners do business in Asia; (4) expanding theater security cooperation in Latin America and the Caribbean to bolster the U.S. position as partner of choice, in the face of growing military cooperation activities by China and other extra-hemispheric actors; (5) giving priority to the functionality of an inter-American system, in which the OAS is the multilateral vehicle to engage China and resolve regional security issues;[130] and (6) articulating a clearer vision of what the U.S. stands for in the hemisphere, and why the U.S. approach best advances broad-based development, prosperity, and human dignity.[131]

A P.R.C. that is weak, in crisis, or excluded from the Western Hemisphere is not necessarily in U.S. interests, nor those of the region. If TPP had gone ahead and China had joined, Latin America and the Caribbean, as well as China, would stand to benefit mutually from robust international engagement.

For the United States, responding effectively to the challenges presented by Chinese engagement in the Western Hemisphere is not merely a policy option, but a necessity, for the ties of geography, economic interdependence, and family that link the U.S. to the region also bind it to the negative and positive consequences of Chinese engagement there.

NOTES

1 The author is Latin America Research Professor with the Strategic Studies Institute of the U.S. Army War College. The views in this article are strictly his own.

2 "China's Policy Paper on Latin America and the Caribbean (Full Text)," Government of the People's Republic of China, November 2008, http://in.china-embassy.org.

3 "1st China-CELAC Ministerial Forum: Big Deal or Missed Opportunity?" *Dialogo Chino*, January 9, 2015, www.dialogochino.net.

4 "Xi Jinping Attends China-Latin America and the Caribbean Summit," Ministry of Foreign Affairs of the People's Republic of China, July 18, 2014, www.fmP.R.C.gov.cn.

5 For a detailed discussion of these objectives, see R. Evan Ellis, *China and Latin America: The Whats and Wherefores*, Boulder, CO: Lynne Rienner Publishers, 2009. See also R. Evan Ellis, "China's Activities in the Americas," Testimony to the Joint Hearing of the Subcommittee on the Western Hemisphere and the Subcommittee on Asia and the Pacific, U.S. House of Representatives Foreign Affairs Committee, September 10, 2015, http://docs.house.gov.

6 The literature on Chinese "investments" in the region, including statements by Chinese leaders, regularly conflates loans and contracts to supply products or services (such as major construction projects paid for through loans by Latin Ameri-

can and Caribbean states) with investments. Moreover, commitments for future investments, such as the billions of dollars that may be invested over the course of a decade to develop a mine or oilfield for which a Chinese company has been given an operating license, are sometimes referred to as investments. Even within the financial literature, mergers and acquisitions are often reported as investments in the region, although the benefit of such transactions goes to stockholders, few of which may be located in the region, although the change in ownership may open the door for later investment in the newly acquired asset.

7   "China's Military Strategy," State Council Information Office of the People's Republic of China, May 26, 2015, http://eng.mod.gov.cn.

8   "China Continues to Bring Citizens Evacuated from Libya Back Home," *Xinhua*, March 5, 2011, http://news.xinhuanet.com.

9   Kevin Wang, "Yemen Evacuation a Strategic Step Forward for China," *Diplomat*, April 10, 2015, www.thediplomat.com.

10 "China's Military Strategy," State Council Information Office.

11 "Another 'Great Game': Why China's PLA Is Jostling for Position with the World's Armed Forces in Tiny Djibouti," *South China Morning Post*, April 4, 2016, www.scmp.com.

12 Harry Kazianis, "China's Oversized Aircraft Carrier Ambitions," *Diplomat*, June 20, 2014, www.thediplomat.com.

13 "Posible relación con China Continental," *ABC Digital* [Paraguay], June 7, 2007, www.abc.com.py.

14 Jenny W. Hsu, "Panama Respects Taiwan, China 'Truce': Ambassador," *Taipei Times*, February 6, 2010, www.taipeitimes.com. See also "Taiwan corteja a Martinelli," *La Prensa*, December 27, 2009, www.prensa.com.

15 "Honduras abrirá relaciones diplomáticas con China," *La Prensa*, December 8, 2009, www.laprensa.hn.

16 "El Salvador anuncia que restablecerá relaciones con Cuba," *Hoy*, March 18, 2009, www.hoy.com.ec.

17 See Ellis, "China's Activities in the Americas."

18 "China Warns Taiwan over New Law Governing Cross-strait Relations," *Reuters*, March 31, 2016, http://uk.reuters.com.

19 Rudroneel Ghosh, "Diplomatic Tussle: China's Resumption of Official Ties with Gambia Resurrects the Ghost of Dollar Diplomacy between Taipei and Beijing," *Times of India*, March 19, 2016, http://blogs.timesofindia.indiatimes.com.

20 "Venezuela y China suscriben acuerdo para adquisición de radares," *El Universal*, April 8, 2005, www.eluniversal.com.

21 "Chávez recibe primeros aviones chinos portadores de misiles, cohetes y bombas," *El Espectador*, March 13, 2010, www.elespectador.com.

22 "Venezuela adquiere aviones chinos de entrenamiento de combate L15," *Infodefensa*, April 4, 2014, www.infodefensa.com. See also "Venezuela habría cerrado la compra del avión de entrenamiento chino L15 'Falcón' y piensa también en Sukhoi," *Defensa*, April 9, 2014, http://defensa.com.

23 "La Armada de Venezuela fortalecerá sus medios de combate y apoyo en 2014," *Infodefensa*, January 7, 2014, www.infodefensa.com. See also "Venezuela activa un nuevo Grupo de Artillería armado con sistemas de la china Norinco," *Defensa.* September 13, 2013, www.defensa.com.

24 Richard D. Fisher and James Hardy, "Venezuela Signs Up for VN1, Hints at Chinese Amphibious Vehicles Buy," *IHS Janes 360*, November 23, 2014, www.janes.com.

25 Zhang Fan, "LatAm Turns to China for Security Projects," *China Daily*, October 25, 2014, http://usa.chinadaily.com.cn.

26 Santiago Rivas, "Venezuela Receives More Chinese K-8 Trainers," *IHS Janes 360*, March 14, 2016, www.janes.com.

27 "FAE desiste de comprar aeronaves a China por un 'desacuerdo técnico,'" *El Universo*, July 4, 2011, www.eluniverso.com.

28 Edward Fox, "China Loans Ecuador $240 Mn for Security Program," *Insight Crime*, October 22, 2012, www.insightcrime.org.

29 Zhang, "LatAm turns to China."

30 "Aclaran que 10.000 fusiles fueron donados por China," *Los Tiempos*, June 27, 2008, www.lostiempos.com.

31 "Bolivia: U.S. Subterfuge in Missile Destruction," *China Post*, March 30, 2006, http://chinapost.com.tw.

32 See R. Evan Ellis, "China—Latin America Military Engagement: Good Will, Good Business, and Strategic Position," Carlisle Barracks, PA: U.S. Army War College Strategic Studies Institute, August 2011, www.strategicstudiesinstitute .army.mil, p. 27.

33 One Chinese donation of road construction and engineering equipment reportedly generated bad will in the Bolivian armed forces when almost all of the vehicles donated quickly broke down. See "China Dona Equipo de Ingeniera a las Fuerzas Armadas de Bolivia," *Infodefensa*, June 1, 2012, www.infodefensa.com.

34 "Bolivia comprará aviones chinos para lucha antidroga," *El Universo*, October 2, 2009, www.lostiempos.com.

35 "Bolivia estrena helicópteros militares H425 de China, los primeros en América," *El Confidencial*, September 13, 2014, www.elconfidencial.com.

36 "Bolivia define esta semana compra de radares para proteger su espacio aéreo," *Los Tiempos*, October 28, 2016, www.lostiempos.com.

37 "Gobierno suspende indefinidamente compra del tanque chino MBT-2000," *La Republica,* April 7, 2010, www.larepublica.pe.

38 "Problemas con los camiones chinos del Ejército de Perú," *DefensaSur*, February 12, 2013, www.defensasur.com.ar.

39 "El Ejército de Perú retira por problemas la munición china," *Tecnología Militar*, April 5, 2013, tecnologamilitar.blogspot.com.

40 "Perú selecciona el sistema táctico de lanzacohetes múltiples Norinco tipo 90B," *Infodefensa,* January 10, 2014, www.infodefensa.com. See also "El Ejército de Perú adquiere sistemas de artillería chinos por 38 millones de dólares," *Defensa.* December 27, 2013, www.defensa.com.

41 Cesar Cruz Tantalean, "Peru Receives Chinese Tactical MRLs," *IHS Jane's 360*, July 21, 2015, www.janes.com.

42 "Negocia la Argentina comprar helicópteros militares a China," *La Nación*, May 17, 2007. www.lanacion.com.ar.

43 "Analysis: China Looks to Break into Latin American Market via Argentina," *IHS Jane's 360*, February 10, 2015, www.janes.com.

44 "La Fuerza Aérea descartó la compra de un caza chino (III)," *Desarrollo y Defensa*, August 29, 2015, http://desarrolloydefensa.blogspot.com.ar.

45 "China entregará un buque patrullero a Trinidad y Tobago," *Infodefensa*, March 11, 2014, www.infodefensa.com.

46 "Mindefensa recibió puentes militares de China avaluados en 3 millones de dólares," *El Espectador*, October 12, 2013, www.elespectador.com.

47 "JDF Gets Military Aid from China," *Jamaica Observer*, August 24, 2011, www.jamaicaobserver.com.

48 For background on the criticism of the Jamaica government and the JDF over the Tivoli Gardens incident, see Marc Wignall, "Something Went Horribly Wrong in Tivoli Gardens," *Jamaica Observer*, May 30, 2011, www.jamaicaobserver.com.

49 Wendell Minnick, "Argentina, China Could Jointly Develop Fighters," *Defense News*, February 22, 2015, www.defensenews.com.

50 Danilo Valladares, "China llega a América Central con satélites y megaobras," *IPS Noticias*, November 1, 2012, www.ipsnoticias.net.

51 For background on China's bid to participate in the program, see Jamie Hulse, "China's Expansion into and U.S. Withdrawal from Argentina's Telecommunications and Space Industries and the Implications for U.S. National Security," U.S. Army War College Strategic Studies Institute, September 2007, www.strategicstudiesinstitute.army.mil. For Information on the failure of that bid, see "Arianespace to Launch Argentine Satellite Arsat-1," *Arianespace Official Website*, June 28, 2010, www.arianespace.com.

52 "Successful Operation of a Cooperative SLR Station of China and Argentina in San Juan," *Science Bulletin*, Vol. 53, No. 16, 2008, www.sciencemeta.net.

53 Despite publicly expressed concerns stemming from the secrecy of the program, the size and position of the satellite dish are consistent with communication with satellites and reception of signals from beyond the vicinity of earth, rather than any terrestrial military tracking purposes. Martin Dinatale, "Un documento de China reavivó la polémica por la base de Neuquén," *La Nación*, June 15, 2015, www.lanacion.com.ar.

54 "China's Policy Paper on Latin America and the Caribbean."

55 See, for example, the Posture Statement of General John F. Kelly before the Senate Armed Services Committee, 114th Congress, March 12, 2015, www.southcom.mil.

56 Colum Lynch, "In Surprise Move, China Withdraws Riot Police from Haiti," *Foreign Policy*, March 25, 2010, www.foreignpolicy.com.

57 "Saludan fortalecimiento de cooperación militar entre Fuerzas Armadas de Perú y China," *Andina*, November 23, 2010, www.andina.com.pe.

58 "Vicepresidente de Costa Rica destaca misión humanitaria de buque," *Xinhua*, November 25, 2011, http://spanish.news.cn.

59 "PLAN Taskforce Conducts Maritime Joint Exercise with Chilean Navy," Ministry of Defense of the People's Republic of China, October 12, 2013, http://eng.mod. gov.cn. See also "Armadas de China y Chile realizaron ejercicios navales," *Noticias FFAA Chile*, October 16, 2013, http://noticiasffaachile.blogspot.com.

60 "PLAN Taskforce Conducts Joint Maritime Exercise."

61 "China's Naval Hospital Ship Arrives in Barbados for Service, Visit," *Xinhua*, November 28, 2015, http://news.xinhuanet.com.

62 For a detailed list of such activities, see R. Evan Ellis, *The Strategic Dimension of China's Engagement with Latin America,* Washington, DC: Center for Hemispheric Defense Studies, October 2013, http://chds.dodlive.mil, pp. 85–116.

63 See Ellis, "China's Activities in the Americas."

64 Ellis, *Strategic Dimension.*

65 See, for example, Jane Perlez, "Leader Asserts China's Growing Importance on Global Stage," *New York Times*, November 30, 2014, www.nytimes.com.

66 In addition to conducting the sixth annual BRICS summit, and the first ministerial level summit between China and the nations of CELAC during this visit, President Xi signed a significant number of bilateral deals with each of the countries involved, although almost none of the signature projects announced during this visit, such as a regionwide development fund and a transcontinental railroad, have yet been realized. For a more in-depth analysis of the trip, see R. Evan Ellis, "China's Advance in Latin America Has More Challenges than Xi's Visit Suggests," *Manzella Report*, July 18, 2014, www.manzellareport.com.

67 "China-Latin America Finance Database," Inter-American Dialogue, accessed April 10, 2016, www.thedialogue.org.

68 "Ecuador recibe $1.400 millones de un crédito chino," *La Republica*, February 26, 2013, www.larepublica.ec.

69 Charlie Devereux, "China Bankrolling Chavez's Re-Election Bid with Oil Loans," *Bloomberg*, September 26, 2012, www.bloomberg.com.

70 Mariano Obarrio, "Cristina y Xi Jinping acordaron inversiones por US$ 7500," *La Nación*, July 19, 2014, www.lanacion.com.ar.

71 Javier Blanco, "Para evitar que caigan las reservas, le pidieron más crédito a China," *La Nacion*, September 28, 2015, www.lanacion.com.ar.

72 Chinese and Venezuelan experts consulted for this study confirmed that there was only one $5 billion loan, announced multiple times, and not two separate loans. Moreover, the loan would be principally used to repay other obligations incurred by Chinese companies operating in the country, with very little disbursement of new funds. See "Venezuela recibirá al cierre de 2015 préstamo por $5.000 millones de China," *El Universal*, September 25, 2015, www.eluniversal .com.

73 See, for example, "U.S. Embassy in Nicaragua Voices Concerns over Chinese-led Canal" *Reuters*, January 7, 2015, www.reuters.com.

74 See, for example, Axel Meyer and Jorge A. Huete-Pérez, "Conservation: Nicaragua Canal Could Wreak Environmental Ruin," *Nature*, February 19, 2014, www.nature .com. Indeed, Environmental Resources Management, the otherwise reputable company commissioned to perform the environmental impact analysis on the proposed canal, has, in contradiction of norms for such studies, released very few details. See Ivan Castro, "Nicaragua Canal Project Study Delivered, Details Scarce," *Reuters*, June 1, 2015, www.reuters.com.

75 For a discussion of the complex financial relationships surrounding the canal, see Octavio Enríquez, Santiago Villa, and Wilfredo Miranda, "La 'telaraña' de Wang Jing y la conexión militar con China," *Confidencial*, November 3, 2014, http://confidencial.atavist.com.

76 For a good, brief overview of challenges associated with the canal, see Richard Feinberg, "A Transoceanic Canal for Nicaragua?," *Brookings Institution*, June 9, 2014, www.brookings.edu. See also R. Evan Ellis, "Los negocios detrás del canal," *Confidencial*, December 14, 2014, www.confidencial.com.ni.

77 Rezaye Álvarez M, "Ronald MacLean Abaroa fuera de HKND Group," *La Prensa*, March 17, 2015, www.laprensa.com.ni.

78 John Gallagher, "Nicaragua Canal Start Delayed Again," *IHS Maritime 360*, September 23, 2015, www.ihsmaritime360.com.

79 The official project schedule of the canal indicates that work on a temporary port on the Pacific coast entrance for the canal at Brito and initial earth-clearing work were to begin during the first half of 2015, as well as the implied acquisition of land from persons along the canal route and solicitations for major infrastructure projects associated with the canal. As of the time this article went to press, no such activities had begun. See "Nicaragua Canal Project Description," HKND Group, December 2014, http://hknd-group.com, pp. 36–37.

80 Gallagher, "Nicaragua Canal Start Delayed Again."

81 For a more in-depth discussion, see R. Evan Ellis, "The China-CELAC Summit: Opening a New Phase in China-Latin America-U.S. Relations?," *Manzella Report*, January 13, 2015, www.manzellareport.com.

82 UNASUR and CELAC are multilateral institutions of recent creation, promoted by anti-U.S. regimes such as those of ALBA, as well as independent actors, such as Brazil. By design, UNASUR and CELAC exclude the United States and Canada. By extension, the use of these two institutions, rather than the OAS (in which the U.S. is a member), to address important regional security weakens the voice of the United States in such matters.

83 For further discussion of such possibilities, see R. Evan Ellis, "La relevancia estratégica de América Latina para los Estados Unidos," *DEF*, February–March 2015, pp. 125–131.

84 "Terminal Intermodal Logística de Hidalgo," Hutchison Port Holdings, accessed April 10, 2016, www.tilh.com.mx.

85 K. Quincy Parker, "Hutchison Principal May Sell Stake in HPH," *Nassau Guardian*, February 9, 2015, www.thenassauguardian.com.

86 See R. Evan Ellis, "China, S.A. como empresa local en América Latina," *Temas de Reflexión*, No. 7, May 2013, www.eafit.edu.co.

87 Miguel Lazcano, "Gobierno busca convertir a Viru en una mega terminal aérea," *La Razón*, October 20, 2015, www.la-razon.com; and "China financiará Mutún y vía de Rurrenabaque," *Los Tiempos*, October 1, 2015, www.lostiempos.com.

88 For a more detailed discussion of Chinese activities in the telecommunications sector of Latin America and the Caribbean, see Ellis, *Strategic Dimension*, pp. 52–63.

89 "Investigative Report on the US National Security Issues Posed by Chinese Telecommunications Companies Huawei and ZTE," U.S. House of Representatives, 112th Congress, October 8, 2012, http://intelligence.house.gov.

90 For a detailed discussion of the range of logistics and other projects controlled by Hutchison on Grand Bahama island, see Carey Leonard, "Hutchison's Investments on Grand Bahama . . . Have They Performed?," Speech to the Grand Bahama Chamber of Commerce, February 28, 2014, http://freeport.nassauguardian.net.

91 Joshua Goodman, "China's Xi Offers Caribbean Nations $3 Billion in Loans," *Bloomberg*, June 3, 2013, www.bloomberg.com.

92 For an overview of Chinese organized crime activities in the region, see R. Evan Ellis, "Chinese Organized Crime in Latin America," *Prism*, Vol. 4, No. 1, December 1, 2012, pp. 67–77.

93 See, for example, Elyssa Pachico, "Zetas' Control of US-Mexico Border Slipping: Report," *Insight Crime*, January 29, 2013, www.insightcrime.org.

94 See, for example, Bryan Harris, "Hong Kong Triads Supply Meth Ingredients to Mexican Drug Cartels," *South China Morning Post*, January 12, 2014, www.scmp.com.

95 See, for example, Bryan Harris, "Mexican Drug Cartels Eye Asian Markets," *CNBC*, September 24, 2015, www.cnbc.com.

96 See, for example, Laurence Culliver, "How Chinese Companies Sustain Organized Crime in Mexico," *Vice News*, June 25, 2014, http://news.vice.com.

97 R. Evan Ellis, "New Developments in China-Colombia Engagement," *Manzella Report*, October 27, 2014, www.manzellareport.com.

98 "China dice que carguero detenido en Cartagena llevaba material militar 'ordinario,'" *El País*, March 4, 2015, www.elpais.com.co.

99 Carrick Mollenkamp, "HSBC Became Bank to Drug Cartels, Pays Big for Lapses," *Reuters*, December 11, 2012, www.reuters.com.

100 Bruno Riberio, "PCC envia dinheiro do tráfico para Estados Unidos e China," *O Estado de São Paolo*, January 15, 2015, http://sao-paulo.estadao.com.br.

101 Arron Daugherty, "Colombians Charged in Massive China-based Money Laundering Scheme," *Insight Crime*, September 11, 2015, www.insightcrime.com.

102 Erika Kinetz, "From Israel to Colombia, Who's Laundering Money in China," *Washington Post*, March 28, 2016, www.washingtonpost.com.

103 "Russia with Plans for Military Bases in Nicaragua, Cuba and Venezuela," *Mercopress*, February 27, 2014, http://en.mercopress.com.

104 "Countering Iran in the Western Hemisphere Act of 2012," H.R. 3783, 112th Congress, 2nd Session, January 3, 2012, www.gpo.gov.

105 For a detailed discussion of such projects, see "Iran-Venezuela after Chávez, Still an Indissoluble Bond?," *Alice News*, July 6, 2013, http://alice.ces.uc.pt.

106 See, for example, R. Evan Ellis, "El Islam Radical en Latinoamerica y el Caribe," *Air & Space Power Journal en Español*, http://airpower.us9.list-manage1.com, 2nd Semester 2015, Vol. 27, No. 2, pp. 4–15.

107 See "China's Initiation of the Five Principles of Peaceful Co-Existence," Ministry of Foreign Affairs of the People's Republic of China, accessed September 16, 2015, www.fmP.R.C.gov.cn.

108 Juan Pablo de Santis, "Belgrano Cargas: el tren que une a Cristina, Macri, los chinos y Moyano," *La Nación*, June 26, 2012, www.lanacion.com.ar.

109 "Secuestran a tres chinos en Caquetá," *El Tiempo,* June 9, 2011, www.eltiempo.com.

110 "Estancadas las obras en la represa hidroeléctrica Patuca III en Honduras," *La Prensa*, August 15, 2013, www.laprensa.hn.

111 "Petrolera china desestima que protesta en Tarapoa haya afectado sus intereses," *El Universo*, November 14, 2006, www.eluniverso.com.

112 "Matanza en Oriente sería por petroleras," *El Universo*, August 16, 2009, www.eluniverso.com.

113 "Colquiri aún dialoga y denuncian más tomas," *Los Tiempos*, June 9, 2012, www.lostiempos.com.

114 Aldo Miguel, "Expulsan pobladores de Zautla a mineros chinos," *El Sol del Puebla*, November 22, 2012, www.oem.com.mx.

115 "Las Bambas: Declaran estado de emergencia en provincias de Apurímac y Cusco," *Peru21*, September 29, 2015, http://peru21.pe.

116 R. Evan Ellis, *China on the Ground in Latin America: Challenges for the Chinese and Impacts on the Region*, New York: Palgrave-Macmillan, 2014.

117 Omar Santana, "Protestan contra 'nuevos comerciantes chinos,'" *Diario Libre*, July 30, 2013, www.diariolibre.com.

118 "Police to Ramp Up Security Measures for Chinese Community in Jamaica," *Gleaner*, August 27, 2013, http://jamaica-gleaner.com.

119 See, for example, R. Evan Ellis, "Intensificación de las Relaciones de China con América Latina y el Caribe En el Contexto de la Política Estadounidense Hacia la Región," *Air & Space Power Journal en Español,* 1st Semester 2014, Vol. 26, No. 1, pp. 9–24.

120 "Clinton Warns of Iranian, Chinese Gains in Latin America," *CNN*, May 1, 2009, www.cnn.com.

121 Roger F. Noriega, "China's Influence in the Western Hemisphere," Statement before the House Subcommittee on the Western Hemisphere, April 6, 2005, http://2001–2009.state.gov.

122 See, for example, "China 'Not a Threat' in L. America," *People's Daily Online*, August 19, 2010, http://en.people.cn.

123 Roberta S. Jacobson, "China's Latin America Presence Not a Threat: U.S. Official," *Xinhua*, November 13, 2013, http://news.xinhuanet.com.

124 See, for example, Jiang Shixue, "Triangulation between China, Latin America and the US?," *Xinhua*, July 19, 2014, www.china.org.cn.

125 Experts close to the decision, interviewed off the record, suggested that the gesture reflected a sincere desire by those involved to forge a more positive, respectful relationship with the region, but did not necessarily contemplate its impact as a "signal" to those outside the region contemplating a stronger relationship.

126 "Kerry Makes It Official: 'Era of Monroe Doctrine Is Over,'" *Wall Street Journal*, November 18, 2013, http://blogs.wsj.com.

127 See, for example, Philip Ewing, "DOD Insists Sequester Dangerous," *Politico*, February 3, 2013, www.politico.com.

128 "Trans Pacific Partnership Trade Deal Signed in Auckland," *BBC News*, February 4, 2016, www.bbc.com.

129 This list of policy recommendations was originally presented by the author to the U.S. Congress in his testimony before a joint hearing of the House Foreign Affairs Committee Subcommittee on the Western Hemisphere, and the Subcommittee on Asia and the Pacific, September 10, 2015, http://docs.house.gov.

130 Such support for the OAS may involve resources and spending the time and political capital to achieve real institutional reforms, as well as imposing political and economic costs on those states who seek to prevent the OAS from addressing important regional security issues, and who seek instead to advance institutions that exclude the United States, such as CELAC or UNASUR.

131 Indeed, the U.S. State Department advocated such value-based leadership in its 2015 Quadrennial Diplomacy and Development Review (QDDR), stating, "America is strongest when our optimism, integrity, ideals and innovation are a model for the world." *Enduring Leadership in a Dynamic World*, Quadrennial Diplomacy and Development Review 2015, U.S. State Department, www.state.gov, p. 8.

PART IV

Conclusion

15

Conclusions and Comparisons to Developments in Central and Southeast Asia

DAVID B. H. DENOON

Overview

This chapter will focus on two sets of conclusions: (a) those related to Latin America and this volume per se, and (b) some general observations about the interaction of China and the United States in the three regions being analyzed (Central Asia, Southeast Asia, and Latin America) in this three-volume set of books.

Latin America and the Caribbean (LAC)

Since 1823, and the pronouncement of the Monroe Doctrine, the U.S. has been the preeminent power in Latin America and the Caribbean. Although, early in his first term, President Obama pledged an "equal partnership" with LAC and, in the second Obama term, Secretary of State Kerry said, "the era of the Monroe Doctrine is over," these commitments do not necessarily reduce the preponderant influence of the U.S. in the region.[1]

For example, although China's total trade with Latin America has expanded 22 times between 2000 and 2014 (from $10 billion to $257 billion), U.S. total trade with the region in 2014 was $875 billion, so still more than three times China's total.[2] The figures for foreign direct investment(FDI) are even more lopsided, with China at $86 billion and the U.S. with $375 billion.[3]

One area where China leads the U.S. is in aid commitments. Between 2005 and 2014 China made $119 billion in aid pledges.[4] It should be noted that many of the Chinese commitments are for large projects, some of which, like the Trans-Andean Railway, have not yet come to fruition (See Chapter 2 of this volume, by Osvaldo Rosales, for an overview of the LAC economic scene).

Thus, in Latin America and the Caribbean (LAC), we see a pattern that repeats itself in other regions of the globe: the U.S. is the preeminent power, but China's influence is growing quickly. What is uncertain is whether China will be able to maintain its high economic growth rate and whether the U.S. will be able to sustain its leadership with a 1–2% GDP growth rate and a growing percentage of the American population becoming skeptical about overseas commitments.

What we will do below is summarize some of the key issues that will permit the reader to make a judgment about the likely future positions of the U.S. and China.

The discussion will focus on two broad themes:

1) China is the rising power in LAC and is using a combination of economic and political incentives to explore how best to maximize its interests in a region that was formerly completely dominated by the U.S.
2) The U.S. is the status quo power in LAC and finds low levels of Chinese trade and investment unthreatening. However, if China were to establish military bases in LAC or to finance direct challenges to U.S. interests, the U.S. is likely to respond by undercutting China's newfound influence.

China

China's strategy in LAC has been to identify key energy supplies, raw materials, and food sources and, if possible, combine those economic interests with ties to governments willing to take an anti-U.S. stance.[5] In Venezuela under Chávez and Maduro, Brazil under Lula da Silva and Rousseff, and Argentina under the Kirchners (husband and wife), China found both an economic and political set of allies. Although this seemed like a brilliant approach in the first decade of the 21st century when those regimes were doing well, it now seems like an over-concentration on risky investments. (These issues will be discussed in greater detail below in the section on China's links to the Latin American political Left).

China doubled down on this strategy by also supporting new multilateral organizations in LAC that had strong anti-U.S. orientations. Since the U.S. has long dominated the Organization of American States (OAS), it is not surprising the some Latin states would want to establish new organizations that they could control. Yet the two new entities that the Latin states promoted, the Bolivarian Alliance of the Americas (ALBA) and the Community of Latin American and Caribbean States (CELAC), have few accomplishments to their credit. Moreover, by warmly welcoming China's participation in these two organizations (and excluding the U.S.), the Latin states have put themselves in an awkward position should it prove that ALBA and CELAC are ineffective.[6]

Obviously, if the Latin Left were to revive politically or were ALBA and CELAC to show more promise, China's investment in them would appear to be foresighted. Yet, at present, that looks unlikely, so it will be interesting to see what stance the successor governments in Venezuela, Brazil, and Argentina take toward China and how ALBA and CELAC are positioned in the near future.[7]

The United States

Analysts of great power behavior have long noted that, in addition to military capability, influential states must maintain a vibrant economy. For a state to be an anchor of a major security grouping, it must also provide broader economic benefits to the countries it wants to lead.[8] There is little doubt that, from the latter part of the 19th century until today, the United States has provided both a security and economic framework for LAC. Much of this time the U.S. role was resented and led to many anti-U.S. activities and protests. Nevertheless, since World War I, the U.S. dollar has been the region's major currency for international transactions, the U.S. has remained the leading trade partner, and the U.S. military has provided implicit security guarantees.

The U.S. provision of this security and economic environment has meant that LAC central banks could rely on the U.S. dollar to settle accounts and that the region could be safe from outside invasion and spend, on average, a small percentage of GDP on defense.[9] Also, the LAC states could cede responsibility to the U.S. for designing and negotiating the relevant trade agreements: the General Agreement on Tariffs and Trade (GATT), the World Trade Organization (WTO), the North American Free Trade Agreement (NAFTA), and the Central American Free Trade Agreement (CAFTA). Although many times the terms of these agreements were disputed, none of the LAC states would have been able to design and negotiate these treaties on their own.

Similarly, for the last seven decades, the U.S. played the lead role in the OAS and the Inter-American Development Bank (IADB), which both facilitated multilateral activities in the LAC region. The principal alternative to these two institutions has been the Economic Commission for Latin America (ECLA), which was completely controlled by the Latin states and provided a different intellectual and political orientation.[10] ECLA played a key role in developing the "Dependency School" in the 1960s and has provided a statistical basis for challenging the claims that the U.S. economic role in the region was benign.[11]

Skepticism, and even outright hostility to the U.S. role in LAC, has been led by Cuba since the advent of Fidel Castro and by Nicaragua since the rise to power of the Ortegas and the Sandanista movement. The Chinese have built on that resentment and have widened the coalition of anti-U.S. states as regimes with related views arose in Argentina, Brazil, Bolivia, and Venezuela. For analysis of the particularly large investment China made in Venezuela, see the chapter in this volume by Anthony Spanakos.

Thus, as a status quo power, the U.S. has faced a dilemma under both Republican and Democratic administrations. What should the U.S. do when Latin states intentionally foil U.S. initiatives? For example, during George W. Bush's first year in office, Brazil gleefully blocked a proposed Free Trade Agreement for the Americas and, during Barack Obama's first term, the subsequent president of Brazil refused to visit Washington when she found out (to no one's surprise) that her mobile phone had been tapped by U.S. surveillance.[12] The usual answer by policymakers in Washington has been to ignore the annoyance on the grounds that the Latin state will lose more than the U.S. That answer alone reinforces the recognition of the asymmetry in power and economic strength between the U.S. and the LAC states.[13]

After exploring these two themes (a) China as the challenger experimenting with different tactics; and (b) the U.S. as the confident preeminent outside power, we will now turn to several additional issues that are critical in LAC and affect the way that China and the U.S. interact in the region.

Economic Autonomy from the U.S.?

Trade and trade dependence have been two of the most volatile issues in U.S.-LAC relations. Starting with the import-substitution industrialization strategy during World War II, and proceeding from the 1960s to the 1990s with the Latin effort to avoid "dependency," many of the Latin American states have seen autonomy as a central policy objective. Since the U.S. was the leading trading state in the region, avoiding dependence meant avoiding dependence on the U.S. China initially provided a vehicle for this change of direction because it could be a different export market. What many Latin American states found out, however, was that China was not just a growing export market but a strong competitor to local industries with its manufactures.[14] While it was good to have an alternative export market to forestall dependence on the U.S., China no longer looked so attractive when it began to flood Latin American domestic markets with low-cost consumer and intermediate goods. Also, some U.S. concerns about losing key markets were excessive as China still cannot compete on quality or in most high-tech products.[15]

Thus, overall the LAC states see China's growing presence as both an opportunity and a challenge.[16] In the periods when China's GDP was growing rapidly, agricultural and raw material exports were finding a buoyant market. Now, however, as China's GDP growth is slowing, the trade balance has turned against the LAC countries and China's economic role is seen as a mixed blessing.

Migration and higher education also play key roles in U.S. ties to LAC whereas they have a limited role in ties to the People's Republic of China (PRC). Migration of unskilled workers from Mexico and Central America has been massive and the controversy surrounding them has tended to obscure the trend of higher-income Latin American families sending their sons and daughters to U.S. universities.[17] In both cases, the Latin individuals involved learn about the U.S., learn at least some English, and develop ties that can affect their location and family choices throughout their lifetimes. China, on the other hand, is a great distance away; and, despite its scholarship programs, learning Mandarin is a formidable task. So, this means that the U.S. has a distinct advantage in creating personal and professional ties with Latin America. Also, as much as many Latin Americans say they want autonomy from the U.S., few are willing to give up the opportunities for a North American education or working in the U.S.

Military Links

As mentioned above, most LAC states spend a modest amount of their GDPs on the military and, since the 1960s, military rule has faded from the scene. Nevertheless, one important form of influence that both China and the U.S. can try to cultivate is through supplying military equipment and dual-use technology like satellite and related telecommunications equipment.[18]

As R. Evan Ellis notes in Chapter 14 of this volume, China has supplied middle-tier military platforms and equipment to Venezuela, Bolivia, and Argentina.[19] The PRC has also launched satellites for Venezuela, Bolivia, Brazil, and Ecuador. Moreover, near the end of Mrs. Kirchner's presidential term, China negotiated a secret deal with Argentina to build a satellite downlink station for its own use. Apparently, this was linked to financial support for the Kirchner government, but the terms of the arrangement were kept highly secret and not even released to members of the Argentine parliament. It remains to be seen if the successor Macri government will permit the arrangement to go forward.

Given its history of having supported some of the military regimes in Latin America and its desire to limit military expenditures in the region, U.S. military assistance has gone mostly to the governments of Peru and Colombia to help them deal with drug trafficking. The U.S. also runs a variety of officer training courses that are designed to teach U.S. values and procedures.[20] Hence, it is fair to say that neither China nor the U.S. plays a major role as a military supplier in the LAC states.

The Caribbean

Much of the discussion about Latin America considers the Caribbean as an afterthought.[21] Part of this is because the population in the Caribbean is modest, but part of it is cultural. Although Cubans and those in the

Dominican Republic speak Spanish (like most in Latin America), the colonial heritage of the rest of the islands means that French, English, Dutch, and Danish are spoken elsewhere. So, there is a certain cultural distance between much of the Caribbean and the rest of Latin America. Also, in general, the Latin American states became independent in the 19th century while most of the Caribbean became independent in the 20th century. These differences in culture and historical experience produce different reactions to the arrival of a new outside power in the region.[22]

The most notable difference, politically, between the Caribbean and the rest of the Latin American countries is the high percentage of the island states that diplomatically recognize Taiwan instead of the PRC.[23] It is also interesting to see that six of the Central American countries recognize Taiwan.[24] This may have been partly due to energetic diplomacy by Taiwan in the early 1970s after the U.S. formally recognized the PRC, but it also reflects the sympathy that small states have for another small "country" that is being coerced by a larger state.

Finally, small states, generally, do better economically if they specialize, so they tend to be less protectionist and concentrate their exports in a limited number of products. Though tourism is the largest sector of many of the Caribbean states, their manufacturing is highly specialized and they find China's open import markets appealing.[25] Since the larger Latin American states have more diversified economies, they are more threatened by imports from China and their domestic producers may not be efficient enough to compete in China's import markets.[26]

Thus, although the Caribbean and Latin states are often grouped together in regional organizations, their cultural and historic backgrounds are different and their preferred economic strategies differ as well. So it is not surprising that they take varying approaches to the arrival of China in the hemisphere.

Regionalism in the LAC States

As discussed above, one of the key goals of many LAC states has been to become less dependent on the United States. Aid, trade, and foreign direct investment from China has been one route to greater autonomy and forming regional groupings that can speak for a cluster of countries has been another.[27] The BRICS (Brazil, Russia, India, China, and South Africa) grouping has gotten a great deal of publicity but has only one Latin state (Brazil) and lost influence as all of its members face slowing economies and assorted difficulties.

ALBA (the Bolivarian Alliance of the Americas) probably comes closest to the archetype of an anti-U.S. grouping; but, like the BRICS, as its members face serious economic setbacks, ALBA countries have few resources in reserve to promote the agenda.[28] Moreover, although China has been willing to provide the ALBA countries with aid and encouragement, policymakers in Beijing have been cautious about promoting a blatant anti-U.S. program in a region where the U.S. still predominates.

CELAC is a more inclusive grouping, and thus speaks for broader range of countries. It produces well-documented research and promotes open forums on a number of development topics. Although Chinese observers have been welcomed at CELAC sessions, they could not count on their views being endorsed in CELAC, as they could in ALBA.

So, regionalism is a means for generating more leverage for small countries; and, given the long history of anti-U.S. sentiment in many Latin American states, it is not surprising that groups like ALBA get established. Yet, to date, there have been limited results for such ventures.

Comments Comparing China-U.S. Relations in Central Asia, Southeast Asia, and Latin America

Since 1979, much of the mainstream American commentary on Chinese foreign policy has stressed that China's principal objectives have been to defend the homeland and neighboring waters and to obtain adequate food, hydrocarbons, and natural resources.[29] Thus, many observers saw China's goals as basically defensive.

However, in the last decade, several important changes in Chinese policy have taken place. First, China has been more willing to use force to achieve its objectives.[30] Second, the Chinese government has launched its "going out" strategy of encouraging overseas investments and purchases of foreign corporations that could help in upgrading China's technological skills. Third, China has restated a number of its key military objectives, most notably its commitment to become a great "maritime power."[31] These changes, combined with Chinese president

Xi Jinping's highly nationalistic depiction of "The China Dream" warrant a new assessment of Chinese objectives. The shift toward a "going out" economic strategy and from a "near seas" to a "far seas" naval posture indicates a far more assertive stance by Beijing.

What we do below is to examine current Chinese and U.S. foreign policy in Central Asia, Southeast Asia, and Latin America to see how these respective policies are changing. It appears that, under president Xi's leadership, China has an overall strategy of pursuing a more assertive foreign policy, but the tactics being selected in each of the three regions are quite different.

In Central Asia, China has long-term strategic interests and may well want to eclipse both the U.S. and Russia in influence. However, at the moment, Beijing's focus is on extracting hydrocarbons and in building out the transport links necessary to tie Western China to Central Asia and Europe. Thus, China has avoided any significant involvement in the use of force. Also, China's signature program in Central Asia is the "One Belt, One Road" concept with its ambitious plans for highways, railroads, and ports, plus oil and gas pipelines inside and on the periphery of the region.

In Southeast Asia, China not only has long-term strategic interests, but also major economic and territorial claims. Although China took a non-confrontational stance toward the region in the 1990s and early 2000s, by 2007, Beijing had begun to shift its approach. In the non-confrontational period, China offered highly concessionary terms to the Southeast Asian countries that joined the China-ASEAN Free Trade Agreement and did not back up its territorial claims with force.

Nevertheless, after 2007, China's tactics changed dramatically. Beijing authorized hostile actions by its navy, coast guard, and maritime militia to back up is territorial claims and began its current process of building naval and air bases on atolls where there are claims by multiple states. Although the United States takes no position on the territorial claims in the South China Sea, it has a 200-plus-year record of defending "freedom of navigation." The U.S. also has made highly visible ship visits close to islands and atolls that China currently occupies. Thus, we have a situation in Southeast Asia where both China and the U.S. perceive they have vital interests and where both are willing to use force to protect those interests. Economic concerns come into play as well, when the U.S. proposed the Trans-Pacific Partnership (TPP) and China favored the Regional Comprehensive Economic Partnership (RCEP) as a competing form of trading arrangement.

In Latin America, the United State is the predominant outside power, in terms of military capability, foreign investment, and cultural ties. Nevertheless, China has now become the leading trading partner for important economies like Venezuela, Brazil, and Argentina, and China is the largest aid donor and lender for many countries. Also, a China-based company, Hutchison-Whampao, now manages the Panama Canal. In addition, there is some possibility that China will fund a new Pacific to Atlantic canal through Nicaragua.

So, though China has no military bases in Latin America, it is clearly making a major economic investment in the region. By supporting Latin countries that have anti-U.S. regimes, China is showing that it wants to cause political difficulties for the United States.

Thus, we have a situation in Latin America where the U.S. still leads in influence, but China is making significant inroads and could become the dominant outside economic actor if it keeps up its investments in the region. In Table 15.1 below we see rankings for levels of commitment and willingness to use force for the U.S. and China in the three regions.

Hence, we see some interesting patterns, which we will explore in greater detail below. As a rising power, China is experimenting with how to expand its influence from its direct borders to the global arena. Both Central Asia and Southeast Asia border China, but neither area received much attention from Beijing until the 1990s. Central Asia, of course, did not become independent from the USSR until 1991 and Southeast Asia only became more important as China's economy boomed and it needed

TABLE 15.1.

Levels of Commitment

	Central Asia	Southeast Asia	Latin America
U.S.	Low	High	Medium
China	High	High	Medium
Willingness to Use Force			
U.S.	No	Yes	No
China	No	Yes	No

more raw materials for manufacturing. The big turning point in China's ties to Southeast Asia was in 2002, with the start of the China-ASEAN Free Trade Agreement.

In the last decade and a half, circumstances have changed dramatically. As the Soviet Union collapsed, China saw an opportunity for both economic and strategic influence in Central Asia; and, as U.S. attention focused on the Middle East under the George W. Bush administration, possibilities for a greater role in Southeast Asia developed as well. Yet China approached the two regions very differently. In Central Asia, China has avoided getting involved militarily and sought its influence through trade, direct investment, and loans. Whereas in Southeast Asia, China has achieved a combination of political, economic, and military influence. Also, in the South China Sea, China has been willing to deploy significant military assets.

In Central Asia, China has been careful not to offend the sensibilities of the newly independent states there. On the other hand, in Southeast Asia, China has been willing to offend the other South China Sea claimants and even use force to expel competing claimants. This demonstrates that China's leaders see the economic and strategic aspects of Southeast Asia as sufficiently important to risk offending most or all of the ASEAN states.

For the United States, which is withdrawing from Afghanistan and no longer needs the oil and natural gas in Central Asia, the priorities are different. Central Asia has lost some of its luster and the Obama administration recognized that it is perceived by the ASEAN states as playing an ineffective role in Southeast Asia. So Central Asia has declined in its importance to the U.S., while Southeast Asia has recently risen in significance. Latin America, long a safe area in the U.S. "backyard," still ranks of middle-tier importance, but the Chinese arrival is not as it is concerning as in Southeast Asia.

China's Links to Anti-.U.S. Latin American States

Although China's leadership functions through the Communist Party of China (CPC), the party no longer stresses communism and is quite pragmatic about its choice of partners for implementing its foreign policy. For example, in the Middle East, China maintains a close working relationship with both Iran and Saudi Arabia even though one is a Shiite regime and the other is an ultra-conservative Sunni one and both countries normally scorn communist governments. In the Middle East, China's main goals are to obtain oil and to avoid antagonizing any faction of Islam so it can remain on good terms with the Muslims within its borders and those in neighboring states. This means that ideology is secondary to pragmatism and that low-keyed relations are emphasized with Middle Eastern states.

In Latin America, the circumstances are different. In addition to purchasing hydrocarbons, metals, ores, and food, China has sought out regimes that were critical of the U.S.—so Beijing could form "strategic partnerships" with governments that would challenge Washington's positions on a variety of issues. In the first decade of the 21st century, China was able to achieve its objectives in both the economic and political arenas. China's soaring exports generated so much foreign exchange that Beijing could make attractive offers for the items it wished to purchase.[32]

Moreover, China could use its foreign exchange to offer grants, loans, and appealing financial terms for its foreign direct investments as well. Also, since there was a long record of resentment toward U.S. firms in Latin America, China found a welcome environment for its approach. Finally, it happened that, in the early years after 2000, Left-wing, anti--U.S. governments got control of several major states and were prime candidates for China to court.

Presidents Nestor Kirchner in Argentina, Lula da Silva in Brazil, and Hugo Chávez in Venezuela were all sympathetic to the entreaties of the Chinese. This made it feasible for the Chinese to create the type of links they wanted with large Latin American states. Wheat and beef from Argentina; oil, soybeans, and ores from Brazil; and oil from Venezuela were key imports for China, and all these states became prime export markets for Chinese manufactures. Also, each of the three original presidents, in the early 2000s, was followed by an equally anti-U.S. successor: Kirchner's widow in Argentina, Dilma Rouseff in Brazil, and Nicolás Maduro in Venezuela. This meant that for at least a decade in each country China could count on access to vital imports, a vibrant export market, and a government that would share key aspects of Beijing's policy toward the U.S.

These features made for a powerful combination just as China was receiving so much attention as a rising power. One part of its Latin

American strategy was to focus on its bilateral ties with kindred states. However, a second part of its approach was to establish multilateral institutions that would be rivals of the multilateral architecture created in the West in the early years following World War II. The BRICS grouping was the most visible entity, but its companion, the New Development Bank, provided key resources the Latin American countries could plan on borrowing from.[33] Also, instead of trying to join the West's new trade pact, the Trans-Pacific Partnership, China set up its own trade grouping, the Regional Cooperation Economic Partnership, which has less demanding terms for membership than the TPP. In addition, in many situations, China uses its seat on the United Nations Security Council to block Western initiatives.[34] Therefore, China's rise and its desire to thwart various Western goals has made its economic and political clout a formidable adversary for the U.S. and the West more broadly.

Yet China is by no means invincible. Several developments in the post-2010 period have combined to limit China's influence. The first, discussed above, is the slowing of China's economy. It is important to note that China's economy is not now in recession; it has just had a major slowdown in its growth rate. After having its GDP grow at an average rate of 10% per year for 30 years, China is now growing at a 6–7% annual rate. That is still faster than Japan, the U.S., and the European Union. Nevertheless, with its growth rate cut roughly in half, many of the projects in supplier countries that were based on assumptions of a 10% growth rate are no longer viable.

Second, China's hyper-growth spurt (1980–2010) was based on soaring exports and internal investment that buttressed demand during periods of slowing demand. As the CPC's Third Plenum in 2013 concluded, China can no longer count on either exports or countercyclical investments to sustain growth; and a shift toward services requires a fundamental rebalancing of the economy and will take decades.[35] Thus, it is reasonable to assume that the China market will remain an attractive export destination for many years to come, but it will be a more competitive, slower-growing venue.

Third, and most important, is that China is now seen as an assertive regional power and a budding global player. Hence, China's actions and policy positions are getting more scrutiny. Several examples stand out: China has differences with North Korea on its nuclear program; with

South Korea on territorial questions related to the Koryo dynasty; with Japan over sovereignty in the East China Sea and the Senkaku/Diao-yu islands; with a growing number of Southeast Asian states in the South China Sea; and with India over Arunachal Pradesh. Related to this is China's refusal to abide by the ruling of the International Tribunal on the Law of the Sea (ITLOS) on July 12, 2016.[36] Not only is this a serious violation of international law, but it puts China in the position of being the aggressor rather than the victim (which has been a Chinese claim for much of the period since 1842).[37]

So, as China's growth slows, it is a less attractive economic partner; and, as China becomes more aggressive, there are more states that see it as a potential threat rather than as a partner or champion of small countries. The U.S. has the advantage that it is located across the Pacific Ocean and does not seek new territory to add to its current boundaries.

Ironically, just as China has lost some of its allure as a challenger to Western institutions, the major states in Latin America have lost much of their influence and bargaining power. China's largest debtor in Latin America is Venezuela, to which it has lent about $50 billion. Given the economic chaos, at present, in Venezuela under the Maduro administration, there is frequent speculation in China about whether Venezuela will default on its debt.[38] Under these conditions, Venezuela is hardly in a position to lead a strong coalition of countries against the United States.

Remarkably similar circumstances have befallen Brazil. Former president Lula initiated a host of domestic, redistributive schemes and it made him very popular with low-income voters in Brazil. Yet, by the time of his second term, as the oil price started to plateau and the public became more aware of the extent of governmental corruption, the appeal of his Leftist policies came into question.[39] Lula managed to get Dilma Rousseff elected as his successor, yet the malfeasance of his administration became a burden for her. (Rousseff was subsequently removed from office on August 31, 2016.) Moreover, the International Monetary Fund estimates that the Brazilian economy will shrink by over 7% between 2015 and 2017. Corruption, indictments, and a collapsing economy do not make an appealing model for other states to follow.

In Argentina, the era of the two Kirchners featured many of the same polices tried in Venezuela and Brazil. This led, in December 2015, to the election of Mauricio Macri, who promptly announced a reversal of most of the Kirchners' policies.

This leaves China in a difficult position in Latin America. Even its ties to the Bolivian regime may be affected as President Evo Morales is leaving office with a mixed record as well. It will be interesting to see if China's new tactics of courting the more conservative regimes in states like Chile, Peru, and Colombia can succeed. If Beijing does focus on that, it will be a sign that economic issues are foremost in China's calculus. On the other hand, if China continues to give substantial aid and make large loans to Brazil and Venezuela, it will indicate that political and strategic matters are the principal Chinese concerns.[40]

U.S. Policy in Central Asia, Southeast Asia, and Latin America

Central Asia is an interesting test of American pragmatism in foreign policy. In the 1990s, the Central Asian states had just gotten independence from the Soviet Union and there was considerable optimism that they would become pro-Western democracies. This led to increased U.S. and European Union aid and activities by non-governmental organizations to encourage political change (which, on balance, did not come to pass).

Then, after September 11, 2001, the U.S. took a particular interest in the region as a route to provide access for troops and supplies going to Afghanistan.[41] This raised the strategic significance of Kazakhstan, Tajikistan, and Kyrgyzstan and their ability to provide key overflight rights and air bases. Yet once President Obama announced that U.S. troops in Afghanistan would be reduced to 5,000 soldiers by the end of 2014, the importance of overflight and transit rights declined dramatically.[42] Also, in the 2010 to 2015 period, the development of shale gas in the U.S. meant that, in general, American oil companies had adequate supplies of hydrocarbons. U.S. firms were thus less interested in paying the high costs of finding and transporting oil and gas out of Central Asia.[43]

So, within a 15-year period, U.S. interest in Central Asia went from minimal to intense and back to modest again. Both Russia and China had a different pattern: for them, attention to Central Asia has grown steadily in the last decade. President Putin has placed a very high priority on Central Asia as a key region in the "near abroad."[44] Since marriage, education, and migrant worker ties are still close between Russia and Central Asia, Putin has a strong base to build upon. The Chinese have fewer cultural ties in Central Asia but Beijing's aid and investment has gotten them an important seat at the table. Also, supporting various multilateral organizations, like the Shanghai Cooperation Organization (SCO), is a low-cost way to increase visibility.[45]

The Obama administration was loath to make any new overseas commitments, so lowering the U.S. profile in Central Asia fits this overall strategy. It remains to be seen what the U.S. president elected in November 2016 will do, particularly if the situation in Afghanistan deteriorates.

Southeast Asia presents a totally different set of circumstances. Not only did president Obama make a commitment to "pivot" and "rebalance" toward East Asia but the South China Sea has become the focus of intense competition between China and its neighbors. Also, with the ITLOS ruling going against China on all of its substantive issues, it is difficult for China to portray itself as a friendly neighbor if it continues to reject the ITLOS determination.[46]

The circumstances put the U.S. in a curious position because the U.S. has not even ratified the United Nations Convention on the Law of the Sea (UNCLOS), including its arbitration provisions. Thus, it would be a major setback for international law and norms if China was able to reject the ITLOS findings and to use force to continue to occupy rocks and atolls that its neighbors claim as theirs. Also, since the U.S. has security treaties and executive agreements with five states in Southeast Asia, it would be a major loss of influence for the U.S. if China were to prevail in its current behavior.[47] Moreover, if China prevails, its dominant position in the Northern Tier states of Southeast Asia, especially Laos and Cambodia, would be reinforced.[48]

Latin America is quite distinct from the other two Asian regions that we have analyzed. Because the U.S. has long been the major outside power in Latin America, it is more difficult for a new challenger to gain traction. As noted above, China has made major commitments of trade, aid, and direct investments, but these initiatives have produced limited results. Although the food and raw materials have been important imports for China, the anticipated political gains have been modest. Also, given the political changes in Argentina and the problems in Venezuela, Brazil, and Bolivia, China's investment in the region may be seen as a disappointment. The question will be: will China fundamentally change its tactics?[49]

* * *

In sum, great power politics is alive and well in these three regions. The U.S. is diminishing its role in Central Asia; China and the U.S. both see Southeast Asia as a region of vital interest; and China's assets in Latin America are looking less promising. Whether China can maintain its economic growth rate is probably the most critical variable in determining if it will continue its high-visibility commitments to these three regions. For the U.S., moderate economic growth seems plausible, so future commitments to these regions will draw on a strained budget and be shaped by an American public that is increasingly skeptical of overseas involvement.

NOTES

1 *Remarks on U.S. Policy in the Western Hemisphere*, Secretary of State John Kerry, Organization of American States, November 18, 2013, www.state.gov.

2 Sullivan, M., *Latin America and the Caribbean: Key Issues for the 114th Congress* (Washington, DC: Congressional Research Service, January 2015).

3 The $86 billion for Chinese FDI in Latin America and the Caribbean (LAC) includes Chinese investment in the Cayman Islands, which is mostly a transit point for investment transfers (much of it returning to Hong Kong and China), so the figure substantially overestimates the actual FDI in the LAC region. The Chinese Ministry of Commerce *Bulletin* in 2014 stated that Chinese investment in LAC that year was $10.58 billion.

4 Hornbeck, J., *U.S.–Latin American Trade and Investment in the 21st Century: What's Next for Deepening Integration?* (Washington, DC: Inter-American Dialogue, 2014).

5 See the chapters in this volume by Li He and Haibin Niu for differing views on China's strategy in LAC.

6 Ellis, R. E., *China on the Ground in Latin America: Challenges for the Chinese and Impacts on the Region* (New York: Palgrave-Macmillan, 2014).

7 *Economist*, "Latin America's Economies: Learning the Lessons of Stagnation," June 27, 2015.

8 For a discussion of how major powers form these groupings and what it means to be a "hegemon," see C. Kindleberger, *The World in Depression, 1929–39* (Berkeley: University of California Press, 1973), pp. 291–308.

9 Denoon, D., *Constraints on Strategy—The Economics of Western Security* (Washington, DC, and New York: Pergamon-Braseys, 1986), chap. 1.

10 For a discussion of this background, see S. Babb, "The Washington Consensus as Transnational Policy Paradigm: Its Origin, Trajectory, and Likely Successor," *Review of International Political Economy* 20(2), 2013, pp. 268–297.

11 One of the principal early articles that shaped the thinking of the "Dependency School" was Andre Gundar Frank's "The Development of Underdevelopment," *Monthly Review*, 1966.

12 In the case of the Free Trade Agreement of the Americas, the Brazilian opposition played a key role in the collapse of the entire negotiations.

13 Bagley, B., and M. Defort, *Decline of the U.S. Hegemony? A Challenge of ALBA and a New Latin American Integration of the 21st Century* (Lanham, MD: Lexington Books, 2015).

14 Kynge, J., and J. Wheatley, "Emerging Markets: Fixing a Broken Model," *Financial Times*, September 10, 2015.

15 Nolte, D., "The Dragon in the Backyard: U.S. Visions of China's Relations toward Latin America," *Papel Político* 18(2), 2013, pp. 587–598 (see p. 589).

16 China is a particular challenge to the more advanced LAC manufacturing economies. See the chapter in this volume by Enrique Dussel Peters.

17 In the chapter by Daniel Restrepo and Frank Mora, see the discussion of cultural issues. Also see student data in K. Ross, "Study: U.S. Sees Increase in Number of Students from Latin America," *U.S. News & World Report*, November 16, 2015.

18 Hilton, I., *China in Latin America: Hegemonic Challenge?* (Oslo: Norwegian Peacebuilding Resource Center, 2013).

19 In 2009 China sold trucks and ammunition to Peru but the items were faulty and this led to a cancellation of an order for Chinese MBT-2000 tanks.

20 Horta, L., "Uncle Sam's Backyard: China's Military Influence in Latin America," *Military Review*, September–October 2008, pp. 47–55.

21 See the chapter by Amb. Richard Bernal for an overview of China's relations in the Caribbean.

22 Aronson, C., and J. Heine with C. Zaino (eds.), *Reaching Across the Pacific: Latin America and Asia in the New Century* (Washington, DC: Woodrow Wilson Center for International Scholars, 2014).

23 Five of the 22 states that recognize Taiwan are in the Caribbean: Dominican Republic, Haiti, St. Lucia, St. Kitts and Nevis, and St. Vincent and the Grenadines.

24 As of March 2017, the six were: Belize, El Salvador, Guatemala, Honduras, Nicaragua, and Panama.

25 Loser, C., *The Growing Economic Presence of China in Latin America* (Miami: Center for Hemispheric Policy, University of Miami, 2006).

26 Silverstein, M., and A. Singhi, *The $10 Trillion Prize: Captivating the Newly Affluent in China and India* (Boston: Harvard Business Review Press, 2012).

27 See the chapter by Christopher Sabatini for a detailed discussion of the traditional and new regional organizations in LAC.

28   Erikson, D., "U.S. Perceptions of China's Inroads in Latin America," in A. Hearn and J. Leon-Manriquez, eds., *China Engages Latin America: Tracing the Trajectory* (Boulder, CO: Lynne Reiner, 2011).

29   For an elaboration of these themes, see H. Harding, *A Fragile Relationship: The U.S. and China since 1972* (Washington, D.C.: Brookings, 1992), and K. Lieberthal, *Governing China: From Revolution through Reform* (New York: W.W. Norton, 2010).

30   Several examples: interference with the U.S. survey ship *Impeccable* in 2009; damage to two Vietnamese hydrographic ships in 2011; occupation of Scarborough Shoal and expulsion of Filipino sailors in 2012; and contested entry of a Chinese oil rig, HY54–981, into Vietnam's Exclusive Economic Zone in 2014.

31   McDevitt, M., *Becoming a Great "Maritime Power": A China Dream* (Alexandria, VA: Center for Naval Analyses, June 24, 2016).

32   By 2000, China had over $1 trillion in foreign exchange reserves, which was unparalleled for an emerging economy.

33   China pledged massive launch capital of $100 billion for the New Development Bank.

34   A recent example, at the UN, was China's efforts during 2012–2014 to block Western plans to remove the Assad regime in Syria.

35   This rebalancing will shift Chinese demand to internally produced consumer products and will reduce dependence on imported items to be assembled for export from China.

36   The ITLOS ruling was adverse for China in several regards: (1) the court dismissed China's claims to all the territory and water inside its "9-Dashed Line"; (2) it reiterated that atolls and isles that are not above high tide are not entitled to a 12-mile territorial sea; (3) it ruled that no rock feature that is below high tide can claim an exclusive economic zone of 200 miles; and (4) it decided that if a rock cannot claim a territorial sea, it is not permitted to block entry of foreign shipping within a 12-mile limit. These determinations essentially undercut the legitimacy of China's claims in the South China Sea and make its occupation of numerous features there subject to legal challenge.

37   Since 1842 and China's loss to Great Britain in the Opium Wars, the various infringements of China's sovereignty by Western countries and Japan were presented to the Chinese people as the "Century of Humiliation."

38   For a summary of the commentary in China about Venezuela's economic situation, see C. Jenkins and Ting Shi, "In China, Venezuela Default Talks in Front Page News," *Bloomberg News*, June 15, 2016.

39   Porter, E., "Mistakes in Policy Dash Hopes in Brazil," *New York Times*, May 4, 2016, p. B-1.

40   At the time of this drafting, negotiations are underway between the Chinese and Venezuelan governments over the terms of Venezuela's repayment of Chinese loans. See L. Hornby and A. Schipani, "China Seeks to Renegotiate Venezuela Loans," *Financial Times*, June 19, 2016.

41 Although the Khyber Pass (from Pakistan to Afghanistan) was the ideal sup- ply route for Afghanistan, it was often blocked by Pakistan when Islamabad was bargaining for assorted benefits. This meant it was critical for the U.S. to have overflight and landing rights for supplies coming through Central Asia.

42 In 2016, President Obama reversed himself and ordered that U.S. troops in Afghanistan be redeployed and increased to 10,000.

43 The exception to this pattern was Chevron, which had smaller domestic supplies than some of the other major U.S. oil companies. Chevron has gone ahead with an enormous expansion of the Tengiz field in Kazakhstan. See S. Reed, "Chevron Approves $37 Billion Kazakh Oil Expansion," *New York Times*, July 11, 2016, p. B-3.

44 Lukyanov, F., "Putin's Foreign Policy: The Quest to Restore Russia's Rightful Place," *Foreign Affairs*, May–June 2016, pp. 30–37.

45 See, for example, the Xinhua News Agency's infomercial in the *New York Times* promoting the SCO on June 28, 2016, p. A-5.

46 Ironically, the South China Sea controversy raises the importance of the Trans- Pacific Partnership. If the Chinese are successful at occupying atolls in the South China Sea *and* the U.S. Senate fails to ratify the TPP, then the ASEAN states will have stark evidence of the U.S. being unwilling to maintain its influence in South- east Asia.

47 The treaties are with Thailand and the Philippines and the executive agreements are with Singapore, Malaysia, and Indonesia.

48 The Obama administration made Southeast Asia a high priority, including several presidential visits, appointing a special ambassador to ASEAN, and signing the regional Treaty of Amity and Cooperation.

49 Also, the Obama administration's decision to grant diplomatic recognition to Cuba should strengthen the hand of the U.S. in dealing with Left-wing Latin states.

Richard L. Bernal is Pro-Vice Chancellor of Global Affairs at the University of the West Indies, Jamaica. He was a former member of the Board of Directors of the Inter-American Development Bank. Dr. Bernal was Jamaica's Ambassador to the United States of America and Permanent Representative to the Organisation of American States (OAS) from 1991 to 2001. Previous to his diplomatic posting, he was chief executive officer of a commercial bank. He has also worked in the Bank of Jamaica and the Planning Institute / Agency of Jamaica and as Advisor to the Minister of Finance on external debt management and stabilization and adjustment policy. He is the author of *Dragon in the Caribbean: China's Global Re-Dimensioning—Challenges and Opportunities for the Caribbean.*

Lucio Castro is Secretary of Productive Transformation of the Ministry of Production of Argentina. He has held numerous positions in global finance, civil service, and international organizations such as the World Bank and the Inter-American Development Bank (IDB). He was a professor at the University of Tres de Febrero, University of San Andrés, FLACSO, and Universidad Catolica Argentina, and a visiting researcher at Harvard University. Castro holds a PhD in economics from Sussex University and a Master's degree from the Program in Economic Policy Management at Columbia University.

Benjamin Creutzfeldt is Resident Postdoctoral Fellow on Sino-Latin American-U.S. Affairs with the SAIS Foreign Policy Institute. A China scholar of German and British extraction, he has been a lecturer for Chinese studies and international relations in Colombia for the past eight years. He received his PhD in political studies in 2015. Creutzfeldt's publications include *China en América Latina: reflexiones sobre las relaciones transpacíficas.*

David B. H. Denoon is Professor of Politics and Economics at New York University and Director of the NYU Center on U.S.-China Relations. He served in the federal government in three positions: Program Economist for USAID in Jakarta, Vice President of the U.S. Export-Import Bank, and Deputy Assistant Secretary of Defense. Professor Denoon is a member of the Council on Foreign Relations, the National Committee on U.S.-China Relations, the Asia Society, the U.S.-Indonesia Society, and is Co-Chairman of the New York University Asia Policy Seminar. He is the author and editor of eight books, most recently *The Economic and Strategic Rise of China and India, China: Contemporary Political, Economic, and International Affairs,* and the first two volumes in the U.S.-China Relations series.

Enrique Dussel Peters is Professor at the Graduate School of Economics, Universidad Nacional Autónoma de México (UNAM). He is the author or editor of more than 30 books and many articles in books, journals, working papers, and newspapers in Chinese, English, German, Portuguese, and Spanish.

R. Evan Ellis is Research Professor of Latin American Studies at the U.S. Army War College Strategic Studies Institute (SSI), with a focus on Latin America's relationships with China and other non–Western Hemisphere actors, as well as transnational organized crime and populism in the region. He has published more than 170 works, including *China in Latin America: The Whats and Wherefores, The Strategic Dimension of Chinese Engagement with Latin America, China on the Ground in Latin America,* and *Honduras: A Pariah State, or Innovative Solutions to Organized Crime Deserving U.S. Support?.*

Ruben Gonzalez-Vicente is University Lecturer at Leiden University. His research explores the internationalization of Chinese companies and the Chinese state, China's foreign policy, Chinese mining investment and its development impacts, and, more recently, the rise of populism and nationalism under late capitalism. His work has been published in journals such as *Political Geography, The China Quarterly, The Pacific Review,* and *Latin American Politics and Society.*

José Augusto Guilhon-Albuquerque is Professor of International Relations at University of São Paulo, Brazil and currently Special Advisor to the President of the Brazilian Trade and Investment Agency (Apex-Brasil). His researches focus on the analysis of foreign policy, regional integration and Brazil-China bilateral relations. He has published and edited numerous books and dozens of scholarly articles in English, Spanish, French, German and Portuguese. He also served in public administration at local, state, and federal levels.

He Li is Professor of Political Science at Merrimack College, North Andover, MA. Li is the author of several books, including *Political Thought and China's Transformation: Ideas Shaping the Reform in Post-Mao China, From Revolution to Reform: A Comparative Study of China and Mexico, Sino-Latin American Economic Relations*, co-editor of *The Chinese Labyrinth: Exploring China's Model of Development*. Li has also been a Fulbright Scholar and the recipient of fellowships and grants from Ford Foundation, Tinker Foundation, Henry Luce Foundation, and Chiang Ching-Kuo Foundation. He worked at the Chinese Academy of Social Sciences from 1981 to 1985 and served as Visiting Senior Research Fellow at National University of Singapore in 2008 and 2011.

José Luis Machinea is Professor at the Torcuato di Tella University and the University of Buenos Aires. He is former Executive Secretary of the Economic Commission for Latin America and the Caribbean (ECLAC), and held multiple high-ranking positions in the government of the Argentine Republic: Minister of Economy, President of the Central Bank, Under Secretary of Economic Policy, and Under Secretary of Development Program. He has also worked as a Distinguished Visiting Researcher at the Inter-American Development Bank (IDB) and as a consultant for the World Bank, as President of the Argentina Foundation for the Development with Equity, and as Research Director of the Institute for the Industrial Development of Argentina's Industrial Union. Machinea has a PhD in economics from the University of Minnesota.

Frank O. Mora is Director of the Kimberly Green Latin American and Caribbean Center and Professor of Politics and International Relations at Florida International University (FIU), Miami, FL. Prior to arriving at FIU, Dr. Mora served as Deputy Assistant Secretary of Defense for the Western Hemisphere from 2009 to 2013. Dr. Mora is the author or editor of five books and numerous academic and policy articles, book chapters and monographs on hemispheric security, U.S.–Latin American relations, civil-military relations, Cuba's politics and military, and Latin American foreign policy. He is a recipient of the 2011 Outstanding Public Service Award from the Department of Defense.

Haibin Niu received his PhD in international relations at Fudan University in 2006. Currently he is Senior Fellow and Deputy Director of the Center for American Studies and Assistant Director of the Institute for International Strategic Studies at the Shanghai Institute for International Studies. He has published and translated several books on international studies. From 2010 to 2011, he worked at the Foreign Affairs Office in the Shanghai Municipal Government.

Daniel A. Restrepo is Senior Fellow at the Center for American Progress. For nearly six years and through two presidential campaigns, Restrepo served as the principal advisor to President Barack Obama on issues related to Latin America, the Caribbean, and Canada, serving as special assistant to the president and senior director for Western Hemisphere affairs at the National Security Council from March 2009 to July 2012 and as an advisor to and surrogate for Obama for America during the 2008 and 2012 campaigns. Previously, Restrepo created and directed The Americas Project—focused on Latin America and on the role of Hispanics in the United States, their future, and the implications for public policy—at the Center for American Progress. Restrepo is a graduate of the University of Virginia and the University of Pennsylvania School of Law.

Osvaldo Rosales was Director of the Division of International Trade and Integration of the Economic Commission for Latin America and the Caribbean (ECLAC) from 2005 to 2015. Formerly, he was the General Director of International Economic Relations of the Ministry of Foreign Affairs of Chile (DIRECON), Chief Negotiator of Chile for the FTA between Chile and the United States, Chief Negotiator (Trade Pillar) of

Chile at the Political and Economic Association Agreement with the European Union, and Chief Negotiator of the Chile and Korea FTA. Mr. Rosales has authored numerous publications, including *China and Latin America and the Caribbean: Building a Strategic Economic and Trade Relationship*.

Christopher Sabatini is the founder and editor of a recently launched news and opinion website, LatinAmericaGoesGlobal.org, and Adjunct Professor at the School of International and Public Affairs (SIPA) at Columbia University. From 2005 to 2014, he was the senior director of policy at the Americas Society and Council of the Americas (AS/COA) and the founder and editor-in-chief of the hemispheric policy magazine *Americas Quarterly*. From 1995 to 1997 he was a Diplomacy Fellow with the American Association for the Advancement of Science, working at the U.S. Agency for International Development's Center for Democracy and Governance. He has served as an advisor to the World Bank and the U.S. Agency for International Development and has published numerous articles on Latin America, democratization, political parties, and U.S. policy in the region. He has a PhD in government from the University of Virginia.

Anthony Petros Spanakos is Associate Professor of Political Science and Laws at Montclair State University and Adjunct Professor in the Department of Politics at NYU. His PhD is from the University of Massachusetts Amherst. He is the co-editor of *Reforming Brazil*, a special issue of *Latin American Perspectives* on the "Legacy of Hugo Chávez," and of the *Conceptualising Comparative Politics* book series. He was a Fulbright Fellow at the University of Brasilia and the Institute of Superior Study of Administration in Venezuela and a visiting research fellow at the East Asia Institute in Singapore.

INDEX

active and with head held high (Ativa e
Altiva), 163, 173
Africa, 6, 78–79, 130, 133, 236
Agnew, John, 212
Ahmadinejad, Mahmoud, 71
aid pledges, 373–74
AIIB. *See* Asian Infrastructure Investment
Bank
aircraft carriers, 343
ALBA, 55, 352, 375; activities sponsored
by, 140; as anti-American grouping,
11, 69–71, 380; Chávez creating, 71;
Chinese financial support and, 87;
FTAA and, 139–40; human rights and,
73–74; Obama partnerships and, 76–
77; populist agenda and, 330; regional
organizations and, 84; soft-balancing
and, 143; trade possibilities and, 141;
U.S. as good partner and, 321; Venezuela promoting, 7, 99
Alcântara Satellite Launch Base, 164–65
Almagro, Luis, 321
Amorim, Celso, 66, 164
Andean Pact, 7
the Andes, 209–11, *211*, 227n4; commodity
boom and, 221; financing in, 223–25;
FTAs in, 223; global economy of,
225–26; market opportunities in, 217;
mining projects in, 218–19; natural
resources of, 226; trade of, 220–23
Andes Petroleum, 214
ANDI. *See* National Industry Association
anti-Americanism: ALBA and, 11, 69–71,
380; China and, 376, 383–87; Ecuador

and, 80–81; Maduro, 305, 374, 384;
Rousseff, 384; of Venezuela, 80–81,
305–6
antidumping measures, 198, 207n7,
292n22
Antigua, 249
APPRI (Agreement for the Promotion
and Reciprocal Protection of Investments), 115
Arbenz, Jacobo, 63
Argentina: antidumping measures used
by, 198, 207n7; balance of payments,
202, 204; bilateral relationships of,
199; business opportunities in, 57;
China and exports from, 185, *197*, 199;
Chinese arms purchased by, 347–48;
Chinese bilateral agreement with, 199;
Chinese economic relationship with,
204; Chinese FDI in, 199–202, *200*;
Chinese loans to, 287–88; Chinese
relationship with, 193–95; Chinese
strategic relationship with, 203, 206;
Chinese trading partner with, 195–99;
CONAE of, 194; Corralitos in, 58n3;
creditor agreements of, 192; deep space
antenna of, 194–95; deregulation in,
188; domestic economy of, 22; economic measures in, 189–91; economic
policies of, 186–89; economic turbulence in, 23; EU-MERCOSUR agreement and, 56; exchange rate controls
in, 204; exports of, 195–98, *196*, 205;
external debt of, 188–89; financial market return of, 192; financing for, 201;